# STUDIES IN
# CRITICISM AND AESTHETICS
## *1660–1800*

# STUDIES IN CRITICISM AND AESTHETICS, 1660–1800

## ESSAYS IN HONOR OF
## *Samuel Holt Monk*

EDITED BY HOWARD ANDERSON AND JOHN S. SHEA

10031

*UNIVERSITY OF MINNESOTA PRESS, Minneapolis*

# Acknowledgments

THE editors wish to thank Mr. John E. Neill and his associates at W. W. Norton and Company, Inc., for providing a generous grant that helped in the compilation of the index to this book. For their advice and encouragement we are grateful to Professors M. H. Abrams, Herbert Davis, Rensselaer W. Lee, Marjorie H. Nicolson, Robert C. Rathburn, Martin Steinmann, Jr., H. T. Swedenberg, and Willard Thorp, and, especially, to Professors John W. Clark and Franz J. Montgomery. Professor Montgomery and Professor Richard Stang read portions of the manuscript and made valuable suggestions. We are grateful to E. K. Waterhouse for a photograph of *Old Peasant with Donkey*, to Mrs. David Brower for compiling the index, to the University of Minnesota Photographic Laboratories for the photograph of Mr. Monk, and to our wives for help with the proofs. Finally, we acknowledge the gracious editorial assistance of Mr. William Brimi, and of Miss Marcia Strout of the University of Minnesota Press.

# Table of Contents

# STUDIES IN
# CRITICISM AND AESTHETICS
## *1660–1800*

❦ HOWARD ANDERSON AND JOHN S. SHEA

# Introduction

THESE essays were written to mark the thirtieth anniversary of Samuel Holt Monk's influential study in the history of a critical idea, *The Sublime.* To observe that anniversary is to recognize as well Mr. Monk's consistent accomplishment as a scholar and his humane influence as a teacher. It could scarcely have been an accident that he first chose to study an idea which affected the experience of an age in both art and life, for throughout his career he has been intent upon establishing the lively and subtle context within which an understanding of art can flourish. As a teacher and as a scholar, he has revived regions of the past which would not otherwise have existed for students of literature.

The concentration of the essays in this book upon criticism and aesthetics in the period from Dryden to Wordsworth reflects Mr. Monk's continued interest in the conventions and inventions which shaped that literature. In *The Sublime,* largely conceived during his graduate days at Princeton, Mr. Monk studied the mutations of the idea of sublimity from Longinus through the English eighteenth century. He showed how Boileau's interpretation of Longinus, which more than any other discussion turned the attention of English critics to sublimity, involved the radical transformation of an essentially rhetorical idea into an aesthetic one. *Peri Hupsous* had treated sublimity as a matter of style, as a certain heightening of discourse by linguistic means. Boileau distinguished the sublime style from what he thought the true sublime, consisting not of rhetorical patterns but of less tangible qualities of thought, existing often in the simplest language, that move readers to emotion. If Boileau deserves the blame that Keats assigned him for some of the sterilities of eighteenth-century English criticism and poetry, he deserves credit for the fruitfulness of his discussion of sublimity. It was under his influence that critics began to explore the inner processes of literary creation and the aesthetic response. Having established Boileau's importance, Mr. Monk went on to the heart of his book, an account of the slow evolution of the idea of the sublime in the writings of English critics from Dennis and Addison at the beginning of the century to Alison and Reid at the end of it. Two facts emerged with especial clarity from his study: first, that the elevation of sublimity as a literary ideal tended to subvert the orthodox neo-classical canons of taste; second, that as English critics explored the sublime they were making their way to an explanation of literary psychology. While Mr. Monk had not set out to write a general history, he provided such a rich context around his central idea that *The Sublime* remains one of the most valuable surveys of literary criticism in the eighteenth century.

At the same time, Mr. Monk's first study demonstrated the vast knowledge of literature, the philosophical grasp, the awareness of the relations among the arts, which have marked all his scholarship. Yet his erudition was — and is — controlled by his sense of proportion and by an intense effort of clarification, qualities that reflect how much he has learned from those writers who have been his life study. The clear, uncluttered prose of *The Sublime* was a model of the way in which difficult and complex ideas may be expounded without offense to readers and without falsification of the subject.

Mr. Monk's particular interest down through the years has been the history of ideas, in which *The Sublime* is a classic study; in a briefer example of the scope of his work, "A Grace beyond the Reach of Art," he pursues the sources of Pope's critical dictum through literary and philosophical writings in five languages over a period of two thousand years. In these studies, as in his later attention to the critical opinions of Dryden and Temple, Mr. Monk has upheld the position that no work of art, however unique, can be properly evaluated apart from an understanding of the traditions within which it has been produced. But *The Sublime* established the complementary truth that convention is constantly in the process of being made new by invention. It is not surprising, then, that Mr. Monk's interest has extended to those forms of literature which embodied and engendered new ideas about the techniques and purposes of art in the eighteenth century. His studies of the novels of Defoe and Sterne, and of that book which comes so tantalizingly close to being a novel, *Gulliver's Travels*, have focused on the potentialities of form as a creator of meaning.

The breadth and seriousness of Mr. Monk's scholarship have been recognized by his colleagues: he has held fellowships from the American Council of Learned Societies and from the Scribner, Rockefeller, and Guggenheim Foundations. Most recently, he has been research fellow at the William Andrews Clark Memorial Library and at the Folger Shakespeare Library. He has been, for several years, a member of the editorial board of the California edition of the Works of John Dryden, and an advisory editor of the Augustan Reprint Society. From 1960 through 1963 he served on the Executive Committee of the Modern Language Association of America.

As a teacher, his achievement has been equally honorable. He taught at his alma mater, Southwestern at Memphis, until he joined the Army Air Corps in 1942. After the war, he came to the English Department of the University of Minnesota, where he has served as Chairman, Director of Graduate Studies, and representative to the departmental council. He has been Visiting Professor at Columbia University (Summer, 1951), New York University (the Berg Professorship, 1954–1955), and the University of California, Berkeley (the Beckman Professorship, 1961).

Because Mr. Monk's mind has always been attuned to productive scholarship, it would be understandable had only secondary energies remained for the classroom. On the contrary, for a generation of students at the University of Minnesota, Samuel Monk has been one of the greatest of teachers, whether in the lecture hall, the close quarters of a seminar meeting, or the individual conference. The unquestioned master of the literature, intellectual background, art, architecture, and society of eighteenth-century England, Mr. Monk is equally the master of speaking eloquently about them. Students invariably pack his lecture courses and seminars; students and colleagues, from English and other departments, overflow into the hallways when he gives a public lecture. Like his readers, his students have learned to understand the literature of the Augustans because he has been able to re-create for them the context of the age itself. None of his students will be surprised that "The Pride of Lemuel Gulliver," in which Mr. Monk brings a wealth of background to bear on a text of great intrinsic importance, originated in a classroom discussion, was later pre-

Samuel Holt Monk

sented as a public lecture, and only afterwards appeared in print. The critical essay exemplifies Mr. Monk in another way: it shows the sympathetic comprehension of the ideals of the great Augustans which has made it possible for his students to see Dryden and Swift and Pope and Johnson as mortal men, certainly, but as men whose minds are as alive in the twentieth century as they were in the eighteenth.

Samuel Monk's excelling qualities are of the spirit as well as of the mind. If his students, colleagues, and friends were asked to single out his chief strengths, they would probably think of the moral ones first: perhaps, above all, his commitment to knowledge, his sense of responsibility to his profession. Indeed, his teaching and writing are what they are because he has always exercised that commitment and that responsibility. Among Mr. Monk's favorite men of the eighteenth century are, significantly, Samuel Johnson and John Wesley; both sensed deeply the need of these qualities for a fully achieved life.

While Mr. Monk has done justice to many writers in the act of teaching, he has perhaps talked best about literary theory, about which there are not many men as learned as he. But in a class some years ago, after a stunning clarification of the cruel complexities of early eighteenth-century critical ideas, he stopped suddenly, shook his head, and flung his papers on the desk. "Lies, all lies!" He had not, he felt, been able to tell the full truth, and anything less than the full truth was a lie. The incident seems representative of him. Yet the complement to this tenacious honesty is his perspective; for, in spite of a nagging sense of incompleteness, he has found the resources to do much. His response to the difficulty of telling the truth has never been to abandon the attempt.

Samuel Monk will retire from teaching in a few years, but, if his activities over the last half dozen years give any indication of the future, he will continue to make available to scholars and students the rich values of his learning. This volume, then, while recognizing especially the first of Mr. Monk's studies, implies a tribute to all that he has accomplished and all that he will accomplish.

ﻼ    ﻼ    ﻼ

The essays in this book largely share Mr. Monk's view of the eighteenth century as a time of movement, change, and complexity. The study of the Augustans to which he has contributed so much reveals that the best that they thought and said about literature and the other arts comes to something quite different from the combination of formulas and smugness which once was thought to have dominated the age. As Bertrand Bronson's essay suggests, the classical precept that art imitates nature proved as adaptable as it was venerable, providing authority for unfamiliar realms of nature (notably the sublime) as proper subjects for art. Even in the earliest decades of the century, Mr. Bronson shows, poets attempted to express intense emotions, not merely to represent external reality. The determination to include states of feeling as part of the reality to be communicated through art can scarcely be considered a romantic innovation when it is essential to the doctrine and practice of artists so Augustan as Pope and Handel. And it is surely the inclusiveness of the Augustan concept of mimesis — as well as of the familiar doctrine that art instructs by pleasing — that permitted criticism to remain as generous and assured in the writings of Johnson as it had been in those of Dryden and Pope.

The frequently conflicting artistic impulses toward emotional expression and toward classical order which the eighteenth century tried to reconcile were already apparent in the baroque and neoclassical art of the seventeenth century. Rensselaer Lee describes the results of the conflict in two paintings of an episode from Tasso by the Italian Guercino, discussing as well the relation between the pastoral interlude in literature and the developing form of the landscape-with-figures in painting. William Halewood argues that baroque expressionism was in fact far better established in the theory of the visual arts than in poetics, and that the traditional relation between literature and painting may have helped to expand the acceptable limits of poetic representation. If painting might have literary significance, poetry also gained by borrowing from seventeenth-century theories of painting a recognition of the passions as legitimate objects of representation. The irregular genius of such an artist as Michelangelo was cited during the period as an example for both painters and poets.

To insist upon the importance of such a critical influence is not to deny the preeminence of classical example and precept. Yet Earl Miner and Lillian Feder remind us in their essays on Dryden and Pope that these artists adapted to contemporary needs what they learned from the Greek and Roman past. Dryden, revising Chaucer in the light of classical theories of narrative poetry, incorporated into his medieval tales historical and philosophical elements highly relevant to the Restoration. Pope's translations of Horace, Miss Feder points out, are frequently more Juvenalian in tone than Horatian; Pope combined the methods of the two satirists to serve his own purpose of attacking Hanoverian corruption. James Thomson, the subject of Ralph Cohen's essay, modified classical georgic conventions by the use of biblical metaphor and modern scientific imagery. Thomson's poetry, though still recognizably georgic, presents a new image of man's position in the universe, notably through new methods of expressing space and time.

Visual artists also reshaped their inheritance from the past for individual uses. "The mind," said Sir Joshua Reynolds, "always desires to entertain two objects at a time." Reynolds conceived his artistic subjects in this double way: both as representatives of mankind and as particular living persons. He frequently managed to make his figures representative by placing his sitter in a setting or costume suggesting timeless action. Particularity of characterization he achieved by concentrating on the precise likeness and expression. Reynolds is shown in Robert Moore's essay to be the type of the classical artist: equally concerned with representing a subject and with commenting upon it. On the other hand, Emilie Buchwald's essay follows the development of Gainsborough's style toward the late years when, with the aid of long study of seventeenth-century landscape, he fused portrait and background in an idealized relationship. Each artist made his own use of the past; it is perhaps surprising to find the supreme classicist, Reynolds, the more intent on portraying the individual and realistic, as well as the ideal, in his paintings.

These five essays discuss the adaptation of traditional techniques to modern problems. Irvin Ehrenpreis argues that great poetry succeeds to the extent of its engagement with relevant human concerns; he analyzes the contribution made to Augustan poetry by its allusion to the recognizable contemporary scene. Pope's *Epistle to a Lady* is typical of great eighteenth-century art in the intentional clarity of its reference to real people and real events, which makes actual social life the most important basis of the poem's structure. The relative failure of Young's satires may be due to their abstract impersonality, just as Gray's *Bard* suffers because its protagonist and setting have no connection with a real world.

Pope's openness to complex reality appears in his criticism as in his poems. Paul Ramsey discusses important passages in *An Essay on Criticism* showing that the context of critical statements (a context existing within the poem and within literary tradition) modifies their seeming dogmatism and simplicity. Mr. Ramsey argues that the absolutism of Pope involves subtle, alert, and perceptive judgment, not rules simplistically applied. And such, he continues, is the nature of true critical absolutism in the twentieth century as in the eighteenth. To compare this analysis of Pope with Ernest Mossner's discussion of Hume is to see, once again, how correct Bertrand Bronson has been in his contention that unity within diversity is the defining characteristic of that century. For, different as some of Hume's basic assumptions and particular judgments are from Pope's, both men share the conviction that criticism is grounded in philosophy, and literature in life. For both, criticism requires perception of the general and the particular, the objective and the subjective; and both pay close attention to the role of individual genius and individual feeling in poetry. Hume's description of the character of a true critic — "strong sense, united to delicate sentiment, improved by practice, perfected by comparison, and cleared of all prejudice" — is almost precisely that which Pope draws in the *Essay*.

The greatest critic of the century, Samuel Johnson, adhered to the tradition that the poet should be a universally learned man, and, as Geoffrey Tillotson remarks, Johnson was often conservative when faced with critical innovation. But if the *Dictionary* definition of the sublime dismisses the new conception of the word, Johnson elsewhere reveals his full understanding of its power. In his discussion of Dover Cliff in *King Lear*, Mr. Tillotson further suggests, Johnson achieved the fullest expression of sublimity in the eighteenth century.

Even so negligible a critic as William Warburton cannot be characterized as merely dogmatic and hidebound; as Robert Ryley shows, he analyzed *An Essay on Man* very closely in search of complexity and ambiguity in patterns of imagery, so anticipating by nearly two hundred years the practical critics of the twentieth century. And Scott Elledge's study discloses that precisely where we might most expect to find theoretical dogmatism and prescription — in the study of language itself — we discover a field dominated by men aware that language cannot and should not be fixed and codified. Johnson, in the Plan for the *Dictionary*, is concerned with the conflict between his roles as "discoverer" and as "law-giver," his functions in "ascertaining" and "preserving" language; he is prescriptive only in discussing pronunciation. Nor is Johnson an exception among students of language in the period: Mr. Elledge follows the development of comparable ideas in numerous works appearing after the middle of the century.

Much of the flexibility and inventiveness of the best Augustan literary theory and practice may have been an accommodation to the threat to poetry from the new science and philosophy. Poetry had required apology even at the height of the Renaissance; by the end of the seventeenth century its value as a means to truth was denied not only by many scientists but by the most influential philosopher of the age. Faced with the assumption that unadorned prose is the exclusive vehicle of reality, artists and critics were forced to look at poetry in new ways. The justification of poetry as something more than amusement took various forms. Shaftesbury argued that sensibility, the faculty that perceives harmony and disharmony, is the essential human endowment. Man is to be considered not primarily as rational, but as a perceiver of values; this position implies that moral and aesthetic distinctions are made on the same basis. As Ernest Tuveson makes clear, Shaftesbury did not argue that the mere possession of sensibility assured the benevolence of human responses; he urged that this faculty be trained to see harmony and to seek it. The value of art in such training is a corollary of Shaftesbury's view.

Shaftesbury is representative of eighteenth-century aestheticians in holding the relation between perceiver and object to be more complex than Locke had believed. Walter Hipple traces the establishment of a theory of beauty upon apparently objective phenomena outside the human mind; at the same time, however, he shows that beauty as a concept is created through associations residing only in the perceivers' minds. Associational psychology may, indeed, be said to have restored some of the prestige of which art had been deprived by empirical philosophy. While associationism is essential to the aesthetic theory of the century, it is even more strikingly obvious in the novelistic techniques of Laurence Sterne. Ian Watt considers the unity of *Tristram Shandy* dependent upon a consistent narrative voice. That voice, created in part through a singular system of punctuation, is defined by its association of ideas rather than by the rational subordination of one to another.

Associationism was a means of qualifying or of denying Locke's views of the operation of the mind and the function of art. But some critics preferred to justify art by using Locke's own ideas about the nature of language. The idea that the evocation of an emotional response is the essential aim of poetry, inherent in the developing idea of the sublime, provided grounds for considering profound simplicity rather than complex allusiveness to be the essential quality of poetic language. David Hansen's essay describes how Joseph Addison moved from the belief that poetry is ornamental to the contrasting belief that, although images have their uses, poetic greatness depends first upon the impressive, direct statement of great ideas.

Addison's perception could lead to the recognition that great poetry in fact involves the simplest possible statement. More often, however, its effect was not to establish simplicity in the language of eighteenth-century verse but, instead, to give authority to a system of poetic diction considered necessary for the expression of great thoughts and great emotions. If the critics and artists studied in this book, together with their lively contemporaries, were generally more impressed by reality than by doctrines in art, less imaginative minds frequently controlled influential positions in the literary world. By the end of the century, popular criticism was inclined to be satisfied with classifying poetry according to its type — sublime, beautiful, or picturesque; and it is against such oversimplification of eighteenth-century theory that Wordsworth's ideas in the Preface to *Lyrical Ballads* are most surprisingly new. As James Scoggins demonstrates, Wordsworth was determined that poetry must assert a new relation between the external world and the mind of man. From the point of view of the second-rate criticism that Wordsworth's own books encountered, this aim was revolutionary. From the perspective established by the studies in this book, Wordsworth's criticism is an original and valuable contribution to a struggle in defense of the worth and reality of art which had begun at least a century before.

✹ B. H. BRONSON

# When Was Neoclassicism?

CHAMBERS, in his provocative book *The History of Taste*, pointed out that when the greatest monuments of classic art — the Parthenon, the Athena Parthenos, and other glories of Periclean Athens came into being, no appreciation of these masterpieces was expressed in writing. No literary evidence survives to show that the aesthetic consciousness of that golden day had reached a level more sophisticated than that of admiring "gold-and-glitter." [1] Art, to be sure, had value, but it was prized for irrelevant reasons, reasons potentially inimical to a free development of the artistic impulse. The reasons were moral, idealistic, or civil: concerned, that is, with useful instruction, or regulative norms, or polity. Art was always to serve some ulterior, public purpose. The artist was of little account or interest in himself but the impersonal object in view was important. Thus the name of Ictinus, and his part in designing the Parthenon, were only of local and immediate concern and were soon forgotten. Pericles could propose divesting the Athena Parthenos of her gold, should the city need the money. The vandalism of such an act he ignores, as he ignores the name of the sculptor, Phidias, his friend. But piety, he allows, would of course require restitution to the goddess. Likewise Herodotus, a world traveler exactly contemporary, estimates the weight of the gold he has seen and carefully inquired about, in famous temples and statues, but says nothing about the aesthetic properties — unless mere size be such — of the works he describes. Thus, for instance: "there was in this temple the figure of a man, twelve cubits high, entirely of solid gold." Or again, Thucydides, on any question of beauty, is equally noncommittal.

1. Frank P. Chambers, *The History of Taste* (New York, 1932), pp. 273ff.

Plato, we remember, judges art as the excellence of a *copy* thrice removed from the original, and justifies it only so far as it instructs. Aristotle, in the *Poetics*, also bases the arts on imitation, and our pleasure in them in recognition — that is, of the object represented, whether actual, probable, or ideal ("such as it was or is, such as it is supposed, or such as it ought to be").[2] Led by the Sophists, eventually we approach an art appreciation loosened from the tether of pedagogy and religion, and flowing toward the Hellenistic Renaissance and the consequent Alexandrian efflorescence of patron, collector, connoisseur, antiquary, and dilettante — *id genus omne*. In due course, Rome abandons her earlier puritanic asceticism, is drawn into the Hellenistic current, and imbibes culture and corruption from the vanquished. By the time of Augustus, Rome has little more to learn, though the process continues "as streams roll down, enlarging as they flow."

Classicism, then, as a conscious theory of art, as doctrine defensible and defended, was, in the ancient world, Hellenistic, not Hellenic. May we not proceed to hazard the generalization that there can hardly be such a phenomenon as a primary, original classicism? For by the time we meet conscious formulations of aesthetic principle, it is always Neoclassicism that we confront. The doctrinal motivation is always traditional, invoking established norms, and to these the artist's individuality is subservient. Subservient, but not servile nor suppressed by them — rather, inspired — for the attitude is one of worshipful acceptance. Tradition is Law, in fullest realization of which lies the artist's supreme satisfaction. When this frame of mind has become self-conscious and deliberate, with allegiance acknowledged, we are in the presence of Neoclassicism.

Thus, the Augustan classicism of the first century B.C. was an integral part of the Hellenistic cultural renaissance: it was a neoclassical movement, consciously recreative of older and purer models. Terence remembered Menander, Catullus Sappho, Vergil Homer and Theocritus. Similarly, of course, the Italian Renaissance is a gradual recovery of the values and ideals of antiquity. Brunelleschi, Alberti, Vignola, Palladio, Lomazzo were neoclassicists in the fullest sense, votaries of ancient order and system, profound students of the Vitruvian precepts. In the following century, the learned genius of Poussin, the encyclopedic labors of Junius, and the poetical treatise of Dufresnoy led to the crystallization of the classical code by the French Academy, establishing the example of the Ancients as "one clear, unchanging, universal light." Under these auspices, English Neoclassicism is launched; and here begins *our* more particular field of inquiry.

✶   ✶   ✶

The elder of us were bred up in the critical conviction that the eighteenth century was one century we needn't worry about: we knew precisely where it stood, and what it stood for. It was fixed in its appointed place, and there it would always be when we cared to look again. We understood its values, and they bored us. The interesting thing was to see how the human spirit struggled out of that straitjacket into new life. As students of English literature, we knew that its tenets had reached their probably ultimate exemplification in the work of Pope, and that what followed in his track was only feebler and more arid imitation, while the buds of fresh romantic promise were beginning here and there to peep out timidly. That this view, or something like it, is still current is suggested by a front-page article on Christopher Smart in the *Times Literary Supplement*, entitled "Lucky Kit?" "To us," we read, "Smart seems one of the first rebels against the rational behaviour and rationalist thought which have come down like a bad debt from his century to ours."[3] One might have thought that a statute of limitation could ere now have been invoked in such a case.

However the debt may lie, certain it is that that century no longer looks so placid as formerly, whether because we have done more reading, or because events of recent decades have affected our eyesight, or because the newer telescopic lenses have altered the range of visibility and brought things into sharper focus. More seems to have been going on formerly than we had suspected. The painstaking and systematic research of our minute topographers has left seemingly few corners of the eighteenth-century terrain unscrutinized. The net result of this turning over of all such reading as was never read — well, hardly ever — has been to reveal a region of the most baffling complexity and self-contradiction, in which can be found almost anything we choose to seek. Wherever we pause, we are bewildered by the diversity that surrounds us: not alone in the conflict of opinion but shot through the very texture of every considerable author's or artist's work. Of even the chief spokesmen this is probably true. Pope is no exception. The difficulty of making a consistent pattern of Johnson's thinking is notorious. Yet when we look at the au-

2. *Poetics* 1460b 10.
3. *Times Literary Supplement*, December 29, 1961, p. 921.

thoritative surveys of critical historians, such is not the impression we receive. Their momentum bears us stoutly forward, and at any point they tell us where we are, how many miles we have traveled, how far we have still to go. Best safety lies perhaps in maintaining our speed; but there might be something deceptive in this sense of undeniable progress: "The rough road then, returning in a round, / Mock'd our impatient steps, for all was fairy ground."

All the authoritative guides tell us — and we believe them, do we not? — that the road sets out from "Neoclassicism" and in due course arrives at "Romanticism," taking roughly a century to cover the distance. As we trace it, the landscape visibly alters: it grows less cultivated, more picturesque, wilder. The vegetation is ranker, the hills are higher and more precipitous; the road begins to wind, first in graceful curves (the "line of beauty"); then, adapting itself to the ruggeder country, skirting torrents overhung with jagged rock and blasted old trees, becomes ever more irregular and full of surprises. The wayfarer is at first likely to be struck with solemn awe; later, he finds himself almost breathless and gasping with fearful joy; and at last, in self-surrender, now with streaming eyes, now with shouts of apolaustic abandon, identifies himself with the spirit of what he beholds — or rather, perhaps, identifies what he beholds with his own exalted and pathetic state.

But we have been snatched aloft on the wings of metaphor. Let us decline from the resulting oversimplification and try to regain our composure. And first, returning to Neoclassicism, let us acknowledge that, if regarded as a distinct phase of Art, separate in time and visible effects, in England it never really existed. Or, if it ever took palpable shape, that was only in the pages of certain bloodless theorists, whose formulations, when themselves regarded as efforts of the imagination or works of art, are the sole extant examples of its wholehearted enforcement. Conceptually, it exists as a theoretical terminus that was not and could not be reached in practice, a *reductio ad absurdum* of valid and defensible ideals.

We observed that Classicism, wherever it achieves self-consciousness, in works of art or in underlying doctrine, is always retrospective and therefore essentially neoclassical. Now we have declared that in actual fact a truly neoclassical work of art, as the term is usually employed, was never created in England. The solution of this apparent contradiction is that for practical purposes the troublesome term Neoclassicism is otiose and expendable. It pretends to a distinction without a difference, for the

difference is only in degree, not in kind; while the instances of it are hy-
pothetical. The simple term Classicism, then, with occasional inflections,
will answer all our needs, and the tautological *neo-* may be dismissed un-
lamented.

We know pretty clearly what we mean by Classicism, and therefore
need not be overelaborate in definition. Briefly to recapitulate: Man, being endowed with ratiocination, has as his birthright the key to proper
conduct. What he does ought to be in conformity with the best use of the
faculty that so far as he can tell distinguishes him from all other living
things. If he so employs it, he may arrive at reasonable inferences about
his relation to the universe, and his limitations; about his responsibilities
and obligations to himself and to society — "Placed on this isthmus of a
middle state." He ought thereby to be led to the recognition of those
ideals of truth, morality, order, harmony, which he shares with his fellow man.

In Art, the classical ideals follow from these premises. All the arts — the
nobler ones especially — imitate nature, in the sense that they search for a
norm, or an ideal, that shall perfectly fulfill and express the natural capabilities or potentialities of the entities, or class of entities, represented: not
for the worse but for the essentially typical, or for the better. Analysis has ranked the categories and genres from high to low, has differ-
entiated their characteristic excellences and shown their special objectives. It has noted the appeal of simplicity, the charm of variety within
perspicuous unity, the desirability of balance and proportion. And it has
discerned a large number of proprieties great and small which can be
drawn up and codified at will under the general head of Decorum. The
latter are what provide the Dick Minims with their chief exercise and
they are, to be sure, the readiest subjects for discussion and debate.

From the ancient classical world we have by a miracle of good fortune
inherited a body of literature in many kinds, a large amount of sculpture
and sufficient remains of architecture to serve as enduring models of such
shining merit that they can hardly be surpassed. They establish the moral
and rationally ideal bases of art, teach virtue, and provide inexhaustible
illustration of aesthetic beauty and truth . . . So much may suffice by
way of summary.

᙮    ᙮    ᙮

Whatever date may be chosen to mark the beginning of the new age of
classicism, in England the emotional state of the last decades of the seven-

teenth century, like the political situation, is in equilibrium highly precarious. Everywhere the dominant impression is one of instability and insecurity, of which the Stuarts in their brilliant undependability are almost the paradigm. A music characteristically of poignant, nostalgic sweetness, frequent change of tempo, brevity of movement. An architecture eclectic and experimental in its major examples, inclining to the theatrical and grandiloquent. A poetry incapable of broad definition, containing Milton, Butler, Marvell, the pyrrhonism of Rochester, the sweep of Dryden: in over-all summary uncommitted and capable of anything from the sublime to the obscene. Classic control is an ideal then but seldom exemplified and, in a society standing in need of the strong purgatives of Swift's satire, most often perceptible only through a screen of negative images. On the heels of the brittle artificiality of Restoration comedy, and subsiding from the stratosphere of Dryden's heroic drama, the tumultuous rant of Nat Lee, the passionate distresses of Southerne, and the pathos of Otway, the last decade of the century sees the rise of sentimental comedy and the stage is committed to the new era with irresistible parting tenderness, tears of welcome, abundance of fine feeling and flown phrasing. "'Tis well an old age is out, And time to begin a new." The air is heavy with *un*restrained emotion. John Dennis, the foremost dramatic critic of the new decade, and no contemptible judge when all is said, puts Otway next to Euripides for "a Faculty in touching the softer Passion" [4] — a rating which will be repeated when, much later, Joseph Warton exalts him among "sublime and pathetic poets." [5]

Sublimity is constantly in the thought of Dennis and his contemporaries, made vividly aware of Longinus by Boileau. With consequent editions, translations, and commentaries arriving post with post, Longinus in the front of the eighteenth century is a name to conjure with, in the defense of irregular genius and unbounded Nature. The critics invoke him with a fervor not often accorded the tame Quintilian, who "the justest rules and clearest method joined." The six lines devoted to Longinus in that handbook of Augustan orthodoxy, Pope's *Essay*, are a timely corrective of too rigid notions of that school:

> Thee, bold Longinus! all the Nine inspire,
> And bless their Critic with a Poet's *Fire*.
> An *ardent* Judge, who *zealous* in his trust,
> With *warmth* gives sentence, yet is always just;

Whose own example strengthens all his laws;
And is himself that great Sublime he draws.

(ll. 675–80)

Pegasus spurns the common track, takes a nearer way, and all his end at once attains. Here Pope cites an interesting analogy:

In prospects [i.e., natural scenery] thus,
  some objects please our eyes,
Which out of nature's common order rise,
The shapeless rock, or hanging precipice.
Great Wits sometimes may gloriously offend,
And rise to faults *true* Critics dare not mend.

(ll. 156–60)[6]

A quarter of a century earlier, Dennis, crossing the Alps, called Longinus to mind. Walking, he says, "upon the very brink . . . of Destruction," he was moved to introspection:

. . . all this produc'd . . . in me . . . a delightful Horrour, a terrible Joy, and at the same time, that I was infinitely pleas'd, I trembled . . . Then we may well say of her [Nature] what some affirm of great Wits, that her careless, irregular and boldest Strokes are most admirable. For the Alpes are works which she seems to have design'd, and executed too in Fury. Yet she moves us less, where she studies to please us more.[7]

This passage, penned in the very year when Pope was born, and published in 1693, must surely have lain in the poet's mind, to produce the same comparison between "great wits" and wild Nature at the opportune moment. But the coincidence failed to sweeten the personal relations of the two men.

Along with frank emotional outbursts, preoccupation with the appearance of Nature is one of the traditional signals, as all know who gladly teach and all who docilely learn, of the rising tide of Romanticism. Yet here at the outset of the century, in the very Citadel of the Rules, we observe these full-fledged extravagancies. Loving description of a gentler Nature fills early pages of Pope, in the 1704 half of *Windsor Forest*, in the *Pastorals* — recall the extremes of empathetic trees and blushing

4. "Remarks upon Mr. Pope's Translation of Homer" (1717), *Critical Works*, ed. Edward Niles Hooker (Baltimore, 1943), II, 121.

5. Joseph Warton, *An Essay on the Genius and Writings of Pope* (London, 1756), I, dedication. Otway was demoted in later editions.

6. Ed. Warburton, 1744. Earlier editions place the last couplet at ll. 152–53; Warburton returned to that order in 1764.

7. *Miscellanies in Verse and Prose* (1693), ed. Edward Niles Hooker, II, 380–81.

flowers: these springing under the footfall of beauty, those crowding into a shade. Pathetic tenderness, heightening to overwhelming passion, suffuses the *Elegy* and the amazing *Eloisa to Abelard*. And later, of course, praise of Nature and of God in Nature finds supreme expression in the first Epistle of the *Essay on Man*. Already, however, by the date of the latter, Thomson had published the most extended paean to Nature in all her moods that his century, or probably any century, was to see in verse. But, as we shall increasingly observe, it is significant of a trend that, as the years passed, Thomson tried to intellectualize his spontaneous overflow of powerful emotion by injecting more and more sociological, philosophic, politico-economic, and other filler: "untuning the sky," to borrow a phrase from an elder poet, by cerebration.

ɟ ɟ ɟ

During these same decades external Nature was receiving tribute in other art forms as well as in poetry. By this time, a great tonal poet, Handel, had written work that both in quantity and quality sets him high among those artists of all time who have made Nature an important part of their subject matter. I do not speak metaphorically but with literal truth. To illustrate, an example may be cited, convenient because brief and universally familiar, though all but unrecognized in such a connection. In the opera *Serse*, there is an aria mistakenly called the "Largo from *Xerxes*," or more popularly, "Handel's Largo." As we know, Handel was a dramatic composer, which means that his creative imagination went hand in hand with textual idea. This is not to say that the process of translating consisted of choosing particular notes to represent named objects — though, in its place, he did not disdain particular imitation of that kind. His genius, however, lay in finding musical equivalents for moods, emotions, scenes coming to him in verbal form. Thus, in the aria mentioned, he is calling up the musical image of a tree: a tree which has grown with the seasons, in the favoring sun and air, and has put forth spreading branches that provide a cool, rustling delight in which to respire and be thankful, "Annihilating all that's made / To a green thought in a green shade." The verbal statement is perfectly explicit about this:

*Recitative*: Fair, soft, leafy branches of my belovèd sycamore, for you may fate shine brightly. Let thunder, lightning, and storm never outrage your precious peace, nor desecrate you with violence.

*Larghetto* (not *Largo*): Never gave tree a dearer, sweeter, more lovely shade. (Ombra mai fù di vegetabile cara ed amabile soave più.)

The world, of course, has taken that larghetto to its heart for a talisman against mischance in all weathers. But when we return to the stated literal meaning, could (we ask) that total experience, sensuous, sensible, spiritual, be more satisfyingly evoked?

Nature in Handel's music is a topic large enough for extended study. *L'Allegro ed Il Penseroso*, for example, contains abundant responses, from the obvious sound effects of the chirping cricket, the fluting bird song, the ringing round of the merry bells, and the "bellman's drowsy charm," to the subtle impressionism of the "whisp'ring winds soon lull[ing] asleep" in a D minor cadence hushed with twilight, and the rising moon evoked by a voice-line that climbs slowly for an octave and a half. Our total sense of the work, to quote Winton Dean, "is not a matter of pictorial embellishment, but of a creative sympathy transfusing the entire score, a sympathy with English life and the English scene which is perhaps the profoundest tribute Handel ever paid to the land of his adoption." [8] But on the larger subject of Handel's intense susceptibility to nature's more permanent features, Dean declares, with a just disregard of irrelevant temporal considerations: "There is something Wordsworthian in Handel's view of nature, and a strong element of Hellenic pantheism; a consciousness of the immanence of some superhuman power, aloof yet omnipresent, is often combined with a sense of mystery and awe." [9]

To understand Handel's music as description inevitably requires a little concentrated study. Our contemporary notions of the true and proper functions of music are so opposite to the traditions out of which his art grew that at first it seems almost belittling to suggest that he intended his compositions to be understood so literally. But it will not do to ignore the fact, or to laugh off the theory behind it as the midsummer madness of an era now happily outgrown. The problems of imitation in the arts are basic to all classical theory and practice. It is especially important for us to realize that the kind of imitation involved in Handel's work is not a mere invitation to free subjective reverie on the listener's part, the uncontrolled Träumerei, beginning anywhere, to which the latter-day concertgoer is all too prone. If we wish to converse in this tongue, we must learn it. Simply to follow it at all, we have to know its scope and purpose.

The musicians of that period believed that music could and should be

8. Winton Dean, *Handel's Dramatic Oratorios and Masques* (London and New York, 1959), p. 320.
9. *Ibid.*, p. 63.

a kind of sound-language, precise in the expression of ideas, emotional states, conceptions. But they always started from verbal language, and built an accompanying system of tonal equivalents. Motion swift or slow, rough or even, unbroken or interrupted, was easy enough, given the verbal clue; so too were onomatopoetic concepts, ideas of sound or sound-producing agents, water, wind, animal noises — as exemplified, for instance, in Vivaldi's *Seasons*. Place relations like high or low, near or far, found ready musical equivalents — again if words confirmed them. Handel's contemporary and boyhood friend, Johann Mattheson, who developed this language with extreme elaboration (1739), made a useful classification.[10] He divided the "figures" or *loci topici* into two sorts, *loci notationis* and *loci descriptionis*. The first were the abstract technical devices of music, like inversion, repetition, imitation in its compositional sense. The second were the devices with nonmusical implication, emblematic in meaning, allegorical, metaphorical, of pictorial similitude. In practice, of course, the two kinds were mutually collaborative and consubstantial. The metaphysical and ethical significance of Music had not yet faded from memory. Music had once been next to Divinity in importance because on earth it was the image of celestial order, harmony, and proportion: the Higher mathematics, in fact, with a capital H. It *must* therefore have intellectual meaning, and there ought to be no unbridgeable gap between the physical and metaphysical in music. To give it ideational significance and coherency was not merely right but almost an obligation. As Bukofzer admirably stated the case: "Music reached out from the audible into the inaudible world; it extended without a break from the world of the senses into that of the mind and intellect . . . Audible form and inaudible order were not mutually exclusive or opposed concepts . . . but complementary aspects of one and the same experience: the unity of sensual and intellectual understanding."[11] *Die Affektenlehre*, then, was not the quaint, Shandean aberration it is commonly reported to be. It strove to bring a little more of the unknown within the bounds of the knowable; to introduce evidences of order at the frontiers of rational experience. It became absurd only when it was pushed to extremes — as happened also to rules vainly imposed on other forms of aesthetic expression.

One of its benefits was to describe and objectify emotions in such a way that our private feelings could be shared — identified, experienced, and made generally available in a recognizable musical shape. This, I take it, is the impulse behind all allegory. The process of personifying the passions in *descriptio*, by means of rhythm, tonality, modes, and keys with an established significance, renders music continually allegorical and thereby intellectually viable. This is the rationale of Handel's music, and, basically, it embodies a profoundly classical ideal. Let us not be intimidated by the term Baroque, which in music is a neologism of perhaps mainly negative utility. So universal a man as Handel will not be contained in a narrow room, and we must be wary of trying to impound him. But one thing is certain: it is not for being a revolutionary that he was exalted in his own century. Nor, on the contrary, when in the days of Mannheim and Vienna the classical forms of that great musical age were reaching perfection, was it for being reactionary that Handel's towering genius was arriving at full recognition. From the middle of the century on, whatever school was in the ascendant in England, his fame never ceased.

To emphasize Handel's firm classic alignment is not to do him any injustice. Apart from external nature, the themes that seldom fail to strike fire in his imagination, from *Acis and Galatea* and *Esther* to the very end, were drawn from two sources, the Old Testament and Greek myth. His chief formal innovation lay in the use he made in the oratorios — but not the operas — of the chorus, where his debt is to Greek tragedy via Racine's imitative handling of it. In him appears a similar deployment of choral participation on two levels: that is, both within and above the dramatic action. The chorus concentrates the issues and sums them up; and they rise in and out of that involvement and not as a moral tag superimposed from without. This important insight I owe again to Winton Dean. "With Handel," Dean declares, "as with the Greeks, the force of such pronouncements varies in proportion with their dramatic motivation. The central themes of *Saul, Belshazzar, Hercules,* and *Jephtha*, round which the whole plot revolves, are envy, *hubris*, sexual jealousy, and submission to destiny — all favorite subjects of the Greeks — and it is no accident that those works are conspicuous both for the grandeur of their choruses and for the overriding unity of their style. Handel in this temper reminds us again and again of Aeschylus." [12]

᛭ ᛭ ᛭

Without leaving problems of imitation, and still pursuing the classical ideals, we may shift now to the subject of landscape gardening, wherein

10. Johann Mattheson, *Der volkommene Capellmeister* (Hamburg, 1739).
11. Manfred Bukofzer, *Music in the Baroque Era* (New York, 1947), p. 369.
12. Dean, *Handel's Dramatic Oratorios and Masques*, p. 41.

the mid-century is seen to have defined its sympathies and characterized itself in especially typical fashion. Not the least characteristic fact here is the confluence of contradictory impulses that blur the purpose and direction of changes taking place. Are we watching the gradual repossession of England by Nature with the approach of the Romantic Age, or is the motivation behind this movement quite another thing? Which, it may be asked, is the more romantic, in the deepest sense, the appeal to the eye or the appeal to the mind which "creates, transcending these, / Far other worlds and other seas?"

Several kinds of imitation are involved here, of which we may distinguish two or three in what may have been the order of their emergence. Under the guidance of Sir William Temple, who led away from the stiff, geometrical garden patterns in vogue at the end of the seventeenth century, with their radiating or parallel straight walks, clipped hedges, trees shaped in balls, cones, pyramids symmetrically balanced, the century opened with a strong impulse toward the "Sharawadgi," the supposed sophistication of oriental irregularity. Pevsner has shown the political overtones of English "liberty" in this movement. Shaftesbury's declared approbation of the "horrid graces of the wilderness" indicates British restiveness under too strict control, and also reflects anti-Gallic sentiment in opposition to the rule of Lenôtre.[13] The English Constitution was a *natural* growth, was it not?

This tendency soon broadened and blended with Augustan ideas of classical attitudes toward Nature. The great Roman poets were all poets of nature, assuming the pastoral frame of mind, reveling in country philosophizing, cultivating the natural delights of their rural retreats. The mood was inherited from the Hellenistic development of natural parks and gardens, associated with the Muses and philosophical discussion, and carried on in the Sicilian pastoral tradition and its Alexandrian sequel. Country life in the sumptuous villas of the later Roman nobles, statesmen, generals, not to mention emperors, had much of what the English landed gentry emulated in their great estates; and similar attitudes toward the natural scene seem to have been generated in both worlds.

Even before William Kent came the experiments of Vanbrugh and Bridgman at Castle Howard, Blenheim, and Stowe in romantic gardening. H. F. Clark observes:

The triumph of the irregular occurred during the rise of Palladianism in architecture. Both were derived from classical sources filtered through the work of Italian Renaissance scholarship . . . Irregular gardens were as classical and correct as the buildings of the Burlington group . . . [Sir Henry Wotton's precept that] "as fabrics should be regular, so gardens should be irregular," was a truth which classical authority was found to have practiced . . . [This, it was asserted] was "the method laid down by Virgil in his second *Georgic*." Addison, whose vogue as a leader of taste was enormous, brought the weight of his authority to the side of change by claiming that his own taste was Pindaric, that in his garden it was difficult to distinguish between the garden and the wilderness.[14]

Chiswick Park, begun after Burlington's first visit to Italy, was one of the first of the new irregular gardens, in which, it appears, Pope himself had a hand along with Bridgman. Kent continued it, and Pope theorized the work in his Epistle to Burlington.

Nothing is clearer than that these designers painted primarily to the mind's eye, and aimed at presenting to the observer temporal vistas. "What an advantage," exclaims Shenstone,

must some Italian seats derive from the circumstance of being situate on ground mentioned in the classicks! And, even in England, wherever a park or garden happens to have been the scene of any event in history, one would surely avail one's self of that circumstance, to make it more interesting to the imagination. Mottoes should allude to it, columns, &c. record it; verses moralize upon it.[15]

Like the poets with their bejeweled incrustations of literary quotation, they enriched the scene by setting up as many echoes as possible, by every variety of associational device that might stimulate the imagination and excite emotion. Urns and obelisks, statues and temples evoked the classical nostalgia on three levels: through the recollection of actual classical scenes; through such scenes idealized in the idyllic canvases of Poussin and Claude; and by recalling images and sentiments from the ancient poets with whose work so much of their literary experience was impregnated. This art, then, was an imitative art not only in a pictorial sense but also in its close kinship to literature.

The art of music and the art of gardening are alike in the fact that specific meaning in both must be introduced from another medium. Music,

13. Nikolaus Pevsner, "The Genesis of the Picturesque," *The Architectural Review*, November 1944; also the same author's *The Englishness of English Art* (London, 1956), p. 156.

14. H. F. Clark, *The English Landscape Garden* (London, 1948), pp. 12–13.

15. William Shenstone, "Unconnected Thoughts on Gardening" in *Works* (1768 ed.) II, 113.

we have seen, expresses ideas by developing a metaphorical language that must depend on verbal assistance for correct interpretation of any but the most rudimentary conceptions. But modes and keys acquire independent meaning from repetitional use; and conventional rhythms, meters, and musical figures will convey an accepted sense without the help of intermediaries. Obviously, we must have been tutored in order to understand: it is not enough to be sensitive to musical impressions. Similarly, now, gardening developed its own *Affektenlehre*. The language of flowers has always been a very arbitrary one that had to be memorized; but the toughness and durability of oaks, the dark foliage of yews, the cadent habit of willows, have supplied an obvious symbolism that by association is generally known and acknowledged.

It may be that in some parts of the Orient the language of vegetation has been pursued to such a degree of cerebral sophistication that complex ideas can be formulated by its means alone. If so, it would of course presume in the recipients equal study, knowledge of conventions, and fastidious discrimination in their use. Among the English, poets have been the earliest interpreters and moralizers of natural phenomena. Topographical poetry was already in vogue by the time the landscape artists began to elaborate the extrasensory content of nature in their pictorial compositions. "So," writes Dyer in "Grongar Hill,"

> So we mistake the future's face,
> Ey'd thro' hope's deluding glass,
> As yon summits soft and fair,
> Clad in colours of the air,
> Which, to those who journey near,
> Barren, brown, and rough appear . . .
> Thus is nature's vesture wrought
> To instruct our wand'ring thought.
>
> (ll. 121–26, 99–100)

The landscape designers determined to make equally certain, by the employment of adventitious means, by architecture, sculpture, inscriptional mottoes, artful scenic punctuation,[16] and control of point of view, that the significance of their statements should be rightly understood. Indeed, it sometimes seems as though they resent the pulse of life and would fix the scene in a single moment of time, like the garden in Chaucer's dream, where the sun was always temperate and never set, and change of seasons was unknown. "To see one's urns, obelisks, and waterfalls laid open,"

Shenstone reflects, "the nakedness of our beloved mistresses, the Naiads and the Dryads, exposed by that ruffian Winter to universal observation: is a severity scarcely to be supported by the help of blazing hearths, chearful companions, and a bottle of the most grateful burgundy." [17]

But, as the decades passed, purposes were clarified, subtler meaning was directed to a wider "literate" public, and taste altered. Imitation grew more sophisticated and in a sense more philosophical. The classical idea of what nature herself intended in an imperfect realization of purpose in any given local effort, struggling with intractable elements, became the overriding concern. The genius of place held the secret, and it was the duty of the artist to consult this genius and liberate it into perfect expression. The art, however, lay in ridding it of local idiosyncrasy and domestic encumbrances, which were like bad personal habits, the uncouth awkwardness of village speech, dress, or manners. It was a generalized, ideal beauty that was sought, the perfect classical statement that did not imply stereotyped repetition or dull platitude but became a fresh and living realization of universal truth. "Great thoughts," Johnson said, "are always general."

To reconstitute the face of nature in this way was to compose three-dimensional paintings not from devotion to the charms of nature but according to an intellectual conception as classical as the modeling of antique sculpture. Truth to an ideal beauty, essentialized from a myriad of imperfectly beautiful particulars, was the object here as there: to be real but not realistic, natural but not naturalistic — "the artifice of eternity," the mind's embodiment. "Objects," Shenstone wrote, "should indeed be less calculated to strike the immediate eye, than the judgment or well-formed imagination." To be sure, there are natural proprieties, rules derived from Nature's own practice, "discovered, not devised." "The eye should always look rather down upon water." "The side-trees in vistas should be so circumstanced as to afford a probability that they grew by nature." "Hedges, appearing as such, are universally bad." "All trees" (that is, species of them) "have a character analogous to that of men . . . A large, branching, aged oak is perhaps the most venerable of all inanimate objects." [18]

It must be apparent, then, that what we have been tracing is not the development of a more and more romantic love of an external Nature un-

16. The neat word is A. R. Humphreys's in *William Shenstone* (Cambridge, 1937), p. 100.
17. Shenstone, "Unconnected Thoughts," II, 121.
18. *Ibid., passim.*

contaminated by the hand of man; but rather a more and more subtly refined Art, working with natural phenomena as its plastic elements, on the same classical principles that had been operative in literary art, sculpture, architecture, and were now coming to new and vigorous life in English painting, and, soon after, in the classical revival in France. How, then, is it permissible to use this art of landscape gardening as proof of the continual progress toward Romanticism? Brown's notorious "capabilities" were basically a classical theory — a point too seldom acknowledged.

So far as concerns the cult of the Picturesque, it may be fair to say that it is the belated psychologizing stepchild of the much earlier cult of irregularity, via the theories of Burke at the mid-century and concerned to rationalize, not to retreat into, wilderness. It set up "savage" Rosa, who had not lacked earlier admirers — note Walpole's outburst, going over the Alps with Gray in 1739: "Precipices, mountains, torrents, wolves, rumblings, Salvator Rosa!" [19] — on a higher pedestal than Claude, partly in conscious protest against a late classicism that it felt had become too pure. The asymmetry of the older Baroque tradition, continued on the Continent in the Rococo, no doubt also helped to familiarize sensitive spirits with these "Gothic" tastes.

✦    ✦    ✦

The connection between the landscape gardener's and the painter's point of view was patent to all. Shenstone pronounced: "Landskip [which he distinguishes from 'prospects,' or distant views] should contain variety enough to form a picture upon canvas; and this is no bad test, as I think the landskip painter is the gardiner's best designer. The eye requires a sort of balance here; but not so as to encroach upon probable nature." [20] But there was as yet no school of English landscape painters to provide models, and of course Shenstone was looking toward Italy. Not until the seventh decade, when Richard Wilson translated the English scene into classical terms, was the need supplied. Hitherto, no painter of the English natural scene had appeared who could hold a candle to Claude or the Poussins. And, in fact, when we look for classicism of any sort among *early* eighteenth-century British painters, it is very hard to find. The sequence of names, Holbein, Van Dyck, Lely, Kneller, covers in symbolic outline much of the earlier history of British art. Against this long tradition of foreign lawgivers, and the current snobbery of the Connoisseurs, Hogarth fought with every weapon he could find or invent. He managed to loosen the soil for a British planting. He was no traditionalist and neither by precept nor practice did his influence tell in the direction of Classicism. It was not, however, ancient art he was tilting against but snobbery and pseudo-connoisseurs.[21] But neither would anyone be likely to attach a Romantic label to him. Although he was a theorist, he was by temperament an improviser more interested in facts than in formulas. His masterpieces, e.g., Captain Coram's portrait, his Mrs. Salter, the sketches of the Shrimp Girl, and his Servants, do not set up for "ideal nature," though the Coram has been called one of the great original landmarks of British portraiture.

Ellis Waterhouse dates the beginning of the classical age in British painting precisely at 1760, with the accession of George III and the first public exhibition of the newly incorporated Society of Artists.[22] To this exhibition Reynolds contributed his "Duchess of Hamilton as Venus." The following year Hogarth sent his ill-starred "Sigismonda"; in 1764, Benjamin West entered his first classical history picture. But matters were already getting out of hand because the rules were so permissive that anything sent in was eligible to be shown — even paper cutouts; and the Academy was inaugurated in 1768 to introduce some needful measures to control rights of entry.

Thenceforward, after the establishment of the Royal Academy, throughout Reynolds's presidency, in spite of shortcomings and backslidings, the principles of the Grand Style predominated. During the decade of the seventies, Reynolds made his most determined effort to emulate the old Renaissance masters. This was also the time of his greatest influence. From the late seventies through the early eighties, Barry was doing his big work ("Progress of Human Culture") for the Royal Society of Arts, the logical fulfillment, if not the triumph, of the doctrine. The history picture, in full panoply and classical costume, stood up for the main, and West, with crown patronage, Gavin Hamilton, Copley, Opie, Northcote, and Reynolds as well, strove to realize the ideal. But other winds were blowing, and the mesmerism of Raphael and Michelangelo lost compulsion with the passing years. By 1790, the history piece had been, if not declassicized, then refurbished in modern guise, and "ideal nature" in the

19. Horace Walpole to Richard West, September 28, 1739.
20. Shenstone, "Unconnected Thoughts," II, 115.
21. J. T. A. Burke, "Classical Aspect of Hogarth's Theory of Art" in *England and the Mediterranean Tradition* (Oxford, 1945).
22. Ellis K. Waterhouse, *Painting in Britain, 1530–1790*, Pelican History of Art (Baltimore, 1953), p. 157.

Grand Style, though still a noble ideal, no longer compelled assent — at least in England.

Nonetheless, with the presidential addresses of Reynolds, we are given the *first* great *literary* statement of the classical ideal in painting. Professor Bate goes even further, declaring that "Reynolds' *Discourses* comprise perhaps the most representative single embodiment in English of eighteenth-century aesthetic principles." [23] The *Discourses* were delivered over a very long span — from January 1769 to December 1790 — and were first published complete in 1794. They had a cumulative power; and it is beyond contradiction that eighteenth-century classical *doctrine* reaches its climactic formulations in the last decades of the age.

As for Reynolds's own enormous achievement on canvas, it is very difficult to confine. "Damn him," exclaimed Gainsborough in grudging acknowledgment, "how various he is!" At the end of his life, Reynolds simply and regretfully confessed that Michelangelo's example had been too lofty for imitation: "I have taken another course, one more suited to my abilities, and to the taste of the times in which I live." [24] Nevertheless, this clear and uplifted spirit, this "very great man," as Johnson justly called him, did incontrovertibly succeed, without violating the bond of individual portraiture, in typifying and idealizing for all time a class, a portion of society, a way of life, in dozens of his numberless subjects. In the abundant best of his canvases, we seem to have been shown, not merely so many named personages, but a great deal of the age in which they lived. In a subtle way, he reconciled the individual portrait to the generalized, ideal history piece, a marriage most fully exemplified in his monumental *Family of the Duke of Marlborough*, but demonstrated as well in many of his more informal works.

ʃ    ʃ    ʃ

If there were stirrings against the classical teaching of Reynolds in the art of painting, the doctrine was hardly questioned when applied to sculpture. Reynolds devoted his Tenth Discourse to this subject. In it he rebukes all attempts to include elements of the picturesque, or such pictorial effects as flying drapery or wind-swept hair, or contrasts of light and shade, or imbalance, as a child against a full-size figure, or a stooping figure as companion to an upright one. The delight of sculpture, he declares, is an intellectual delight in the contemplation of perfect beauty, in which the physical pleasure has little part. This art only partly represents nature. "Sculpture," Reynolds pronounces, "is formal, regular, and austere; disdains all familiar objects, as incompatible with its dignity, and is an enemy to every species of affectation. . . . In short, whatever partakes of fancy or caprice, or goes under the denomination of Picturesque . . . is incompatible with that sobriety and gravity which is peculiarly the characteristic of this art." [25]

It is plain that the work of the previous generation of sculptors, even the great Roubillac in his funerary monuments, would not have been approved by Reynolds, because their work was semidramatic, and aimed to make a theatrical statement. But the new members of the Royal Academy, Nollekens, Flaxman, Banks, and Bacon, received the doctrine *con amore*. Nollekens persisted, after his years in Rome, in modeling even Johnson without benefit of wig, evoking (it is said) Johnson's growling protest: "Though a man may for convenience wear a cap in his own chamber, he ought not [in a bust] to look as if he had taken physic." Flaxman's work is filled with the distillation of eighteenth-century ideas of "the just designs of Greece." [26] He worked in Rome 1787–1790. Bacon's statue of Johnson, in St. Paul's, in toga and cropped head, perfectly fulfills Reynolds's notion of "ideal nature." Indeed, Katherine Esdaile, the historian of British sculpture, is filled with indignation at the lamentable triumph achieved by classicism over the native tradition of good homely realism. It is certain that in this art, if naturalism means the tendency toward Romantic individualism, the last two decades of the eighteenth century were a palpable retrogression from its arrival.

A kindred spirit is visible in architecture. The Burlingtonian tradition, carried past 1750 by Isaac Ware, James Paine, and Sir Robert Taylor, was reinvigorated, reoriented, and archaeologized, in part through the excitement over Pompeii at the mid-century, and by investigation all the way from Paestum, Sicily, Athens, as far eastward as Palmyra. The fifties were a decade of strenuous field work by both English and French in Greek and Roman antiquities. Soufflot and Leroy, the Comte de Caylus, Stuart and Revett, William Chambers, Winckelmann, Clérisseau, were some of the best known, and Piranesi, who published three sets of Roman engrav-

23. Walter Jackson Bate, *From Classic to Romantic* (Cambridge, Massachusetts, 1946), Chapter III, §6, p. 79.
24. Conclusion of the Fifteenth Discourse, December 10, 1790.
25. Conclusion of the Tenth Discourse, December 11, 1780.
26. An offshoot of this impulse is to be observed in the sudden flood of Homeric illustration after 1750, reaching its classical climax about 1790. See Dora Wiebenson, "Subjects from Homer's Iliad in Neoclassical Art," *Art Bulletin*, XLVI (March 1964), 23–37.

ings by 1754 — not to mention the official volumes on Herculaneum beginning to appear in 1757. Robert Adam's first tour lasted from 1753 to 1758. He filled notebook after notebook with archaeological studies. His brother James followed his example in 1760. James Stuart's and Nicholas Revett's *Antiquities of Athens*, published in 1762, was based on their investigations of the previous decade. Lord Anson's London house, in the Greek style, was the first conspicuous result. Between the two stricter modes, the Palladian and Athenian, falls the revolutionary Adam work, more various, freer, but classical in inspiration, and enormously successful, influential, and fashionable. Fiske Kimball, in fact, our most painstaking authority on the Rococo, credits Adam's vogue with being responsible for the demise of that style even in France, its originator.[27] Sir William Chambers likewise throws his weight solidly behind the classical tradition (apart from sowing his wild oats in Chinese gardens); so did the Woods of Bath; and even James Wyatt, although flirting occasionally with the Gothic, began and continued throughout his career with classically designed buildings. Fashions in architecture are not easily overturned. But the Adam brothers were thoroughgoing, and did really change the look of things. And their regulation, of course, affected all the interior appointments, from carpet to ceiling, wall decoration, furniture, and lighting. Wedgwood, who belongs to the same decades, with his Etruscan and classical pottery adorned with charming antique luting modeled by Flaxman, fitted in beautifully here. Moreover, thanks to the practical improvements of Caslon in type-founding, and the fanatical perfectionism of Baskerville in the middle decades, fine printing was moving on a parallel course. Along with the extreme beauty and refinement of his Roman type, Baskerville was learning how to manipulate the white space on his page, until his Latin titles sprang out three-dimensional, like antique urns and pedestals standing in the open air, bearing classical inscriptions. His example was not lost on his immediate successors, and in the hands of the Foulis brothers, of Bensley, and Bulmer — with the aid of such designers as Wilson, Fry, the Martins, and Figgins — printing became more classically splendid right to the end of the century. It would be hard to conceive of any piece of furniture more thoroughly at home in the library of an Adam house than some of the magnificent quartos and folios that were published in the years when those great houses were built or remodeled: Syon, Osterly, Kedleston, Kenwood, Luton Hoo, Mellerstain, Newby Hall, and many another. Appropriately, some of the most sumptuous volumes were works of the line of architects already named, Burlingtonians and Classicists both: Campbell's *Vitruvius Britannicus*, Burlington's *Fabbriche Antiche*, Chambers's *Treatise*, Stuart's and Revett's *Antiquities of Athens*, Robert Adam's *Ruins of Diocletian's Palace* and the Adam brothers's *Works in Architecture* are only a few of the most distinguished. They had, moreover, an international circulation and international influence.

If, in summarizing our impressions of the latter decades of the century we recall that Goldsmith then showed in his two great essays in decasyllabic couplets how freshly the Augustan music could be reembodied in the hands of a master of that tradition; if we add to Reynolds's *Discourses* Johnson's *Lives of the Poets* (1779–1781): we shall be in no danger of attributing to Classicism an early demise. If we set beside these masterpieces Gibbon's magnificent elegiac monument to ancient Rome (1776–1787), a supreme embodiment of the Augustan spirit — an epic, as Lewis Curtis demonstrates, reared to celebrate Wisdom and Moral Virtue guiding Power, and warning against surrender;[28] and if, moreover, we remember Burke's nobly conservative defense of the principle of continuity and tradition: we shall not imagine that the Classical Age dwindled or died from anemia and decay. Classicism is a faith, and, being a faith, therefore never fully realized but demanding constant effort from its devotees to attain the values it essentially embodies: the humane ideals of rational truth, moral virtue, order, and beauty expressive of these goods. The community of artists and thinkers with whom we are here concerned, whatever their individual variance, ardently professed and diligently sustained these convictions in art and in life. Burke's *Letter to a Noble Lord* (1796) is not the least splendid expression of that spirit, and George Sherburn's sentence upon it is finely appropriate: "The echo from Virgil may serve to remind us that Burke's art came from the ancients, and that with the figured and fervent mood of his last works eighteenth-century prose goes out in a blaze of noble artifice."[29]

*    *    *

In studying the past, we have grown so habituated to our progressive way of anticipating the future in its earliest premonitory signs that we

27. Fiske Kimball, *The Creation of the Rococo* (Philadelphia, 1943), pp. 207ff.
28. "Gibbon's Paradise Lost" in *The Age of Johnson: Essays Presented to Chauncey Brewster Tinker*, ed. F. W. Hilles (New Haven, 1949), pp. 73ff.
29. George Sherburn, "The Restoration and Eighteenth Century" in *A Literary History of England*, ed. Albert Baugh (New York, 1948), p. 1094.

seldom allow a moment's reflection to the oversimplification and really gross distortion of the historical truth of any actual moment of the past which this practice entails. To the people who are living in it, the present seldom looks like the future. Very few have the leisure for prophecy — except of calamity — or the power of disinterested observation and detachment. The present is always a confused muddle of conflicting values and doubtful issues, and the battle never ceases.

Much earlier, I quoted a dubious couplet: "The rough road then, returning in a round, / Mock'd our impatient steps, for all was fairy ground." It would not be surprising if no one recognized the lines, which intrinsically are hardly memorable. They are part of Johnson's crafty demonstration that in Pope's celebrated onomatopoetic description of the labors of Sisyphus —

> With many a weary step, and many a groan,
> Up a high hill he heaves a huge round stone;
> The huge round stone, resulting with a bound,
> Thunders impetuous down, and smoaks along the ground.

—"the mind governs the ear and the sounds are estimated by their meaning." [30] They do not make very good sense; but I intended to impose on them a kind of symbolic sense, to suggest that the looks of the road and the speed of the passage were highly subjective matters, largely dependent upon — or at least radically affected by — the purpose and preoccupations of the passenger. I have wished in this paper to spend an hour looking at the eighteenth century as if it were a spatial rather than a temporal panorama. For a while I was tempted to take as my title, "From Romantic to Classic," thinking thereby to point the moral in a ready and easy way. The pretty paradox seemed to provide a sort of compass or a means of escape from the bewildering complexities wherein I was stumbling. And indeed it was a help, though insufficient, by its inherent magnetic property of lifting by attraction one sort of matter from the indiscriminate mass.

But, in the end, it had to be rejected because the truth is that, as historians, we are not obliged to travel the road either in one direction or in the other. Both ends of the panorama are equally open to our elevated, timeless vision. A topographical map does not itself move: it lies open to inspection. It is not like Rabelais's Island of Odes, "où les chemins cheminent, comme animaux." Its roads, on the contrary, stay exactly where they are laid down.

It is worthwhile, I think, and corrective of the distortions arising from our obsession with interpretation *ex post facto*, to try to look at an Age in the richness of its complexities and contradictions. If we did not know — or if we could awhile forget — that the Age of Romanticism followed on the heels of the Age of Enlightenment, should we not quite naturally be seeing the eighteenth century in quite another than the customary view: as in fact a period when the spirit of Classicism steadily *refined* its values, grew increasingly *assured* in its declaration of them, and never knew better their true and vital meaning and importance than when on the verge of losing them?

> This thou perceiv'st, which makes thy love more strong,
> To love that well which thou must leave ere long.

Hence, I have been concerned to call to mind the emotional ferment, the resistance to rule, the communion with external nature, all those signs and signals of "Romanticism" that complicate the *opening* of the Age of Reason; next, the irregular and disconcertingly rhythmless horizon line where at unpredictable intervals the different arts thrust up their temporal peaks; and, toward the close of the century, the passion for order, the lofty vision of a timeless beauty, the powerful affirmations of faith in man's ability to define and by strenuous effort to approximate it by the rational use of his human endowment, his shared inheritance, native and natural: the persistent and lasting devotion to the Classical Ideal.

30. Johnson, Life of Pope, paragraph 332 (*Lives of the Poets*, ed. G. Birkbeck Hill [Oxford, 1905], III, 231).

❧ RENSSELAER W. LEE

# Erminia in Minneapolis

A FEW YEARS ago in a masterly essay on its nature and significance, the late Renato Poggioli remarked that the pastoral is the triumph of the "days" over the "works," of the bucolic over the georgic, and that literary shepherds form an ideal kind of leisure class.[1] Certainly they inhabit no land of Cockaigne "where the sausages hang on trees and people indulge in a perpetual kermess." But they enjoy nonetheless a perpetual Eden where nature is a benign and generous mother, yielding them all that they need for nourishment and bodily comfort provided they practice a moderate and distinguished form of Epicureanism to which, in fact, they are entirely predisposed. In this economic idyll, fruit and water, milk and cheese suffice for food, and these are acquired, to say the least, through no painful exertion. Straw easily gathered covers their humble cottages and sheep provide wool for rustic clothes as well as chief articles in a wholesome diet. Literary shepherds generally do not farm, for that is hard work — the hard work of the peasant and the georgic — nor do they hunt, for that is both unsedentary and dangerous and means confronting savage beasts in the wilderness of forests far from leisure and from home. They fish occasionally, but in safe and pleasant ponds and nearby streams, or even not far from shore, but never on the perilous and multitudinous seas. Nor does the weather interfere with their unlaborious and agreeable life, for nature is not only generous, but also merciful and

NOTE: This essay provided the main substance of the second of the three Harris Lectures entitled "Tasso in Art" which were given at Northwestern University in April, 1966. The material had earlier been used in a lecture at the Pierpont Morgan Library in New York.

the literary shepherd is spared "the penalty of Adam, the seasons' difference." Since nature provides all that is necessary and since the shepherd,
frugal Epicurean that he is, "Seeking the food he eats / And pleas'd with
what he gets," delights in the simplicity of his life and in the sobriety of
his pleasures — milk is his drink, not alcohol — he is, unless tormented by
love, the most contented of men. And greatly valuing his peace of mind
(however artificially acquired), he is opposed, often very articulately, to
those passions that are related to the misuse or even the ownership of
property. Greed and avarice are not in him: well he knows that "radix
malorum est cupiditas." Material prosperity and possessions he does not
aspire to. And, since his desires are his needs, since production equals
consumption, and since there are no money, credit, debts, or taxes in his
world, he is under no compulsion to be thrify in a practical sense. "He
never saves," says Poggioli, "for a 'rainy day' that supposedly will never
come"; the shepherd is not "the wise and prudent ant," but the "carefree
grasshopper."

But although the literary shepherd is a contented stay-at-home, despis-
ing worldly pelf, eschewing, as all readers of pastoral literature know, the
mundane iniquities of courts and marketplaces and averse to danger and
adventure, his peace is not sloth and his ease can be anything but ignoble.
He may, especially if ripe in years, have a philosophic turn of mind, he
can on occasion give excellent advice, he may even, *paulo maiora cana-
mus*, "rend dignes d'un consul la campagne et les bois." [2] Very fascinating in this connection is Poggioli's suggestion that the idea of pastoral
leisure is an imaginative projection of the classical and humanistic antino-
my of the mechanical and liberal arts. Since the former are the natural activities of the slave, the latter of the freeborn, the shepherd becomes in
this sense "the symbol of the scholar and humanist in his moments of leisure and ease — when he is no longer a learned man, but rather a sage,
reaching not for knowledge, but for beauty and wisdom." [3]

The "inherent improbability" of one pastoral, at least, aroused the ire
of Samuel Johnson, who found its images artificial and outworn and its
disguises insincere, [4] and it has often been accused of insincerity and arti-

1. "The Oaten Flute," *Harvard Library Bulletin*, XI (1957), 147–84. My debt to
Poggioli in this article, particularly in its first section, is very great indeed.
2. Nicolas Boileau, *L'Art Poétique*, II, 36; cf. Vergil's Fourth Eclogue, 3: "Si
canimus silvas, silvae sint consule dignae."
3. Poggioli, "Oaten Flute," 167.
4. See his famous comment on *Lycidas* in his *Life of Milton*.

ficiality by those who questioned its truth to life. But Johnson with his manly and unromantic good sense was not the one to perceive that the pastoral dream, however fragile, is recurrent, and that it grows out of a tenacious human longing for unclouded happiness or peace of mind. And the literary shepherd who incorporates this longing finds it easier to possess his soul by quitting the tiring complexities of human fellowship and "the great town's harsh heart-wearying roar" for a country paradise exempt from public haunt "where," as Tennyson said in *Guinevere*, "beyond these voices there is peace." Here in the midst of a kindly and unexacting nature, supported by a propitious (though improbable) pastoral economy, enjoying

> The simple ayre, the gentle warbling wynde,
> So calme, so coole as no where else I fynde
> The grassye ground with daintye daysies dight,
> The bramble bush, where byrds of every kynde
> To the waters fall their tunes attemper right . . .[5]

and always in reach of sheep bells, he may recover a sense of moral evil and of good and even speak a more philosophic language.

But Johnson's charge of "inherent improbability" nonetheless sticks, and it is true that much pastoral literature, however deep its pristine roots in human psychology, fails to satisfy us precisely because, as he says in his *Pope*, pastorals, "not professing to imitate real life, require no experience." Hence it is that although the pastoral as a form may be judged improbable, artificial, or insincere, or set down as mere conformity with the tradition of literary imitation, the pastoral ideal often finds deeper and more poignant expression, indeed its most valid expression, in other forms of literature, in epic or chivalric poetry, in romance or tragicomedy, where the pastoral episode occurs as an interlude or passing experience of unforeseen happiness or repose, as a restorative pause in a life of demanding action or exhausting emotion. Thus the pastoral oasis, as Poggioli calls it, is a period of refreshment and recreation in the midst of the heavy business and manifold cares of life. It occurs, as he points out, in the *Aeneid*, *The Divine Comedy*, the *Orlando Furioso*, *Don Quixote*, *As You Like It*, and the *Gerusalemme Liberata*. It achieves vitality not only through dramatic contrast with the main action and prevailing tone, let us say, of a heroic poem, but also because "a breathing spell in the fever and anguish of being" is not only infinitely desirable, but a normal and legitimate part of life. A brief sojourn in Arcadia may, in fact, from time to time be a human necessity. It is only the unlimited extension of Arcadia that becomes enervating and unreal.

✓ ✓ ✓

In 1962 the Minneapolis Institute of Arts acquired a handsome painting by Giovanni Francesco Barbieri (1591–1666) (following page), known from a squint in his vision as Guercino. A native of Cento, a small town in the Duchy of Ferrara whose dukes had been the patrons of Ariosto and Tasso, he was one of the most eminent painters of the Italian Seicento and in the course of his life achieved an international reputation which brought him invitations that he did not see fit to accept to the courts of England and France. The painting in Minneapolis illustrates the famous episode of Erminia and the Shepherd [6] from the beginning of the seventh canto of Tasso's *Gerusalemme Liberata*. This is a perfect example of the pastoral oasis and one of the finest expressions in literature of the pastoral dream.

The *Gerusalemme Liberata*, published in 1581, is, as all the world knows, a heroic poem of high seriousness, its argument being the siege and capture of Jerusalem by the Crusader Godfrey of Boulogne. Yet it does not owe its fame to its epic machinery for which the *Aeneid* and the *Iliad* served as models or to its main action, but rather to those amorous and idyllic episodes like Erminia and the Shepherd, Erminia and Tancred, or Rinaldo and Armida where Tasso put aside an often mannered and imitative style and wrote with the ease and naturalness of great poetry. These episodes, concerned with star-crossed lovers, a company to which Tasso himself belonged, so compel the imagination with their beauty of language, their high poetic sensitivity, their characteristic vein of tender melancholy, and their rich human interest that the serious central argument with its pious speeches, its indefatigable prayers, its divine interventions and its mechanical battle scenes cribbed from Vergil appear by contrast stilted and insincere. These are the passages that became at once the inspiration of art [7] and music; they are Tasso's most authentic utterance

5. Edmund Spenser, *The Shepheardes Calendar, June*, 4–8.
6. I want to thank Anthony Clark, Director of the Minneapolis Institute of Arts, for courteously providing me with a photograph of the painting, the opportunity to study it, and valuable information concerning it.
7. Tasso's influence on the history of painting has been variously considered by scholars in recent years. See my "Armida's Abandonment: A Study in Tasso Iconography before 1700" in *De Artibus Opuscula XL: Essays in Honor of Erwin Panofsky* (New York, 1961), p. 336, note 3, and my "Van Dyck, Tasso and the Antique" in *Studies in Western Art, Acts of the Twentieth International Congress of the His-*

Giovanni Francesco Barbieri (il Guercino), *Erminia and the Shepherd*.
Courtesy of the Minneapolis Institute of Arts

and bear the thoughtful, melancholy, or voluptuous imprint of his own soul.

The story of Erminia, the most tenderly appealing of Tasso's heroines, breaks the main action of marches, ambassadorial parleys, duels, and fierce skirmishes in the middle of the sixth canto. A pagan princess of Antioch, she had earlier been captured, chivalrously entertained, and generously set free by Tancred, the noblest spirit among the Christian warriors. With him she had fallen secretly and hopelessly in love and he can never return her love because of his own fatal passion for Erminia's friend, the warrior maiden Clorinda, modeled on Vergil's Camilla, who is a brave champion of the Saracens. Erminia takes refuge within the walls of Jerusalem and from their ramparts sees Tancred engaged in a bloody single combat with Argante, a Saracen Ajax, which is halted by the coming of night. Tormented by love and fear and thinking to cure his wounds with healing herbs whose secret virtues she had learned from her mother, she resolves to quit Jerusalem and to seek her beloved in the Christian camp. Clad in the stolen armor of her friend Clorinda, who is inactive at the moment, she deceives the guard and rides forth from Jerusalem at night. But her armor gleaming in the moonlight attracts the attention of a Christian patrol who, recognizing it as Clorinda's, give chase, as they think, to a powerful foe. The unhappy Erminia flees, her swift horse outdistancing pursuit, and at the beginning of the poem's seventh canto, she enters an antique forest, in which she wanders, weary and grieving, for the rest of the

tory of Art (Princeton, 1963), III, 14, note 4, for the titles of other articles dealing with this subject.

Guercino ranks with Poussin and Tiepolo as one of the most copious illustrators of Tasso's Gerusalemme. Besides the canvases dealing with the story of Erminia discussed or mentioned in this article (see note 29 below), between 1615 and 1617 he frescoed a room in the Casa Chiarelli-Pannini in Cento, his birthplace, with ten subjects from epic and romantic literature, six of which illustrate the story of Rinaldo and Armida (see G. Atti, Intorno alla Vita e alle Opere di Gianfrancesco Barbieri detto il Guercino da Cento [Rome, 1861], pp. 26–27); they have been transferred to canvas and are now in the Pinacoteca in Cento. Another fresco cycle, comprising thirteen subjects from the story of Clorinda, was painted for the Villa Giovannina near Cento; heavily repainted, they are still there (ibid., pp. 36–39). The sources record a few other paintings of Tasso subjects which have disappeared: a drawing of two half-length figures in the collection of Fritz Lugt in Paris representing Rinaldo preventing Armida from committing suicide might be related to a painting paid for in 1636 of two half-length figures of Rinaldo and Armida (see J. A. Calvi, Notizie della Vita e delle Opere del Cavaliere Gioan Francesco Barbiere, detto il Guercino da Cento [Bologna, 1808], p. 77). An engraving by Bartsch after a drawing by Guercino of Tancred Baptizing Clorinda may indicate that the painter executed or planned to execute a picture of this subject.

night and the following day. At evening she arrives at the clear waters of the river Jordan, beside which she dismounts and sleeps an unquiet sleep, troubled with dreams of Tancred.

At this point we enter the pastoral atmosphere. A cheerful choir of birds saluting the dawn awakens Erminia and she hears the murmuring waters and the morning air moving in the trees, musical and sympathetic voices of nature, "secretari del suo amore antico," which recall her grief and cause her to lament again. Looking about, she sees nearby the solitary abodes of shepherds and her grieving is interrupted by the sound of pastoral songs accompanied by the music of rustic wood pipes. This is the remote and restful place in the country, the kindred loneliness of which echoes Erminia's (and Tasso's) loneliness of heart, the *locus amoenus* which provides the setting for the idyll which follows.

The first scene of this idyll, Erminia's encounter with the shepherd, is the subject of the Minneapolis Guercino (page 40). Its pastoral charm and tender humanity made it from the beginning a favorite among Italian painters, some of whom (to say nothing of their cultivated patrons) are recorded as having read Tasso with enthusiasm, and it remained a popular subject among Italian and French artists for well over two centuries, enlisting the talents of such distinguished names as Annibale Carracci,[8] Domenichino, and Lanfranco, all of whom painted it before Guercino, and later of Claude Lorraine, Solimena, Fragonard, and Delacroix, not to mention other painters of less renown. Hearing the rustic music, Erminia walks with slow steps in its direction and discovers a white-haired shepherd seated where trees crowd into a pleasant shade, weaving baskets of osier and listening to the song of three boys. These are frightened by the strange sight of arms — this is symbolic, says Poggioli, of the pastoral fear of might and power — but Erminia, greeting them graciously, reassures them and, removing her helmet, discloses her beautiful golden hair, thus proving that she is no warrior, but only a maiden in distress. She bids them all, blessed by heaven as they are, to continue their "bel lavoro," since her arms bring no threat of war to their work or to their songs.[9] Thus she makes the point that the shepherd's life of peace and solitude is exempt from one of the chief dangers besetting man.

The Minneapolis picture illustrates the precise moment when Erminia, who has surprised the shepherd and the boys with her sudden appearance, removes her helmet, revealing her gentle womanhood.[10] An effective use of light falling from the left and striking her face and hair, her armor and the white drapery below, and her arms and hands upraised to remove her gleaming silver casque, sounds the note of dramatic surprise; striking not only Erminia, but also the face and right shoulder of the shepherd as he turns quickly from his work to regard her, and touching with strong accents the group of boys at the right, it also connects Erminia with the group of rustic dramatis personae, emphasizing the swiftly established human relationship between them. A tree on the left and a rustic house with thatched roof on the right frame the composition. The pastoral background which owes something to the rendering of the subject by Guercino's early Baroque predecessor, Annibale Carracci,[11] shows a stream

8. Annibale Carracci may have been the first to paint it. His picture, probably dating about 1595, is in the National Gallery in London (see H. Voss, *Die Malerei des Barock in Rom* [Berlin, 1924], p. 502).

9. Stanzas 6 and 7 of this seventh canto provided Guercino with the subject of the Minneapolis picture:

> Ma son, mentr'ella piange, i suoi lamenti
> Rotti da un chiaro suon ch'a lei ne viene,
> Che sembra, ed è, di pastorali accenti
> Misto e di boschereccie inculte avene.
> Risorge, e là s'indrizza a passi lenti,
> E vede un uom canuto a l'ombre amene
> Tesser fiscelle a la sua gregge a canto,
> Ed ascoltar di tre fanciulli il canto.
>     Vedendo quivi comparir repente
> L'insolite arme, sbigottîr costoro;
> Ma gli saluta Erminia, e dolcemente
> Gli affida, e gli occhi scopre e i bei crin d'oro:
> Seguite, dice, avventurosa gente
> Al Ciel diletta, il bel vostro lavoro;
> Chè non portano già guerra quest'armi
> A l'opre vostre, ai vostri dolci carmi.

10. A good school copy of the figure of Erminia is in the Galleria Cámpori at Modena where it is attributed to Guercino's nephew, Benedetto Gennari. He was, however, only fifteen in 1648 and presumably too young to have made it before its journey to Naples the following year. See *La Galleria Cámpori* (Modena, 1929), p. 40, and Plate LXVII.

11. Annibale's painting (see note 8 above) shows the actors reversed with Erminia at the right, the shepherd and boys at the left. His and Guercino's paintings have pastoral and landscape features in common: the stream of water, flocks, trees, the distant mountain, and both show considerable similarity in the arrangement of these features. In both, though differently, a house closes the composition on one side, a tree on the other. A drawing at Windsor Castle attributed to Domenichino has striking features in common with Guercino's picture: in both the figure of Erminia is seen at the left in the act of removing her helmet; the landscape features in the center are similar; and the group of cattle at the right show marked similarities. This drawing looks like a study for the Minneapolis picture and certain stylistic features might tempt one to attribute it to Guercino. I am greatly indebted to Richard Spear of Oberlin College for calling it to my attention and for suggesting the possibility that Guercino is its author (cf. John Pope-Hennessey, *The Drawings of*

of water flowing behind Erminia, flocks in the middle distance, and farther back to the right a herdsman driving cattle. More distant still are trees
and a barn with steeply sloping roof and in the farthest distance a blue
mountain.

This painting, one of two Erminias which Guercino completed in the
second half of 1648, was probably executed for Don Antonio Ruffo of
Messina,[12] whose important collection contained not only splendid examples of Italian Baroque painting but notable paintings of other centuries and schools as well. It is a handsome example of Guercino's late
manner, which, as Denis Mahon has pointed out, had its earliest beginnings soon after his arrival in Rome from Cento in 1621 and most probably as a result of his exposure to the classic theory of art then current
among the Roman letterati. The chief exponent of the theory was Mon-
signore Giovanni Battista Agucchi, secretary of state during Guercino's
two years in Rome to Pope Gregory XV, who as Archbishop of Bologna
had been one of Guercino's principal patrons. Agucchi was a friend of
Annibale Carracci and Domenichino, Baroque painters with strongly classicizing tendencies. Probably between 1607 and 1615 he wrote a *Trattato
della Pittura*, an important fragment of which, discovered by Mahon,
demonstrates that Agucchi was an exponent of the theory of ideal imitation, based ultimately on Aristotle's *Poetics*, some fifty years before Bellori expounded the theory in 1664 in his famous lecture *Idea* before the
Accademia di San Luca in Rome. It is also probable that Agucchi suggested to Guercino that he might improve the style he brought with him
to Rome, a strongly personal style which was no doubt provincial in
Agucchi's eyes, by studying the paintings of his friend, the classicistic
Domenichino, then architect of the Papal Palace. And there is clear evidence of the influence of Domenichino's art on Guercino during his years
in Rome and for a short time after his return to Cento.[13]

In the Minneapolis picture one may see how Guercino has sought to
accommodate his art to the formal and theoretical precepts of classicism.
He carefully balances the left half against the right half of the picture; in
particular the tall, active, strongly lighted figure of Erminia, the arresting
movement of her arms as she doffs her helmet, seen in clear silhouette
against deep space, equals in pictorial emphasis the denser and less spacious
side of the picture showing the compactly constructed group of the shepherd and the boys with the herds and the screen of trees behind them. The
composition is closed: on the left by the standing figure of Erminia fac-

ing into the picture, its curve echoed in the tree cut by the frame, on the right by a vertical of the architecture and the straight back of the shepherd boy who also faces inward. There is strong architectonic emphasis on verticals and horizontals throughout the picture: one may note, for instance, how the group of the shepherd and boys which forms in itself an inverted, almost equilateral triangle is brought to a nearly perfect square by the basket close to the lower edge of the picture which is in a vertical line with the shepherd's head and by the white sheep in the right-hand corner which lies in a vertical line with the back and head of the boy on the right, the base of the square being precisely established by the horizontal line running through the bowl, the shepherd's feet, and the sheep's snout, the top by the near isocephaly. Recession in the painting is accomplished not by characteristic Baroque diagonals extending forcefully into depth, but by a rather careful arrangement of receding planes seen in the figures who, in spite of their turning movements which create some depth, lie very much in a single plane like a frieze; in the sheep behind

*Domenichino in the Collection of His Majesty the King at Windsor Castle* [New York, 1948], p. 105, no. 1265). I might also note here that the London *Erminia*, long attributed to Annibale Carracci, has been recently given by Donald Posner of New York University, in an unpublished thesis on Annibale, to his pupil, Panico. Professor Eugenio Battisti (*L'Antirinascimento* [Milan, 1962], pp. 532–33 and Plate 36) is inclined to identify the London picture with an *Erminia* which Giovanni Battista Agucchi (see above, p. 44) ordered from Annibale's cousin, Ludovico Carracci, in 1602, and which there is reason to believe Annibale repainted in part. But the picture does not bear the marks of Ludovico's invention or execution.

12. The other was painted for Cardinal Fabrizio Savelli, the papal legate at Bologna. Denis Mahon, to whom I am greatly indebted for a mine of information concerning Guercino's paintings of subjects from Tasso, has reasonably conjectured, on the basis of Guercino's letters to Ruffo and of the entries of his brother, Paolo Antonio Barbieri in their joint account book, that the painting begun for Ruffo appealed so much to the cardinal who saw it in Guercino's studio that he worried the artist into giving it to him and painting a different version for Ruffo (for the documentation, see Vincenzo Ruffo, "La Galleria Ruffo nel Secolo XVII in Messina" in *Bolletino D'Arte*, X [1916], 61–63, and Calvi, *Notizie della Vita*, pp. 120–21). The journey of Ruffo's picture to Messina is amply documented by letters of Guercino and the agent (see Ruffo, "Galleria Ruffo," 95–96). That the Minneapolis picture is, in all probability, the Ruffo, not the Savelli, picture is borne out by the fact that the Guercino *Erminia*, which was among pictures of the Ruffo collection brought to Naples and perhaps dispersed during the first half of the nineteenth century, came from a collection near Naples in southern Italy and that an engraving by Guglielmo Morghen, one of a family of engravers active in southern Italy in the eighteenth century, corresponds exactly with the Minneapolis picture. The engraving is reproduced in A. Calabi, *L'Incisione Italiana* (Milan, 1931), Plate 139.

13. For a full account of Guercino's relations with Agucchi and Domenichino, see Denis Mahon, *Studies in Seicento Art and Theory* (London, 1947), pp. 58–102; for Agucchi's *Trattato*, pp. 111–54.

Erminia and the shepherd; in the herds and trees; and finally in the distant mountain. There is, in fact, a tendency to mitigate the effect of the space-creating diagonal in the figures themselves. Thus Erminia, the shepherd, and two of the boys are swung round so that the upper parts of their bodies tend to face the spectator and this increases our sense that the action takes place in a single plane across the picture, as in a classical frieze. The drawing of the figures is firm, their individual contours being generally precise and clear. The use of light is dramatic but not so expressively dramatic as to prevent it from being a constructive agent in the picture: emphasizing the forms and having a certain rational evenness of distribution across the canvas. The beautiful figure of Erminia in its idealization and its posture is related to classical sculpture, and even the shepherd, however rustic his attire, has a *non so che* of nobility about him. In brief, this handsome picture has a closed composition, a linear clarity, an architectonic structure, and a balance of parts that reflect the formal principles of classical art. It has, furthermore, those qualities of embellishment, decorum, and grace which, as Agucchi had probably instructed Guercino some twenty-five years before, should attend the ideal imitation of nature. How well it interprets Tasso's subtle and introspective poetry is an interesting question. Although Erminia is, as she should be, every inch a princess, there is nothing wayworn or heart-weary, as there should be, about her as she stands in a posture of active beauty and in strong light, like a goddess, before a shepherd whose mild surprise shows decorous restraint, and before the three children who give scant impression of having been frightened at all. What we actually have is a finely painted and attractive picture, an urbane, carefully planned, not very animated, and somewhat pedestrian picture in which Tasso's poetry has become a not ungracious prose. This is what we should expect from a narrative painting in Guercino's late manner in which, as Waterhouse has said, there is no loss of artistry, but a loss of fire.[14] For Guercino, during his stay in Rome many years before this *Erminia* was painted, had already begun to alter the early Baroque manner that was congenial to his talent, in an effort to conform to classical taste and theory and classicizing practice. His high reputation does not, in fact, rest on works produced during what has been called the classical *détente* in the Baroque century of the 1640's and 1650's, but on his early expressive style, impressionistic rather than constructive, luministic and richly pictorial, and concerned not with ideal imitation but wich the dramatic, momentary, and authentically real in human action.

In this nativ: early style, the famous dark manner of his youth, when his natural genius was unattenuated by the precepts of classicism, he painted another *Erminia*,[15] illustrating this time the conversation with the shepherd which succeeds the moment of surprise. This picture (following page) recently acquired by the City Museum and Art Institute of Birmingham, England,[16] shows Erminia as no ideal type but as a young Italian woman of the people, seated informally on the Arcadian earth by an ancient countryman of once vigorous physique, but now stooped and wizened and very old, in contrast to the fresh youth of the romantic figure clad in armor who turns her gentle, candid face to listen intently to the words of the bent, expressive figure at her side.

They are seated before a thoroughly rustic structure with no pretensions even to the post-and-lintel distinction of the Minneapolis dwelling and there can be no question of the poignant reality of the human interchange between them. In its homely types which have no trace of idealization and in the sense it gives of the immediate reality and importance of the communion between Erminia and the shepherd, this early picture is far removed from the Minneapolis painting with its accent of ideal beauty in the figure of Erminia and its more contrived and rhetorical drama. These differences in content are matched by significant differences of style. Where at Minneapolis the figures take their place in ample space, at Birmingham they crowd the space and are placed so close to the spectator that the large left foot of the shepherd nearly touches the picture plane (the gorget which Erminia has removed actually does touch it). This dynamic compression of large forms within a small space heightens the mood of concentration on something important which the protagonists with their active postures and their expressive gestures and glances themselves convey. The sense of concentrated drama is again in-

14. Ellis K. Waterhouse, *Italian Baroque Painting* (New York, 1962), p. 116.
15. It was painted for the Duke of Mantua, not in 1618 as recorded by C. C. Malvasia, *Felsina Pittrice* (Bologna, 1841), II, 259 (1st ed., 1678), but in 1620 — it is signed and dated 162[0] on the shepherd's knife blade, the last figure of the date being obliterated. Mahon (*Seicento Art and Theory*, p. 70, note 113) makes it clear that the picture could not have been begun before 1619 and that Guercino's visit to Mantua with his picture which he presented in person to the Duke was deferred until 1620.
16. I am indebted to Miss Patricia M. Butler of the City Museum and Art Gallery of Birmingham for a photograph of the picture and for valuable information about it.

Giovanni Francesco Barbieri (il Guercino), *Erminia Conversing with the Shepherd*. By permission of the Museum and Art Gallery, Birmingham

creased by a vigorously expressive use of light and shade characteristic of Guercino's early manner and not found in the later Minneapolis picture. The light does not appear to be placed carefully in certain parts of the picture merely to emphasize the forms or for the sake of a balanced pictorial structure; it also flashes and flickers over flesh and draperies, over armor, architecture, and landscape, having an independent pictorial virtue of its own and making its own dramatic contribution to the picture's moving content. And a consequence of this free luministic style is that the linear definition of the figures is less clear than in the later, classically oriented picture. Finally, the informal diagonal arrangement of the figures in space — characteristic of the Baroque pictorial idiom — is in contrast to the more formal symmetry and frieze-like arrangement at Minneapolis. The late picture has a quality of distance from reality which, without doubt, Guercino, conforming to classical principles, wished to convey. But the Birmingham painting, cast in the early Baroque style congenial to him, is more real, more intimate, more intense, and a truer interpretation of Tasso's idyll than the later picture.

In the conversation between Erminia and the shepherd, Tasso develops the theme of the pastoral of innocence [17] in a scene which also perfectly illustrates the pastoral economy. How is it possible, asks Erminia, that the shepherd and his clan are able to live in peace in a country devastated by war? The shepherd has several answers to this question: first, the clangor of war never reaches a spot so remote and obscure; then, just as the lightning strikes only the loftiest summits (here the literary shepherd remembers his Horace), but spares the lowly plain, so, by heaven's grace, enemy swords descend only on the lofty heads of kings; last, predatory soldiers are not tempted by poverty which, indeed, the shepherd cherishes and which is a kind of guarantee of a tranquil life untroubled by ambition or avarice. And his simple needs, since he lives in Arcadia, are well provided for. Water, pure and clear, quenches his thirst. His flock and orchard supply unbought food for his humble table. His three boys to whom he points as he talks with Erminia — "Ch'addito e mostro" —

17. Poggioli, "Oaten Flute," 157–58, distinguishes between the pastoral of innocence in the episode of Erminia and "the other side of the picture, or the pastoral of happiness" in Tasso's earlier work, the pastoral drama *Aminta*. In this type of pastoral, happiness is equated with the fulfillment of man's erotic wishes unfrustrated by anything. "Thus," says Poggioli, "he projects his yearning after free love . . . into a state of nature that exists nowhere, or only in the realm of myth." Thus the famous first chorus of the *Aminta*, beginning "Ò bella età de l'oro," is a praise of the only time when love was really free.

this explains the gesture of his left hand in the Birmingham picture — guard his sheepfold and he manages well without the bother of servants. Thus he lives "in solitario chiostro," in his sequestered vale where the welcome frugality of his diet is equaled by the simplicity of his pleasures: contentedly he watches the goats and stags bound across the landscape, the fish gleam in the river, and small birds spread their wings to the sun.

Since the shepherd has little to do in this pastoral Eden, he has plenty of time for Erminia. Continuing his discourse, he makes it clear that he appreciates his paradise all the more because he once lost it and regained it. Like old Meliboee, in the episode of Calidore and Pastorella in Spenser's *Faerie Queene*,[18] itself a pastoral oasis of great beauty which owes much to the story of Erminia, Tasso's young shepherd had abandoned his flocks and gone to court. There, serving as a gardener, he had come to know the iniquities of life among the proud and great and the vanity of human wishes. But after a time, deluded with idle hopes and sighing for his lost peace, he bade adieu to courts and returned to his sheep and his lowly quiet life in the country, where he now passes tranquil days amidst his friendly glades. Erminia hangs on the shepherd's words, intent and quiet: "Mentr'ei così ragiona, Erminia pende / Da la soave bocca, intenta e cheta . . ."[19] It is from these lines and those which follow that the Birmingham picture, a true interpreter of the gentle seriousness of her character and of the impression which the shepherd's discourse has made on her weary and love-distracted heart, takes its tone. She decides to remain with the shepherd's family "in quella solitudine secreta" congenial to her loneliness — of which it is, indeed, the image — hoping that the pastoral shades may alleviate her sorrow. We should note, however, and the point is important, that she will sojourn with the shepherd, not abide. She will sojourn only until fortune facilitates her return to the burden and the heat of active living. Thus she fulfills the requirement of the pastoral oasis that the bucolic experience be an interlude of recovery or refreshment, nothing more.

After the sympathetic and kindly shepherd has consoled Erminia and welcomed her to his house, his wife helps her to remove her armor and to clothe herself in the lowly weeds of a shepherdess. But the pastoral disguise cannot hide the true woman: neither the look in her eyes, nor the movement of her limbs seem those of a dweller in the woods, nor can a vile habit conceal "la nobil luce / E quanto è in lei d'altero e di gentile." This moment in the story, or rather a combining of this moment with the shepherd's previous discourse, was depicted by the high Baroque artist Pietro da Cortona in a painting in the Doria Gallery in Rome (following page).[20] Here an old but athletically built shepherd, whose "age is as the lusty winter," talks and points to the landscape while an absorbed Erminia allows his aged wife to remove her helmet and hands her sword to one of the boys. Baucis and Philemon, the aged couple in Ovid's fable,[21] are the literary ancestors of the shepherd and his wife whose hearts, like theirs, beat as one and who extend to Erminia the simple, kind hospitality with which they entertained Jupiter and Mercury. Tasso here gives us a glimpse of a domestic idyll, the natural outcome, Poggioli points out, of the pastoral of innocence and generally presented in literature in terms of old age, rather than of youth.

So Erminia abides for a therapeutic season in the country where she lives the daily life of a shepherdess, guiding her flocks to pasture in the morning, and bringing them to the fold at night. Often in the heat of summer when her lambs are resting in the shade, she follows the ancient pastoral custom,[22] everywhere observed in the Renaissance, of carving her lover's name on trees, and on many more she retraces the events of her piteous story. Thus we see her in a charming and spacious landscape by Salvator Rosa in the Galleria Estense in Modena (see page 53)[23] with her flocks nearby in the chequered shade. She is carving the name of Tancred on the bark of a magnificent tree and has finished the letters TAN which are clearly visible. A shaft of sunlight strikes the upper part of her body, revealing her action, while at the right three shepherds with their flocks variously illustrate the pastoral leisure, notably one who is stretched out in an attitude of full repose. Behind them extends a far view over the bucolic Eden: the cooling waters of a placid stream in the foreground and beyond the never-ending afternoon of an Italian landscape. In the succeeding moment, the last of her idyll, in stanzas of exquisite sensibility, in which, as Francesco De Sanctis well remarks, "reminiscences of Pe-

18. Book VI, Cantos IX and X.
19. Canto VII, stanza 14. The shepherd's discourse had occupied stanzas 8–13.
20. Painted 1635–1640 (see Giulio Briganti, *Pietro da Cortona o della Pittura Barocca* [Florence, 1962], pp. 220–21).
21. *Metamorphoses*, VIII, 628–724.
22. It goes back to Vergil's Tenth Eclogue, 52–54, where Gallus will carve the name of Lycoris.
23. See R. Pallucchini, *I Dipinti della Galleria Estense di Modena* (Rome, 1945), p. 233. The exact date of the painting is 1640 and it belongs to Rosa's youthful, Tuscan period.

Pietro da Cortona, *Erminia Being Divested of Her Armor*. Rome, Doria Gallery; Photograph Alinari

Salvator Rosa, *Erminia Carving Tancred's Name*. Modena, Galleria Estense;
Fotografía Soprintendenza alle Gallerie — Napoli

Michelangelo Cerquozzi, *Erminia Addressing the Trees*. Tivoli,
Villa d'Este; Fotografía Gabinetto Fotografico Nazionale

trarch and poetical commonplaces are set to a new music, mysterious, with a quality in its melody impossible to define," [24] Erminia bids the graven trees preserve for future lovers who may stop to rest in their shade, and reading, pity her misfortunes, the memory of her sorrowful history. In a painting by Michelangelo Cerquozzi (opposite page)[25] in the Villa d'Este at Tivoli, we see her in a setting of full country activity and atmosphere, surveying her handiwork and addressing the trees. Despite a certain superfluity of barnyard detail, the artist gives full attention to Erminia and is able to suggest her pathetic loneliness of spirit and the wistful melancholy of her lament. After these stanzas, Tasso's epic — canto l'armi pietose e il Capitano — resumes its predestined course and the pastoral interlude is at an end.

⚹ ⚹ ⚹

In a beautiful passage near the end of the *Purgatorio* [26] Beatrice tells Dante that his time will be short as a woodland dweller in the Earthly Paradise, but without end in the heavenly city, and in an earlier canto Matilda had supposed that "the ancient poets who sang the age of gold and its happy state perhaps dreamed on Parnassus of this place" [27] of fresh flowers, clear streams, murmuring air, and bird songs, of everlasting shade and perpetual spring. But in this Eden, lost through man's default, Dante can abide no more than Adam of old, and Beatrice hurries him on to loftier experience. Thus for the Christian poet of the Middle Ages, an Arcadia of the spirit could not be endless, but only a brief resting place in an arduous pilgrimage. In this sense Dante's Earthly Paradise resembles the pastoral oasis in the poetry of later centuries, where Arcadia, with its

24. *History of Italian Literature,* trans. Joan Redfern (New York, 1931), II, 658.

25. Cerquozzi (1602–1660) was one of the strong coterie in Rome who painted lower genre subjects, the so-called *Bambocciate.* The Dutchman Pieter van Laer, in Rome from 1625 to 1639, was largely responsible for the introduction of this type of painting and greatly influenced Cerquozzi. Naturally these painters aroused the ire of the academicians. See Rudolf Wittkower, *Art and Architecture in Italy, 1600 to 1750* (Baltimore, 1958), pp. 172–73. Cerquozzi painted no less than four examples of Erminia encountering the shepherd.

26. Canto XXXII, 100–2:

> Qui sarai tu poco tempo silvano,
> e sarai meco, senza fine, cive
> di quella Roma onde Cristo è Romano.

27. Canto XXVIII, 139–41:

> Quelli che anticamente poetaro
> l'età dell' oro e suo stato felice,
> forse in Parnaso esto loco sognaro.

The Earthly Paradise is described in the first half of this canto.

atmosphere and economy of the Golden Age, is only a place to stop and breathe in the fitful rush of life. Spenser's pastoral paradise in the *Faerie Queene* where Sir Calidore finds innocence and "happy peace" is short-lived; human brutality destroys it and the knight is driven once more to resume his quest. Don Quixote, after his strenuous follies as a knight-errant, resolves to lead the peaceful life of a shepherd for a year, though his sensible niece remarks that "the corn is too old to make oaten pipes of." [28] But his pastoral intermezzo is no sooner begun than it is ended by his death. At the close of *As You Like It*, the Duke and his lords, who have learned much from nature during their enforced vacation in the forest of Arden, return to the city and the court. Occupied once more with the normal business of living, they will no longer "lose and neglect the creeping hours of time." As for the gentle Erminia, in due course she leaves the shepherds, the better prepared by her bucolic sojourn to meet her destiny. This is to discover Tancred lying in a remote place, unconscious and near death, to stanch his blood with her veil and with her hair and in time to heal his wounds. [29] After this she disappears from Tasso's poem, her love unfulfilled. For the great poets, at least in their full maturity, "poco tempo silvano" is all that life allows, or ought to allow, anyone. Thus the pastoral interlude has its refreshing or healing value, but its prolongation into something more is incompatible with serious living and becomes a wishful and unsubstantial dream.

Still, Arcadia, like summer, "hath all too short a date." Nicolas Poussin and Guercino before him have warned us that even in that ideal country death holds sway. [30] "Ne certes mote he greatly blamed be" — no more than Spenser blamed Sir Calidore — who in the unremitting midst of life, requires from time to time a pastoral retreat, a few calm, unhurried days or weeks, or, happily, a longer relaxation of the spirit, somewhere in the realms of gold. A captive of the city, perplexed and wearied by its rush and noise, and dulled by routine, he might be pardoned for crying with Arthur in *King John*,

> So I were out of prison and kept sheep
> I should be as merry as the day is long!

28. Part II, Book IV, Chapters LXIII–LXXIV.

29. Canto XIX, stanzas 102–19. Guercino twice depicted Erminia's discovery of Tancred wounded, first in an early picture in the Doria Gallery in Rome, painted in 1618, not very long before the Birmingham *Erminia* (see Malvasia, *Felsina Pittrice*, II, 259), second, in a late picture at Castle Howard, Yorkshire, painted in 1649 for Cardinal Savelli, which is a pendant to the *Erminia* painted for the Cardinal (see

note 12 above). This painting was paid for in 1652 by the Archduchess of Mantua (*ibid.*, II, 333), who in 1651, as Denis Mahon first pointed out to me, visited Guercino's studio, undoubtedly saw the *Erminia and Tancred* there, wished it for herself, and eventually got it (*ibid.*, II, 267, and A. Luzio, *La Galleria dei Gonzaga* [Milan, 1913], p. 106). This subject, though not to the same extent as Erminia and the Shepherd, was popular among the painters.

30. In Guercino's arresting painting in the Corsini Gallery, Rome, executed in his early manner, not later than 1623, two shepherds come suddenly upon a death's-head which is placed on a decaying block of masonry inscribed "Et in Arcadia ego." In Poussin's picture of about 1630 in the Duke of Devonshire's collection at Chatsworth the masonry has been changed to a sarcophagus bearing the same inscription and surmounted also by a death's-head. Panofsky, in a famous article ("Et in Arcadia Ego: Poussin and the Elegiac Tradition" in *Meaning in the Visual Arts* [New York, 1955], pp. 295–320), has demonstrated that in these paintings, both of which have the significance, *memento mori,* it is death himself who speaks, and that the inscription must be translated "Even in Arcadia, there am I." In Poussin's painting in the Louvre, executed about 1636, the death's-head is no longer present, and the meaning of the inscription has changed. "Et in Arcadia ego" is no longer a warning spoken by death; it is spoken by the person buried in the tomb and means "I, too, lived in Arcadia." This interpretation, as Panofsky has eloquently testified, accords with the contemplative and elegiac character of the Louvre painting as compared with the sharply dramatic character of the earlier Chatsworth picture which is derived from the even more startling Guercino.

❧ EARL MINER

# Chaucer in Dryden's FABLES

SOME of Dryden's comments in the Preface to the *Fables* have so much warmth and rightness that his criticism has become part of the very meaning of the *Canterbury Tales*. His translations of the five Chaucerian poems, however, have had a less even reception. Widely acclaimed in the decades after their appearance in 1700, they lost importance when such great Chaucerian scholars as Tyrwhitt made sound texts of the originals accessible toward the end of the eighteenth century, and they suffered in the general fall of Dryden's reputation in the nineteenth. With his merits, both as poet and translator, growing more conspicuous again in this century, they have drawn more favorable attention. Their place in the history of Baroque style has been characterized.[1] Their divagations from the medieval texts have been studied minutely.[2] And their place among Dryden's other translations has been examined.[3] It now seems time to assess Dryden's conception of Chaucer and the poems and to define the purposes guiding his numerous alterations.

To understand Dryden's approach to the earlier poet it is necessary to take account of the three major conceptions of Chaucer that were current in the seventeenth century.[4] That most often met with considers him a poet given to broadness and freedom in treating love, with the Wife of Bath the great exemplar. Because of the strength of this impression, and the growing moralism of the English public, Dryden finds himself unable to excuse Chaucer's "ribaldry, which is very gross in many of his novels," and rejects the apology in the General Prologue.[5] Least often encountered of the three chief conceptions is the one that we today are apt to feel is the most important — Chaucer the creator of character. The appreciation of his humanity and his literary art is transformed by Dryden into some of the most memorable passages of the Preface. A third view, increasingly expressed after mid-century, can best be called historical. When Dryden says that "from Chaucer the purity of the English tongue *began*," both the verb and the stress of syntax imply elements missing in Spenser's famous phrase, "well of English vndefyled" (*Faerie Queene*, IV.ii.32). The historical conception of growth or progress, which is perhaps first applied to Chaucer by Thomas Fuller in his *Church History of Britain* (1655), is later reflected in such references to Chaucer and linguistic change as the famous stanzas in Waller's "Of English Verse" (1668), and is almost fully developed in progress-pieces like Addison's "Account of the Greatest English Poets" (1694).

The historical conception is of very great importance to Dryden. It is at the basis of his title, *Fables, Ancient and Modern*, since it groups Chaucer with Boccaccio and Homer with Ovid. The famous comparison of Chaucer, Ovid, and Boccaccio defines their places in their own historical traditions as much as their absolute literary qualities. More revealingly still, Dryden distinguishes two lines of English nondramatic poetry, one from Chaucer to Spenser to Milton, the other through Fairfax and Waller.[6] We have heard so often of the role of Waller and Denham in refining English versification that we have forgotten that Dryden defined the really great line of English poets differently. That line accounts for the great English achievement in narrative poetry, and it is to this form that all the poems translated for the *Fables* belong.

1. See Wolfgang Jünemann, *Drydens Fabeln und ihre Quellen* (Hamburg, 1931), which, in spite of its title, is concerned chiefly with Dryden's style and his versions of Chaucer. It has a useful bibliography. Further titles may be found in the Notes and Additional Notes of George R. Noyes, ed., *The Poetical Works of Dryden*, rev. ed. (Boston, 1950), the edition quoted in this discussion.

2. See W. H. Williams, "*Palamon and Arcite* and *The Knightes Tale*," MLR, IX (1914), 161–72, 309–23. As might be expected from one of Dryden's best students, this is the most careful discussion we have of Dryden's changes.

3. The standard work is William Frost, *Dryden and the Art of Translation*, Yale Studies in English, No. 128 (New Haven, 1955).

4. My generalizations are based upon examination of the material referred to in Vol. I of Caroline Spurgeon, *Five Hundred Years of Chaucer Criticism and Allusion*, 3 vols. (Cambridge, 1925), with some other evidence not noted there. It may be added that the major Elizabethan conceptions of Chaucer can also be found, although considerably altered, in the Preface to the *Fables*.

5. *Of Dramatic Poesy and Other Critical Essays*, ed. George Watson, 2 vols. (London, 1962), II, 285–86; hereafter cited as *Critical Essays*.

6. *Critical Essays*, II, 270–71.

Perhaps the very title tells as much. It would at least seem to be the most generic and usable Dryden could discover. In a letter to Pepys, he writes that he is translating "Fables from Ovid," "Novills from Boccace," and "Tales from Chaucer." [7] We have seen that he also spoke of the "ribaldry" of Chaucer's "novels." Each of the terms is applied somewhere to Chaucer, and each applies to narrative poetry. What the possibilities of narrative poetry might be is explained by the traditional rhetorical subdivisions of *narratio*: *fabula* ("non a veritate modo sed etiam a forma veritatis remota"); *argumentum* ("falsum sed vero simile"); and *historia* ("in qua est gestae rei expositio").[8] Given Dryden's choice of poems, their collective title, *Fables*, seems inevitable as the most attractive and applicable. Certainly it will be found that the three major thematic changes he makes in the Chaucerian poems involve the historical, the fabulous, and the argumentative — the last in the senses either of philosophy, satire, or panegyric. It is also the case that these traditional forms of narrative account for all the poems he has chosen to include in the *Fables*.

Although Dryden's changes vary in nature — as in quantity they defy enumeration [9] — sometimes one, two, or all three of what I have called the thematic changes mark his translations of individual Chaucerian poems. His *Flower and the Leaf* and *The Wife of Bath, Her Tale* almost wholly emphasize the fabulous. The former was in Middle English a vision and is changed by him into a dream vision. The latter had been a Breton lay. Both represent forms of Romance literature that Dryden had not practiced (at least outside his plays) earlier in his career, and yet his changes heighten the very elements of Romance. Some alterations in *The Flower and the Leaf* extend the tendency to description in the Romance by recalling Chaucer's love of spring scenery:

> When first the tender blades of grass appear,
> And buds, that yet the blast of Eurus fear,
> Stand at the door of life, and doubt to clothe the year;
> Till gentle heat and soft repeated rains
> Make the green blood to dance within their veins:
> Then, at their call, embolden'd out they come,
> And swell the gems and burst the narrow room;
> Broader and broader yet, their blooms display,
> Salute the welcome sun, and entertain the day.
> Then from their breathing souls the sweets repair
> To scent the skies, and purge th' unwholesome air;

Joy spreads the heart, and, with a general song,
Spring issues out and leads the jolly months along.[10]

Some additions, like the following to *The Wife of Bath's Tale*, increase
the element of magic and faery:

The king of elfs and little fairy queen
Gambol'd on heaths, and danc'd on ev'ry green;
And where the jolly troop had led the round,
The grass unbidden rose, and mark'd the ground:
Nor darkling did they dance; the silver light
Of Phoebe serv'd to guide their steps aright,
And, with their tripping pleas'd, prolong'd the night.
Her beams they follow'd, where at full she play'd,
Nor longer than she shed her horns they stay'd,
From thence with airy flight to foreign lands convey'd.
Above the rest our Britain held they dear;
More solemnly they kept their sabbaths here,
And made more spacious rings, and revel'd half the year.[11]

The changes in conception further the same ends. In *The Flower and the
Leaf*, Dryden not only changes the waking to a dream vision; he also
changes the knights and ladies to "a fairy show" (481). Both changes
distance with dream or magic what must have seemed to him already distant and magical. There is a similar change in his rendering of *The Wife
of Bath's Tale*. Lounsbury objected to Dryden's version on the grounds
that it "is essentially a fairy story." In Chaucer, he says, the heroine has

7. Charles E. Ward, ed., *The Letters of John Dryden* (Durham, North Carolina,
1942), no. 61; also in *Critical Essays*, II, 263.
8. Quintilian, *Institutio Oratoria*, II.iv. On *argumenta* see also V.x. The definitions quoted are translated by H. E. Butler in the Loeb Library ed. of the *Institutes*,
4 vols. (London and Cambridge, Massachusetts, 1953), I, 225: *fabula*, that "which is
not merely not true but has little resemblance to truth"; *argumentum*, that "which,
though not true, has yet a certain verisimilitude"; and *historia*, "an exposition of actual fact." See also Cicero, *De Inventione*, I.xix, ed. and trans. H. M. Hubbell, Loeb
Classical Library (London and Cambridge, Massachusetts, 1949), pp. 54ff.
9. Williams ("*Palamon and Arcite*," 162) states that "there are only about seven
lines in *Palamon and Arcite* adopted from the *Knightes Tale* without change." In
discussing what seem to me the major principles or conceptions governing Dryden's changes, I do not mean to suggest that there are not other important kinds of
change. Those Williams observes in *Palamon and Arcite* account for almost all not
mentioned here.
10. *The Flower and the Leaf*, ll. 7-19. Dryden is recalling the opening of the
General Prologue to *The Canterbury Tales*, but with more conceited imagery. Except where otherwise specified, my quotations from Dryden are of passages he adds
or alters almost wholly from the original.
11. *The Wife of Bath, Her Tale*, pp. 3-15. Cf. *The Hind and the Panther*, I, 212-
15.

been transformed into a crone by an "unmentioned, but evidently malignant agency." In Dryden, "She is herself a proficient in magic art. . . . When her offer is accepted by the knight, she spreads her mantle on the ground, and transfers him with furious rapidity to King Arthur's court, while his horse is also brought thither by some devil subject to her will." He finds such freedom "objectionable because it was false to the original, false to the belief upon which the original was founded . . . and false to the central idea of the story." [12] Whether the supplanting of an "unmentioned, but evidently malignant agency" with a magical power based upon character is such an enormity may be open to question. Certainly Chaucer has his magic flights and his Canacee has her magic ring. Whatever our attitude should be, Lounsbury's initial point holds: Dryden has rendered Chaucer's tale of a magical transformation into yet a greater faery.

It cannot fail to strike a reader with both the medieval and Dryden's texts before him that in such alterations Dryden has "medievalized" the stories in a manner more often associated with the Romantics. Some readers may find this surprising; if so, they may be assured of finding other additions that better accord with stock conceptions of Dryden. There is the ironic vein — of women: "Like leaky sieves no secrets we can hold"; and of fools:

> For fools will prate, and, tho' they want the wit
> To find close faults, yet open blots will hit;
> Tho' better for their ease to hold their tongue,
> For womankind was never in the wrong.
> So noise ensues, and quarrels last for life;
> The wife abhors the fool, the fool the wife.

There is also a historical passage of a familiar kind.

> Then courts of kings were held in high renown,
> Ere made the common brothels of the town:
> There, virgins honorable vows receiv'd,
> But chaste as maids in monasteries liv'd;
> The king himself, to nuptial ties a slave,
> No bad example to his poets gave;
> And they, not bad, but in a vicious age,
> Had not, to please the prince, debauch'd the stage.

To be sure, the criticism of the court of Charles II (rather than of William III, as so often in additions to poems in the *Fables*) may render the familiar strange. We also find Dryden's simple style:

> The King of Heav'n was in a manger laid,
> And took his earth but from an humble maid;
> Then what can birth, or mortal men, bestow,
> Since floods no higher than their fountains flow? [13]

Because "The Character of a Good Parson" is a professed imitation, its contemporary allusions are more to be expected. It is well known that the last thirty-five lines are an addition in which the deposition of Richard II is introduced as a parallel to that of James II, and in which the too easy accommodation of divines like Gilbert Burnet and William Sherlock — who had once professed Erastian doctrines of loyalty to the throne and passive obedience — is contrasted with the nonjuring principles of a "good parson." Dryden's positive values of a philosophical or theological nature — another aspect of argumentation — have more often eluded attention. His parson's eyes shine with *grace*. He shows only "sweet regards and pleasing sanctity." In his sermons he "lov'd to dwell" upon "eternal mercy." And "He taught the gospel rather than the law." Such are the qualities Dryden found in true religion — grace rather than will, assurance rather than fear. Grace, or mercy, is to him the prime attribute of God (as reason or wisdom is His essence):

> To threats the stubborn sinner oft is hard,
> Wrapp'd in his crimes, against the storm prepar'd;
> But, when the milder beams of mercy play,
> He melts, and throws his cumbrous cloak away.
> Lightnings and thunder (heav'n's artillery)
> As harbingers before th' Almighty fly:
> Those but proclaim his style, and disappear;
> The stiller sound succeeds, and God is there.

> (34-41)

The stress on mercy recalls the creation passage in *The Hind and the Panther* (I, 247–62). Dryden does not merely translate. Nor does he merely score some political hits on unprincipled contemporaries. The historical and philosophical tendencies of his "Character of a Good Parson" naturally allow for the affirmation of his most deeply held religious beliefs.

In *The Cock and the Fox*, as again in *Palamon and Arcite*, the same dwelling upon personal beliefs and introduction of historical matters are

12. Lounsbury's remarks are called just, with some reservations, by Noyes, ed., *Poetical Works of Dryden*, p. 1034.

13. The four quotations are from *The Wife of Bath, Her Tale*, pp. 155; 143–48; 61–68; 386–89. The last is part of a long addition of a philosophical nature (pp. 386–457).

joined with a greater stress upon the mythic qualities of fable. The most familiar historical passage in his translation of *The Nun's Priest's Tale* is that on Chanticleer's consorts.

> This gentle cock, for solace of his life,
> Six misses had, beside his lawful wife;
> Scandal, that spares no king, tho' ne'er so good,
> Says they were all of his own flesh and blood,
> His sisters both by sire and mother's side;
> And sure their likeness show'd them near allied.
> But make the worst, the monarch did no more,
> Than all the Ptolemies had done before:
> When incest is for int'rest of a nation,
> 'Tis made no sin by holy dispensation.
> Some lines have been maintain'd by this alone,
> Which by their common ugliness are known.
>
> (55-66)

Chaucer's joke on Chaunticleer's incestuous relations with his "sustres" involves a simple, delightful contrast between the innocent barnyard and sophisticate humanity. Dryden's *monarch*, like his altering of *sustres* to *misses* (mistresses), makes clear a historical intent. The complexity of allusion reminds one tonally of the opening lines of *Absalom and Achitophel*. Noyes follows Saintsbury in believing the last two lines to refer, not to the "cousinhood of William and Mary," but perhaps to "the Hapsburgs and the 'Austrian lip' " (Noyes, 1032). Both suggestions seem likely, although the last two lines follow logically from the instance given, "the Ptolemies." James Kinsley suggests (*The Poems of John Dryden*, IV, 2076) that the opening lines refer to Henry VIII, who married "Catherine of Aragon, his brother's widow," and effectively compares the passage with one in *The Hind and the Panther* (I, 351-69). Henry had had his misses, although only "scandal" would have held them "of his own flesh and blood." Yet it is not necessary to go back to the Tudors to discover a promiscuous "monarch." Dryden is rejecting what "scandal" said of Charles II. In his *History of His Own Time*, Gilbert Burnet insinuated that Charles had had incestuous relations with his sister, the Duchess of Orleans.[14] Burnet appears to be voicing a rumor which Dryden feels calls for reply. Moreover, "make the worst," Charles did "no more" than Henry VIII, whom Dryden thought to be kingly, if not entitled to his justification.

"Monarch" Chanticleer is, then, like Dryden's other literary characters which allude to historical figures. Chanticleer merges several individuals and periods into one whole, which may be defined in various ways, but which here focuses upon the libidinous typology of the Cock.[15] As in the opening lines of *Absalom and Achitophel*, here the historical is blended with the metaphorical. Instead of biblical history, there is the typology of the Cock: in behaving promiscuously and incestuously man is playing the part of a beast, lowering himself from his created station. But it is after all Chanticleer being described, and applied to him, the historical details only increase the gaiety — he seems all the more prodigious and important. It is ultimately nearly impossible to isolate a single dominant tone, because both barnyard and court are considered in a metaphorical relationship of which we cannot say that one stands primarily for the other. A later addition to the tale shows what is involved. Chanticleer tells Partlet:

> "See, my dear,
> How lavish nature has adorn'd the year;
> How the pale primrose and blue violet spring,
> And birds essay their throats disus'd to sing:
> All these are ours; and I with pleasure see
> Man strutting on two legs, and aping me:
> An unfledg'd creature, of a lumpish frame,
> Indued with fewer particles of flame.
> Our dame sits cow'ring o'er a kitchen fire;
> I draw fresh air, and nature's works admire;
> And ev'n this day in more delight abound,
> Than, since I was an egg, I ever found." [16]

In Chaucer's version the effects depend upon keeping the barnyard and the human world as far apart as possible in order that the periodic short-circuitings carry the maximum literary shock. In Dryden's version, as this quotation very clearly shows, the terms of the metaphor — or the strands of history — often fuse or exchange dominant roles.

There are other historical, satirical touches added. As has long been noticed, the Fox is treated as a Commonwealth "Saint" (480–88, 492, 796).

14. *Bishop Burnet's History of His Own Time*, ed. Osmund Airy, 2 vols. (London, 1897), I, 538–39, and II, 468–69, makes the insinuations of Charles's incest.

15. See Wolfgang Franzius, *Historia Animalium Sacra* (Wittenberg, 1612; there were other editions), p. 405, for the libidinous typology of the Cock: "[Gallus] est libidinosissimus. . . . Cumque reliqua animalia omnia Venere enerventur & debilitentur, & sic omnia post Venerem contristantur, ipse solus gallus cantat post coitum." Dryden used Franzius for typological material in *The Hind and the Panther*.

16. Unlike most of the passages quoted, this (pp. 455-66) is not wholly Dryden's; some details will be found in Chaucer.

The conception leads to further development in his protest of good intent to Chanticleer:

> "So loyal subjects often seize their prince,
> Forc'd (for his good) to seeming violence,
> Yet mean his sacred person not the least offense."
>
> (790–92)

Charles I and James II take the hand (see 124) of monarch Chanticleer. Most of the additions tend, however, in another direction: a mingling of lyricism, history, and elevated amplifications of Chaucer's concern with the issue of divine prescience and human free will. The historical details sometimes contribute to an ironic tone, sometimes to an elevated. The range includes "Mercia's king, / Whose holy life the legends loudly sing" (360–61); "Venerable Bede" (374); Joseph (383–84); Orpheus (601–7); the Greek and Roman poets (631–38); the Olympiad (668); and the splendid addition to Chaucer's mock woe on the destruction of Carthage, "And all the Punic glories at an end" (709). Religion, poetry, and history merge in these additions to elevate (even where the local effect is ironic) a comic tale into serious realms.

These realms can be best understood in terms of the philosophical additions, the *argumentum*. Although his Nun's Priest takes no stand, and in spite of the wonderful individuality of his characters, Chaucer appears to endorse the belief that man has no true free will. Dryden, whose characters are usually more typical, rejects Chaucer's tacit endorsement of necessity and, although he is absorbed by astrology and fate, argues for free will. Neither writer can be described simply. When the Cock is caught by the Fox, Dryden has an ironic lament like Chaucer's. It begins,

> Alas, what stay is there in human state,
> Or who can shun inevitable fate? . . .
>
> (see 675–84)

The poetic force betrays an emotion not wholly ironic. But the irony is there. In other passages, the irony is even more pervasive and must be viewed in context if the total direction is to be clear. (See 207–8, 237, 242, 325–26, 330–31, 335–41, 383–84.) The direction is revealed by the emphases in the passages added on prescience and freedom (513–22 and 533–51). The first follows the spirit of Chaucer's writing on this dilemma; the second argues freedom.

> Thus galley slaves tug willing at their oar,
> Consent to work, in prospect of the shore,

But would not work at all if not constrain'd before.
That other does not liberty constrain,
But man may either act or may refrain.
Heav'n made us agents free to good or ill,
And forc'd it not, tho' he foresaw the will.
Freedom was first bestow'd on human race,
And prescience only held the second place.
If he could make such agents wholly free,
I not dispute, the point's too high for me;
For Heav'n's unfathom'd pow'r what man can sound,
Or put to his omnipotence a bound?
He made us to his image all agree;
That image is the soul, and that must be,
Or not the Maker's image, or be free.

(533–48)

Faith in the merciful goodness of God is the basis of his rejection of necessity: "Good Heav'n whose darling attribute we find / Is boundless grace, and mercy to mankind" (281–82).

Dryden's additions to *The Nun's Priest's Tale* suggest in enumeration a strange tonal and thematic medley: it includes history, both ironic and elevated; it embraces "argument," ranging from satire to such philosophical issues as the proper use of imagination and reason as well as the problem of freedom of the will; and it involves fable in the heightening of Chaucer's beast allegory. It is an intellectual and tonal complex that undoubtedly deprives the story of some of its Chaucerian simplicity of line and human immediacy, as variations on a musical theme are apt to be more complex, less sweetly satisfying than the original melody. For this complex of tone and idea there is but one other example in English, *The Hind and the Panther*. That too is a beast fable, like this a plea for religious faith in Grace and for religious toleration (see 737). There are also differences in emphasis. Both poems reject private reason. The earlier favors the reasonableness of an infallible church and a God whose essence is wisdom or reason. The latter favors "fancy," the imagination or the subconscious operations of the psyche, which also have their truth (see, with attention to irony, 207–8; 237, 242; 325–41). Although in the translation fatality is confirmed by the truth of dreams — the future is fixed to the extent that Chanticleer is caught — the fact that he is saved by "fancy," the creative imagination (757ff.), proves that in practice free will may by God's Grace overcome destiny. The differences are slight, after all. Faith and imagination belong to the same realm. Certainly both poems reject private reason, which is exemplified in the Chaucerian tale by Partlet, and in both it and *The Hind and the Panther* by the Fox, who is an emblem of heresy, hypocrisy, and political disruption.[17]

Dryden's changes in *The Knight's Tale* are in some ways more significant than those in the other Chaucerian poems. Most obviously, he has fashioned *Palamon and Arcite* into three narrative divisions to Chaucer's four. Chaucer ends his first *pars* with Arcite's banishment; Dryden brings him back to Thebes and his three years in disguise before ending his first book. In Dryden the very division gives a sense of the passage of time and keeps the main action situated in Athens. Such division also integrates the whole of the first part of Arcite's adventures and begins the second book with attention upon Palamon. Chaucer's second part ends with Palamon and Arcite going off to Thebes to enlist their centuries of knights; here it is Chaucer who gives the sense of time passing with a division. Dryden continues his second book beyond this point, describing the building of Theseus's costly amphitheater, while the heroes gather their knights. Once more the focus is on a greater unity of place, and the building gives perhaps a better illusion of time passing than would a mere division. Dryden's third book begins at the same point as Chaucer's fourth part, with the arrival in Athens of the two retinues from Thebes. The refashioning gives a much clearer narrative line, stressing a beginning (love and quarreling friendship — the problem), a middle (preparations for resolution — the first duel and the building of the amphitheater with its pagan deities), and an end (the battle, Arcite's death, the marriage of Palamon and Emily). No doubt Chaucer had his reasons for his structure, but artistic design is something in which Dryden excels. His division into books rather than parts also stresses the conception he shares with Chaucer: the action is that of an epic.

The difference between the high comedy of *The Cock and the Fox* and the epic of *Palamon and Arcite* leads to certain fundamental alterations in stress, especially upon what may generally be termed history (II, 436) and reason (II, 349). Both help explain Dryden's more Homeric sense of the horrors of war (cf. Dryden I, 135–40 with Chaucer, 1001–8). They help explain why his imagery possesses a clearer logic (Dryden I, 326–30, 464–69; Chaucer, 1163–68, 1299–1302). Two other kinds of change, often reflected in but the smallest departure from Chaucer's text, contribute to the elevation of Dryden's version. One is a concern with fate and fortune exceeding even Chaucer's. The alteration is sometimes to be found in the addition of a casual "inevitable" (I, 232) or a sentence (II, 209) or simply in an extension of Chaucer (III, 1-2). The effect is not simply explained, since the alterations are absorbed into astrology, and astrology into myth.

> For Mars was early up, and rous'd the sky.
> The gods came downward to behold the wars,
> Sharp'ning their sights, and leaning from their stars.
>
> (III, 440-42)

The Homeric participation of the gods is very much more developed in Dryden's version, but fused as here with their Christianizing in astrology. Such a stress upon myth may have differing effects. It makes such fables as that of *The Flower and the Leaf* or *The Wife of Bath, Her Tale* yet more fabulous. In the epic and pagan context of *Palamon and Arcite*, one major effect is the transformation of allegorical deities into the familiar epic "machines" of Homer and Vergil. Chaucer's detailed allegorical descriptions of the temples (with "auter" and "oratorie") of Venus, Mars, and Diana become *fanes* (to use Dryden's exact, repeated word) of the pagan gods. He also shows them far more active and less allegorical (cf. Dryden II, 553-55; Chaucer, 1990). Such an alteration becomes yet clearer in Palamon's prayer to Venus, which in Dryden is beautifully merged with elements from Lucretius's hymn to the goddess at the beginning of *De Rerum Natura* (Dryden III, 129ff.). Thereafter numerous details show the gods in greater activity (e.g., in III, 273-74, 296-98).

The changes in structure, with the alterations to greater concern with fortune and to depiction of pagan deities given to heightened mythic activity, lead to emphases resembling Chaucer's but somewhat different. To both poets, Theseus is a good king, a representative of stability, law, and yet mercy. Dryden enlarges him to stress a certain cruelty at the outset of the poem (in the depredations upon Thebes) and philosophy in his long speech at the close. In Chaucer, Palamon and Arcite seem almost equally to be good men led into trouble by amorousness and wrath. Of the two, it is Arcite who conveys Chaucer's sense of human suffering. In Dryden, the fault in them seems to be youth, and they are distinguished almost along the Homeric lines (given, that is, the traditional preference for Hector and Troy). Arcite is a cunning, valiant Achilles, devoted to Mars. Palamon is a more sensitive, moral Hector, devoted to Venus. In neither does Emily cut much of a figure. Both Chaucer and Dryden are

17. The outlines of the typology are clear in *The Cock and the Fox*, and clearer still in the Fox of *The Hind and the Panther*.

led by their concerns to reflect upon man's lot in two crucial speeches, Arcite's while a-dying, and Theseus's in reconciling the living to the tragedy they have participated in. In Chaucer, Arcite's speech (2765–96) contains the more moving lines, fraught as they are with the famous human cry over the instability of human life — "What is this world? what asketh men to have? . . ." Dryden is less moving here (III, 778–835). There are some more telling images, real action on Emily's part (804), but less human intensity. In Chaucer, Theseus's long speech (2987–3093) is premised upon an attitude of *contemptus mundi*. The divine and human comedies, as it were, intersect and man finds his reconciliation to the human by reference to the divine. In Dryden (III, 1024–1139), the speech affirms rather a continuous beneficence of divine purpose through all the orders of creatures. What seems tragic in man's unstable lot is recognized and expressed in terms of the ruins of time. But Dryden finds reconciliation in the pronounced Stoic cast given to Theseus's speech. He prepared for this change by an alteration in the counsel given by Theseus's father Egeus. The pertinent passages read:

> "This world nys but a thurghfare ful of wo,
> And we been pilgrymes, passynge to and fro.
> Deeth is an ende of every worldly soore."
>
> (A, 2847–49)
>
> Like pilgrims to th' appointed place we tend;
> The world's an inn, and death the journey's end.
> Ev'n kings but play; and when their part is done,
> Some other, worse or better, mount the throne.
>
> (III, 887–90)

The Stoic image of the inn, adapted from Epictetus, governs the tone and prepares for the humanistic Stoicism of the speech Dryden gives Theseus. As with the speech of Egeus, Dryden starts with Chaucer but ends with a very different tone, that of Renaissance Christian humanism. Dryden's version of Theseus's speech rises to great heights of beauty, excelling Chaucer and completing the meaning of the poem "As jarring notes in harmony conclude." To Dryden, man's end is not ultimately tragic, because it is governed by a destiny directed by a kind God (1024–37). At the same time, the divinely ordained natural law is sober, like the decrees of Aeschylus's just Zeus (1054–56). The ruins of time are treated with particular beauty and with little debt to Chaucer:

So wears the paving pebble in the street,
And towns and tow'rs their fatal periods meet;
So rivers, rapid once, now naked lie,
Forsaken of their springs, and leave their channels dry.
So man . . .

(1062ff.)

The speech ends with the Vergilian sense of the epic life in which dignity is earned by suffering, and in which pride in the achievement of the dead reconciles us to their loss: "Nihil O tibi, amice, relictum." To Chaucer's "To dyen whan that he is best of name" (3056) is added, "And leave no more for fortune to dispose" (III, 1093).

Dryden's alterations in the Chaucerian poems are quite clearly of a degree and nature unexpected in ordinary translation. Yet they can easily be defined in terms of the *historia, fabula,* and *argumentum* of classical narrative. Most simply, with *The Wife of Bath, Her Tale,* the pseudo-Chaucerian *Flower and the Leaf* exemplifies the heightening of fable. Dryden's "Parson" incorporates history and satiric *argumentum.* His *Palamon and Arcite* merges history with philosophic *argumentum.* Finally, *The Cock and the Fox* gives added increments of history, beast fable, and *argumentum* both philosophical and satiric.

If there is in these refashionings any element more common than the others, or more capable in Dryden's style of embracing the others, it is history. Such poems as *Absalom and Achitophel* or *The Hind and the Panther* are historical in subject and narrative method; yet in them Dryden's use of history allowed fable and "argument" full scope. Certainly it would be a mistake to underestimate their importance in attesting to his imaginative powers with metaphor and his capacity to delight at the very end of his life in the faery of Romance, or in showing how closely related is his satire to a secure philosophical and religious ethos. But the historical conception, which had provided him with a realm in which he excels our other great English poets, also made possible his admission of Chaucer for the first time to a plausible pattern of English literary history and to the select group of authors in the *Fables.* This is to say that he was the first to conceive of Chaucer as a classic, with all that implies in humanistic and specifically Drydenian practice. For him, at least, a classic possesses three attributes. It has first of all permanency. A product of history and of a specific national culture, it is also enduring, immortal. Dryden wrote, in poetry and prose, so many progress-pieces that we can see he regarded history as a process of growth leading to permanency or to transcendence of time.[18] Chaucer's relation to the growth of English literature is obvious in the Preface: it is from him that our language "began" and it is he who originates the great line of English nondramatic poetry. His permanence is demonstrated by the proof that he is superior to Ovid and Boccaccio, two recognized classics of different eras. The second attribute is worthiness for translation. If permanence implies value in an order of greatness above time, the necessity for translation implies the historical accident of major linguistic change or difference. The third attribute is value as a source of allusion. Dryden had shown his respect for Chaucer in this way thirteen years before the *Fables*, when in the fable of the Pigeons in the third part of *The Hind and the Panther* he shapes an Æsopian fable by allusion to *The Nun's Priest's Tale* in the frame and some details absorbed into his fable.[19] Chaucer fulfills, then, each requirement, and if Dryden's alterations in his translations are more extensive than in his renderings of other authors, it is a matter requiring other explanations. But we can at least see a certain justice in Scott's inclusion of the renderings of Chaucer among Dryden's "Poems." It is difficult to believe that either Chaucer or Dryden would have objected strenuously. Both would have had cause for rejoicing over the *Fables* and its Preface. And not the less Dryden, whose death so soon after their publication, at the height of his powers as critic and poet, and exactly three centuries after Chaucer's, would have seemed to both poets with their absorption in human destiny events doubly fortunate.

18. I tried to discuss Dryden's conceptions of growth and permanency as aspects of history in "Dryden and the Issue of Human Progress," *PQ*, XL (January 1961), 120–29. I neglected there to consider *The Hind and the Panther*, in whose opening lines can be seen a clear distinction between that which is immortal and mortal, both of them found in history, but the immortal rising above it.

19. This, and some other details treated in this discussion, will be developed in my notes to the California *Works of John Dryden*, III.

⚓ ERNEST TUVESON

# Shaftesbury and the Age of Sensibility

Ezra Stiles, then president of Yale College, composed in 1783 his famous sermon "The United States Elevated to Glory and Honor." He reviewed the momentous decisions the new nation would have to make, and set forth a prospect of its future (even including a remarkably accurate forecast of the population two centuries later); and, as might be expected, the moral and religious issues were specially emphasized. The United States, he believed, would have to choose among three forms of religion: "idolatry" (which for him meant Roman Catholicism); Deism; and the pure "unidolatrous" worship. Needless to say, he favored the third; but his remarks on Deism, that complex of beliefs so characteristic of his century, are of more than passing interest.

The orthodox — even if relatively liberal — Stiles presents a surprisingly sympathetic account of the Deistic faith, intending, he says, "to give the idea the most candid extent, perhaps beyond the desires of a *Tindal*, or even a *Shaftesbury*, the amiable *Confucius* of deism, not to mention the smaller and more desultory geniuses of a *Hume*, or a *Voltaire*; neither of whom had any more taste or judgment in religious or moral reasoning than *Cicero* in poetry, or *Cibber* for the drama."[1] In this noble theology there is no need for pardoning mercy, "such being the excellency and dignity of man, who, as *Phocilides* saith, is the *image of God*, that he well answers the end of existence, merits reward, and must hereafter be happy under the all-comprehending, the most benevolent administration of the universal FATHER: How pure and sublime is natural religion!" Stiles, who

1. *The United States Elevated to Glory and Honor* (New Haven, 1783), p. 78.

himself had for a time been seduced by Deism, may have been more deeply affected than he realized. How attractive does the prospect of a nation of Deists seem! — if only, alas! harsh reality did not bring us back, even in this new world of hope and promise, to the ever-present and persistent evil in human nature.

Stiles's account of Shaftesbury is both misleading and, if accurately interpreted, illuminating. It is misleading in that like many other statements of Shaftesburian philosophy, it makes the author seem more idealistic, more removed from reality than he actually was (although here Stiles hints at a reservation). Three expressions taken together, however, almost epitomize the purpose and significance of Shaftesbury's message. First, the statement "that he well answers the end of existence," as we shall see, is the essential point Shaftesbury makes about the human being: not that he is "good" in some absolute moral sense, but that he has the mental equipment enabling him to play his appointed part in the great operating whole. Second, it is unusual to say the least for an orthodox theologian to employ "taste" as the criterion for ideas about religion and morality. Stiles here unconsciously spoke as a Shaftesburian, even in rejecting Shaftesbury; for "taste," when understood in all its connotations, is the key word of the *Characteristics*, and in addition a key word of the age itself.

Finally, the comparison of Shaftesbury with Confucius has a special and specific significance. The Chinese sage, whose work the Jesuit missionaries had begun to describe in the preceding century, became an intellectual hero, the prophet, to a fuller extent than any Greek or Roman author, of the *philosophes*. They envisioned him as a great moralist, a beautiful soul, a gifted writer of prose, but, above all, the reformer who, by bringing his countrymen back to the natural and therefore true principles of human conduct, established a strong and lasting nation. Professor Rowbotham says that Confucius was introduced to Europe at a time when advanced thinkers were beginning to ask, "Can man's relation to the universe and to his fellow men be solved in any other terms than that of Revelation?" Confucian teaching "had thoroughly explored the questions of the relation of man to man and of man to the infinite without too great a preoccupation with the esoteric and metaphysical but with a strong emphasis on the art of living." [2] Plato, in contrast, was theoretical and metaphysical. Further, Confucius had emphasized the social nature of man's being, as contrasted with the individualism of the Renaissance.

Shaftesbury likewise distrusted metaphysics and "system," and held that virtue is essentially and ultimately social, since man, by his very biological nature, is made to live in society. We may reasonably speculate that Stiles had the reforming function in mind when he conferred on the modern the mantle of the ancient.

The third earl of Shaftesbury, as the textbooks say, wished to reassert the dignity and native moral endowment of man against the dehumanizing tendencies of Lockian empirical philosophy, Hobbesian materialism, skepticism, and the fanaticism of religious sects.[3] All this is true enough; but we have not recognized that his primary purpose was not that of a philosopher. His works belong to rhetoric rather than to philosophical discourse, for their intention is to incite men to action: nothing less than a sweeping reform of themselves and of society. We still have not corrected Mandeville's caricature of Shaftesbury as a "good-natured," retiring connoisseur, who painted in his fancy a beautiful portrait of man as he never was. Not in this way did such men as Rousseau, Diderot, Herder, Schiller, Winckelmann, Goethe, think of him: for them he was the prophet of a moral and social revolution. Like his grandfather, he was an innovator, and he intended to bring about pragmatic results, not merely to inspire contemplation. He intended to change the world, not by engaging in party conflict, but by changing the motives of statesmen; and far from being ineffectual, he was one of the most important founders of a movement which we still cannot evaluate perfectly, for it has shaped and colored our own opinions far more than we may realize.

We cannot properly understand Shaftesbury's work unless we see it as one of many expressions of alarm about the condition of "society" (meaning the class that conducted government). Shaftesbury in reality was one of the many writers who tried to effect changes in morals and manners, another of whom was Steele. The latter's complaints are typical of the general attitude: wit has been perverted, and the disappearance of serious conversation testifies to a common mood of skepticism and triviality; "what seemed at first a conspiracy" only against Virtue is now grown into a "general Insurrection"; and "instead of employing their Passions in the service of Life, [men] spend their Life in the service of

2. A. Rowbotham, "The Impact of Confucianism on Seventeenth Century Europe," *Far Eastern Quarterly*, IV (1945), 239. See also H. G. Creel, *Confucius: The Man and the Myth* (New York, 1949), pp. 256ff.

3. See, for example, Ernst Cassirer, *The Platonic Renaissance in England*, trans. J. E. Pettegrove (Austin, Texas, 1953), especially Chapter VI.

their Passions." [4] The evil teachings of Hobbes, fanaticism, and party factionalism all exacerbated the situation.

If all agreed as to the symptoms, there was an important divergence about the cause and cure. Two very different types of treatment, reflecting very different ideas of human nature, were proposed and tried. (The fact that writers in one group were mostly Tories while those in the other tended to be Whigs may be suggestive.) First, there was of course what might be called the traditional Christian-classical view of man as a being endowed with reason and potentially rebellious passions. A radical evil infects human nature. Timothy Nourse, who wrote toward the end of the seventeenth century, may be cited as representative of this, certainly the most common view. In man's prelapsarian state, Nourse says, man "had all the means of safety in his own power; his Understanding was pregnant and clear, his Will was most free and unbyass'd, and all his Passions were in a quiet and dutiful Obedience thereto." But now, his faculties being in "perpetual disorder," man shows "generous Courage" in even attempting to follow the way of Virtue.[5] It follows from this attitude toward human nature that one important function of literature is that of purging evil moral humors which may be reduced but never extirpated. It seemed necessary to increase the caustic as the disease waxed, and the last Voyage of Gulliver and the close of the *Dunciad* represent perhaps the most extreme and the final great efforts in this enterprise of moral physic.

But some had begun to think that another kind of therapy might be more effective. It may be that man is not deeply and incurably scarred. It may be that his nature is essentially unchanged, and that he is still, as he was in the beginning, a moral being. A crust of evil customs and beliefs may have deceived both orthodox theologians and Hobbesians into assuming that they are the permanent and unchangeable qualities of humanity. Shaftesbury, in his uncompleted manuscript "Second Characters," remarked that modern clothing has so distorted the human body that it is hardly possible to find an example of man's natural figure: the analogy with the condition of his moral form is clear.

Benjamin Whichcote's sermons (which Shaftesbury edited) began to set forth the proposition that the principal function of Christianity is to restore man to his true self. Isaac Barrow, that remarkable man who made a career of pioneering in both natural philosophy and religion, began about 1660 to set forth a new version of the Gospels, reminiscent of the old Pelagian heresy; yet no less a person than Archbishop Tillotson later edited these sermons. Significantly, his preaching centered not on right reason but on the virtue of charity. "Wit," he indeed implied, is characteristically associated with "malice and uncharitableness"; we achieve virtue by letting our souls respond, immediately, without instruction of conscience, to the situations and needs of others.[6] Charity is the "sum and abridgment of all other duties," for "every man is of a divine extraction, and allied to heaven by nature and by grace"; and the evidence of this high lineage is the impulse to sympathize with other human beings.[7] In all Christian thought, the virtue rather inaccurately named "charity" — better, love — had been supreme; but it was grounded in the conception of the Body of Christ, and was considered the gift of grace. Barrow in effect locates "charity" in man's original nature, where it had remained, even after the Fall. The human race, he says, has sunk into a "drowsie state," morally, and religion can awaken it — surely a much modified conception of original sin. Charity, moreover, begins to assume its common present-day meaning — benevolent action. "All Men (I suppose) feel in themselves (if at least not harden'd by villainous custom) a disposition prompting them to commiserate, yea . . . to succour and relieve them who are in want, pain, or any distress." To paint the portrait of human nature as "drawn over with dusky shades, and irregular features of base designfulness, and malicious cunning" actually is a sign of infidelity (leaving Calvin, one fears, in a parlous state).[8] Charitable action is then a means of redemption in itself.

Steele's *Christian Hero* is a notable piece of propaganda for this kind of salvation. Although he stresses in a rather more orthodox manner than Barrow's the "hereditary Disease" afflicting human nature, he regards it as curable here and now; the natural condition of the soul is still health, although a persistent infection, caught from the environment, needs to be overcome. The Christian teaching, and a conscious effort to strengthen the emotion of sympathy, will effect our soul's cure. From natural sym-

4. *The Christian Hero* (London, 1701), Preface. The best succinct account of the ideological background is Rae Blanchard's introduction to her edition of this work (Oxford, 1932).

5. *A Discourse upon the Nature and Faculties of Man* (London, 1697), p. 110.

6. Ser. xxviii, "Motives and Arguments to Charity" in *Works*, ed. J. Tillotson (London, 1700), I, 339f.

7. Barrow, ser. xxvii, "The Nature, Properties, and Acts of Charity," I, 323.

8. *Ibid.*, ser. vii, "The Frame of Human Nature," II, 99; and ser. i, II, "Of Infidelity."

pathy "is kindled that noble spark of Coelestial Fire, we call Charity or Compassion, which opens our Bosoms and extends our Arms to embrace all Mankind, and by this it is that the Amorous Man is not more suddenly melted with Beauty, than the Compassionate with Misery." [9] The "weeping comedy," by arousing this powerful feeling in the spectator, would tune the heart. Thus charity, guided by prudence derived from ordinary experience and sanctioned by Christian teaching, would be the basis of morality.

One reason for the stress on the emotional response, which hitherto had been suspect, was the distrust of right reason.[10] Are there in fact any innate moral principles which can be observed in all peoples? Worse, is reason, for so long thought to be the reliable mentor of judgment and taste, itself an interested party, secretly committed to man's essentially selfish amorality? [11] Locke's description of the understanding as a faculty which has the power of comparing and combining simple ideas into knowledge and opinions, but which lacks a native moral bias and indeed any real feeling for values per se, furthermore, left much out of any full account of the human psyche: left out, indeed, those things that most people in their hearts believe make them "human" and not mere biological machines, however intricate.

The mind was being absorbed into nature. Throughout the tradition which Europe had inherited there had been a tacit assumption that the mind, although physically located in the natural world, is yet outside and above it. Even Aristotle, the objective student of human phenomena, concluded that the rational soul differs "as what is eternal from what is perishable; it alone is capable of existence in isolation from all other psychic powers." [12] The new philosophy was revealing nature as a harmoniously operating process, in which each participant moves like a component of a great machine: the whole operation, not the individual actions of the wheels and gears, is the end. Can the human mind remain alone and self-contained above such a system?

One of the most influential Deistic works, Wollaston's *The Religion of Nature Delineated* (1722), starts from the premise that the mind really is a mechanism, rather like a computer, designed to operate within the world machine. The individual is happy only when he acts in strict accord with the "truth" of each situation in which he finds himself; the mind determines what that truth is by obtaining and objectively evaluating all the relevant data. Wollaston out-Locked Locke; all we can know we receive from our sensory experience, and we have no moral guide from divine revelation.

Thus there were two diametrically opposed solutions to the moral problem which I described before. The ethic based on sympathetic emotion led to sentimentalism; the moral philosophy of impersonal understanding looked forward to the young Godwin. Each has obvious limitations; emotion provides an unstable and narrow foundation for all the complex moral judgments men must make in a complex civilization. On the other hand, the suppression of emotion, as Godwin was to find out, is difficult. There is, moreover, an objection to such a system in its own terms. The young Franklin, then a printer in London, composed Wollaston's book, and wrote a brief critique of it, which he published in 1725 under the title *A Dissertation on Liberty and Necessity*. He perceived that Wollaston demanded the impossible: "In order to know which is best to be done, and which not, it is requisite that [men] should have at one View all the intricate Consequences of every Action with respect to the general Order and Scheme of the Universe, both present and future." No, man must have in his nature some kind of moral direction, for "How exact and regular is every thing in the *natural* world!" Is then man alone to be left to "blunder about" in the universal scheme? "And can we suppose less Care to be taken in the Order of the *moral* than in the *natural* system?" He implies that we must be directed by faculties analogous to those that assist the animal creation. We shall simply have to absorb this blow to our pride, which "tends to exalt our Species above the rest of the Creation . . . What! bring ourselves down to an Equality with the Beasts of the Field!" But "truth will be Truth."

Happily it may not be necessary to bring ourselves to such a mortifying conclusion. Perhaps we have natural, nonrational functions in our psychic make-up, corresponding to the instincts of animals, but on a higher level. It may be that man realizes his potentialities fully not when he rises above nature to an "intelligible" world, but when he fully utilizes all his natural endowment, both as an individual and as a member of the great consort of nature. The confusion about morality has arisen because

9. Steele, *The Christian Hero*, p. 8of.
10. See Robert Voitle, "The Reason of the English Enlightenment," *Studies on Voltaire and the Eighteenth Century*, XXIV/XXVII (1963), 1735ff.
11. See the discussion by Rae Blanchard cited above.
12. *De Anima*, cited in R. Hoopes, *Right Reason in the English Renaissance* (Cambridge, Massachusetts, 1962), p. 27.

of a false notion that the soul is in a constant state of warfare between good and evil principles; the truth is that the personality is intended to be a harmonious whole, in which every aspect is intended to participate. The universe, Shaftesbury says, must be created and governed by one Mind, which can neither be at war with itself, nor be demonic in purpose.

Shaftesbury, then, began his call for reform by urging that his contemporaries take a good look, without preconceptions and without pride, at the behavior of their own species. Men should observe themselves as sedulously and impartially as they study their hunting dogs. Shaftesbury, then, aspired to be a truly naturalistic philosopher, to "inquire what is truly *natural* to each Creature: and whether that which is *natural* to each . . . be not withal its *Happiness* or Good." [13]

When we look at ourselves in this Baconian mirror, what do we see? Most philosophers had concluded that "reason" is the form, the distinguishing and determining element in the human being. But the mind has been integrated into nature, and reason no longer has its old independence and supranatural involvement. Shaftesbury's conclusion, in effect, was that the human animal is to be defined as a value-perceiver. Our reactions to objects, to situations, as beautiful or ugly, good or "ill" in themselves — this, and not our capacity for ratiocination (which we in the twentieth century share with machines) makes us "human." As a species we may be defined as those animals that possess *sensibility*. Hobbes (and, by implication, Locke), referring all basic motivations to self-interest, were shallow observers. Taste, disinterested taste, is a hard fact; it is ultimately the fact that makes man a moral being, and not merely an organism striving to survive.

This point is of course the foundation of Shaftesbury's program for the reformation of society. If many elements contributed to it, nevertheless the idea was a stroke of genius, and a new development in the history of thought. It has been said that the Greeks discovered the mind itself. Since then, there has been a division of the intellectual process — so long an unseparated whole — into distinct parts. Shaftesbury singled out the response to values as an activity of the mind with at least partial autonomy. It was in this century that the word and concept "aesthetic" first appeared; and the isolation of sensibility from the process of knowing and of logical thinking made possible the romantic doctrine of the imagination.

The immediate inspiration for Shaftesbury's idea may have been the fact that, from the Renaissance onwards, refinement of taste rather than strength of judgment or warlike accomplishment had increasingly become the mark of the true aristocrat. *An Essay on Criticism* is evidence that, early in the eighteenth century, the rage for virtuosoship had become nearly a mania. Shaftesbury regards the critical function as highly important, and extends it to the ethical area. Nor was the connection between courtesy and good taste by any means new. There had also been intimations that the joy the virtuous man feels is similar to purely aesthetic pleasure. Barrow had said that "The practice of benignity, of courtesie, of clemency do at first sight, without aid of any discursive reflexion, obtain approbation and applause from men; being acceptable and amiable to their mind, as beauty to their sight, harmony to their hearing." [14] In Barrow, however, this remains an analogy. It applies literally the expression "beauty of holiness," that quality now being interpreted as pragmatic charity. Thomas Burnet, in 1699, took a momentous step beyond this point, suggesting that a kind of sensation similar to the aesthetic is actually a criterion for the goodness of action. We have what he called a "principle" in the natural conscience which, when it has matured, enables us to distinguish "one thing from another in Moral Cases, without ratiocination," and which is comparable to sensitivity to tastes, odors, and the like.[15] Shaftesbury expanded this suggestion into a moral theory. He reversed the traditional test of truth and goodness. An object we call good, Plato had observed, is appropriate for its use, and pleasing; hence we say it is beautiful. The intimate connection of the true and the beautiful has always seemed dubious, although there is in Neoplatonism an intimation that the perfectly "true," the First Being, as imperfectly reflected into the material world, creates the impression of beauty. Shaftesbury's test, however, is explicit. "That what is BEAUTIFUL is *harmonious* and *proportionable*; what is harmonious and proportionable, is TRUE; and what is at once both *beautiful* and *true* is, of consequence, agreeable and GOOD" (*Miscellany*, III.ii).

For Shaftesbury, no less than most of his contemporaries, had no doubt as to the reality and consistency of fundamental aesthetic responses; they

13. *Miscellany*, IV.ii. I have used the fourth edition, 1727, of the *Characteristics*. Citations are of parts or chapters and sections.

14. Barrow, ser. xxviii, "Motives and Arguments," I, 339.

15. *Third Remarks upon an Essay concerning the Human Understanding* (London, 1699), p. 8. I have more fully discussed the intellectual background of the "moral sense" theory, in *The Imagination as a Means of Grace: Locke and the Aesthetics of Romanticism* (Berkeley and Los Angeles, 1960), Chapter II.

are more dependable, he implies, than the operations of reason. "Nothing surely is more strongly imprinted on our Minds, or more closely interwoven with our Souls, than the Idea or Sense of *Order* and *Proportion*. Hence all the Force of *Numbers*, and those powerful *Arts* founded on their Management and Use. What a difference there is between *Harmony* and *Discord! Cadency* and *Convulsion!*" (*The Moralists*, II.iv). He proceeds to the momentous step of moving moral philosophy from its old foundation of reason, and inaugurates the "moral sense."

Shaftesbury's conviction that nature demonstrates an aesthetic order as its fundamental characteristic was no mere fanciful notion, as the following statement by a distinguished twentieth-century scientist indicates:

One thing we can discern about Nature . . . at least it is a harmony. Now that for us the magical has been exorcised from it we can feel the vast unbroken harmony it is. Where tragedy and where comedy and where both it is at least a harmony all its own. . . . This world with all its sweep of content and extent taxes utterance to indicate. Yet it is given us in so far to seize it, and as one coherent harmony. More: it is revealing to us the "values," as Truth, Charity, Beauty.[16]

The last sentence is especially important; Sir Charles Sherrington, with Shaftesbury, sees the unique human sense of value as resulting from the uniquely human ability to appreciate the aesthetic wholeness of the universe. Shaftesbury's description of the planetary system and its relation to the cosmos reflects Newtonianism. Universal laws relate an infinity of diverse objects; he was neither an emanationist nor a pantheist — hence his emphasis on the need for an "organic unity" created by a pervading mind, uniting what otherwise would be only a congeries of separate objects. But, as Sherrington implies, to know the scientific account of nature is only a beginning; to appreciate the quality of the universe, one must combine empirical knowledge and sensibility. An earlier scientist, who lived in the period of high Romanticism, exemplifies this combination. Alexander von Humboldt, in a kind of prayer, says of his own magnum opus, *Cosmos*: "May the immeasurable diversity of the elements which crowd together into the picture of nature not be found to impair the harmonious impression of repose and unity, which is the ultimate aim of every literary or purely artistic composition." The following statement could be a gloss on the apostrophe to nature in *The Moralists*:

The external world only exists for us so far as we receive it within ourselves, and as it shapes itself within us into the form of a contemplation of nature. As intelligence and language, thought and the signs of thought, are united by secret and indissoluble links, so in like manner, and almost without our being conscious of it, the external world and our ideas and feelings melt into each other.[17]

*Characteristics of Men, Manners, Opinions, Times*, the gathering of Shaftesbury's published writings, went through many editions. Superficially, it seems like the other collections of essays, often rambling and verbose, that appeared during this period. It has, however, an underlying unity, which we can recognize only if we see that the whole constitutes a manifesto for reform of character and society. Although there is not space for an extensive analysis here, a brief consideration of some of the individual works may indicate Shaftesbury's intention.

The heart of the doctrine which Stiles recognized as resembling a new religion is contained in *An Inquiry concerning Virtue or Merit*, and *The Moralists*, which were published in one volume. The first-named sets forth the proposition that man's nature is an integral part of the harmony of the universe, and should in its behavior reflect that harmony. The ideal is not the Man of Feeling. Balance, proportion, symmetry of thought and action — these are the desiderata, and there are many classical quotations and ideas. The new element is the fact that everything grows out of an inner sensibility; the ideal life is an evolving work of art, nature's art, rather than a creation of the judgment. On the moral side, man is equipped with two kinds of "affections" — themselves forms of sensibility, ways of reacting to the social environment. The "private" group furnishes the natural tendencies necessary to impel the human creature to conserve his life and well-being. The "public," sometimes misleadingly called "natural," affections (both in truth are natural unless carried to excess), impel the individual to act in the interest of his fellows and of his species. Shaftesbury should be clearly understood: his is not a prescriptive moral system. Man is endowed with the social passions, not as means to elevate him spiritually or to redeem him from the curse of sin, but because he has to have them to play his part in the natural system. Shaftesbury realized that humanity has to be "social" in order to survive; the common picture of man as naturally a complete and ruthless individualist must be biologically false.

16. Sir Charles Sherrington, *Man on His Nature*, Gifford Lectures, 1937–1938, reprinted in Mentor Books, p. 280.
17. *Cosmos: Sketch of a Physical Description of the Universe*, trans. E. Sabine and others (New York, 1847), I, 68, 64.

The imbalance of affections, where it exists, predictably is on the side of the private ones. There is in most men no inherent bias to produce such a defect, but lack of thoughtfulness and failure to mature combine with many influences from society to produce a habit of selfishness, which is another word for narrowness of soul. Shaftesbury thought, like Locke and most other post-Restoration thinkers, that mankind has been cursed by overactivity of the abstract reason, which has erected vast and false theories on insubstantial or mistaken assumptions. He deeply suspected all abstract, logical formulations of human nature, where each loose end is neatly tucked in. Any local set of beliefs, elevated to the position of a divine revelation, he considered contrary to the universality of truth. He was one of the contributors to the Whig belief in liberty of thought. Attacking the newly risen false theory that human nature is essentially bad, and consequently can be held in control only by harsh measures, he noted as one of its results that "'tis hard to find in any Region a human Society which has human laws. No wonder if in such Societys 'tis so hard to find a Man who lives NATURALLY, and as a Man" (*Inquiry*, II.i.3).

It is a mistake, however — one that many have made from his time to the present — to suppose that this kind of theorizing leads to glorification of the spontaneous and untutored — e.g., the Noble Savage. He says indeed that the human being in a primitive state was but "the rough *Draught* of Man . . . A Species *in the Birth*," "ere yet he enter'd into Society, and became in truth *a human Creature*" (*The Moralists*, II.iv). Like most writers of the Enlightenment, he really means by the "natural" person one who has been trained to realize the potentialities of his own nature. Taste in aesthetics, no matter how sophisticated, must always presuppose a basic, unlearned response to colors and forms — but that response in itself is not taste. By analogy, the perfected moral taste presupposes an immediate, unreasoned, unlearned reaction to or aversion from acts of cruelty and injustice, and immediate admiration for obvious generosity. But the reactions of the heart are not sufficient to guide one in deciding what he should do in a complex and difficult situation; the statesman (and it was the leaders of society whom Shaftesbury particularly addressed) must be developed. Thus the instrumental reason should be the servant and counselor of the moral sensibility. Shaftesbury intimates, however, that there is a kind of "reason," itself a form of sensibility — a power of appreciating the proportions and shape of a situation, corresponding to informed artistic taste. This over-all sensibility would regulate the affections and moral and aesthetic senses. For even the "public" affections can be excessive (*Inquiry*, II.i.3).

This conception of ethics is founded on a theory of nature. *The Moralists*, which seeks to educate men in the right apprehension of the universal order, is, therefore, the center of Shaftesbury's whole work. The key to the great puzzle of our world is the fact that its plan represents an artistic creation. Aesthetic appreciation is not merely an aid in seeking to find the design of the whole; it is the only way to do so. Experience of an aesthetic type in the contemplation of nature enables us to establish a rapport with the creating mind. The aesthetic experience, moreover, should lead to that result; when it becomes an end in itself, it fails to fulfill its function. Thus it is misleading to associate Shaftesbury with "art for art's sake." Theocles, in Shaftesbury's Platonic conversations, finally brings Philocles to understand that "the *Beautiful*, the *Fair*, the *Comely*, were never in the Matter, but in the *Art* and *Design*; never in *Body* it-self, but in the *Form* or *forming Power* . . . What is it you admire but MIND, or the effect of *Mind?*" (*The Moralists*, III.ii). The work of art can make us aware of the harmony of our own minds as we sense this quality in the minds of others; and nature, the supreme masterpiece in which all other masterpieces have their being, brings us to the full realization of what we are as we sense the nature of the divine mind.

When Shaftesbury calls the artist the "second maker under Jove," he subtly changes the traditional meaning of this ancient phrase. The artist is not imitating an ideal reality, but expressing the "Harmony, Proportion, and Concord," to use Shaftesbury's favorite words, of his own mind. The work of art is valuable, in the end, not as a masterpiece of artistic achievement but as the successful expression of the artist's quality of soul. In literature, it would follow, such terms as "invention," "disposition," and "genre" would have a changed significance, for in the classical tradition they relate to objective creation according to impersonal norms. One might say, indeed, that each poet is his own subject, which he realizes more or less well in his own genre. In a larger sense, all poets have one subject, and eventually one genre: all, insofar as they share it themselves, reflect and set forth the harmony of the universe. One of Shaftesbury's most suggestive remarks is that nature has a Self, with which our own limited selves come into relation. The poet at his best overcomes some of our limitations and thus provides an invaluable service: for, alas, most of us live our lives deaf to the great universal music. No wonder we live in discord. The poetic sensibility brings together in unity and harmony, like the divine being itself, a vast diversity of apparently unrelated things. Hazlitt, whose belief that "disinterestedness" is the central motive for action is in accord with Shaftesburian principles, thus explains the unifying possibilities and power of the intellect:

The mind of man alone is relative to other things, it represents not itself but many things existing out of itself, it does not therefore represent the truth by being sensible of one thing but many things (for nature, it's object, is manifold) and though the things themselves as they really exist cannot go out of themselves into other things, or compromise their natures, there is no reason why the mind which is merely representative should be confined to any one of them more than to any other, and a perfect understanding should comprehend them all as they are all contained in nature, or *in all*. No one object or idea therefore ought to impel the mind for it's own sake but as it is relative to other things . . .[18]

The poet, it would seem, should neither select nor pass judgment, but rather evoke the "many things" in the universe, which he has in his experience comprehended; he might well be, as Whitman says of himself, "a kosmos," and like Whitman he could boast, "I am large, I contain multitudes."

The first purpose of *The Moralists* is to convince the average, intelligent, well-meaning but confused man of such propositions as those I have described. It goes beyond persuasion, however; it attempts, as a work of literature in its own right, to exemplify the harmony of the universe as apprehended by the rightly attuned sensibility. Theocles's hymn of praise to nature, the center and climax of the whole composition, is the ancestor of the long line of poems describing the natural order. Although there are traces of lyric, especially pastoral, and even epic in it, nevertheless it was truly a new departure in literature; it dealt a disastrous blow to the system of genres so long accepted by literary theorists. Pope pointed out that it could be written as blank verse — no accident, probably, for Philocles enthusiastically speaks of this "number'd Prose." Description, tableaux, scenes, which previously had been subordinate to the argument of any longer poem at least, now become ends in themselves. Theocles exclaims "But see!" and proceeds to limn a landscape; but he is supposed not to compose it, only to reproduce faithfully the art of the Maker. Accompanying the evocations is a kind of running commentary, like an enthusiastic guided tour of an art exhibition.

Technically, Shaftesbury is in the line of natural theologians, but with a significant difference. Natural theology attempted to show that the artfully contrived system of things conclusively proves the work of a great Mind. Emphasis was on perfect adaptation of means to obvious ends, among which were man's needs. Even after the new philosophy had undermined the anthropocentric conception, there still was a feeling that God had had a special care for man. John Ray argued that the great variety of insects, most of them nuisances, argued no malice in the Creator: they afford men material for entomological study.[19] But Ray's main argument is that, if a "curious Edifice or Machine" indicates the design of some "intelligent Architect or Engineer," should not the "grandeur and magnificence, that excellent contrivance for Beauty, Order, Use, &c." in the world, lead us to infer the "efficiency of an Omnipotent and All-wise Creator"?[20] Although most writers of this type — the Boyle lecturers, for example — observe the beauty and grandeur of the heavens, these are largely by-products of the work of the great Engineer. But sheer efficiency often seems to be the only real purpose. One frequently gets the impression that the great system resembles that obsession of this period, the perpetual motion machine — wondrously made but without commensurate significance except as it shows the skill of its·designer. The ancient idea that God in creation, by a spontaneous outpouring of creative energy, manifested His infinite love, loses much of its point when the universe is represented as a vast mechanism.

Barrow, in "The Being of God Proved from the Frame of the World," strikes a somewhat different note. All created things, he says, "joyn together in one universal consort, with one harmonious voice" — not only, as in the *Te Deum*, to praise the Maker, but to create a perfect harmony. The poems in honor of St. Cecilia's Day suggest, often, that harmony is an end in itself. Again, Barrow says, "this whole Systeme of things what is it, but one goodly body (as it were) compacted of several members and organs."[21] This return to the metaphor of the world as a living body anticipates the later conception, held by such Romantics as Diderot and Goethe, that the universe is a complex of active processes rather than a mechanism composed of dead matter.

18. "Remarks on the Systems of Hartley and Helvetius" in *Complete Works* (London, 1930), I, 73.
19. *The Wisdom of God Manifested in the Works of the Creation*, 4th ed. (London, 1704), p. 32.
20. *Ibid.*
21. Barrow, ser. vi, II.

The wonderful contrivance is present in Shaftesbury's apostrophe to nature, too, but it is subordinate; and he drops the remnants of crude anthropocentrism. Nature is the supreme achievement of the artist continuously expressing His mind, which we comprehend in part through our sensibility, aided by the understanding. "All Nature's Wonders serve to excite and perfect this Idea of their *Author*. 'Tis here he suffers us to see, and even converse with him, in a manner suitable to our Frailty. How glorious is it to contemplate him, in this noblest of his Works apparent to us, the System of the bigger *World*" (*The Moralists*, III.i).

If there is an element of mystical experience in this, there are also differences from most kinds of mysticism. There is indeed a contact with — not only a conception of — the great Being, but not a loss of the self in the Whole. The result, in fact, is rather the opposite — the individual finds and realizes his own individuality. It is a cure for the limitations our experience imposes on us. We realize "that neither *Man*, nor any other Animal, tho ever so compleat a *System* of Parts, as to all *within*, can be allow'd in the same manner compleat, as to all *without*; but must be consider'd as having a further relation abroad to the *System of his Kind*" (*The Moralists*, III.i). We become more, not less "social" as the consequence; for Shaftesbury, contemplation is a means, not an end. Nor is this properly a spiritual ascent. We do not, as in Plotinian mysticism, rise from the material state to pure Being. We comprehend more and more of the natural world. Nor do we rise, as Plotinus recommends, from "process" to "essence." [22] And, of course, the experience is affected by the fact that it has more in common with the aesthetic than with the spiritual: logically enough, for if the essential characteristic of the universe is harmony, it is to be grasped by a form of sensuous activity.

Another means of reform is the development of true artistic taste in such a manner that it will lead on to the perfection of taste in ethics. One of the principal themes in Romanticism was the intoxicating idea that development of the feeling for the beautiful and the sublime could be a means of reforming society. The main distinction between this idea and the Horatian *utile dulci* is that, in the former, the emphasis is on the moral effect of the aesthetic impression itself, apart from and beyond the content or subject matter.

This too is certain; That the Admiration and Love of Order, Harmony and Proportion, in whatever kind, is naturally improving to the Temper, advantageous to social Affection, and highly assistant to *Virtue*; which is it-self no other than the Love of Order and Beauty in Society. In the meanest Subjects of the World, the Appearance of *Order* gains upon the Mind, and draws the Affection towards it. (*Inquiry*, I.iii.3.)

Even Poe, while insisting on the necessary separation of "Poetry and Truth," adds that the faculty of taste displays the "charms" of duty, "waging war upon Vice solely on the ground of her deformity — her disproportion — her animosity to the fitting, to the appropriate, to the harmonious — in a word, to Beauty" (*The Poetic Principle*).

If the social order has for the most part been "unnatural," an ideal society can exist, and one has existed — as we might expect, in classical Greece. The Greeks, Shaftesbury says, had no masters. By this statement he denied the still common belief that pagan wisdom was a fragmentary recollection of Old Testament revelation, and he insinuated that the Hebrews had shared the universal barbarousness of pre-classical times. The Greeks discovered beauty. "Whatever flourish'd, or was rais'd to any degree of Correctness, or real Perfection in the kind, was by means of GREECE alone, and in the hand of that sole polite, most civiliz'd, and accomplish'd Nation" (*Miscellany*, III.i). Taste there was perfected, and "simplicity and nature" were revealed in all forms of thought and action. "And thus the Nation was evidently *Original* in Art; and with them every noble Study and Science was . . . self-form'd, wrought out of Nature, and drawn from the necessary Operation and Course of things, working, as it were, of their own accord, and proper inclination" (*ibid.*). Under the wise guidance of critics (forerunners, perhaps, of a Shaftesbury) society created works and institutions that were "Muse-like, graceful and exquisite." The Greek spirit was characterized by "SIMPLICITY and NATURE," for "this *natural* Growth of Arts" was peculiar to Greece. This account suggests those qualities to which Schiller later was to give the rather misleading name "naïve." And when Schiller described the Laocoön as the model of truth and beauty and as "an indescribable harmony," he was using favorite Shaftesburian terms.[23]

22. The soul's seeing is hindered "by its decline into Matter, by its very attention no longer to Essence but to Process — whose principle or source is, again, Matter, the Kind so evil as to saturate with its own pravity even that which is not in it but merely looks towards it." Plotinus, *The Enneads*, trans. Stephen MacKenna, 3rd ed. (London, 1962), p. 69. The tone as well as the substance of such a passage indicates how misleading it is to call Shaftesbury the "restorer of ancient philosophy," even though he shared the moral idealism of the Platonic school.

23. "Shaftesbury's idea of the organic unity of the artist's work and of the artist as a second Creator was immensely potent, and the implications of this idea are found

There was a dilemma in Shaftesbury's own aesthetics which later writers were to reflect. On the one hand, his own formal canon of taste featured such rational and classical (by any definition) qualities as balance, symmetry, serene control of power. Although he rehabilitated "enthusiasm," it was always, he made clear, to be under the firm control of the sense of harmony and balance. Yet the need for apprehending the universe in all its parts as an aesthetic whole led inescapably to other standards. He condemns the "Gothic" as barbarous, and states that a pile of sand has no aesthetic qualities, being shapeless. Yet since we must believe as an article of faith that the art of the great Self everywhere in nature is perfect, we are compelled to admit that "the wildness pleases." "The Objects of the Place, the scaly Serpents, the savage Beasts, and poisonous Insects, how terrible soever, or how contrary to human Nature, are beauteous in themselves, and fit to raise our Thoughts in Admiration of that Divine Wisdom, so far superior to our short Views" (*The Moralists*, III.i). And in the next section Philocles has been so far converted that he now regards even "rude *Rocks*," and "all the horrid Graces of the *Wilderness*" as having a special appeal. In his "Second Characters," fragmentary notes for an uncompleted treatise on painting, he says that a landscape should never seem composed; nature to be sure sometimes appears to be a painter herself, but then the artist should imitate "not the picture, but *herself* only." [24] What *is* her "pure self"? — the graceful, proportioned Greek statue, or the Alpine landscape, certainly pure nature, with its uncontrolled power and unclassical proportions? Which is the ideal: Apollonian, or Dionysian?

The practical technique for a "do-it-yourself" reformation of taste was what Shaftesbury called the "colloquy" and sometimes "soliloquy." Since this part of Shaftesbury's thought, although long neglected, has at length received attention, I shall not discuss it in the detail its importance would suggest.[25] Shaftesbury would have us imagine ourselves observed by another person — a device adumbrating Adam Smith's theory of conscience. There was, "among the Antients, that celebrated *Delphick* Inscription, RECOGNIZE YOUR-SELF: which was as much as to say, *Divide your-self*, or *Be* TWO. For if the Division were rightly made, all *within* wou'd of course, they thought, be rightly understood, and prudently manag'd. Such Confidence they had in this Home-*Dialect* of SOLILOQUY." (*Advice to an Author*, I.ii.) This procedure is explained in Lockian terms. Man, having reasoning power, must "be forc'd to receive Reflections back into his Mind of what passes in it-self, as well as in the Affections, or Will; in short, of whatsoever relates to his character, Conduct or Behavior amidst his fellow-Creatures, and in Society." We should call before this inner power those notions, tastes, dogmas which we have come to accept without examination.

Doing this, we shall inevitably realign things in the order of true importance. We really see — not merely think about — our attitudes: "by a certain powerful Figure of inward Rhetorick, the Mind apostrophizes its own FANCYS, raises 'em in their proper *Shapes* and *Personages*, and addresses 'em familiarly, without the least Ceremony or Respect" (*Advice*, I.ii). The procedure seems to be one form of that "raillery," which, Shaftesbury maintained, is an effective test of true ideas. This evocation of thoughts as "personages," moreover, is in line with the eighteenth-century mode of personification, and may suggest one reason for its popularity.

A means of effecting self-reformation is to develop the awareness of nature as a whole; it is one way to correct preoccupations with trivialities and artificialities, such as "Dress, Equipage, the Tiring-Room, or Toy-shop" (*Miscellany*, III.ii). There is a pattern proposed for this meditation, which begins with the "inanimate" world, "from beautiful Stones, Rocks, *Minerals*; to *Vegetables*, Woods, aggregate Parts of the World, Seas, Rivers, Mountains, Vales. . . . The higher *Architecture* of Nature." The "animate" is the next level, and finally we combine all to apprehend the "Union and Harmony" of the aesthetic and the moral, exemplified in the noblest ideas, "Home, Family, Country." The century engaged in a great "colloquy," aimed at a vast renovation of taste and

throughout the aesthetical writings of German classicism, for Shaftesbury's influence in this and in other respects permeated the eighteenth century in Germany." R. Hinton Thomas, *The Classical Ideal in German Literature, 1755–1805* (Cambridge, England, 1939), p. 80. René Wellek has informed me that Winckelmann's MS commonplace book contains large excerpts from Shaftesbury. It has not been observed, however, so far as I know, that Shaftesbury actually set forth the essential idea of the eighteenth-century classical revival.

24. *Second Characters; or, The Language of Forms*, ed. Benjamin Rand (Cambridge, England, 1914), p. 139. Since this edition was the first publication of this material, it could not have influenced aestheticians and critics of the two centuries following Shaftesbury's death: a remarkable fact, since his critique of painting and sculpture often anticipates Ruskin's approach.

25. See Gardner D. Stout, Jr., "Yorick's Sentimental Journey: A Comic 'Pilgrim's Progress' for the Man of Feeling," *ELH*, XXX (1963), 395ff.; and Robert Marsh, "Shaftesbury's Theory of Poetry: The Importance of the 'Inward Colloquy,'" *ELH*, XXVIII (1961), 54ff.

opinions. One form it took was the poetry of natural description. Here, for example, are echoes of Shaftesbury's ideas and favorite words in Joseph Warton's *The Enthusiast: or, The Lover of Nature*:

> O taste corrupt! that luxury and pomp,
> In specious names of polished manners veiled
> Should proudly banish Nature's simple charms!
> All-beauteous Nature! by thy boundless charms
> Oppressed, O where shall I begin thy praise,
> Where turn th' ecstatic eye, how ease my breast
> That pants with wild astonishment and love!
>
> (ll. 142ff.)

In poetry of this kind there is a new emphasis on aesthetic experience as such; but, I think it is safe to say, this experience frequently was intermingled with a sense of moral teaching according to a new method.

The creed and the mission of the modern Confucius may be summed up in two quotations:

Upon the whole then, we may justly as well as charitably conclude, that it is truly *our Author's* Design, in applying himself with so much Fairness to the Men of Looser Principles, to lead 'em into such an Apprehension of the Constitution of Mankind and of human Affairs, as might form in 'em a Notion of *Order in Things*, and draw hence an Acknowledgment of that Wisdom, Goodness, and Beauty, which is supreme; that being thus far become Proselytes, they might be prepar'd for that *divine Love* which our Religion wou'd teach 'em, when once they shou'd embrace its Precepts, and form themselves to its sacred Character. (*The Moralists*, II.iii.)

. . . even *here* HUMAN NATURE shews it-self, such as it is; not perfect, or absolutely successful, tho rightly tending, and mov'd by proper and just Principles (*ibid.*, II.iv).

Perhaps the greatest teacher of the Shaftesburian kind of moral philosophy was to come long after Shaftesbury, and in a world which the English nobleman would have considered strange indeed. Thoreau's life and works enacted the "colloquy," and in *Walden* he assumed the role of Theocles to his time. This is not to say that Shaftesbury was the directly inspiring influence, but that the *Characteristics* expressed a mood and a belief about man and the universe that permeated the eighteenth and much of the nineteenth centuries. "If, then, we would indeed restore mankind by truly Indian, botanic, magnetic or natural means, let us first be as simple and well as Nature ourselves, dispel the clouds which hang over our own brows, and take up a little life into our pores" (*Walden*, "Economy"). To cure men, to restore them to the spiritual health which is their rightful heritage, Nature herself being the physician — nothing could be more in keeping with Shaftesbury's vision.

If there was a central current in the Romantic movement, it may well have been this enthusiasm for the restoration of humanity through cultivation of sensibility and awareness of the natural harmony. If so, Shaftesbury may well be a major prophet. But, even if the claim is exaggerated, there is no doubt that we track him everywhere in the Age of Sensibility. Nothing could more surely demonstrate the truth of this statement than the fact that the president of a New England college could apply to ideas about religion and morality the test of taste.

❦ DAVID A. HANSEN

# Addison on Ornament and Poetic Style

Aᴅᴅɪsᴏɴ's first critical essay, the preface to the *Georgics* in Dryden's translation of Vergil (1697), advances the view that poetry requires ornament. He bases this requirement on the premise that while poetry must please and instruct, pleasure is its distinctive end.[1] "There are," he says, "several ways of conveying the same truth to the mind of man, and to choose the pleasantest of these ways is that which chiefly distinguishes poetry from prose."[2] The prose writer states a truth in as direct a manner as possible. By contrast, the poet expresses the same truth in an indirect manner by means of such ornaments as description, illustration, circumstance, or metaphor.[3] Addison explains why the poet's indirect, figurative style is more pleasing to the imagination and understanding than the prose writer's direct, plain style. This explanation may be set aside for the moment while we stress that Addison values ornament not as an end in itself but as a means of forming the style that has the most pleasing effects. Skillfully used, ornament enables the poet to gain the distinctive end of his art and to attain the highest achievements in it.

In later critical essays Addison expressed divergent opinions on ornament while performing such critical tasks as orienting his concept of poetic style toward theories of the sublime advanced by Longinus, Boileau, and Dennis; defending poetry against the charge of being mere wit incapable of expressing truth; justifying Milton's use of ornament to form the sublime style; and speculating on the pleasures of the imagination produced by poetry. The present essay aims to show how Addison changed his opinions about ornament and poetic style and yet always defended ornament.

In the preface to the *Georgics* Addison establishes the distinctive features of a georgic with reference to the principles of poetry. He explains the pleasing effects of the indirect style, and defines both the style of a georgic and the unique excellence of Vergil's language. Thereafter, he shows how Vergil, while succeeding in this genre, succeeds also in creating great art. The *Georgics*, Addison concludes, is "more perfect in its kind" than the *Aeneid* and is " the most complete, elaborate, and finished piece of all antiquity." [4] Addison's preface may have exerted influence on criticism and poetry during the eighteenth century.[5] But as a critical document it belongs to the seventeenth. Addison's remarks on style are little more than the commonplaces of the century, and his assessment of Vergil's style is similar to Dryden's in the preface to *Annus Mirabilis* (1667). Although Addison expresses conventional opinions on style, he develops them into a premise that is central to his theory of the pleasures of the imagination.

Addison's discussion of a georgic turns on the principle that poetry must be useful and pleasing. "A georgic," he says, "is some part of the science of husbandry . . . set off with all the beauties and embellishments of poetry." [6] In the best georgics, the poet selects only those precepts of husbandry which "are useful and at the same time most capable of ornament." In elaborating on the unique features of a georgic, Addison emphasizes pleasure as its chief purpose. It is the least improving kind of poetry because it does not encompass, for example, the precepts of morality or the abstractions of natural philosophy. But these subjects "seldom give an opportunity for those beautiful descriptions and images which are the spirit and life of poetry." A georgic takes as its province the fields and woods, or, more generally, "the most delightful part of na-

1. Addison's emphasis on pleasure is conventional. See M. H. Abrams, *The Mirror and the Lamp: Romantic Theory and the Critical Tradition* (New York, 1953), p. 16; René Wellek, *A History of Modern Criticism: 1750–1950* (New Haven, 1955), I, 21. This conventional emphasis did not escape censure. See Joseph Trapp, *Lectures on Poetry* (London, 1742), pp. 24–25.

2. Joseph Addison, "An Essay on Virgil's *Georgics* (1697)," *Eighteenth-Century Critical Essays*, ed. Scott Elledge (Ithaca, 1961), I, 2.

3. *Ibid.*, 2–3.

4. *Ibid.*, 8.

5. See Elledge, "Notes," *Eighteenth-Century Critical Essays*, I, 489.

6. This quotation and all others in this paragraph appear in the same place, Addison, "On Virgil's *Georgics*," 2, 4.

ture," and this province affords ample opportunity for beautiful descriptions and images. Addison defines the style of a georgic with reference to the manner in which the poet must describe things: "We now come to the style which is proper to a georgic, and indeed this is the part on which the poet must lay out all his strength, that his words may be warm and glowing, and that everything he describes may immediately present itself and rise up to the reader's view. He ought in particular to be careful of not letting his subject debase his style and betray him into a meanness of expression." Addison, then, requires of a georgic both vividness in its descriptions and propriety in its diction, the one to produce the most pleasing effects on the imagination, the other to sustain the style of poetry. Both vividness and propriety depend on ornament — the tropes and figures traditionally recommended as poetic devices.

In Addison's discussion of Vergil's use of ornament, we can see the commonplaces of rhetoric adapted to a discussion of poetry. The seventeenth century inherited and perpetuated a critical tradition in which poetry was associated closely with rhetoric, and in which the discussions of both arts often revolved around style.[7] Throughout the century, "style" referred generally to a manner of expression that departs from the ordinary patterns of speaking.[8] It is a manner formed by the use of tropes and figures. Addison leads into his remarks on Vergil's use of them by emphasizing the principle of propriety. As the "serious poem" ought not to admit the familiar phrase or saying from common talk, so the georgic "is not to appear in the natural simplicity and nakedness of its subject, but in the pleasantest dress poetry can bestow on it." Addison remarks: "Thus Virgil, to deviate from the common form of words, would not make use of *tempore*, but *sydere*, in his first verse, and everywhere else abounds with metaphors, Grecisms, and circumlocutions, to give his verse the greater pomp and preserve it from sinking into a plebeian style."[9] In short, Vergil uses ornament to form the style proper to poetry. Early in the preface, Addison claims that Vergil has excelled all poets before him in the middle style. In light of this claim, Addison's remark that the *Georgics* abound with ornaments is not surprising, since all the ornaments had been regarded by traditional rhetoricians as appropriate to the middle style and as the source of its charm and grace.[10]

Addison speaks of the "just poetical description."[11] The phrase may be taken to encompass both propriety and vividness. Of the two criteria, vividness is the more decisive in determining the excellence of a description and, indeed, of poetry. The criterion of vividness, established firmly in English criticism during the last part of the sixteenth century, had been upheld by seventeenth-century critics.[12] Dryden, for example, applies the criterion to Vergil, and Addison seems to have followed Dryden's example.

In the preface to *Annus Mirabilis*, Dryden says that the wit proper to a heroic or historical  poem lies in "some lively and apt description, dressed in such colors of speech, that it sets before your eyes the absent object, as perfectly, and more delightfully than nature." [13] Dryden, we note, requires of a heroic or historical poem the same vividness of description that Addison requires of the georgic. Neither critic is defining the wit or the style proper to a genre as much as insisting on a quality that marks the best poetry. Dryden, turning to Vergil, can find this quality in the *Georgics* as well as in the *Aeneid*. After remarking on the "many . . . excellent images of Nature" in the *Georgics*, Dryden extols the language of Vergil's descriptions and says that "while we read him, we sit, as in a play, beholding the scenes of what he represents. To perform this, he made frequent use of tropes." [14] Vividness not only brings absent objects into view but also reveals something in them that we ourselves could not perceive. Dryden says, "when action or persons are to be described, when any such image is to be set before us, how bold, how masterly are the strokes of Virgil! We see the objects he presents us with in their native figures, in their proper motions; but so we see them as our own eyes could never have beheld them so beautiful in themselves." [15] In other words, vividness has ultimately the effect of enabling us to perceive the essential property and beauty of things. It is something of this effect

7. This point is made by K. G. Hamilton, *The Two Harmonies: Poetry and Prose in the Seventeenth Century* (Oxford, 1963), p. 94.

8. See *ibid.*, 1–44; Wilbur S. Howell, *Logic and Rhetoric in England: 1500–1700* (New York, 1961), pp. 116–37; George Williamson, *The Senecan Amble* (London, 1951).

9. Addison, "On Virgil's *Georgics*," 5.

10. See, for example, Cicero, *Orator*, trans. H. M. Hubbel, Loeb Classical Library (London, 1939), p. 373.

11. Addison, "On Virgil's *Georgics*," 6.

12. See Rosemond Tuve, *Elizabethan and Metaphysical Imagery: Renaissance Poetic and Twentieth-Century Critics* (Chicago, 1947), pp. 79–116; Jean H. Hagstrum, *The Sister Arts: The Tradition of Literary Pictorialism and English Poetry from Dryden to Gray* (Chicago, 1958), pp. 11–12, 57–150.

13. *Essays of Dryden*, ed. W. P. Ker (Oxford, 1926), I, 15.

14. *Ibid.*, 17.

15. *Ibid.*, 16.

that Addison ascribes to the incomparably excellent language of Vergil's descriptions in the *Georgics*: "And herein consists Virgil's masterpiece, who has not only excelled all other poets but even himself in the language of his georgics, where we receive more strong and lively ideas of things from his words than we could have done from the objects themselves, and find our imaginations more affected by his descriptions than they would have been by the very sight of what he describes." [16] For Addison the decisive criterion of excellence in poetry is vividness because it has the pleasing effect of increasing our apprehension of things.

Vividness, it must be reiterated, depends on the frequent use of ornament. In the preface to *A Parallel between Poetry and Painting* (1695), Dryden praises "the *dictio Virgiliana*," by which he means "the expression of Virgil, his colouring," [17] or his tropes and figures. The parallel permits Dryden, and later Addison, to draw the conventional analogy between ornaments in poetry and the colors in a painting.[18] This analogy, Jean Hagstrum says in *The Sister Arts*, "has often been said to support the view that style is ornamental — that language is color and can be similarly imposed upon already created design or form." [19] Hagstrum, believing otherwise, argues that analogy "does not sanction the doctrine of superficial ornamentalism," but serves as a basis for the censure of gaudy and splendid ornaments.[20] Dryden — nor Addison — approves of laying on gaudy or splendid ornaments. Hagstrum is right. The doctrine of *superficial* ornamentalism in Dryden "does not occupy the central position usually assigned it." [21] But this hardly means that Dryden disapproves of colors. He distinguishes glowing from glaring colors, or daring from foolhardy metaphors, and sanctions the former but censures the latter.[22] Moreover, he argues that if the design of the poem is good, then ornaments can be used for a variety of purposes, such as adorning the design, raising or elevating the plain sense of a passage, or most importantly, giving vividness to a description.[23] In recommending the use of ornament for this last purpose, Dryden — and Addison as well — affirms a principle established by rhetoricians in antiquity and supported by sixteenth-century critics.[24] *Enargeia*, or vividness, can be achieved by the skillful use of such ornaments as metaphor and simile.

As opposed to the view that ornaments are superficial, there is in the critical tradition of the sixteenth century, as K. G. Hamilton says in *The Two Harmonies*, "a doctrine which sees 'poetic ornament' as giving the very life and truth to the subject-matter of poetry." [25] Dryden seems to be writing in this tradition when after admiring the masterly strokes in Vergil's descriptions, he says:

We see the soul of the poet, like the universal one of which he speaks, informing and moving through all his pictures —

> . . . *Totamque infusa per artus*
> *Mens agitat molem, et magno se corpore miscet:*

we behold him embellishing his images, as he makes Venus breathing beauty upon her son Aeneas —

> . . . *lumenque juventae*
> *Purpureum, et laetos oculis afflarat honores:*
> *Quale manus addunt ebori decus, aut ubi flavo*
> *Argentum, Pariusve lapis, circumdatur auro.*[26]

The embellishments of this description, the similes drawn from art, are not extraneous but essential to the image of Aeneas. They enable us to see the kind of beauty that Venus is breathing upon him. The ornaments may be added, but they are also infused by art, and their effect is to bring the creation of his beauty into view. "Imaging is, in itself," Dryden says, "the very height and life of Poetry. It is . . . a discourse, which . . . makes it seem to us that we behold those things which the poet paints, so as to be pleased with them, and to admire them." [27] And Addison, following Dryden, says that "beautiful images and descriptions . . . are the spirit and life of poetry." Addison differs from Dryden in emphasizing that the embellishments of an image, as well as the image itself, increase our apprehension of things.

In the preface to the *Georgics*, the concepts of vividness and the indirect style seem to merge because the nexus of the two concepts is Addison's view that a description, illustration, circumstance or metaphor can convey a truth to the imagination and understanding in the most pleasing manner. After advancing this view, he discusses Vergil's use of "meta-

16. Addison, "On Virgil's *Georgics*," 5.
17. Dryden, II, 148.
18. *Ibid.*, 149.
19. Hagstrum, *Sister Arts*, p. 212.
20. *Ibid.*, p. 213.
21. *Ibid.*
22. Dryden, II, 149, 198, 252–53.
23. *Ibid.*, 150–52.
24. See J. F. D'Alton, *Roman Theory and Criticism* (London, 1931), pp. 113–14; Tuve, *Elizabethan and Metaphysical Imagery*, 109–16.
25. Hamilton, *Two Harmonies*, p. 94; see also pp. 72–74.
26. Dryden, I, 16.
27. *Ibid.*, 186.

phor" (i.e., prosopopoeia) to suggest the truth that "an insolent graft" can transform once barren trees into fruitbearing trees.

. . . Virgil . . . loves to suggest a truth indirectly . . . to let us see just so much as will naturally lead the imagination into all the parts that lie concealed. This is wonderfully diverting to the understanding, thus to receive a precept that enters, as it were, through a byway and to appre-hend an idea that draws a whole train after it. For here the mind, which is always delighted with its own discoveries, only takes the hint from the poet, and seems to work out the rest by the strength of her own facul-ties.[28]

Addison assumes that the metaphor used to suggest part of the truth to the imagination will elicit in every reader the same train or association of ideas, that this association will lead the understanding to discover the whole truth. In a *Spectator* paper on the pleasures of the imagination,[29] Addison qualifies this assumption by admitting that a description will not evoke the same association in every reader. Moreover, Addison argues, the poet's description will please only the reader of imagination, judg-ment, and taste.[30]

Sometime in the sixteen-nineties, Addison made his first attempt to state his theory of the pleasures of the imagination. What seems to be the first draft of the *Spectator* papers on this subject was probably written before Addison left Oxford in the spring of 1699.[31] The first draft sup-plies evidence for two arguments. First, Addison assimilates his views on ornament, vividness, and the indirect style into a main premise for his earliest speculations on the pleasures of the imagination afforded by po-etry. Second, he buttresses this premise by making additions to the first draft, such as qualifying his assumption about the association of ideas and specifying what faculties the reader must possess if the language of poet-ry is to have its effect on him. I shall leave the second argument to the conclusion of this essay, and press the first to emphasize that Addison had a vested interest in the traditional views on ornament, vividness, and style.

In the first draft, Addison says that the poet's description "seems to get y^e better of Nature" since it "often gives us more lively Ideas of a thing, y^n y^e sight of y^e thing itself." [32] While the poet follows nature in painting a landscape, he uses "stronger colours" than nature and gives the landscape "more vigorous [lively] touches, heightens it's beauties, & so enlivens y^e whole piece" that we receive a more vivid image of the land-scape from his description than from the landscape itself.[33] The greater vividness of the poetic image, Addison suggests, may be owing not only to the poet's manner of describing things but also to our own limitations. We perceive in any object perhaps "two or three simple Ideas; but when yᵉ Poet represents it, he may either give us a more complex Idea of it, or mention only such Ideas, as are more apt to affect yᵉ Imagination." ³⁴ As in the preface to the *Georgics*, so in the first draft, the image vivified by strong colors leads to a finer apprehension of things, or what Clarence D. Thorpe has so aptly called "the perceptive response." ³⁵

Addison maintains in the preface to the *Georgics* that the poet's indirect manner of revealing the truth pleases the imagination and the understanding. The pleasure lies in our discovering the whole truth in that part of it which the poet has conveyed by means of a trope. But in the first draft, Addison maintains that our pleasure lies finally in comparing two sets of ideas, one set elicited by the vivid image of an object, the other set by the object itself. The aim of the comparison is to determine whether

28. Addison, "On Virgil's *Georgics*," p. 3.

29. *The Spectator*, ed. G. Gregory Smith, 4 vols. (London, 1911), III, no. 416. This edition has been used throughout the essay; hereafter all *Spectator* references, quotations, and paraphrases will be documented internally in the following manner: (no. 416).

30. See below, p. 127.

31. Elledge, "Notes," I, 499, says, "editors have long assumed that the first draft was written while Addison was still in Oxford." Peter Smithers, *The Life of Joseph Addison* (Oxford, 1954), p. 41, points out that Addison's last period of residence in Oxford, which appears to have been between January 1696 and March 1698, was uninterrupted by trips to London. Addison may have written the first draft during this period. Smithers (p. 34) indicates that Addison wrote the preface to the *Georgics* in 1693. W. J. Courthope, *Addison* (New York, 1884), p. 32, suggests that the notes on Ovid, discussed below, were written in 1697.

32. I have consulted the first draft as described by J. Dykes Campbell in *Some Portions of Essays Contributed to the Spectator by Mr. Joseph Addison* (Glasgow, 1864), p. 13, hereafter referred to as Addison MS, ed. Campbell. There are revisions and additions of the first draft which are clearly indicated by Campbell, but I do not base any of my arguments or suggestions on the revisions or additions. Elledge, "Notes," I, 499-507, indicates the relation between the first draft and *Spectator* papers nos. 411-21.

33. *Ibid.*; the word "lively," enclosed in brackets, has been added as an alternate to "vigorous." Hagstrum, *Sister Arts*, p. 64, n. 25, says, "the word 'liveliness' is usually a synonym for *enargeia*. . . . The use of 'lively' in connection with *enargeia* and the analogy [between ornaments and colors] with painting persisted up at least to the time of Dr. Johnson."

34. Addison MS, ed. Campbell, pp. 13-14.

35. "Addison's Theory of the Imagination as 'Perceptive Response,'" *Papers of the Michigan Academy of Science Arts and Letters*, XXI (1939), 512-13; see also Ernest L. Tuveson, *The Imagination as a Means of Grace: Locke and the Aesthetics of Romanticism* (Berkeley and Los Angeles, 1960), p. 119, for a discussion of Addison's view that "poetry increases apprehension."

or not the ideas we receive from the vivid image have any foundation in nature. Addison finds it difficult to explain why the act of comparison should be so pleasing, but he does say that "the final cause probably of annexing pleasure to yˢ operation of yᵉ Mind was to quicken & encourage us in yᵉ pursuit of knowledge." [36] In moving from the preface to the *Georgics* to the first draft, then, Addison further develops his speculations on the pleasures of the imagination. The two documents are alike in making the style of a poet's description the efficient cause of these pleasures. Poetic style, therefore, is a main premise of his speculations.

It is this premise that Locke and Boileau undermine in radically different ways. Locke condemns discourse dependent on figurative language as incapable of expressing knowledge and truth. Boileau believes that the highest form of the sublime lies in great thoughts expressed in the simplest language, and denies that the sublime depends on the sources of rhetoric. Viewed together, Locke and Boileau reject the doctrine that sees in ornament the very truth and life of poetry. After the preface to the *Georgics*, Addison changes his opinions on poetic style to meet the opinions of Locke and Boileau, yet also continues to defend ornament.

ʃ  ʃ  ʃ

In a biography of Addison written in the last century, W. J. Courthope observes that Addison laid the foundations of his critical method during the latter part of the sixteen-nineties, and that the movement from his early to his later criticism may be seen in a set of notes on his translations of several stories from Ovid's *Metamorphoses*.[37] Early in the notes, Addison announces that he will "only consider Ovid under the character of a Poet, and endeavour to shew him impartially, without the usual prejudice of a Translator." [38] His comments, Addison indicates, will have the twofold aim of improving the criticism of Ovid's poetry and improving the taste of the reader. In the notes that follow these announcements, Addison extends some of his comments into brief essays, which show him orienting his concept of poetic style toward Boileau's sublime and drawing on Locke's account of wit.

Addison, like others of his day, believes that a principal task of the critic is to comment on the beauties and defects of a poem; Ovid lends himself admirably to this task because he has "something of the best and worst poets." A commentary on Ovid, therefore, "would give the reader a truer taste of poetry than a comment on any other Poet." The best in Ovid is the diversity of his styles, which range from the easy and natural to the sublime. The worst lies in his many turns of wit. The "truer taste" that Addison is after requires an appreciation of the sublime and disapproval of wit.

Although Addison says that Ovid's "chief grace is to be easie and natural" in the telling of a familiar story, he observes that there is such a great diversity of argument in the *Metamorphoses* that "who would treat of 'em rightly, ought to be a master of all stiles . . ." [39] Addison cannot agree with critics who "run down Ovid in the gross, for a low middle way of writing." [40] So far as Addison is concerned, Ovid "wants neither strength of thought nor expression, when he endeavours after it, in the more sublime and manly subjects of his poem." [41] As an example of the sublime, Addison cites Ovid's description of Enceladus — a "simple and unadorn'd description" which gives us an image "of a Giant vomiting out a tempest of fire, and heaving up all Sicily, with the body of an Island upon his Breast, and a vast Promontory on either Arm." [42] This image is to Addison "truly great and sublime" implicitly because it has a subject of proper magnitude, and explicitly because it is conveyed in a language that is simple and unadorned. Boileau's influence is present in these comments, since they suggest that the sublime consists in greatness of conception and simplicity of expression.

While the best in Ovid arises from his strength of thought and simplicity of expression, the worst in him proceeds from his extravagant fancy and faulty judgment. [43] They are responsible for several defects: occasional images that exceed all the bounds of probability; an ingenious way of drawing out a single thought that leads him to say more than he should; and an irresistible impulse, so it seems, to "drop the majesty of his verse for the sake of one of his little turns." [44] Ovid's many turns of wit produce one of Addison's longest notes. In this note Addison introduces Locke's account of wit, distinguishes the several kinds of wit (true, false, and

36. Addison MS, ed. Campbell, p. 14.
37. Courthope, *Addison*, p. 32. The notes and translations were published in *The Poetical Miscellanies*, fifth series (1704).
38. This quotation and the others in the next paragraph appear in the same place, "Notes on Some of the Foregoing Stories in Ovid's *Metamorphoses*," *The Miscellaneous Works of Joseph Addison*, ed. A. C. Guthkelch (London, 1914), I, 135.
39. *Ibid.*, 139.
40. *Ibid.*, 134.
41. *Ibid.*, 139.
42. *Ibid.*, 134.
43. *Ibid.*, 139, 145.
44. *Ibid.*, 140, 145.

mixed), identifies the many turns in Ovid as mixed wit, wonders why "so sublime a genius as Milton" could fall into mixed wit "in such a work as an Epic Poem," and explains that Milton fell so low only to humor "the vicious taste of the age he lived in, and the false judgment of our unlearned English readers in general, who have few of them a relish of the more masculine and noble beauties of Poetry." [45] Lucy Aikin and Courthope in their biographies of Addison have observed correctly that the note on wit in Ovid is the embryo of the *Spectator* paper (no. 62) on true wit.[46] Alike as the 1704 note and the *Spectator* paper are in their endeavor to discourage a taste for mixed wit, they differ radically.

The *Spectator* paper on true wit falls into two parts. In the first Addison expands and modifies his earlier discussion of Locke. Addison's revisions have the effect of changing the earlier expository account of wit into a defense of poetry and its figurative language. The second part, none of which appears in the 1704 note, includes the testimony of Dominique Bouhours that wit must be founded in truth; an allusion to Boileau's dictum that truth alone is beautiful and pleasing; Addison's recommendation of "majestic simplicity" as the criterion of the greatest poetry; and his rejection of a definition of wit by Dryden. The two parts of the *Spectator* paper allow us to see that in 1711 Addison could not accept an account of wit that denies truth to poetry because of its dependence on figurative language, or a definition of wit that ultimately requires this language for the sublime.

The *Spectator* paper on true wit was published a few days before Pope's *Essay on Criticism*. Recent studies of the *Essay* have shown how Pope's ambiguous use of "wit" defends poetry against just such derogatory opinions as Locke had expressed.[47] Addison's defense of wit differs from Pope's in at least two respects. First, Addison reckons with Locke himself and qualifies his account of wit. Second, Addison relegates wit to the function of diverting the mind with surprising ideas. Pope, of course, ignores Locke and does not confine wit to a single function. Addison's defense, like Pope's, may have been partly inspired by the hostile opinions toward wit and poetry that were especially current during the first decade of the eighteenth century.[48] According to William K. Wimsatt, Jr., Addison "starts with the assumption that 'wit' is a term of honor." [49] Since the *Spectator* paper on true wit but not the 1704 note counters the hostile opinions toward poetry and wit, one can with some reason disagree with Wimsatt and argue that in 1711 Addison, like Pope, was making a deliberate attempt to redefine "wit" in such a way as to make it a term of honor.

At the outset of the *Spectator* paper Addison quotes Locke's account of wit but omits his explanation of why wit is so pleasing to all people. Wit, Locke says, "strikes so lively on the fancy, and therefore is so acceptable to all people, *because its beauty appears at first sight, and there is required no labour of thought to examine what truth or reason there is in it*." [50] Addison omits the italicized part, no doubt because he rejects Locke's opinion that beauty cannot be present in wit if it lacks truth or reason, and also because he cannot agree with Locke that wit arrests the judgment of all people. The critic's task in antiquity, Addison says, was "to distinguish the several kinds of Wit by Terms of Art, and to consider them as more or less perfect, according as they were founded in Truth" (*Spectator*, no. 61). Addison in the 1704 note distinguishes the several kinds of wit, but only in the *Spectator* does he take pains to examine each of them and to show how even mixed wit has some foundation in reason and truth.

Several of Addison's changes from the 1704 note introduce and emphasize significant qualifications of Locke's account of wit. Locke had said that wit consists "in the assemblage of ideas, and putting those together with quickness and variety, wherein can be found any resemblance or congruity, thereby to make up pleasant pictures and agreeable visions in the fancy." [51] In the 1704 note Addison quotes Locke's observation and says, "Thus does True wit, as this incomparable Author observes, generally consist in the Likeness of Ideas, and is more or less Wit, as this Likeness in Ideas is more surprizing and unexpected." [52] But in the *Spectator* (no. 62) Addison rejects Locke's view that *any* likeness can be

45. *Ibid.*, 144.

46. Lucy Aikin, *The Life of Joseph Addison* (Philadelphia, 1846), p. 33; Courthope, *Addison*, pp. 31–33.

47. See Edward Niles Hooker, "Pope on Wit: 'The Essay on Criticism,' " *The Seventeenth Century . . . By Richard Foster Jones and Others Writing in his Honor* (Stanford, 1951), pp. 225–46; E. Audra and Aubrey Williams, ed., *Pastoral Poetry and An Essay on Criticism*, by Alexander Pope, Twickenham ed., I (London, 1961), 209–13.

48. Hooker, "Pope on Wit," pp. 227ff.

49. *Literary Criticism: A Short History* (New York, 1957), p. 232; cf. Hooker, "Pope on Wit," pp. 230–31.

50. *Essay Concerning Human Understanding*, II, xi; ed. Alexander C. Fraser, 2 vols. (Oxford, 1894), I, 203, my italics.

51. *Ibid.*

52. Addison, "Notes on Ovid" 144.

called "wit," and he stresses that he, not Locke, is restricting the meaning of "wit." After quoting Locke, Addison says, "I shall only add . . . That every Resemblance of Ideas is not that which we call Wit, unless it be such an one that gives *Delight* and *Surprize* to the Reader: these two Properties seem essential to Wit, more particularly the last of them." After thus restricting the meaning of wit, Addison further qualifies Locke. The similarities discovered by wit, according to Locke, produce images that have no foundation in reason or judgment. Addison disagrees. The similarities of wit may "not fill the Mind with great Conceptions," and may only divert the mind with ideas that are novel and surprising, but even these, he insists, must have a "Foundation in the Nature of Things." He agrees with Bouhours: "the basis of all Wit is Truth" (*Spectator*, no. 62). In the 1704 note Addison does not play off the authority of a fashionable French critic against the incomparable Locke.

In the *Spectator* Addison asserts, as he does not in the 1704 note, that true wit — wit in his restricted sense of the term — can be found in metaphor, simile, allegory, enigma, motto, parable, fable, dream, and vision. Implicitly, this assertion runs counter to Locke's opinion that figurative language cannot convey knowledge or truth and has no foundation in reason. Addison makes the case for figurative language, but in such a way as to concede that it can be used to express ideas that depart from truth and to produce images that have no foundation in the nature of things. Addison's view of figurative language is similar to Bouhours's: "metaphors have their truth as well as fictions." [53]

Addison's case for figurative language can be best understood in the context of his concept of the several kinds of wit. The poet, according to Addison, begins with a resemblance between ideas that is obvious, but goes beyond this obvious resemblance to find "some further Congruity" that is surprising. Addison illustrates this point with the following example: "Thus when a Poet tells us, the Bosom of his Mistress is as white as Snow, there is no Wit in the Comparison; but when he adds, with a Sigh, that it is as cold too, it then grows into Wit" (*Spectator*, no. 62). The further resemblance to be an instance of true wit must not only surprise but also have a foundation in the nature of things. Mixed wit consists in further resemblances that surprise the reader but are lacking in the necessary foundation and are, as a result, little more than a senseless play upon words, as in the case of false wit — the pun in particular. "Mixed wit" is therefore "a Composition of Punn and true Wit, and is more or less perfect as the Resemblance lies in the Ideas or in the Words" (*Spectator*, no. 62). The resemblances or conceits of mixed wit arise not from the pun, but from the metaphor; only the metaphor is based on truth.

Wimsatt, examining Addison's treatment of mixed wit, says that its conceits, as in Cowley's *Mistress*, result from the poet's taking "unfair advantage of an authoritative cliché metaphor — or perhaps a mere phonetic accident — 'flame' [i.e., 'the "flame of love"'] and 'flame' ['the "flame" of combustion']." [54] Wimsatt's observation, which is not entirely wrong, blurs Addison's argument that the conceits of mixed wit have a basis in truth or nature, and that they derive not at all from a "phonetic accident" but solely from the ambiguity of metaphor. The pun, Addison says, is "a Conceit arising from the use of two Words that agree in the Sound, but differ in the Sense" (*Spectator*, no. 61). But the conceits of mixed wit do not derive from a play upon homonyms, but from the ambiguity of a single word or metaphor. I. A. Richards has taught us to speak of metaphor in terms of "tenor" and "vehicle," and W. Bedell Stanford to recognize that metaphor "could not possibly consist of one word." [55] But earlier critics from Aristotle through Cicero down to Dryden and Addison believed otherwise.[56] Dryden, for example, says simply enough that tropes "change the nature of a known word by applying it to some other signification," [57] and that a metaphor is "a kind of similitude comprehended in a word." [58] It is this concept of the metaphor that Addison states in the 1704 note:

When in two Ideas that have some resemblance with each other, and are both expressed by the same word, we make use of the ambiguity of the

53. Dominique Bouhours, "The Art of Criticism, or the Method of Making a Right Judgment upon Subjects of Wit and Learning," *The Continental Model: Selected French Critical Essays of the Seventeenth Century, in English Translation*, ed. Scott Elledge and Donald Schier (Minneapolis, 1960), p. 246.

54. Wimsatt, *Literary Criticism*, p. 232, n. 9. For other discussions of mixed wit, see Robert L. Morris, "Addison's *Mixt Wit*," *MLN*, LVII (1942), 666–68; W. Lee Ustick and Hoyt H. Hudson, "Wit, 'Mixt Wit' and the Bee in Amber," *Huntington Library Bulletin*, VIII (October, 1935), 103–30.

55. W. Bedell Stanford, *Greek Metaphor: Studies in Theory and Practice* (Oxford, 1936), p. 8.

56. *Ibid.*, p. 9: "Aristotle, like nearly all his successors until the nineteenth century . . . neglected the true principle of language, that *the phrase or sentence, not the word, is the unit of speech*. For metaphor this is a more vital truth than for any other form of words." Stanford, *Greek Metaphor*, discusses this view in his chapter, "Classical Definitions of Metaphor," pp. 3–21.

57. Dryden, I, 17.

58. Dryden, II, 202.

word to speak [of the] one Idea included under it, which is proper to the other. Thus, for example, most languages have hit on the word, which properly signifies Fire, to express Love by, (and therefore we may be sure there is some resemblance in the Ideas mankind have of them;) from hence the witty Poets of all languages, when they have once called Love a fire, consider it no longer as the passion, but speak of it under the notion of a real fire, and, as the turn of wit requires, make the same word in the same sentence stand for either of the Ideas that is annexed to it.[59]

The conceits of mixed wit, then, according to Addison, arise solely from the ambiguity of a single word, or metaphor.

Addison's parenthetical claim that all languages have hit on the word fire to express love suggests the universal truth of the metaphor — a suggestion that he makes in other terms when he says in the *Spectator* that "the Passion of Love in its Nature has been thought to resemble Fire" (no. 62). Though we may speak of "an authoritative cliché metaphor" or a conventional conceit from amatory verse, Addison seems concerned to have his readers see in the metaphor of fire something of a received truth of mankind.

In the *Spectator*, Cowley not Ovid supplies the example of a poet who exploits the ambiguity of "fire" as the turn of wit requires: "When he resolves to give over his Passion, he tells us that one burnt like him for ever dreads the Fire. . . . His endeavouring to drown his Love in Wine, is throwing Oil upon the Fire. . . . Sometimes he is drowned in Tears, and burnt in Love, like a Ship set on Fire in the Middle of the Sea." (no. 62.) Mindful of the seven types of ambiguity, we do not object to Cowley's conceits. But during the seventeenth century, British philosophers had complained about the ambiguity of language and heaped abuse especially on the metaphor.[60] Hobbes, for example, speaking as a philosopher rather than critic, condemned "metaphors" and other "senseless words" as being so many "*ignes fatui*," and described "reasoning upon them" as "wandering amongst innumerable absurdities." [61] Addison's treatment of mixed wit may be considered as a concession to some part of these charges. He grants the ambiguity of the metaphor, but maintains that in the ambiguity there lies a truth. His major concession is that poets in search of surprising resemblances between ideas will exploit the ambiguity of metaphor, and sometimes, departing from its truth, strike "seeming Resemblances" (no. 62). The images that result from the seeming resemblance are absurd and false, having no foundation in the nature of things. Addison says in the *Spectator* but not in the 1704 note that mixed wit has its foundation partly in truth and partly in falsehood, and adds "Reason puts in her Claim for one Half of it, and Extravagance for the other" (no. 62).

In both the 1704 note and the *Spectator*. Addison claims that the greatest poets — Homer, Vergil, and Horace — scorned mixed wit.[62] He strengthens this claim in the *Spectator*. He changes his mind about Milton — places him among the greatest poets and represents him as having "a Genius much above" mixed wit. More significantly, he says that Boileau, "who formed himself upon the Ancient Poets, has every where rejected it with Scorn" (no. 62). So too does Addison. In both the 1704 note and the *Spectator*, he relegates mixed wit to the epitaph. He goes beyond the 1704 note as he moves, in the second part of the *Spectator*, to the argument that simplicity depends solely on the poet's strength of genius.

After citing Bouhours and Boileau as critics who have advocated that no thought is beautiful that is not founded in truth, Addison remarks:

This is that natural Way of Writing, that beautiful Simplicity, which we so much admire in the Compositions of the Ancients; and which no Body deviates from, but those who want Strength of Genius to make a Thought shine in its own natural beauties. Poets who want this Strength of Genius to give that Majestick Simplicity to Nature, which we so much admire in . . . the Ancients, are forced to hunt after foreign Ornaments, and not to let any Piece of Wit of what Kind soever escape them. (no. 62.)

These remarks represent an attempt to establish a new set of terms to account for the greatest poetry. In the preface to the *Georgics*, Addison speaks of Vergil's wit and bold metaphors, and of all the embellishments of poetry. He speaks now of the natural way of writing and that majestic simplicity we admire in the ancients. And these new terms define a criterion that leads him to depreciate the poets who, lacking in genius, must hunt after foreign ornaments. The simplicity of the greatest poetry puts it beyond the reach of Locke's indictment since the language of this poetry has nothing in it to please only the fancy and arrest the judgment.

Addison rejects the definition of wit that Dryden gives in *The Au-*

59. Addison, "Notes on Ovid," 144.
60. See Richard Foster Jones, "Science and Language in the Mid-Seventeenth-Century," *The Seventeenth Century*, pp. 143–60, especially, pp. 154–55.
61. "Leviathan," *The Works of Thomas Hobbes of Malmesbury*, ed. Sir William Molesworth, III (London, 1839), 37.
62. Addison, "Notes on Ovid," 144.

*thor's Apology for Heroic Poetry and Poetic License* (1677): "it is a propriety of thoughts and words; or, in other terms, thoughts and words elegantly adapted to the subject." [63] Addison, George Williamson has observed, telescopes Dryden's definition and omits the mark of elegance in the adaptation of thoughts and words to the subject.[64] Addison, it may be said, reduces Dryden's definition to the principle of propriety and rejects it on the ground that it "is not so properly a Definition of Wit as of good Writing in general" (*Spectator*, no. 62). To agree that wit is one and the same with propriety can entail admitting the most figurative expressions to the greatest poetry. This is the argument that Dryden makes as he concludes *The Author's Apology*, which is in part a defense of the poet's license to express his fictions by means of tropes and figures. Dryden follows up his definition by arguing:

If our critics will join issue on this definition, that we may *convenire in aliquo tertio*; if they will take it as a granted principle, it will be easy to put an end to this dispute [over the meaning of wit]. No man will disagree from another's judgment concerning the dignity of style in Heroic Poetry; but all reasonable men will conclude it necessary, that sublime subjects ought to be adorned with the sublimest, and consequently often with the most figurative expressions.[65]

Addison's rejection of Dryden's definition is a tacit refusal to accept the conclusion that the sublimest subjects require the most figurative expressions. The third term that Addison finds between the opposites of wit and judgment is genius, to the strength of which he attributes the simplicity of the greatest poetry.

In the second part of the *Spectator*, then, Addison dissociates the greatest poetry from wit and rhetoric. He characterizes this poetry by speaking of its "majestic simplicity" rather than its "sublimity," no doubt because the latter term could be construed to mean the most figurative style.[66] Joseph Trapp, in his Oxford lectures on poetry (1711–42), for example, said that the "remarkable property" of the sublime style is "to be bold and figurative, especially with Metaphors and Hyperboles." [67] Addison, it appears, wanted the remarkable property of the greatest poetry to be not wit and bold metaphors but genius and simplicity.

✦ ✦ ✦

The *Spectator* paper on true wit points to a transition in English literary criticism. The first part of the paper looks back to the seventeenth century in treating poetry as a product of wit and in qualifying earlier definitions of wit. By contrast, the second part looks forward to the criticism of the mid-eighteenth century in seeing poetry as an expression of genius. In adding the second part, Addison moves away from the criticism of Dryden toward that of Joseph Warton in his *Essay on the Writings and Genius of Pope* (1756, 1782). We may see the drift of literary criticism as we move on to Addison's *Spectator* on genius (no. 160). I do not mean to suggest that Addison has a great deal in common with Warton. They are alike mainly in identifying as sublime the poetry of the rare natural genius, and in claiming that its greatness does not depend on art.

Addison's comments on the natural genius, it is well known, show the influence of Longinus.[68] Longinus had recognized five sources of the sublime; the first two are innate powers, the gift of nature: "First and most important is the power of forming great conceptions, . . . Secondly, there is vehement and inspired passion." [69] Addison suggests that the second source is the energy that drives or inspires the sublime of thought when he says that Pindar, a natural genius, "was hurried by a Natural Fire and Impetuosity to vast Conceptions of things, and noble Sallies of Imagination" (no. 160). The natural genius is clearly the writer who has the innate power to form the sublime of thought. Addison describes him as one of those prodigies "who by the mere Strength of natural Parts, and without any Assistance of Art or Learning, have produced Works that were the Delight of their own Times and the Wonder of Posterity" (no. 160). Needless to say, Addison's concept of the natural genius denies that the sublime depends in any way on the other sources cited by Longinus, the sources of art, or rhetoric: the figures of thought and speech; a noble and graceful diction; and harmony in the composition of periods.[70] All of these, to be sure, are present in the poetry of the natural genius, but they are not the source of its sublimity. Moreover, they have not been used according to any principle.

Addison further dissociates the sublime from rhetoric when he treats

63. Dryden, I, 190.
64. *Senecan Amble*, p. 355, n. 2. Addison says that Dryden defines "wit" to mean " 'a Propriety of Words and Thoughts adapted to the subject' " (no. 62).
65. Dryden, I, 190.
66. Samuel H. Monk, *The Sublime: A Study of Critical Theories in XVIII-Century England* (Ann Arbor, 1960), p. 57, makes this point.
67. Trapp, *Lectures*, p. 86.
68. Monk, *Sublime*, p. 56.
69. *Longinus on the Sublime*, trans. W. Rhys Roberts (Cambridge, 1899), p. 57.
70. *Ibid.*

as defective the figurative language of the natural genius. The metaphors and similes in Homer and Solomon produce images without foundation in the nature of things (no. 160). This defect is explained away by the assertion that no rules existed to discipline the natural genius in the noble sallies of his imagination. For the sake of a distinction, Addison forms a second class of writers that includes Vergil and Milton as examples, describing them as having "formed themselves by Rules, and submitted the Greatness of their natural Talents to the Corrections and Restraints of Art" (no. 160). Though in the second class, Vergil and Milton are not inferior to Homer and Solomon. Addison avers that he is making a distinction, not an evaluation. The rules, which are the basis of this distinction, are not disparaged. They produce correct poetry and exact metaphors, but not the force, spirit, and sublimity of thought of the greatest poetry (no. 160). Sublimity of thought has become with Addison not only the criterion of excellence in poetry but also the test of critical discernment. For he reproves the critics of his day who in the name of correctness ridicule the absurd metaphors in the poetry of the natural genius and ignore entirely its sublimity of thought.

Sublimity of thought is Addison's chief criterion of excellence in poetry as he takes up the ballad "Chevy Chase" (no. 70, 74).[71] He speaks about "the essential and inherent Perfection of Simplicity of Thought" (no. 70), and says that "the Sentiments are extreamly Natural and Poetical, and full of the majestick Simplicity which we admire in the greatest of the ancient Poets" (no. 74). His several comments indicate clearly that "simplicity of thought" is a substitute term for "sublimity of thought."

He uses "simplicity" to refer also to the style characteristic of the genuine sublime. He takes exception to Sir Philip Sidney's question that if the ballad is moving when "it is sung by some blind Crowder with no rougher Voice than rude Stile; which being so evil apparelled in the Dust and Cobweb of [an] uncivil Age, what would it work trimmed in the gorgeous Eloquence of Pindar?" (no. 70). Addison's answer is that "there are several Parts in it where not only Thought but the Language is majestick, and the Numbers sonorous," and that one part of it could not "be more sounding and poetical, or resemble more the majestick Simplicity of the Ancients" (no. 74). An ambiguity creeps into his discussion when he "cautions the Reader not to let the Simplicity of the Stile, which one may well pardon in so old a Poet, prejudice him against the Greatness of Thought" in a particular passage (no. 70). The ambiguity

lies in using "simplicity" to refer to a rude diction that must be forgiven
in a poet of an earlier age and also to the unadorned expression that marks
the greatest poetry of the ancients. Ambiguous though Addison's use of
"simplicity" is, his remarks on "Chevy Chase" make the sublime of
thought and simplicity of expression the criteria of excellence in poetry.

C. S. Lewis has argued that Addison may have been slyly giving the lie
to critics who admired Cowley's poetry but disparaged as "Gothic" just
such a ballad as "Chevy Chase." [72] Addison, Lewis suggests, may have
been calling "the neoclassic bluff" by showing how this ballad has "a
great subject, a good moral, unity of action, and truth to Nature." [73]
Following Lewis's line of argument, one could make the case that Addison may also have been calling the Longinian bluff. There are two tests
of the sublime. First, is there in the work a greatness of thought and simplicity of expression that has a great force to affect the mind of the reader? Indeed there is in "Chevy Chase." It had the force to stir Sidney,
though he missed its majestic simplicity by looking for the gorgeous eloquence of Pindar. Secondly, does the work please men of different professions, ages, humors, and inclinations? If it does, then it may be pronounced an example of the genuine sublime. The poem that moved Sidney was so admired by Ben Jonson that "he used to say he had rather have
been the Author of it than of all his Works" (no. 70). "The favourite
Ballad of the common People of *England*," it pleases "a Reader of plain
common Sense," and, indeed, "all such Readers as are not unqualified for
the Entertainment by their Affectation or Ignorance" (no. 70). Since
"Chevy Chase" meets the two tests, it must be an example of the genuine
sublime, and therefore superior to the "Gothic" poetry of Cowley.

The Longinian critic of the period, John Dennis, posed the question
whether the author of the *Spectator* paper on "Chevy Chase" — whom
Dennis believed to be Captain Richard Steele — is in earnest or in jest, and
answered that "he is not in Earnest because he does not believe what he
says; nor in Jest because he does strenuously endeavour to convince the
Reader of the Excellence of that old Dogrel. His Design is to see how
far he can lead his Reader by the Nose." [74] Dennis was not to be led very

71. For another discussion of Addison's ballad criticism, see Lee A. Elioseff, *The Cultural Milieu of Addison's Literary Criticism* (Austin, 1963), pp. 63–73.
72. "Addison," *Eighteenth-Century English Literature; Modern Essays in Criticism*, ed. James L. Clifford (New York, 1959), p. 151.
73. *Ibid.*
74. The quotations and paraphrases in this paragraph and the next appear in the same place, "To H— C— Esq; Of Simplicity in Poetical Compositions, in Re-

far. He refused to believe that "old Dogrel" could be called poetry, let alone the sublime.

In his letter "Of Simplicity in Poetical Compositions, in Remarks on the 70th *Spectator*," written in 1711 but published in 1721, Dennis responded in earnest to the argument that "Chevy Chase" meets the two tests of the sublime. He dismissed as invalid the judgment of the common people, insisting that "the rabble" lack a knowledge of the heroic poem and cannot, therefore, judge a ballad in any perspective or speak sensibly of its language. In addition, "People of Quality are sometimes mistaken as well as the Rabble," he says, and rebukes Sidney for finding anything to admire in "Chevy Chase." The other test, which involves simplicity of thought and expression, leads Dennis to express his firm belief that poetry is an art that excites the passions by means of figurative language for the purpose of satisfying, improving, and reforming the mind of man. Dennis emphasizes that figurative language marks the essential difference between poetry and prose, and that "Figurative Expression is more essential to Poetry than Harmony" since Harmony "it self, if 'tis anything perfect, depends upon Figurative Expression." And he says, "as the Language of Poetry in general is to be bold and figurative, the Language of great and exalted Poetry is to be very bold and very figurative." So far as he is concerned, "Chevy Chase" may have a noble subject, but since the ballad does not have the language of poetry, "'tis plain by consequence that there is nothing great, nothing noble in it; no Magnificence, no Vehemence, no Painting, no Poetry." For Dennis, "Simplicity of Thought is not sufficient to make what we call metre Poetry."

For us, Dennis points up the fact that Addison's ballad criticism sets aside the principle that figurative language is essential to magnificence, vehemence, and painting in poetry. In a paper on another ballad, "Two Children in the Wood" (no. 85), Addison makes clear that the language of a poem is not the only criterion of excellence. He describes this ballad as "a pretty Tragical Story," "a plain simple Copy of Nature, destitute of all the Helps and Ornaments of Art." It pleases solely because it represents nature in such a way as to arouse compassion and pity even in "the most polite Reader." Although it has a meanness of language and "a despicable Simplicity in the Verse," its thoughts are entirely natural, and it will please all men who "have a true and unprejudiced Taste of Nature"; this will be so even though they "are not Judges of Language" (no. 85). Like the concepts of genius and sublimity, that of "a True and unprejudiced Taste of Nature" liberates Addison from judging a poem by the criterion of style or the skillful use of ornament.

We can mark how far Addison has come from the preface to the *Georgics*. Toward the end of the paper on "Two Children in the Wood," he refers to Molière's *Misanthrope* and specifically to Alceste's remark that only those "endowed with a true Greatness of Soul and Genius, can divest themselves of the little Images of Ridicule, and admire Nature in her Simplicity and Nakedness" (no. 85). In the preface to the *Georgics*, Addison portrays Hesiod as an old man who tattles and represents nature in her nakedness and simplicity when he should be bestowing on her the pleasantest dress of poetry.[75] Having cultivated a taste, not to say greatness of soul and genius, since the time when he disapproved of simplicity, Addison can go on to score "the little conceited Wits of the Age" who cannot admire "Productions which have nothing to recommend them but the Beauties of Nature" (no. 85). But Addison, perhaps as catholic in his taste as Lewis argues,[76] also scores these little wits for being unable "to relish even those Compositions that, with all the Beauties of Nature, have also the additional Advantages of Art" (no. 85). Addison's ballad criticism seems to bring him to the position that simplicity and art are not mutually exclusive criteria.

✓ ✓ ✓

Addison, as suggested, revised his early opinion of simplicity. In the preface to the *Georgics*, he derogated the simplicity and nakedness of Hesiod's poetry. In the notes on *Ovid*, however, simplicity became a characteristic of the sublime, and in the *Spectator* papers on true wit and on "Chevy Chase," simplicity emerged as a criterion of excellence in poetry. The change in Addison's opinion points to one of the dominant tendencies in neoclassic criticism — the demand for simplicity at the expense of ornament.

In a study of neoclassic theories of poetic style and form, Francis Gallaway discusses the causes of this tendency, and, distinguishing the most important of them, says, "the rational spirit nurtured by science was the

marks on the 70th *Spectator*," *The Critical Works of John Dennis*, ed. Edward Niles Hooker (Baltimore, 1943), II, 29. Hooker, "Explanatory Notes," II, 442, 446, points out that Dennis believed Steele to be the author. Elioseff, *Cultural Milieu*, pp. 72–73, discusses the differences between Addison and Dennis with respect to "simplicity."

75. Addison, "On Virgil's *Georgics*," 5–6.,
76. Lewis, "Addison," p. 153.

prime cause for the movement toward simplicity. Second in importance was the new aesthetics of the sublime." [77] The primary cause, Gallaway suggests, lies behind the argument that "in the service of truth the gorgeous rhetoric of Browne and Milton must give way to the directness of the scientific analyst." [78] The attack on rhetoric in poetry which came from the new aesthetics of the sublime was more direct. For, to repeat, Boileau had maintained that the highest form of the sublime, which lies in great thoughts expressed in the simplest language, does not depend on the sources of rhetoric. And Boileau was no doubt responsible for changing Addison's early opinion of simplicity.

But Boileau's emphasis on simplicity meets resistance when it comes to Addison's admiration of Milton — an admiration expressed several times over: first in "An Account of the Greatest English Poets" (1694), later in "Milton's Stile Imitated" (1704) and in the notes on Ovid, then again in papers on true wit and genius. Common to all these pieces is Addison's praise for the sublime in Milton. Addison is therefore being entirely consistent with himself when he announces in one of the first papers on *Paradise Lost* that "*Milton's* chiefe Talent and indeed his distinguishing Excellence lies in the Sublimity of his Thoughts" (no. 279). Other poets, modern and ancient, may equal him in every other part of poetry, but none rivals him in the greatness of thought, except Homer (no. 279).[79] Addison was, of course, not the first critic to praise Milton. Dryden had given him his due. A host of lesser critics sang his praises. And Dennis, as early an admirer of Milton as Addison, became, as Raymond D. Havens has said, "the first great protagonist of *Paradise Lost*." [80] Unlike Dryden and Dennis, Addison did not at first find fault with the language of *Paradise Lost* and eventually change his opinion.[81] He acknowledged Milton's faults but pronounced his style "admirable in general" (no. 285). More important, he defended Milton's use of ornament to form the sublime style of his epic. Addison's decision to defend *Paradise Lost* in its most vulnerable part is perhaps the measure of his independence of Boileau, Dryden, and Dennis. So far as I know, Addison is the first neoclassic critic to publish an apology for Milton's style.

Addison emphasizes Milton's sublimity of thought, but he takes it upon himself to defend Milton's sublime style. He grants that Milton is sometimes obscure, labored, and stiff as a result of depending on such ornaments as metaphors, foreign expressions, archaisms, and neologisms (no. 297). Many critics levy this charge against him. So Addison says, adding that while he "cannot wholly refute it," he has "apologized for it" (no. 297). The apology which appears in the first paper on the language of *Paradise Lost* (no. 285) is apparently aimed at critics who have no taste for Milton's sublime style. Addison refers to these critics toward the end of this paper, and dismisses them as being akin to what Dryden used to call his "Prose-Cricks."

Although Addison dismisses Milton's prose critics as unqualified to judge poetry, he takes them seriously enough to present an apology that has five arguments.[82] (1) The language of an epic must be sublime as well as perspicuous. While the plainest and most natural expressions may be used to satisfy the requirement of perspicuity, many of these, having been debased by common use, are inappropriate to the epic. Propriety therefore dictates that a poet "guard himself against idiomatick Ways of Speaking." (2) Aristotle says that metaphors, foreign expressions, and other devices may be used to avoid "the Idiomatick Stile" and to form the sublime. Addison's choice of Aristotle rather than Longinus to sanction the use of figurative language may be owing to the fact that the influential French critic Rapin had pronounced Aristotle the authority on the proper use of figurative language.[83] In addition, Aristotle defends against ridicule the poet who in using metaphors observes the principle of moderation. And it is to this defense that Addison refers those critics who would ridicule Milton's elevated or sublime style. (3) Milton shows great judgment in observing one principle or another of poetic style. For example, his metaphors, which are always beautiful, have nothing of wit in them, "are not thick sown," and are seldom used "where the proper and natural Words will do as well." (4) Poetry, especially when written

77. *Reason, Rule, and Revolt in English Classicism* (New York, 1940), p. 163.
78. *Ibid.*, p. 162.
79. Addison praises Milton in other places. See Raymond D. Havens, *The Influence of Milton on English Poetry* (Cambridge, Massachusetts, 1922), p. 14.
80. *Ibid.*, p. 93.
81. Hooker, "Explanatory Notes," I, 429, makes the point that Dryden and Dennis changed their early opinions of Milton's language.
82. The following paraphrases and quotations appear in the same place, no. 285.
83. René Rapin, "Reflections on Aristotle's Treatise of Poesy in General," in Elledge and Schier, *Continental Model*, p. 288, says: "And because . . . this loftiness which is aimed at by the boldness of a metaphor is dangerous, insomuch that it comes nigh to rashness, Aristotle must be consulted on this matter to employ them with discretion." See Gallaway, *Reason, Rule, and Revolt*, p. 165, who says that "Aristotle, Cicero, and Quintilian afforded classical precedents for decorum of style." Addison no doubt chose the authority of the critic whom he regarded as the most logical man who ever lived (no. 291).

in blank verse, requires ornament to "keep it from falling into the Flatness of Prose," and is "indispensably necessary to support the Stile." (5) The English language was not equal to Milton's sublimity of thought. Of these five arguments, the most important are the third and the fifth. Each deserves further examination.

In the subsequent papers on *Paradise Lost*, Addison buttresses his argument that Milton displays great judgment in using ornament according to one principle or another. A subsidiary argument emerges implicitly from his comments: Milton's proper use of ornament reveals a harmonious operation of judgment and imagination. Speaking of "the noble Similes and Allusions in the first Book," he suggests that these have nothing of wit in them because Milton has the judgment to observe the principle that they must be directed to a proper end: "when *Milton* alludes either to Things or Persons, he never quits his Simile till it rises to some very great Idea . . . The [simile] does not, perhaps, last above a Line or two, but the Poet runs on with the Hint, till he has raised out of it some glorious Image or Sentiment, proper to inflame the Mind of the Reader, and to give it that sublime Kind of Entertainment, which is suitable to the Nature of an Heroick Poem." (no. 303.) Addison emphasizes that Milton's similes and their glorious images or sentiments have nothing in common with "the quaint Similes, and little Turns of Wit, which are so much in Vogue among modern Poets" (no. 303). Commenting on Milton's description of paradise, the most "florid and elaborate" description in the poem, Addison represents Milton as giving free reign to his imagination but only in such a way as to conform to another principle: "In the Description of *Paradise*, the Poet has observed *Aristotle's* Rule of lavishing all the Ornaments of Diction on the weak and unactive Parts of the Fable, which are not supported by the Beauty of Sentiments and Characters. . . . *Milton's* Exuberance of Imagination, has poured forth . . . a Redundancy of Ornaments on this Seat of Happiness and Innocence." (no. 321.) It is this exuberance of imagination and redundancy of ornament that Milton has the judgment to curb in the third book where "the Divine Persons are introduced as Speakers. He dares not give his Imagination its full Play. . . . The Beauties, therefore, which we are to look for . . . are not of a poetical Nature, or so proper to fill the Mind with Sentiments of Grandeur. . . . The particular Beauty of the Speeches in the Third Book, consists in . . . Shortness and Perspicuity of Stile." (no. 315.) Milton's use of ornament thus everywhere gives evidence of his judgment in submitting his great natural talents to the restraints of art. As a result, his style, though sometimes obscure, labored, and stiff, is rich in its diversity, ranging from the plain and perspicuous through the most florid and elaborate to the greatest of them all, the sublime.

Addison's chief argument in defense of Milton's use of ornament is that the English language was not equal to his sublimity of thought. Although he says of Milton's use of foreign assistances that "our Language sunk under him," implying that English could not support all the ornaments he used, Addison says also that our language "was unequal to that Greatness of Soul, which furnished him with such glorious Conceptions." (no. 297). Addison repeated this opinion in such a way as to make clear that our language, not Milton, was at fault. In a passage added to the first draft of the essay on the imagination, Addison says, "If I were to name a Poet that is a perfect Master in all [the] Arts of working on the Imagination, I think that *Milton* may pass for one: And if his *Paradise Lost* falls short of the *Aeneid or Iliad* in this respect, it proceeds rather from the Fault of the Language in which it is written, than from any Defect of Genius in the Author" (no. 417). The question must naturally arise: what is the defect of the English language? Nowhere in the papers on *Paradise Lost* does Addison suggest an answer to this question. In other papers, however, he makes suggestive observations.

In an early *Spectator* (no. 135), Addison observes that the stock of native words is primarily monosyllabic. By contrast to those among us today who believe that poetry gains intensity from such words, he seems to have believed that they are more suitable to the English manner of speaking. They "take off from the Elegance of our Tongue," but at the same time they allow us to express "our Ideas in the readiest manner, and consequently [to] answer the first Design of Speech better than the Multitude of Syllables, which make the Words of other Languages more Tunable and Sonorous" (no. 135). The primary virtues of plain English — brevity, directness, and clarity — are more congenial to conversation and prose than to poetry.

In a *Spectator* paper that appeared shortly after the last on *Paradise Lost*, Addison remarks on another characteristic of English: "there is a certain Coldness and Indifference in the Phrases of *European* languages, when they are compared with the Oriental Forms of Speech" (no. 405). But our language, he further observes, has received innumerable Elegancies and Improvements from that Infusion of *Hebraism*, which are derived to it out of the Poetical Passages in Holy Writ. They give a Force and Energy to our Expressions, warm and animate our Language and convey our Thoughts in more ardent and intense Phrases, than any that are to be met with in our own Tongue. There is something so pathetick in this kind of Diction, that it often sets the Mind in a Flame, and makes our Hearts burn within us. (no. 405.)

Addison asserts that a prayer composed of the most elegant and polite phrases in the English language would seem cold and dead if it were not elevated by Hebraisms drawn from the Bible. The native stock of phrases, then, does not supply the English poet with the means to give force and energy to the expression of his ideas, and to create the pathetic effect of setting aflame the mind and heart. Since Longinus had said that the sublime has the power to conquer the whole man,[84] Addison may have believed that the English language lacked the words and phrases to achieve this effect.

"Addison's reading of Longinus," Elioseff says, "leads him to the conclusion that the pathetic is not one of the principal sources of the sublime. . . . Milton's sublimity does not derive from his ability to work upon the passions, but from his ability to arouse noble thoughts in the minds of his readers."[85] Addison does emphasize Milton's genius for vast conceptions, but he maintains also that Milton "knew all the Arts of Affecting the Mind" (no. 333), and that he is the master of both the sublime and the pathetic ways of writing (no. 339). It is true that he calls on Longinus to sanction the view that the pathetic is not always essential to the sublime (no. 339). That Addison should affirm this view underscores his objection to Dennis's interpretation of the sublime. In *The Grounds of Criticism in Poetry* (1704), Dennis denies Longinus's view, protesting that the pathetic is necessary to the sublime.[86] Once Addison has aligned himself with Longinus — "that great Critick" (no. 339), he goes on to recognize Milton as the master of both the sublime and pathetic ways of writing, and to cite as examples of each way the sixth and seventh books of *Paradise Lost*.

The seventh Book . . . is an Instance of that Sublime which is not mixt and work'd up with Passion. The Author appears in a kind of composed and sedate Majesty; and tho' the Sentiments do not give so great an Emotion as those in the former Book, they abound with as magnificent Ideas. The Sixth Book, like a troubled Ocean, represents Greatness in Confusion; the seventh affects the Imagination like the Ocean in a Calm, and fills the Mind of the Reader, without producing in it any thing like Tumult or Agitation. (no. 339.)

Addison then attributes the pathetic effects of the sixth book to both its magnificent ideas and its image of greatness in confusion.

In the paper devoted to the sixth book, he says that its "Images of Greatness and Terrour . . . are suitable to the Subject," the battle of the angels, and, speaking of Milton's representation of this battle, admires it for being filled with "such Circumstances as should raise and astonish the Mind of the Reader" (no. 333). In addition, he singles out for special praise Milton's use of allegory, description, simile, and personification, noting his debts to particular episodes and sublime passages in the Bible. The sixth book is an example of Boileau's sublime. It consists in magnificent ideas and has the effect of awakening the strong emotions of astonishment and terror. But it is also an instance of the sublime *style* formed by such devices as Longinus had recommended: image, circumstance, allegory, personification.[87] Hence it is that Addison praises its great "Variety of sublime Ideas" yet also its "many wonderful Stroaks of Poetry" (no. 333).

Boileau, as is well known, separated the sublime from the sublime style, and interpreted the sublime to mean the extraordinary, the surprising, and the marvelous.[88] A discourse to be sublime must have these qualities, and must elevate, transport, and ravish. But Boileau denied that these qualities depend on rhetorical devices or the noblest diction. As Samuel Holt Monk has shown, Boileau dissociated the sublime from the sublime style. When comparing Moses's account of the creation of light and his own paraphrase of this account written in the sublime style, he concluded that "the greatest thought in simple language is the highest form of the sublime, since the thought operates directly and with no let or hindrance to the reader's mind, filling it with awe and awakening emotions of a very intense kind." The several terms that Boileau uses for these emotions — the extraordinary, surprising, astonishing, and marvelous "may be vague and unsatisfactory," Monk further observes: "but they indubitably tell us that the sublime, apart from the sublime style, must be a great thought

84. *Longinus*, p. 43.
85. Elioseff, *Cultural Milieu*, p. 97.
86. Hooker, *Dennis*, I, 359; Monk, *Sublime*, p. 53, makes this point.
87. *Longinus*, 83–97, 123–27, 139.
88. My discussion of Boileau is a summary of Monk's and all the quotations in this paragraph appear in *Sublime*, pp. 31–32.

and that it must awaken strong emotions in the mind of the reader. This is the new, the eighteenth-century sublime for which Boileau is responsible."

In discussing the sublime of *Paradise Lost*, Addison is eclectic but also independent, and, taking note of this fact himself, he emphasizes his independence. On the basis of critical disagreement over "some particular Points in an Epic Poem," he exempts himself from the rules laid down by any single critic (no. 321). He claims that he is at "Liberty sometimes to join with one [critic], and sometimes with another, and sometimes to differ from all of them." (no. 321). He joins with Boileau to define the distinguishing excellence of *Paradise Lost* — its vast conceptions, and also its power to astonish the reader. But he joins with Longinus and Dennis to argue that this effect has its source in the sublime style as well as in the sublime, as in the example of the sixth book. And he joins with Dennis in regarding terror as a strong emotion altogether appropriate to the sublimity of an epic poem.[89] But Addison differs from all of them when he argues that there is a sublime that does not evoke strong emotions.

Of the seventh book of *Paradise Lost*, Addison says that it "affects the Imagination like the Ocean in a Calm, and fills the Mind of the Reader, without producing in it any thing like Tumult or Agitation" (no. 339). The seventh book is "an Instance of the Sublime that is not mixt and work'd up with Passion" (no. 339). The vast conceptions of the seventh book do not agitate the mind of the reader. They have quite the opposite effect. They calm the mind. In discussing this book, Addison touches on Moses's account of the creation of light and refers to Longinus's rather than Boileau's dicussion of this account. Addison's reference to Longinus rather than to Boileau is perhaps significant.

Longinus had said that Moses, "having formed and expressed a worthy conception of the might of the Godhead, writes at the very beginning of his Laws, 'God said' . . . 'Let there be light, and there was light.'"[90] In its broad context, this example illustrates Longinus's view that the first and most important source of the sublime is the poet's power to form vast conceptions. Now what is particularly suggestive about this example is that it illustrates Moses's power to form and to express a worthy conception of the might of the Godhead. In imitating Moses, "*Milton*, tho' his own natural Strength of Genius was capable of furnishing out a perfect Work, has very much raised and ennobled his conceptions" (no. 339). Not any conceptions, but specifically conceptions of God's might. For

Addison's first example of the sublime in the seventh book is that of the Messiah coming forth "in the Power of his Father, surrounded with a Host of Angels, and cloathed with such Majesty as becomes his entering upon a Work, which, according to our Conceptions, appears the utmost exertion of Omnipotence" (no. 339). The sublime of the seventh book consists in the vast conception of God's power in creating order out of chaos, and this conception, Addison seems to be arguing as he moves from the sixth to the seventh book, calms the mind of the reader.

In his discussion of the seventh book, Addison returns to his argument that the English language, unequal to Milton's glorious conceptions, put upon him the necessity of resorting to foreign assistances. A description that Addison finds more sublime than any other in the poem is that of "the Messiah . . . looking down into the *Chaos*, calming its Confusion, riding into the midst of it, and drawing the first Out Line of the Creation" (*S.* 339). From this description, Addison chooses to discuss these lines:

> He took the Golden Compasses, prepar'd
> In God's Eternal Store, to circumscribe
> The Universe, and all created things. . . .
>
> (VII, 225–27)

It is "the Thought of the Golden Compasses" that Addison describes as "conceived altogether in Homer's Spirit," and also as a "very natural instrument in the Hand of him, whom Plato somewhere calls the Divine Geometrician." The conception of the golden compasses elicits from Addison the principle that "Poetry delights in cloathing abstracted Ideas in Allegories and sensible Images" (no. 339). Although he does not explain what effect the allegory of the golden compasses has on the mind of the reader, one may assume that it produces the pleasures of the imagination.

In a passage that appears in the first draft of the essay on the imagination, and also — but with significant changes — in the last *Spectator* paper on this subject, Addison says that "Allegories when well chosen, are like so many Tracks of Light in a Discourse, that make everything about them clear and beautiful" (no. 421). And he says of metaphors and allegories:

By these Allusions a Truth in the Understanding is as it were reflected by the Imagination; we are able to see something like Colour and Shape in a Notion, and to discover a Scheme of Thoughts traced out upon Matter.

89. Monk, *Sublime*, p. 54, makes the point that Dennis introduced the emotion of terror.
90. *Longinus*, p. 65.

And here the Mind receives a great deal of Satisfaction, and has two of its Faculties gratified at the same time, while the Fancy is busie in copying after the Understanding, and transcribing Ideas out of the Intellectual World into the Material. (no. 421.)

The well-chosen allegory, according to Addison, will draw analogies between abstract ideas and the great or beautiful works of art or nature. The allegory of the golden compasses, which is well chosen, reveals the hand of the Divine Geometrician creating order out of chaos and giving a design to his creation from the very beginning. The allegory enables Milton to express his conception of God's might and wisdom, and, so Addison might argue, to produce an image that has the effect of bringing the imagination and understanding into harmony. In claiming that the seventh book fills the reader's mind with great calm, Addison may well have meant that its truth brings the peace that comes with a knowledge of divine power and wisdom. There is no question that Addison believes Milton discovers this truth to the reader in the sublime style.

*        *        *

I have suggested that Addison made significant changes in his statement about metaphors and allegories as he moved from the first draft to the *Spectator*. In the first draft, he does not say that their truth is reflected by the imagination to the understanding. He has it the other way around: "By these allusions a truth in y$^e$ Understanding casts, as it were, a shadow on y$^e$ Imagination." [91] Slight change to be sure, yet it reveals how he revised an observation to add dignity to both figurative language and the imagination.[92] Unlike Locke, Addison believes that both convey a truth to the understanding.

In the first draft, Addison says, "It is y$^s$ art of affecting y$^e$ Imagination, y$^t$ gives a lustre & embellishment to good sense, & makes one Man's compositions so much more charming & delightfull, y$^n$ another's. It sets off all writings in general; but is in particular y$^e$ very life, & highest perfection of Poetry." [93] Revising this passage for *Spectator*, no. 421, he decides to say that the very life and highest perfection of poetry lies not in the "art" but the "Talent of affecting the Imagination." The substitution of "talent" for "art" reflects the important change in his critical thinking. It epitomizes his attempt and, indeed, that of others after him, to remove the discussion of the life and perfection of poetry from the province of wit and rhetoric to the sphere of genius and talent. Although Addison in making this attempt surrenders the skillful use of ornament as the decisive criterion of excellence in poetry, he upholds the view that ornament may be used for a variety of purposes.

Our survey of Addison's criticism reveals that he assigns a variety of functions to ornament. In his earliest criticism, he assigns it the twofold function of painting vivid images and of giving the imagination and the understanding the pleasure of discovering in the image some truth or complex idea about the nature of things. Later on, he acknowledges that function which won the admiration of everyone but philosophers and scientists, namely, the function of diverting the mind by discovering surprising similarities between ideas. At the same time, he advances the traditional argument that ornament should be used to depart from the idiomatic way of speaking and to form the sublime style, and he assigns to this style the functions of filling the mind with such strong emotions as astonishment and terror, and of revealing such vast conceptions as the power and wisdom of God in the creation and design of the universe. Ornament can be used also to represent such scenes as Paradise in the most florid and elaborate manner, and — this applies only to personification — to express such passions as man has suffered after the fall (no. 363). Finally, personification, which Vergil uses to suggest a truth about the nature of things, has been used by other poets to represent "any Passion, Appetite, Virtue or Vice, under a visible Shape, and [to] make it a Person or an Actor in his Poem," Addison says, citing the examples of "Hunger and Envy in *Ovid*, of Fame in *Virgil*, and of Sin and Death in *Milton*" (no. 419). He goes on to say, in a passage added to the first draft: "Thus we see how many ways Poetry addresses it self to the Imagination, as it has not only the whole Circle of Nature for its Province, but makes new Worlds of its own, shews us Persons who are not to be found in Being, and represents even the Faculties of the Soul, with her several Virtues and Vices, in a Sensible Shape and Character" (no. 419). Given these provinces in their variety and scope, poetry requires a language of greater flexibility than that provided either by the idiomatic way of speaking or

91. Addison MS. ed. Campbell, p. 16.

92. Elioseff, *Cultural Milieu*, p. 171, makes the point that Addison added dignity to the imagination. Addison appears also concerned to dignify figurative language. For example, he says in the first draft that allegories and metaphors should strike comparisons that are "very surprising and very beautiful," adding later that they should be "exact" and "agreeable," Addison MS, ed. Campbell, p. 17; he decides on the latter (no. 421). In a "surprising" metaphor, there is wit; not so in an "exact" metaphor, which appeals more to the reason than fancy.

93. Addison MS, ed. Campbell, p. 18.

by a lexicon of the proper words in plain English. In maintaining that ornaments supply poetry with the language it requires to achieve its end, Addison upholds a traditional opinion.

Addison, we know, was partly responsible for eighteenth-century views on poetic diction, especially the view that the language of poetry is never the language of the people. Since this view came to be misunderstood, scorned, and rejected, one would do well to emphasize that Addison recognized the abundant possibilities of figurative language. Although he supported the principle that figurative language can be used for the purpose of awakening and expressing emotions, he had little to do with the tendency in the eighteenth century, beginning perhaps with Dennis, to make the language of poetry unique in being the language of the passions. This tendency, as Hamilton suggests, leads to an emphasis on the lyric, to an expressive theory of poetry, and, ultimately, to the end of "the whole medieval and Renaissance tradition of poetry as an art of ornamentation." [94] It is this tradition properly understood that Addison upholds in defending Milton's use of ornament against prose critics of the day. Addison's views on genius, talent, and the imagination may point to the mid-century and, beyond, to romantic criticism, but his views on taste and judgment bring us back to his problem of justifying the ornaments of art in an age of reason.

In a major addition to the first draft of the *Spectator*, no. 416, Addison introduces an argument in defense of poetic descriptions that has its parallels in arguments in earlier *Spectator* papers. He accepts the fact that poetic descriptions may transport one reader or impress him as being extremely natural and leave another cold or strike him as having no likeness or conformity to things in nature. He argues, "This different Taste must proceed either from the *Perfection of Imagination* in one more than in another, or from the *different Ideas* that several Readers affix to the same Words" (no. 416). As I remarked earlier, he changes his assumption about the association of ideas leading to a discovery of the whole truth that a poet suggests in a metaphor; he now argues that a reader must meet certain requirements before he can appreciate the poetic description. He must have by birth a good imagination, and he must have a knowledge of the force and energy of the words in his language, and the resulting judgment to distinguish which of them "are most significant and expressive of their proper Ideas," or "to cloath and adorn them to best Advantage" (no. 416). A parallel to this last argument may be found in Addison's advice to the critics of his own day that they should study Locke's *Essay* to learn the distinction between words and things, and yet, like the critics of antiquity, study also their native language to become masters of all its elegancies of expression (no. 291). A closer parallel may be found in the *Spectator* paper on taste (no. 409); this parallel allows us to see another main tendency of eighteenth-century literary criticism in Addison.

The tests for determining whether or not one has "taste," the faculty that "discerns the Beauties of an Author with Pleasure, and the Imperfections with Dislike," require an ability to perceive and appreciate, for example, Livy's style and Cicero's brilliant language. Lacking this faculty yet having others, one can profess, as did an eminent mathematician, that his "greatest Pleasure . . . in reading *Virgil*, was in examining *Aeneas* his voyage by the Map," or, as might the modern chronicler-historian, that his sole delight in Vergil was in little more than "the bare Matters of Fact" (no. 409). Similarly, in *Spectator*, no. 416, after explaining the requirements a reader must meet in order to appreciate a poetic description, Addison says that one who is deficient in either imagination or judgment "may receive the general Notion of a Description, [but] can never see distinctly all its particular Beauties." Addison's apology for poetry comes to this: to be able to perceive the particular beauties of poetry and to be receptive to its manner of conveying ideas or revealing a truth, one must have a unified sensibility.[95] One needs imagination, judgment, and taste. Thus does Addison defend poetry and oppose the man of reason who has a mind only for the bare matters of fact. It may be said, finally, that Addison's case for the language of poetry and its diverse functions and effects rests on the premise of imagination, judgment, and taste. Of these premises, taste eventually became a basis of the eighteenth-century critic's demand for elegance as well as simplicity. Addison advocated simplicity and succeeded in establishing a basis for elegance.

94. Hamilton, *Two Harmonies*, p. 193.
95. For another view, see Tuveson, *Imagination*, p. 123.

⚜ PAUL RAMSEY

# The Watch of Judgment: Relativism and AN ESSAY ON CRITICISM

REGARDING the *Essay on Criticism* as "rich and complex,"[1] the editors of the Twickenham edition point also to its "great and noble design."[2] Reuben Brower talks of "the bounce and go of verse by a terribly bright young man who has recently acquired all the 'right ideas,' which he gets off with dazzling verbal skill and cheerful superiority."[3] That is a dreadful thing to say of anyone, especially when true. The poem has earned something of its violent disparities of reputation.[4] At its best it is better than a system: brilliant, profound, and delightfully tuned. At its worst it is trivial, frivolous, timidly dull, and disorderly. In this essay I shall explore some real and apparent discrepancies in the hope of telling some truths about the poem, its defects and doctrine, and at least some partial truths about the vexed topics of absolutism and relativism.

Pope had an enormous gift to see, to versify, brilliantly to shade, to dance a metaphor to frequent and penetrating truth. He had less power of artistic coherence (*The Rape of the Lock* is a magnificent but finally unique exception) and, as has often been said, not much talent for philosophical coherence. But in this poem he was working in a tradition which had, for all its variety and flexibility, a great deal of coherence. Nor should literary criticism become a philosophical "system," though it needs good theory. Density, nearness to experience, ability to deal with the singular are strengths of literary criticism; abstraction and self-complicating subtlety can become its enemies. The structure of an essay-poem is by its nature different and in some ways looser than other literary structures.[5] The crucial ordering is the relating of parts to the central ideas, by transition, implication, consistency. In this respect Pope's essay does achieve much order. What defects there are can be smoothed over with the alibi that Pope, like Horace, "without method talks us into sense" (l. 654).[6] It is not just an alibi; a central doctrine of the poem and of Neo-classicism is that "sense" — talented, imaginative, thoughtful, experienced judgment — is more important than method.

Teachers of Pope sadly learn that the patches of timidity and flatness can almost hopelessly prejudice readers against the poem and neoclassical theory. Even when what is said is defensible or true, it can sound superficial, machine-made, cold. "Nature methodized" (l. 89) is one of the worst offenders. The meaning is in important ways true. All good theory is, in the sense Pope meant, "Nature methodized." But what a horrid mechanical click the phrase has! Pope may have had some linguistic ill luck, to be sure; I doubt that the phrase fell so coldly on a contemporary's ear. Still, how "drily plain" (l. 114) can advice be? Other examples follow, capable of defense, unlucky of tone.

> Launch not beyond your depth, but be discreet,
> And mark that point where sense and dulness meet.
>
> (ll. 50–51)

Dullness intrudes on sense, timidity on discretion. In the passage Pope tells us how to win "a Critic's noble name" (l. 47). We say, not thus.

> And rules as strict [as Homer's] his [Vergil's]
>     laboured work confine,
> As if the Stagirite o'erlooked each line.
>
> (ll. 137–38)

1. Alexander Pope, *Pastoral Poetry and An Essay on Criticism*, ed. Emile Audra and Aubrey Williams, Twickenham ed. (New Haven, 1961), I, 227.
2. *Ibid.*, I, 226.
3. Reuben A. Brower, *Alexander Pope, The Poetry of Allusion* (Oxford, 1959), p. 196.
4. Good accounts of the poem's reputation occur in Whitwell Elwin and William John Courthope ed., *The Works of Alexander Pope* (London, 1871–1889), II, 5–24; *Pope's Essay on Criticism*, ed. John Churton Collins (London, 1912), pp. xxxiii–xl; Twickenham ed., I, 207–9.
5. Samuel Johnson discusses with a brilliance extraordinary even for him the structure of the essay-poem, in his Life of Pope, *Lives of the English Poets*, ed. G. B. Hill (Oxford, 1905), III, 99.
6. Quotations from the poem are from *Alexander Pope*, ed. William K. Wimsatt, Jr. (New York, 1951, paper). Line numbers are given in parentheses. I chose to quote from this edition rather than the the standard edition because, like

It takes something of perverse genius to make in a single couplet Homer, Vergil, and Aristotle sound equally and pompously unpleasant.

> True Wit is Nature to advantage dressed,
> What oft was thought, but ne'er so well expressed.
>
> (ll. 297–98)

The traditional metaphor of "dress" always runs some danger of being under-read, but this couplet almost demands that the reader miss Pope's real meaning in context (brilliantly defined by Brower)[7] in favor of a more superficial meaning. Rather than undoing the damage of misreading, the couplet's charm compounds it.

> Be not the first by whom the new are tried,
> Nor yet the last to lay the old aside.
>
> (ll. 335–36)

Once more the question is of tone. Neither Homer nor Shakespeare disobeyed that dictum. But it sounds pinched, and is more often remembered than the gracious "Be thou the first true merit to be-friend" (l. 474).

Pope has been misconstrued often, but one cannot blame merely the misunderstanders. Such flatnesses as these must share the blame. They have shut eyes to what is profound and excellent in the poem.

The poem is also damaged by a conflict of intentions. The aspiring poet-critic and the would-be wit-about-town get decidedly in each other's way. Sometimes it is the poet and critic who is pushed to the wall. One of the most misleading lines may help register my complaint: "For fools admire, but men of sense approve" (l. 391). Only fools, the line seems to say, feel wonder or other passion when reading poetry. Gentlemen condescend to approve or disapprove as rational machines. My parody is gross and true. It grossly misreads what the line means in context; it comes fairly close to the tone. What the line means in context is valid (italics mine):

> Yet let not *each* gay Turn thy rapture move;
> For fools admire, but men of sense approve.

Immature readers are apt to be carried away by mere cleverness of phrase or of conceit; better readers do not confuse the genuinely rapturous with the mildly skillful. Lines 100–1 complement the meaning:

> The generous Critic fanned the Poet's fire,
> And taught the world with reason to admire.

The great poets are magnificent, sublime, astonishing; the good reader responds with wonder, the "admiration" great poems deserve. Pope was such a passionate reader. Awe and rapture are among the emotions in this poem. It is sad that this needs to be pointed out; it is partly the fault of the tone of such lines as 391 that one needs to. And one does need to. Even so observant a critic as Empson quotes the line as a sample of the "grim classical doctrine" Pope inherited, without showing any sense of the line's meaning in context.[8]

Empson in the same essay shows the range of intent in the poem.[9] He argues that, in Pope's light-of-tongue and varied-of-resonance uses of the term Wit, there is usually a "drag towards the drawing-room," [10] even that "there is not a single use of the word in the whole poem in which the idea of a joke is quite out of sight." [11] Empson (not for the first time) overstates by a margin, but he overstates a truth. I find it perturbing that Empson, and Hooker,[12] Brower,[13] and the Twickenham editors [14] find the play on "wit" mostly admirable or unobjectionable. The mixing of intent, the flashing angles of vision, have their excitement and their fun, but the mixture harms, even taints, what is best in the criticism. Gentlemanly ease is one thing, the complex burden of Pope's tones another.

Take for instance the last couplet of part I (ll. 199–200), which ends the high and in the strictest sense Neoclassical praise of the great ancient poets. Help me, he is asking those poets, "to teach vain Wits a science little known, / T'admire superior sense, and doubt their own!" The passage has reverential praise and a fine and genuine humility. Yet something more disturbing enters here, something of fear, of testiness, of harsh emulation. It is not the last time Pope will boast of humility and superior moral virtue. The edge of wit is sharper for the complications. Pope desires

Thomas R. Edwards, Jr., in *This Dark Estate* (Berkeley and Los Angeles, 1963), p. ix, I found the Twickenham edition's use of italics bothersome, particularly in trying to read the poem aloud.

7. Brower, *Alexander Pope*, pp. 202–3.

8. William Empson, *The Structure of Complex Words* (Norfolk, Connecticut, 1951), p. 99. Another example of that frequent misreading of the line occurs in P. A. W. Collins, "Literary Theory and Literary Criticism" in *From Dryden to Johnson*, ed. Boris Ford, 2nd ed. (Baltimore, 1963), p. 181.

9. Empson, *Complex Words*, pp. 84–104.

10. *Ibid.*, p. 94.

11. *Ibid.*, p. 87.

12. Edward Niles Hooker, "Pope on Wit" in *The Seventeenth Century: Studies in the History of English Thought and Literature from Bacon to Pope* (Stanford, 1951); reprinted in *Eighteenth Century English Literature*, ed. J. L. Clifford (Oxford, 1959), pp. 42–61, especially pp. 42–44.

13. Brower, *Alexander Pope*, especially pp. 199–200.

14. Twickenham ed., I, 212–19, especially 218–19.

the poem to be accepted by the wits so that he may be (and be admired for being) in Empson's phrase, "a bright social talker." He wants to join the company of the wits, to be the wittiest of them; he also wants to contemn worldlings and fops, to look down on them from the heights of great poetry and criticism. The mixture is typical enough for a young poet to feel, yet singular in the poem. Few poets can fulfill either dream; Pope fulfills both, but one clouds the other's grandeurs.

What are those grandeurs? What has the poem best to say? Nature. Experience. Tradition. Passion. Judgment. Humility. Not a system, but not an eclectic hodgepodge either. The last item is not the least important nor the most discussed.[15]

Humility is a virtue which Pope genuinely had and was irritably proud of, and the tucks and turns, the realities and illusions of his moral personality are wound into the strangeness of those truths. Humility is also a doctrine, with important meanings. For all his pride, Pope saw, perhaps as well as any other poet, what some of those meanings are.

That insight explains away some of his apparent inconsistencies on the subject of Reason. He writes in this poem of "proud man's pretending wit" (l. 53), yet speaks of "right reason" (l. 211) bringing "resistless day" (l. 212). In short, he rates reason very low and very high. Yet the two views are not inconsistent; they are in fact parts of the same belief. Reason, as Pope understood it (and as Heraclitus and Aquinas and I think finally Plato understood it) begins and ends in mystery; it is a great and divine gift but not a god, a magnificent instrument but not a sufficient one. Prideful reason is dangerous and rapid of error.

Some manuscript lines amplify what he means by "So by false learning is good sense defaced" (l. 25):

> *Good Sense*, which only is the Gift of Heav'n,
> And tho no *Science*, yet is worth the Sev'n.
> Many are spoil'd by that *Pedantic* Throng,
> Who, with great Pains, teach Youth to reason wrong.[16]

Judgment is a gift of Heaven to be humbly accepted and is more important than any branch of learning, since the proper use of any learning requires it. Learning by itself is only too easily perverted by pedantry rooted in pride, in a refusal to recognize the source and limits of reason.

That view of humility and pride penetrates much of the *Essay*; it is the organizing principle of part II, and is implicit in some of the best and most deeply felt passages.[17] It also sets the frame for Pope's aesthetic absolutism. He is an absolutist, in the normal and fundamental sense that he believes with all traditional critics in the reality and intelligibility of literary value, and in the underlying sense that he believes reality and intelligibility to have their source in Nature and in God. God is the source, and end, and test of Nature, which is "the source, and end, and test of Art" (l. 73). One of the central meanings of that remarkable phrase is that aesthetic judgments represent reality: more simply, that such phrases as "Great Homer" can be meaningful and true.

Pope's doctrine of humility precludes easy knowledge or infallible rational systems. Good judgment is difficult, fallible, possible, improvable, corruptible. That general view gives a place, and I am persuaded a fitting place, to the apparent relativism in the poem. The passages which strike a modern ear as strongly relativistic need in every instance (granting a possible slip of phrase or two) to be understood in relation to the general doctrine of the poem. What I shall maintain is that the passages are not relativistic, unless in some vague and innocent sense of the term which does not contradict the absolutism of the poem. Part of the problem comes from the fact that relativism, almost always thought of as opposing absolutism, means a range of things, many of which are compatible with, many of which require, many of which imply the truth of absolutism.

Lines 118–23 show a strong historical sense of the sort frequently linked to relativism:

> You then whose judgment the right course would steer,
> Know well each ANCIENT's proper character;
> His Fable, Subject, scope in every page;
> Religion, Country, genius of his Age:
> Without all these at once before your eyes,
> Cavil you may, but never criticize.

The word "right" and lines 122–23 show that Pope believes that literary judgment of other ages is possible. Other parts of the poem show that comparison of authors of different ages is possible (Homer versus modern witlings). Historical knowledge and historical imagination are needed in

15. Audra and Williams discuss it briefly and well (Twickenham ed., I, 230–31).

16. Quoted (with a trivial exception) as given by R. M. Schmitz as ll. 26–29 in his edition of the manuscript *Essay on Criticism 1709* (St. Louis, 1962), p. 33. The first two of these lines are not quoted in a note giving the passage in the Twickenham ed., I, 242, note 26.

17. Four of the most important are ll. 11–16, 68–79, 181–200, and 215–32, the most important being 68–79 ("First follow Nature").

order to make sound judgments. The passage presumes, entails, and nowhere contradicts Pope's absolutism.

Lines 233–34 and 255–56 enunciate a truth relativists are apt to insist on:

> A perfect Judge will read each work of Wit
> With the same spirit that its author writ.
>
> In every work regard the writer's End,
> Since none can compass more than they intend.

The phrase "perfect Judge" entails absolutism, and nothing in the couplets or their context suggests that to enter into intent is the whole of literary judgment. To understand intent aids and preludes judgment.

Suppose — to abandon Pope's meaning for the sake of making a point — that these couplets did offer their advice as the whole of literary judgment. The first couplet would entail absolutism (there is value to be judged) and lead to the deliciously wry corollary that every literary work is equally valuable, since every literary work is written in the spirit in which it is written. The second couplet would likewise entail absolutism and offer a single, universal, and exclusive standard of judgment: to judge each work solely by how well the author's intent was realized, however trivial or noble, plain or fancy, that intent might be. Line 256 is false, since writers at times build better than they know, but it is not so foolish as that.

Lines 394–97 may seem to suggest universal tolerance and equality in literary judgment:

> Some foreign writers, some our own despise;
> The Ancients only, or the Moderns prize.
> Thus Wit, like Faith, by each man is applied
> To one small sect, and all are damned beside.

If these lines did imply the wisdom of universal tolerance, they would still entail absolutism: if universal literary and religious tolerance is good, then there is at least one moral and aesthetic truth. They would also offer a universal standard which reached across all "cultural" differences, namely universal tolerance. But the context makes clear that Pope does not intend to reduce all literature to equal worth and consequent worthlessness. He is speaking of various ways critics go wrong. The passage points toward lines 406–7, whose meaning is unmistakable:

> Regard not then if Wit be old or new,
> But blame the false, and value still the true.

That sentiment appears to contradict the passage discussed above beginning "Know well each ANCIENT's proper character," but does not. One should regard whether Wit be old or new in making the act of historical imagination necessary to understand the work; one should not make the oldness or newness the sole or overpowering standard of judgment.

Lines 446–47 seem to support the relativistic notion that critical and literary "systems" are fashions which have an equality of transience, and little else.

> If Faith itself has different dresses worn,
> What wonder modes in Wit should take their turn?

The next couplet dispels any such reading.

> Oft, leaving what is natural and fit,
> The current folly proves the ready wit.

The narrow and idle critic is the slave of fashion; the good and generous critic rises above such limitations.

Of lines 712–22 Empson nicely says that "while Pope despises the English for breaking the rules he contrives still more firmly to despise the French for keeping them." [18]

> . . . Critic learning flourished most in France:
> The rules a nation, born to serve, obeys;
> And Boileau still in right of Horace sways.
> But we, brave Britons, foreign laws despised,
> And kept unconquered, and uncivilized;
> Fierce for the liberties of wit, and bold,
> We still defied the Romans, as of old.
> Yet some there were, among the sounder few
> Of those who less presumed, and better knew,
> Who durst assert the juster ancient cause,
> And here restored Wit's fundamental laws.

The context is a history of criticism treated in very unrelativistic fashion. Here the attitude is so complicated that I hesitate to call it inconsistent. Pope does seem in lines 715–16 to imply that it is right and patriotic to ignore foreign laws and hence suggests that different sets of artistic laws are incomparable. To each his own. He also blames the French for their servile obedience to the rules and both praises and blames the English for not keeping the French rules. It is a confusing, if not confused, way to mediate claims, but line 722 lets us know what is intended. There are

18. Empson, *Complex Words*, p. 98.

fundamental laws, known to the ancients, which try both French and English partial and limited rules and practices.

The passage for a moment suggests the notion that Pope was in later years to apply to Shakespeare, that a man should not be tried by the laws of another country, though most of the passage contradicts that notion by precept, implication, and example. Whether the notion was intended here or not, an analysis of it may expose some pertinent issues.

The statement (the phrasing is mine) "A man should not be tried by the literary laws of another country" presumes and implies aesthetic absolutism. For if it is true, at least one literary-critical judgment is valid, namely that he *should* not so be tried. The statement suggests that he should be tried by the laws of his own country, which (once more) entails aesthetic absolutism and even offers a universal procedural rule, a weird one, for making literary judgments: that the literary laws of a country are absolutely and perfectly valid for trying every writer of that country and absolutely and perfectly inapplicable to the writers of all other countries. That implication is historically as well as philosophically preposterous. Of course the statement does carry a truth (the truth Pope saw when defending Shakespeare), that judgment should take place in context and circumstances and that some rules apply in some contexts but not in all. That truth is part and parcel of Pope's absolutism.

The passage also suggests that Pope felt some puzzlement and indecision about the rules.[19] One could gather from it with a little pushing some such putatively relativistic notion as this: that absolutisms of different sorts (construed as neat paradigmatic sets of inalterable and easily applied universal principles) break down when subjected to the test of experience. If absolutism means that all one needs to be a good critic is a neat set of universal rules to be applied by simple logical thumping, then absolutism is plainly false. But such an absolutism bears exceedingly little relationship to the absolutism Pope maintains in the poem. Judgment is necessary and fallible and correctible. He presumes rather than states that there are universal literary principles ("All great poems are passionate" is one), but makes it unmistakably clear that (1) not all rules are universal, and (2) applying the rules is difficult. Further, the notion that tidy absolutism breaks down itself entails absolutism, as it implies that some critical judgments are wrong, which implies that some critical judgments are right. If it is true for instance that Shakespeare's plays are good despite narrow rules they don't fit, then there is at least one aesthetic truth:

some of Shakespeare's plays are good. If absolutisms are inadequate, then absolutism is true.

I have saved for last what for me is one of the most fascinating metaphors in the poem. Attending carefully to the metaphors can reveal much which may go unnoticed, or unsaid, among the abstractions. Pope had a high gift for metaphors of thought (there is much to be said beyond this paper about that).

> 'Tis with our judgments as our watches, none
> Go just alike, yet each believes his own.

(ll. 9–10)

Pope seems to say *De gustibus non est disputandum* (a sentence never uttered except during a dispute about taste, be it noted). Does he? "Each believes his own" is analytically true. To have an opinion is to believe that opinion. Opinions differ, about literature as other matters. This we all know. He says that none go *just* alike. The disagreement between timepieces, while at times frustrating, is seldom great. Further, watches can be set, and would be useless if they couldn't be set. Some timepieces are known to be more accurate than others, hence have a limited and fallible but real authority. Watches of equal accuracy can be used for correction when one has good reason to believe one's own watch wrong (when it's stopped it's apt to be wrong). That is, comparing timepieces or comparing judgments is not a hopeless task. Each man believes his own judgment in the sense I gave above, but it isn't an "absolute" trust (nor does does Pope's view require that judgment should be "absolute" in that sense): a sensible man has enough self-doubt to be willing to compare his judgment with other judgments, his watch with other timepieces. So far the watch metaphor is perfectly compatible with Pope's doctrine and absolutism.

The metaphor can be pushed further, beyond Pope but not beyond the issue at hand. A relativist might complain that a "correct" watch is only arbitrarily correct. Time zones do not represent the detailed facts of sun time, and sun time itself is relative, applying only in our solar system. One time in London is another time in New York (one should not try a man by a watch of another country); the choice of the Greenwich meridian was arbitrary. More important and perhaps nearer the

---

19. So does the famous passage about "a grace beyond the reach of art" (141–60). The phrase "that License is a rule" (149) is worth, I believe, some brooding over for anyone who would understand what literary principles are and do.

analogy to literature, watch time misrepresents subjective time, as critical systems and absolutisms are incompatible with the shifting world of the individual's literary experience.

I hope the invisible opponent is not a straw man; I have tried to give him typical and impressive arguments. To those arguments one can reply somewhat as follows.

There is something fallible and arbitrary in our measurements of time, as there is in our literary judgments; but both point to and depend on what is not arbitrary: nature, reality. Events do have sequential relationships of which our temporal measurements are an abstraction and distortion; our temporal measurements do not create the reality. Events do happen; they go one way in time; we cannot reverse them; events in Paris or on Mars or beyond the furthest visible stars *have* relations, however well or badly our relatings of them represent their reality. Watch time is, to be sure, other than subjective time; but it is not totally and incomparably other; we use our sense of watch time and the real time back of it to discuss, imperfectly, our experience. Time flies, we say. Likewise literary judgment does relate to, does truly represent as well as misrepresent and (mostly) underrepresent our literary and other experience.

The argument could go further yet. Einstein's name has not been sounded, and could lead into some tangled and marshy paths. But I have carried the discussion as far as I now care to go. I think that the connection between aesthetic and moral relativism and Einstein's theory is almost entirely verbal. I shall leave that statement undefended.

I have worked the metaphor beyond any meaning Pope was likely to have consciously entertained, in order to get a little sharper focus on some elusive issues. Like all good metaphors, Pope's metaphor has its truth; like all metaphors whatsoever, it has its limits. Perhaps the greatest limit is that the watch of the metaphor is an unfeeling machine, albeit a delicate one; the judgment of which Pope speaks is neither unfeeling nor mechanical. The metaphor, like the other passages I have looked at, is not relativistic; it is consistent with the central doctrine of the poem. That doctrine, which I have exposed only in part, is traditional, feeling, flexible, well grounded, fundamentally consistent, in large and valuable measure true.

Relativism, I have tried to show, doesn't really exist in *An Essay on Criticism*. When it appears to appear, it has a quaint way of vanishing into the real assumptions of the poem. That is not merely true in this poem. For in the fundamental senses of the terms either absolutism or subjectivism must be true. Either our experience teaches us of genuine value or we are sorely deluded. There is no space between those positions. Relativism tries to occupy that no-space. Insofar as relativism has true things to say, it is implicitly absolutist. Insofar as it is subjectivistic, we who are committed to believe in the reality and intelligibility of literary and other value must in consistency pronounce it false. I do not claim to have proved those last statements in this essay. I have tried to present some evidence and to do some disentangling. More to the major point, I have tried to show something of the faults and very great virtues of a beautiful and important poem. Not the least of those virtues is the coherence of the parts with the central doctrine.

≥ LILLIAN FEDER

# Sermo or Satire: Pope's Definition of His Art

No COMMENTATOR has so successfully elucidated the intention and method of Pope's satire as Pope himself did. Throughout his career as a satirist he explained and defended his own aims and methods: in one respect his whole career can be regarded as an attempt to establish and define the art of satire as he practiced it. In so doing his chief guide and model was Horace, who established satire as an art in ancient Rome. The relationship between Horace and Pope has been treated by many scholars and critics,[1] who have analyzed Pope's use of the *publica materies* that Horace provided for him, but no one has shown that Pope's defense of himself through a Horatian image is actually more than a justification for attacking his contemporaries or exposing the vices of his period: it is a means of defining his own art and establishing a new type of English satire. Pope's departures from Horace, moreover, are as significant as his borrowings in the formation of his own satiric *persona*.

In his attempt to formulate his own method as a satirist it was natural for Pope to turn to Horace for guidance; Horace had been long accepted as one of the chief sources and models for English poets, and Pope felt a profound personal and intellectual tie with him. Furthermore, one of the most interesting and important subjects of Horace's *Sermones* is the art of satire.

As Eduard Fraenkel points out, "Latin poetry, a child of the Hellenistic age, had almost *ab origine* been 'self-conscious' in the primary sense of the word, that is to say given to reflecting upon itself, aware of its own limitations, of the means at its disposal, and of the ends it was aiming at." [2] Of the Latin poets Horace is perhaps the best-known theoretician; he speculated on the nature of satire as he created the form.

Some of Horace's important revelations of his own aims in satire take the form of criticisms of his predecessor Lucilius, for, as G. L. Hendrickson suggests, Horace sought "to create out of the *character Lucilianus* a Roman satire." [3] Horace found Lucilius "witty" and sharp in "smelling out" the faults of others, but unfortunately "durus componere versus," and this "roughness" of style Horace considered his chief fault. Lucilius was too lazy to write "correctly"; because he did not revise his poems, they are wordy; "his stream," says Horace, "is muddy" (*Satires*, I.iv. 7–13). Horace refers to these charges in I.x.1, though in this satire he also defends Lucilius, declaring that one can hardly expect the inventor of a new form also to have perfected it. Horace modestly says that he himself cannot hope to equal Lucilius, but his criticisms of his predecessor and his descriptions of his own efforts to forge his style suggest that actually he hopes to surpass the master and to perfect the genre that Lucilius invented.

In his attempts to refine the "character Lucilianus" Horace emphasizes his concern with correctness, polish, variety, economy, and exactness in meter and diction; in defending himself against his own critics he discloses other principles and techniques which determine his concept of satire. One hears many objections to satire, says Horace, because most people deserve censure; they regard the poet who uncovers their vices as dangerous (I.iv.24–38). Horace's answers to these charges are disarming. First, he declares modestly, he can hardly be regarded as a poet, since his style, like that of comedy, is closer to prose (I.iv.42), a remark that seems intended as much to disarm the critic as to describe Horace's view of himself as a satirist. Reuben Brower's comment on the passage is that

1. See especially R. E. Hughes, "Pope's *Imitations of Horace* and the Ethical Focus," *MLN*, LXXI (1956), 569–74; Reuben A. Brower, *Alexander Pope, The Poetry of Allusion* (Oxford, 1959), especially Chapter IX; G. K. Hunter, "The Romanticism of Pope's Horace," *Essays in Criticism*, X (1960), 390–404; John M. Aden, "Pope and the Satiric Adversary," *SEL*, II (1962), 267–86; Aubrey L. Williams "Pope and Horace: The Second Epistle of the Second Book" in *Restoration and Eighteenth-Century Literature*, Essays in Honor of Alan Dugald McKillop, ed. Carroll Camden (Chicago, 1963), pp. 309–21.

2. Eduard Fraenkel, *Horace* (Oxford, 1957), p. 124.

3. G. L. Hendrickson, "Satura – the Genesis of a Literary Form," *Classical Philology*, VI (April 1911), 133.

in raising "the ugly and unnecessary question as to whether his poems were poetry," Horace's "object seems to have been tactical, a move to exclude his satires from attack by saying that they weren't poems anyway." [4] Whereas there is little doubt that "to the poet and his readers the satire is *sermo*, clearly distinct from the more exacting genres of poetry," [5] the casual conversational style of Horace's *Sermones* is, as he tells us, the product of great care and conscious artistry, and by Horace's own standards is certainly not unpoetic.

C. O. Brink remarks that in *Satires*, I.x, "the attitude of non-committal poetic play seems to clash strangely with the high standards and the strenuous workmanship demanded with so much conviction. . . . Horace seems to be striking two attitudes. He pronounces that poetry is an intricate and serious art: this is one attitude. He also pronounces that poetry is a game which he likes playing: this is another attitude." Brink regards this ambivalence as a characteristic defense of the Augustan poet: like the Hellenistic poet, the Augustan poet was dependent on the patronage of those in political power; thus he guarded his artistic independence by denying the "responsibility of an author." [6]

Significant as this general attitude toward poetry was in shaping Horace's conception of himself as a poet, it only partly explains his insistence that his verse is prosaic in the very satire in which he criticizes Lucilius for his carelessness in poetic technique. In reducing the *Sermones* to the level of the prosaic Horace seems as much concerned with establishing one of his chief satirical techniques, understatement, as with avoiding attacks on his poems. Since his is a "prosaic Muse" (*Satires*, II.vi.17), no one need fear his criticism. Horace begins his defense of himself in I.iv. by denying that his *Sermones* have the intensity and power of poetry. The implication is that these "conversations" cannot really wound: "cur metuas me?" (I.iv.70) One of Horace's main weapons is the denial of the force of his most effective satirical techniques.

Horace contrasts his easy, conversational manner in satire with that of the inspired bard, "cui mens divinior atque os magna sonaturum" (*Satires*, I.iv.43–44), a role he was later to assume in his odes, where he was to describe himself as "Musarum sacerdos" (*Odes*, III.i.3) and to express the hope that he would be placed among the "lyricis vatibus" (*Odes*, I.i.35). Proudly he declares, "Exegi monumentum aere perennius" (*Odes*, III.xxx.1). Of course it is possible that Horace's faith in himself and in his capacity as a poet developed as he grew older and more experienced, but certainly there emerges from the totality of his work a contrast between the satiric poet expressing himself in colloquial, conversational verse and his image of himself as the sacred bard of the lyrics. One should not, however, take too literally his remarks on the prosaic nature of his *Sermones*; his criticisms of the carelessness of Lucilius, his consciousness that he is developing a new genre, his analysis of the poetic requirements of satire, and his hope that his *Sermones* will please Vergil, Maecenas, and other discriminating contemporaries all indicate that Horace thinks of himself as a poet, if not as yet as the "Musarum sacerdos."

When one of Horace's critics accuses him of enjoying hurting others, Horace replies that all he has done is to laugh at "Rufillus who smells of scent and at Gargonius who smells like a goat" (*Satires*, I.iv.91–93). He has no malice, Horace says, he merely teaches by example, as his father taught him. This is one of many autobiographical passages in the *Sermones*. Lucilius, says Horace, entrusted his secret thoughts to his books, which he regarded as faithful friends, and, writing "Lucili ritu," Horace feels free to express his feelings and tell some of the details of his life (*Satires*, II.i.29–34).[7] These self-revelations, however, do not consist of intimate details or records of deep personal conflict. Instead they are the thoughts and feelings that a man might reveal to close friends. Moreover, Horace uses the material of his own life and his personal feelings and attitudes as an important satirical device.

Horace's references to his father in his poems are not simply fond reminiscences of his youth; they are his means of establishing both a *persona* and a standard against which he measures the society he attacks. They are finally a defense of himself in his role of judge and of his right to satirize the faults of his contemporaries. Horace admits he has some minor faults, but, he says, as a result of his father's teachings he is free of vices (*Satires*, I.iv.129–30; I.vi.65–88). Now he takes the "fatherly" role as satirist, exposing follies and vices in order to teach man how to live a good life. Ultimately Horace is a moralist; his aim is to reveal to man the essential sources of happiness: the tranquillity that results from living a life based upon true values. His autobiographical references serve as an

4. Brower, *Alexander Pope*, p. 167.
5. Fraenkel, *Horace*, p. 103.
6. C. O. Brink, *Horace on Poetry, Prolegomena to the Literary Epistles* (Cambridge, 1963), pp. 169–70.
7. For different approaches to the autobiographical references in Horace, see Fraenkel, *Horace*, pp. 152–53 and Brink, *Horace on Poetry*, pp. 172–73.

example of the contentment and pleasure of a simple, honest life founded on self-respect and moderation.

Horace's defenses of himself, his declarations that he leads an upright life, that his heart is pure, suggest not a smug man denying his susceptibility to human frailty, but the satirist defining his role. Horace's own satires are also his critical commentary on the art of satire, which for Horace was actually a *sermo*,[8] an informal, conversational poem in which the poet-moralist revealed and criticized the follies of his society, spoke of his own personality and life, related anecdotes and stories, and felt free to vary his contents and even his style because his art was also "satura," a medley.

Though Alexander Pope was heir to a much richer tradition of satire than Horace was, he felt the need to defend and redefine his art for his own time. Horace, of course, was his model and guide, and Pope's defense of himself is to a large extent a defense of the Horatian image of the satirist. Furthermore, just as Horace emulated and altered the "versus Lucili," so Pope reworked the Horatian *sermo*. Pope's final definition of his art contains many Horatian features, but it also includes significant departures from and even a repudiation of his master.

As early as *An Essay on Criticism*, which Reuben Brower calls "Pope's first 'Horatian' essays,"[9] Pope is conscious of the hostility of inferior writers to true "wit":

> *Pride, Malice, Folly*, against *Dryden* rose,
> In various Shapes of *Parsons, Criticks, Beaus*;
>
> . . . . . . . . . . . . . .
>
> 'Tis what the *Vicious fear*, the *Virtuous shun*;
> By *Fools* 'tis *hated*, and by *Knaves undone!*
>
> (ll. 458–59, 506–7)[10]

Wit is the target of ignorance, says Pope, and he pleads, "Let not *Learning* too commence its Foe!" (l. 509)

In his approach to his main subject, critical theory, Pope's tone is moderate. There is no question that *An Essay on Criticism* is "essentially a compromise, an effort to bring into harmonious accord the various, and sometimes opposing, principles of its sources."[11] Pope, however, does not compromise with his high standards for poetry and criticism: he is harsh in his condemnation of dull poets and ignorant critics, and he seems to be predicting his own future in poetry when he says, "Make use of ev'ry *Friend* — and ev'ry *Foe*" (l. 214).

Certainly this is Pope's attitude in the "Preface of 1717" to the collected volume of his *Works*, where he declares, "The life of a Wit is a warfare upon earth; and the present spirit of the learned world is such, that to attempt to serve it (any way) one must have the constancy of a martyr, and a resolution to suffer for its sake." [12] Early in his career Pope sees himself as a defender of his art, a defender, moreover, not only of learning, taste, and good sense, but of morality: "If I have written well, let it be consider'd that 'tis what no man can do without good sense, a quality that not only renders one capable of being a good writer, but a good man." [13] This early analysis of what makes a good writer contains two elements which are to become consistent attributes of Pope's satiric *persona*: good sense and moral virtue.

It is impossible to use the word *persona* without referring to a recent brilliant essay on the subject by Irvin Ehrenpreis, which should serve to correct the many errors committed through current misuses of this term. Mr. Ehrenpreis argues against the use of the word to separate "the speaker from the author. . . . Through his masterpieces a man defines — not hides — himself. By reading them, we are put in touch with him, not with a series of intermediaries. The nature of his communication may be subtle; his manner, devious. Ultimately, however, he is telling us his truth." [14] I use the word *persona* here to indicate the fairly consistent character of Pope as it emerges from the speaker in his satires, whom Pope uses to represent and reveal himself as a humane Horatian moralist, sustained by his self-respect and his belief in his own values and his own important work, but angry and upset by the vice and folly he sees around him; the speaker is un-Horatian in his determination to withhold nothing, in his pride in his independence, in his forebodings of future spiritual and intellectual darkness, and in his tragic assumption that satire

8. For a discussion of the term *sermo* and the increasing use of the word *satura* during Horace's lifetime, see Hendrickson, "Satura."

9. Brower, *Alexander Pope*, p. 204.

10. Twickenham ed., I, ed. Émile Audra and Aubrey Williams. All quotations from Pope are taken from *The Poems of Alexander Pope*, Twickenham ed., general ed., John Butt (London, 1939–61), I–VI. Volume numbers and individual editors as well as line or page numbers will be cited for the first quotation from any volume of this edition. For subsequent quotations of poetry, line numbers, and, for prose, volume and page numbers, will be given.

11. Twickenham ed., I, 226.

12. *Ibid.*, I, 6.

13. *Ibid.*, I, 9.

14. Irvin Ehrenpreis, "Personae" in *Restoration and Eighteenth-Century Literature*, pp. 33–34.

is a "monument" to testify to his prophetic powers. Pope employs this *persona* to define not only himself but his art.

In the "Preface of 1717" Pope says, "I am altogether uncertain, whether to look upon myself as a man building a monument, or burying the dead." [15] Clearly Pope had in mind Horace's proud declaration in *Ode* III, 30, "Exegi monumentum aere perennius," the sacred bard of the odes rather than the urbane conversationalist of the *Sermones*. Between these ideals Pope alternated for a large portion of his life; he finally resolved the conflict in his satires through a fusion of the two.

*The Dunciad* is, of course, the best known of Pope's defenses of himself, his attempt to "rid" himself of the "insects" who had attacked him. The demands for keys to the dunces provided Pope with an opportunity for further attacks on his enemies and defenses of himself in the notes and commentaries to the *Dunciad Variorum*.[16] These are more than keys to the dunces; ironically, humorously, yet with an occasional serious note, Pope provides in the variorum commentary a key to some of his satirical methods. His defense of himself in the notes and in other additions suggests that he is seeking to defend and define his concept of satire. In retaliating against his enemies Pope is discovering himself.

In the "Advertisement" to the *Dunciad Variorum* Pope says, "Of the Persons it was judg'd proper to give some account: for since it is only in this monument that they must expect to survive, (and here survive they will, as long as the English tongue shall remain such as it was in the reign of Queen Anne and King George) it seem'd but humanity to bestow a word or two upon each, just to tell what he was, what he writ, when he liv'd, or when he dy'd." [17] Once more Pope speaks of his work as a "monument," obviously conscious of the word's traditional associations with Horace, for he qualifies his assertion with his commentary on language. English, as he says elsewhere,[18] does not possess the "universal and everlasting" qualities of Greek and Latin. If one can produce a "monumentum aere perennius" in English, he has done so.

In the *Dunciad* Pope is no writer of *sermones*; he is the poet creating his "monument" — his heroic satire — for posterity. Thus he justifies his identification of the dunces by offering them immortality, an explanation of his method which is, of course, at the same time a sneer at his enemies. In referring to himself Pope speaks of a man whose "humanity" motivates his technique.[19] Another reason for identifying the dunces is his desire to protect the innocent. In "A Letter to the Publisher," signed

William Cleland but no doubt written by Pope himself,[20] Pope is described as an "honest, open, and beneficent Man," whose aim is "to undeceive or vindicate the honest and unpretending part of mankind from imposition." Throughout his notes Pope continues to build up this portrait of the gentle, "humane," even tender Horatian satirist, informing the reader that his harsh comments are not to be taken as motivated by viciousness but rather by the anger of a good and essentially gentle man. Pope "in his very laughter, is not indulging his own ill nature, but only punishing that of others." [21] His humanity, moreover, is a standard against which to measure the cruelty and hostility of his enemies. This emphasis on his humanity and his high moral standards becomes an essential and consistent feature of Pope's Horatian *persona*; he continues to emphasize these qualities in his portrait of himself in the *Imitations of Horace*, *An Epistle to Dr. Arbuthnot*, and *The Epilogue to the Satires*.

There is, however, another feature of Pope's self-portrait in the *Dunciad Variorum* which is un-Horatian and which becomes as important as the Horatian elements in determining his technique in satire. Cleland's letter continues in its praise of Pope's moral qualities: "He has not been a follower of fortune or success: He has liv'd with the Great without Flattery, been a friend to Men in power without Pensions, from whom as he ask'd, so he receiv'd no favour but what was done Him in his friends." [22] Unlike Horace, who is proud to acknowledge the patronage of Maecenas and the approval of Augustus, Pope is proud of his independence, his freedom from the necessities of gratitude. This is not simply a description of Pope's *persona*; it is an essential attribute of the poet who, far from denying the power of his poems, declares that he creates "monuments" in satire; and, as we shall see, it becomes a basic part of Pope's definition of his art in the later satires.

Some of the notes in the *Dunciad Variorum* are specific explanations of particular satiric techniques or comments on language itself. For example, in his note to II, 293, Pope says, "The strength of the metaphors

15. Twickenham ed., I, 9.
16. See Aubrey L. Williams, *Pope's Dunciad, A Study of Its Meaning* (London, 1955), p. 76.
17. Twickenham ed., V, ed. James Sutherland, 8.
18. *Ibid.*, I, 7.
19. *Ibid.*, V, xl, and Williams, *Dunciad*, p. 79.
20. See Twickenham ed., V, xxv, and note 22, p. 19.
21. *Ibid.*, V, 13–19.
22. *Ibid.*, V, 18.

in this passage is to express the great scurrility and fury of the writer [Leonard Welsted] which may be seen, One day, in a Piece of his, call'd (as I think) *Labeo*." Again in the note to II, 356, he makes sure the reader is aware that "all these lines very well imitate the slow drowziness with which they proceed." In a note satirizing the antiquarian language of Wormius, Pope expresses one of his serious concerns as a writer: the need for refinement of the language in order to achieve the purity of diction for which he strove throughout his life (III, 183). In the least personal of the genres in which he wrote, epic satire, Pope reveals something of himself and his aims as a writer. In his later satires there is much more explicit questioning of himself and more self-revelation.

Pope says that he chose a Horatian *persona* to reply to criticisms of his *Epistles* because an "Answer from Horace was both more full, and of more Dignity, than any I cou'd have made in my own person." He is furious at the fools who mistake "a Satyrist for a Libeller," [23] and one of his aims in his *Imitations* is to clarify the difference between the two.

Defending himself and his satirical method in *The First Satire of the Second Book of Horace*, Pope actually uses two *personae*. One, reminiscent of Horace, confesses at the beginning of the poem that he is "Tim-'rous by Nature, of the Rich in awe" (IV, 7); the other, like the "commentator" of the *Dunciad*, declares:

> Could Laureate *Dryden* Pimp and Fry'r engage,
> Yet neither *Charles* nor *James* be in a Rage?
> And I not strip the Gilding off a Knave,
> Un-plac'd, un-pension'd, no Man's Heir, or Slave?
> I will, or perish in the gen'rous Cause.
> Hear this, and tremble! you, who 'scape the Laws.
>
> (ll. 114–18)

The first *persona* loves to talk about himself; he is a simple, direct man who lives a peaceful life; the second regards satire as his "Weapon" (l. 69). Through these two facets of his nature Pope reveals two major techniques of his satire: like Horace he uses himself and his own life as standards for morality and conduct, and he regards satire as a means of combating social and personal enemies; offenders become "Sacred to Ridicule!" (l. 79) His tone may be conversational and humorous, but his anger is real. The verbs Pope uses to describe his art in the following lines clearly show that outrage at vice is an essential part of his satirical technique:

What? arm'd for Virtue when I point the Pen,
Brand the bold Front of shameless, guilty Men,
Dash the proud Gamester in his gilded Car,
Bare the mean Heart that lurks beneath a Star;

(ll. 105–8)

There is little in Horace to account for these lines:

Quid? cum est Lucilius ausus
Primus in hunc operis componere carmina morem,
Detrahere et pellem, nitidus qua quisque per ora
Cederet introrsum turpis;

(Satires, II.i.62–65)

In Horace's poem it is Lucilius who exposes the corrupt. The only real connection between the two passages are the words that Pope had printed in italics to indicate the growth of his own poetic ideas from the suggestions of a few Latin words.

To the question why he does not write in praise of Augustus, Pope employs Horace's rather cautious answer as a kind of ironic excuse for a bitter attack on George II. Horace simply says:

Haud mihi dero,
Cum res ipsa feret: nisi dextro tempore, Flacci
Verba per attentam non ibunt Caesaris aurem,
Cui male si palpere, recalcitrat undique tutus.

(Satires, II.i.17–20)

Horace's caution, his hesitation about the right time and occasion for "the words of a Flaccus" to approach the ear of the great Caesar suggest to Pope the utter impossibility of poetry's ever gaining entrance to the court or mind of George II.

Alas! few Verses touch their nicer Ear;
They scarce can bear their *Laureate* twice a Year:
And justly CAESAR scorns the Poet's Lays,
It is to *History* he trusts for Praise.

(ll. 33–36)

The resigned "Alas!" and the mock acceptance of his tone suggest the hopeless depth of Pope's contempt.

Pope uses the same implied contrast between the two "Caesars" *and* the two poets in his *Imitation* of *The First Epistle of the Second Book of Horace*. In the "Advertisement" Pope praises Horace who "Made his

23. *Ibid.*, IV, ed. John Butt, 3.

Court to this Great Prince, by writing with a decent Freedom toward him, with a just Contempt of his low Flatterers, and with a manly Regard to his own Character." [24] Actually he seems to be more concerned with preparing the reader for his own version of the epistle than with describing Horace's approach to Augustus.

As C. O. Brink points out, Horace's epistle is "a command performance executed with great candour and skill." [25] The first seventeen lines of Horace's poem, which provide Pope with the essential ironic framework for his satire, are the traditional praises of a leader; as Fraenkel suggests, they "contain certain elements of *laudes Caesaris*, first fairly directly expressed in the poem (1–4), then partly disguised (5–12), partly overt (15–17)." [26] The liberty that Horace takes is in disagreeing with Augustus' well-known opinions on literature, especially on Roman comedy.[27] In the parts of the epistle where Horace is most flattering to Augustus, Pope is most contemptuous of George II.

In summarizing the history of Latin poetry, Horace defends and praises his own age. He points to the poetry of Vergil and Varius; and he declares that the poet depicts the glory of great men by revealing their inner qualities as effectively as the sculptor depicts their features in bronze. Then he speaks of his own *sermones* that "crawl along the ground" and of his inability to write in the high style of epic, an explanation for not having addressed an epistle to Augustus earlier (245–59). Pope also traces the history of the poetry of his nation. "For all its irony, the *Epistle to Augustus* is Pope's ultimate evaluation of the Augustan age and its standards in art and life." [28] Like Horace he explains why he cannot praise the king in epic verse; whereas Horace had said that Augustus would scorn "low verses" (258), Pope says that George would scorn all poetry:

> But verse alas! your Majesty disdains;
> And I'm not us'd to Panegyric strains:
>
> (ll. 404–5)

Pope continues to explain why he cannot praise the king in epic strains, and in so doing he explains the method of his whole satire on George II:

> Besides, a fate attends on all I write,
> That when I aim at praise, they say I bite.
> A vile Encomium doubly ridicules;
> There's nothing blackens like the ink of fools;
> If true, a woful likeness, and if lyes,

"Praise undeserv'd is scandal in disguise."

(ll. 408–13)

In the *Imitations* Pope offers clues to his own satiric method by openly inviting a comparison between himself and Horace. "An answer from Horace" offers him not only "dignity" but an opportunity to reveal the seeds of his own themes, characterizations, and points of view, and to exult in the development of his independent voice.

*An Epistle to Dr. Arbuthnot* and the two dialogues of the *Epilogue to the Satires* are also defenses of himself in which Pope deals with the nature of satire. These poems are Horatian in their dramatic structure and use of dialogue, their autobiographical references, their portraits, and their conversational tone, and it is easy to find a great many Horatian parallels and echoes in them. In his remarks on satire, however, Pope alternates between indications of his dependence on the *Sermones* of Horace and deliberate departures from them.

In *An Epistle to Dr. Arbuthnot*, as the helpless victim of dull poets who demand his attention, Pope is the gentle Horatian who offers the traditional advice, "Keep your piece nine years." (IV, 40). He speaks of his "modest satire (l. 189) and, his patience with the criticism of fools, and describes himself as "Poor guiltless I!" (l. 281). His references to the examples of virtuous conduct set by his parents also suggest the Horatian self-portrait. But these are only part of Pope's defense. In speaking of a "poet's dignity" he again expresses his contempt for dependence on the patronage of those in power:

> Above a Patron, tho' I condescend
> Sometimes to call a Minister my Friend.
>
> (ll. 265–66)

Free of all the limitations imposed by patronage, Pope is free to tell the truth. When Arbuthnot asks him why he chooses to attack Sporus,

> "that Thing of silk,
> "*Sporus*, that mere white Curd of Ass's milk?
> "Satire or Sense alas! can *Sporus* feel?
> "Who breaks a Butterfly upon a Wheel?"
>
> (ll. 305–8)

24. *Ibid.*, IV, 192.
25. Brink, *Horace on Poetry*, p. 191.
26. Fraenkel, *Horace*, p. 386.
27. Brink, *Horace on Poetry*, note 2, p. 192; Fraenkel, *Horace*, pp. 295–96.
28. Brower, *Alexander Pope*, p. 305.

Pope's reply to this question is his brilliant "character" of Sporus. In his very description of Sporus as, on the one hand, an insect and, on the other, like Satan, a "familiar Toad" (l. 319), Pope answers the question and points up his method of attack. He attacks Sporus because such weakness is evil and dangerous. His portrait is an example of his method; he must "flap this bug" (l. 309) because he is "Half Froth, half Venom" (l. 320). After emphasizing the pride and servility of Sporus —

> Beauty that shocks you, Parts that none will trust,
> Wit that can creep, and Pride that licks the dust.
>
> (ll. 332–33)

— Pope returns to his own self-portrait, a deliberate contrast with his characterization of Sporus:

> Not Fortune's Worshipper, nor Fashion's Fool,
> Not Lucre's Madman, nor Ambition's Tool,
> Not proud, nor servile, be one Poet's praise
> That, if he pleas'd, he pleas'd by manly ways;
> That Flatt'ry, ev'n to Kings, he held a shame,
> And thought a Lye in Verse or Prose the same.
>
> (ll. 334–39)

The self-portrait here is clearly used as a standard against which to measure the evil he condemns. It is a portrait, moreover, not of Horatian ease and tranquillity, but of the life of an independent man, free to assert the truth because he has never needed to make the compromises of a Sporus or even a Horace.

In "Dialogue I" of the *Epilogue to the Satires*, originally called *One Thousand Seven Hundred and Thirty Eight, A Dialogue Something like Horace*, Pope's adversary complains that his style is too "correct" and he himself is too "moral." Clearly Pope "steals"; "'Tis all from *Horace*" IV, 2–7). He then goes on to speak of and illustrate Horace's familiar technique of understatement in satire and to commend his ability to please Augustus and his court:

> But *Horace*, Sir, was delicate, was nice:
> *Bubo* observes, he lash'd no sort of *Vice*:
> *Horace* would say, *Sir* Billy *serv'd the Crown,*
> Blunt *could do Bus'ness*, H—ggins *knew the Town,*
> In *Sappho* touch the *Failing of the Sex,*
> In rev'rend Bishops note some *small Neglects,*
> And own, the *Spaniard* did a *waggish thing,*
> Who cropt our Ears, and sent them to the King.

His sly, polite, insinuating stile
Could please at Court, and make AUGUSTUS smile:
An artful Manager, that crept between
His Friend and Shame, and was a kind of *Screen*.

(ll. 11–22)

As against Horace's understatement and his friendliness with the powers of the court, Pope contrasts his own directness, his independence, his unwillingness to try to please those in political power:

But 'faith your very Friends will soon be sore;
*Patriots* there are, who wish you'd jest no more —
And where's the Glory? 'twill be only thought
The Great man never offer'd you a Groat.
Go see Sir ROBERT —

(ll. 23–27)

In discussing these lines, John M. Aden says, "the adversary confidently commends Horace for all the wrong reasons," and then goes on to comment in a note, "It is possible of course that Pope might concur in the notion that Horace was guilty of these faults." [29] It seems not only possible but unquestionable that Pope, through the praise of a corrupt and cynical adversary, is criticizing Horace quite severely. The very fact that the adversary praises Horace for his "sly, polite, insinuating stile," which could "please at Court," to the poet who has spoken so often of his pride in his independence and of his contempt for the court is evidence enough. The sources of these lines are also significant. John Butt indicates that in them Pope echoes Dryden's translation of Persius's *Satire*, I, 116–18,[30] but there is another interesting though less obvious parallel that has not been noticed before. In his *Discourse Concerning the Original and Progress of Satire*, Dryden compares the satire of Juvenal and Horace, obviously preferring the work of Juvenal. He says that Horace "insinuates virtue rather by familiar examples than by the severity of precepts." Then fearing that this judgment will make it appear that he prefers Horace to Juvenal, he goes on to say:

But, after all, I must confess, that the delight which Horace gives me is but languishing. Be pleased still to understand, that I speak of my own taste only: he may ravish other men; but I am too stupid and insensible

29. Aden, "Pope and the Satiric Adversary," p. 282. Aden's analysis of Pope's use of a "satiric adversary," particularly in the *Epilogue to the Satires*, is extremely illuminating, and of special importance for any study of the influence of Horace on Pope.

30. Twickenham ed., IV, note 22, p. 299.

to be tickled. Where he barely grins himself, and, as Scaliger says, only shows his white teeth, he cannot provoke me to any laughter. His urbanity, that is, his good manners, are to be commended, but his wit is faint; and his salt, if I may dare to say so, almost insipid. Juvenal is of a more vigorous and masculine wit; he gives me as much pleasure as I can bear; he fully satisfies my expectation; he treats his subject home: his spleen is raised, and he raises mine. . . . His thoughts are sharper; his indignation against vice is more vehement; his spirit has more of the commonwealth genius; he treats tyranny, and all the vices attending it, as they deserve, with the utmost rigor: and consequently, a noble soul is better pleased with a zealous vindicator of Roman liberty, than with a temporizing poet, a well-mannered court-slave, and a man who is often afraid of laughing in the right place; who is ever decent, because he is naturally servile.[31]

Surely Pope knew Dryden's essay, and it is probable that he had in mind Dryden's description of Horace as the "well-mannered court-slave . . . who is often afraid of laughing in the right place" when he wrote this Dialogue. He seems to be referring directly to it in his answer to the suggestion of the adversary that he go to see Sir Robert:

See Sir ROBERT! — hum —
And never laugh — for all my life to come?
Seen him I have, but in his happier hour
Of Social Pleasure, ill-exchang'd for Pow'r;
Seen him, uncumber'd with the Venal tribe,
Smile without Art, and win without a Bribe.
Would he oblige me? let me only find,
He does not think me what he thinks mankind.
Come, come, at all I laugh He laughs, no doubt,
The only diff'rence is, I dare laugh out.

(ll. 28–36)

Unlike the politician and the poet, both afraid to express their honest feelings, Pope holds back neither wrath nor laughter. Thus, when in "Dialogue II" he is accused of pride, he can reply:

So proud, I am no Slave:
So impudent, I own myself no Knave:
So odd, my Country's Ruin makes me grave.
Yes, I am proud; I must be proud to see
Men not afraid of God, afraid of me.

(ll. 205–9)

Pope feels he cannot become a friend of those in power, for to do so would necessitate his imitating not only the hypocritical diplomacy of Walpole but the restrained and "insinuating" manner of Horace. He cannot do so for he regards satire as a "sacred Weapon! left for Truth's defence" (l. 212). He sees his art as a sacred one and himself as the sacred bard of satire. Satire is "To all but Heav'n-directed hands deny'd" (l. 214), and thus it is a sacred charge.

Throughout the *Epilogue to the Satires* Pope defends satire against the attacks of the foolish and the corrupt by justifying his own satirical techniques. He shows up the folly of those who criticize his use of names, and suggests it is impossible to "Spare . . . the Person, and expose the Vice" (Dialogue II, 12). Pope's language throughout these dialogues is strong, his imagery sometimes violent. When in response to his comparison of courtly wits to Westphaly hogs, his adversary objects that Pope's harsh simile "Quite turns my Stomach," Pope's reply is, "So does Flatt'ry mine," and then he goes on to use an even harsher metaphor:

> And all your Courtly Civet-Cats can vent,
> Perfume to you, to me is Excrement. (Dialogue II, 183–84)

Satire and truth become synonymous in these dialogues. Pope defeats his adversaries by relying on the power of truth and virtue:

> Truth guards the Poet, sanctifies the line,
> And makes Immortal, Verse as mean as mine. (Dialogue II, 246–47)

The "mean" verse of the *sermo* becomes the "sacred weapon," the "immortal" poetry of satire, when the poet is free to speak the truth. In his major satires Pope brilliantly unites the casual tone of the *sermo* with the intense and even exalted voice of the "Musarum sacerdos," dedicated to a sacred art, which "the Muse may give thee, but the Gods must guide" (Dialogue II, 215).

31. *Essays of John Dryden*, ed. W. P. Ker (Oxford, 1926), II, 84–87.

❧ IRVIN EHRENPREIS

# The Cistern and the Fountain: Art and Reality in Pope and Gray

FINDING his satires "favourably received at home, and abroad," Edward Young supposed he could account for such good fortune by the remoteness of his derogatory observations — where they occurred — from specific human objects: "I am not conscious," he said (introducing an edition which was published the same year as *The Dunciad*), "of the least malevolence to any particular person thro' all the characters." [1] If Young sounds commonplace in recommending Horatian or "laughing" satire and condemning bitter, Juvenalian violence, he is equally representative of the critical truisms of his era in judging "general" satire to be a higher form than "particular." Like most satirists who flourished during the lives of Dryden and Swift, Young did of course enrich his generalities with a strong infusion of obvious particulars. Yet the structure and meaning of the seven poems never depend upon these changeable parts. In the final impression the reader's mind is occupied with permanent moral truths conveyed by vehicles or arguments that the concrete instances only decorate. The external realities surrounding the living poet are one order; the internal elements that constitute the poem are another.

In these prejudices Young curiously anticipates the widening practice of academic criticism during recent decades, or since the pedantries of philological and socio-historical research were rejected by young American scholars a generation ago. That the true structure of accepted masterpieces never depends upon their reference to nonliterary reality seems a natural law of learned criticism today. Ideally, it is an internal pattern that the "trained" reader hopes to find — a unifying design subtly harmonizing the superficially disparate images in a poem, or connecting the various rhetorical figures with the character of a person supposed to speak the lines. To nourish the literary organism, one may indeed discover that profound intellectual traditions or ancient conventions of symbolism serve as reservoirs of allusion. But they in turn are self-contained imaginative or mythological reservoirs, distinct from factual history or from any science of observed human nature. If a would-be critic should now ask, in the style of Johnson, whether the argument of the *Essay on Man* is intellectually respectable,[2] whether it makes sense according to nonpoetic logic or to principles of psychology, whether it agrees with our knowledge of the external, historical events of the period to which it was addressed, he would probably be censured for confusing literature with documentary evidence. The praise that Johnson devotes to Shakespeare's understanding of human behavior [3] finds only a low-keyed echo in the language of my colleagues. From the study of art and poetry alone, they often imply, we can learn what is most relevant to the appreciation of literary structures, although the accidents of a poem may receive helpful clarification from ancillary knowledge.

In the study of eighteenth-century literature this view has gained coincidental strength from the widely accepted belief that impersonal art is the hallmark of Augustan craftsmanship. The final pages of *Gulliver's Travels*, in which Swift speaks out loud and clear, we are commonly asked to regard as peripheral to the main design. Poems like Johnson's elegy on Levet are passed under our inspection to demonstrate that even the private crises of an author are characteristically generalized and purified before a truly Augustan artist employs them in a work for publication. As an attribute enhancing the ideal of a self-contained literary structure, the value of impersonality is evident.

I am inclined to question the usefulness of these postulates, not with any hope of destroying them but rather in an effort to define the range of their effectiveness. Nobody would like to see us return to that mesozoic era when the biography of an author was indistinguishable from the criticism of his work, or to that later but glacial age when the history of

1. Preface to *Love of Fame, The Universal Passion* (London, 1728), sig. A2.
2. In both the life of Pope and the review of Soame Jenyns.
3. Particularly in the Preface to the edition of Shakespeare.

the language or the social development of the nation was presumed to cast the ultimate illumination upon both the import and the importance of a poem. Yet if internal "literary" coherence has been established, unconsciously, as the highest principle that a scholarly critic can demonstrate in a classic he admires, perhaps it would be profitable to examine some consequences of that assumption. My own hesitant, exploratory effort can hardly generate a conclusive proof or disproof, for my argument is not the sort that knocks down one general proposition and sets up a replacement. Rather I hope by using suggestive examples to encourage others to test my case with evidence of their own picking. In this effort I shall take up a few masterpieces and failures of eighteenth-century poetry, inquiring whether the structural integrity of each does not depend for its cogency, or deepest appeal, upon allusions to reality — whether, in other words, the truly successful imaginative structures do not reach out like a fountain whose glittering shape overflows into and thus vivifies the world around it. Among the specimens to be examined here, two, Pope's *Epistle to a Lady* and Gray's *The Bard*, enjoy a richness of self-contained form that has, I think, seldom been adequately appreciated.

◊　　◊　　◊

Few of Pope's works pretend to exhibit throughout the sort of design which his couplets and his verse paragraphs possess. I wish now to argue that the second "Moral Essay," *An Epistle to a Lady, Of the Characters of Women*, has just this virtue in addition to its others. *To a Lady* is a finished masterpiece such as Pope rarely created. Parts of it have received famous praise from Professor Empson, Dr. Leavis, and Lytton Strachey.[4] Yet little attention has fallen, I think, on the elaborated form of the whole poem. So I should like to consider this in terms of the arrangement of parts and pattern of images, and then to ask how it depends on allusions to reality. Through comparisons with similar poems both by Pope and by Edward Young, I hope to show that the achievement is remarkable.

The *Epistle to a Lady* can be divided into three parts: the first two hundred lines are a group of portraits of women, mostly sinners; the next fifty lines are a didactic analysis of their sins; and the final forty lines are a eulogy addressed to a Lady listener, easily identifiable as Martha Blount. Portraits, analysis, eulogy — among these the connection seems obvious. The concentrated praise in lines 249 to 292 balances the distributed attacks in lines 1 to 198, and the analysis in lines 199 to 248 forms a bridge between the two. The virtues Mrs. Blount owns — modesty, tenderness, fidelity — are conspicuously those the sinners lack; and their vices — vanity, avarice, ambition, lust — have no place in her character.

The structure of the first section will easily be seen to have a formal order. Thus in the series of portraits we find several kinds of rising lines. For one thing, the poet surveys his sinners roughly in order of size: a couplet or two on each of the first few names; four couplets on Silia; six on Calypso; eight on Narcissa; nine on Philomede; seven on Flavia; eighteen on Atossa; and twelve on Cloe, with some very brief profiles interspersed. In the *Epistle to Bathurst*, Pope had used the same rough order of size: one couplet on Colepepper, eight on Blunt, twenty-two on Sir Balaam, and so forth; the principle seems ordinary enough. But in the *Epistle to a Lady* Pope combines it with another, which Professor Elder Olson has noticed in the *Epistle to Dr. Arbuthnot*.[5] There, as the speech progresses, the satire sharpens: the portrait of Atticus is more severe than the ridicule of fools at the beginning, and the portrait of Sporus is more severe than that of Atticus. So in the *Epistle to a Lady*, Atossa's portrait is the climax of violence as well as the climax in length; Philomede's is milder; Narcissa's, still milder. But, as it happens, the sinners are also arranged in degrees of reality. Out of the first six, five seem fictitious: i.e., the poem does not invite us to search for an original. But Sappho, the next, can only refer to Lady Mary Wortley Montagu. Four additional pseudonyms — Philomede, Flavia, Atossa, and Cloe — have been associated with the second Duchess of Marlborough, the Duchess of Montagu, the Duchess of Buckinghamshire, and the Countess of Suffolk. Finally, the Queen is actually named, as is the Duchess of Queensberry (who does not, however, count as a sinner).[6] From the pseudonymous and fictitious, therefore, through the pseudonymous but recognizable, Pope moves to proper public names; and from a countess and an earl's daughter, through duchesses, he rises to the Queen. Admitting many irregularities and interruptions, we may say that he moves roughly through degrees of reality and degrees of rank. In other words, as Pope gets further along in the poem, and strengthens his grip on the audience, he grows bolder.

4. Empson in *Seven Types of Ambiguity*, Leavis in *Revaluation*, Strachey in *Pope*.

5. "Rhetoric and the Appreciation of Pope," *MP*, XXXVII (1939), 13–35.

6. For these identifications see F. W. Bateson's edition of Pope's *Epistles to Several Persons* (III, pt. ii, Twickenham ed.).

There is a further meaning to Pope's order. Those women who can be identified are peeresses or royalty, in contrast to the humble station of Mrs. Blount. Such targets of course give weight to the poem, just as an imperial dramatis personae gives weight to tragedy. They are courtiers, natural focuses of national concern. Lady Irwin had remarked of the *Epistle to Bathurst*, "As the objects of [Pope's] satire are low, people will be less offended, for who cares for [Peter] Waters, Charters, or Ward." [7] One never feels that the figures of *An Epistle to a Lady* are too inconsequential to be worth reading about. As we approach the peak of society, however, we approach the peak of corruption: the poet evokes an urgency suggesting a national crisis.

Young has two satires on women which deeply influenced Pope's work — numbers five and six of *The Universal Passion*, which are commonly judged to be the most satisfactory poems in that book. Yet Young completely misses Pope's effect of urgency because not only does he assign no particular ranks to his group of criminals but he also singles out royalty as the example of virtue:

> 'Midst empire's charms, how *Carolina's* heart
> Glows with the love of *virtue, and of art*? [8]

But Pope, from the long sequence of portraits, swings us up through the passage of didactic analysis into the final eulogy of Mrs. Blount; and there he shifts his point of view; for he addresses the poem to the good woman and holds up the vicious to her examination. Their corrupted natures are described in the third person; her virtuous self, in the second. They are spoken about; she is present, to be saluted directly. The effect gives to goodness, in its limited space, an immediacy and a substance which evil, though intensely realized and extended over hundreds of lines, has lacked. On this drawn-out moral contrast the poem is built. Like the coils of a long spring, the vicious characters are stretched at length and then let go to provide rebounding impetus for the final panegyric.

The moral implications of this relationship bear out the formal order. The Lady is both the positive climax of the entire poem and the justification of the satire. Obviously, Pope wishes to compliment Martha Blount. But in an age when sincerity was the most imitative form of flattery, and in a poem which singled out panegyric as the most suspect kind of literature, he had to exert himself to give force to his praise. By employing most of his lines in condemnation of dangerous women, he adds distinction to the solitary approval bestowed upon Mrs. Blount. Conversely, by loudly recognizing virtue as it appears in a unique specimen, he gives energy to his dispraise of vice. Years earlier, in the *Epistle to Burlington*, Pope had followed the same method; but there the attack on Timon is so much longer than the neighboring eulogy of Burlington, and so far more brilliant, that it submerges the latter. In both cases, however, Pope is especially convincing because as a normal thing he places an envoi or apostrophe, addressed to a primary reader, at the end of a long poem. Since this person is conventionally given his proper name, as the subject of a public tribute, the anonymous Lady inherits such authenticity. Here Pope is in a sense merely expanding and heightening the envoi so that it becomes the positive climax of his poem.

The apotheosis of Mrs. Blount also helps Pope meet a demand normally attached to the production of satire. By what right, a reader naturally wonders, does any author take it upon himself to expose so many faults in others? Most satirists answer by making explicit their moral principles and thereby establishing their own integrity. Thus in *An Epistle to Dr. Arbuthnot*, Pope displays the poet himself as *integer vitae scelerisque purus*, to balance the ignobility of his enemies. This makes sense rhetorically, but the inevitable suggestion of vanity weakens his power as a satirist. In the *Epistle to a Lady* he works less directly but places himself more effectively under the banner of righteousness; for here he embodies virtue in another person and then aligns himself with her. To incarnate his positive values, he invokes not a set of propositions but the concrete description of Martha Blount. Where he does have a long generalizing, didactic passage — and that is to bridge the great series of vicious women and the final portrait of his heroine — he is not expounding virtue but analyzing evil. By establishing his friend as his standard, Pope not only makes his ideal vivid; he also gives us implicit assurance of his own moral elevation. Since she appears as goodness itself, and he makes himself out to be her wholesale and accepted admirer, Mrs. Blount has the effect of a supreme character witness for him, and thereby encourages us to accept his denunciation of the world. Although Pope had employed a similar method at the close of the *Epistle to Burlington*, the tie between the earl and the poet is too thin, and the effect correspondingly weak.

7. Letter of January 18, 1733/4, in Historical Manuscript Commission, *XV Report*, Appendix, pt. vi, p. 97.

8. Young, *Universal Passion*, satire VI, p. 155.

If the formal order of parts thus reveals extraordinary internal coherence directed to a significant rhetorical purpose, the pattern of imagery in the *Epistle* supplies some fascinating reinforcement of that impression. We must remember that *To a Lady* presents a dramatic situation in which the readers overhear the poet as he talks to a woman friend about some paintings. The pair are strolling through a gallery or around a studio hung with portraits and sketches of ladies. As they stop before the various pictures or studies, the poet delivers remarks on the subjects. At the end of the tour and the end of the poem, he turns to his friend and pronounces an encomium contrasting her with the persons whose character he has just unmasked.

It was a traditional literary device, as Professor Jean Hagstrum has shown, to use a gallery of painted portraits as the imagined scene of a disquisition upon moral types.[9] Pierre Lemoyne had employed it in his *Peintures Morales* (1645). Farquhar staged the idea in the *Beaux' Stratagem*, and Addison supplies an instance in a *Spectator* paper (no. 83). Professor Hagstrum also reminds us of the convention of satire formulated as instructions given to a painter. This was established by the Italian, Businello, in his serious panegyric, *Il Trionfo Veneziano*, where the poet does not describe scenes directly but tells an artist how to represent them. Waller, one of Pope's acknowledged masters, naturalized the device to England when he composed a eulogy upon the Duke of York's heroism during a naval battle; here again the poet tells an artist how to bring out the value of the scenes, and Waller entitled his work *Instructions to a Painter*. The formula was soon copied by satirists as a means of pinpointing the corruptions of Charles II's court. Although most of these bitter, libelous pieces seem ephemeral, at least two are by Andrew Marvell.[10] Pope is only tangentially instructing a painter, and his scheme is far more peripheral than either Waller's or Marvell's. However, the tradition was familiar to him; and for the reader who remembers the Restoration poems, the overtone is there:

> Chuse a firm Cloud, before it fall, and in it
> Catch, ere she change, the Cynthia of this minute.
> . . . . . . . . . . . . . . . . . .
> Some wand'ring touches, some reflected light,
> Some flying stroke alone can hit 'em right.
>
> (ll. 19–20, 153–54)

All this is figurative, of course; for we normally treat the Lady of the

poem as a transparent screen between the poet and ourselves; we treat
the poem as a monologue; and we treat the allusions to painting as metaphors. However, I should like to indicate what the figurative setting contributes to the design and rhetoric of the poem. Young, like Pope, states
his theme in terms of painting, and he makes casual use of plastic similes:

> What picture's yonder loosen'd from its frame?
> Or is't *Asturia?* that affected dame? [11]

But he never hints at more, or connects the separate similes to a general
scheme. Pope, however, explores the symbolic value of treating sinners
this way; and he puts his meaning explicitly at the opening of the attack.
In his substitution of paintings for persons he implies the vices of vanity,
deceit, and — above all — fickleness:

> How many Pictures of one Nymph we view,
> All how unlike each other, all how true!
>
> (ll. 5–6)

Pope contrasts the corrupted women's dependence upon visible charms
with the Lady's reliance on virtue within. The theme is a commonplace:
Juba's praise of Marcia in *Cato,* Swift's praise of Biddy Floyd, Welsted's
epilogue to Steele's *Conscious Lovers,* all sing the same tune, exalting not
the visible but the moral, intellectual, and domestic resources of the ideal
woman; yet in Pope's poem the implicit contrast, point for point, with
the tangibilities of the villainous women who have just been observed,
produces a marvelous ironical transformation of the adjectives associated
with them — "art," "pride," etc. — when these are applied to Mrs. Blount:

> Reserve with Frankness, Art with Truth ally'd,
> Courage with Softness, Modesty with Pride,
> Fix'd Principles, with Fancy ever new.
>
> (ll. 277–79)

Young publishes similar aphorisms: "Your strongest charms are native innocence"; "Be kind and virtuous, you'll be blest and wise." But he con-

9. For my discussion of the metaphors drawn from painting I am indebted
to Jean H. Hagstrum's *The Sister Arts: The Tradition of Literary Pictorialism and
English Poetry from Dryden to Gray* (Chicago, 1958), pp. 236–40, and to Robert J. Allen's "Pope and the Sister Arts" in *Pope and His Contemporaries: Essays
Presented to George Sherburn,* ed. James A. Clifford and Louis A. Landa (Oxford,
1949), pp. 78–88.

10. See H. M. Margoliouth's discussion in his edition of Marvell's *Poems and Letters* (Oxford, 1927), I, 268–70, 289.

11. Young, *Universal Passion,* satire VI, p. 141.

fuses his arguments by also praising good women for appearances — for physical beauty and elegant clothes; he never ties the moral contrast to a pervasive metaphor; and his flattery of the highest-born compels him to shun opportunities for irony.

While Pope's objects of satire are present only as paintings, his Lady appears as a living being. The two-dimensional portraits therefore enhance one's sense of positive climax, because it is only after passing over these dozen surfaces that we meet the rounded heroine. To Pope's remark that we distinguish such females by their color — "black, brown, or fair" — Professor Hagstrum applies the principle, accepted by Pope's generation of connoisseurs, that line is more real and stable than color, that color is more changeable and therefore like women.[12] The same motif occurs in the *Essay on Criticism*, where the "faithful pencil" is opposed to "treacherous colours," and where the true lines of sound judgment are contrasted with the deceitful colors of false learning:

> But as the slightest Sketch, if justly trac'd,
> Is by ill *Colouring* but the more disgrac'd,
> So by *false Learning* is *good Sense* defac'd.
>
> (ll. 23–25)

The motif appears again in the lines on Cynthia in the *Epistle to a Lady*:

> Come then, the colours and the ground prepare!
> Dip in the Rainbow, trick her off in air.
>
> (ll. 17–18)

And later in the poem it is employed more generally:

> Pictures like these, dear Madam, to design,
> Asks no firm hand, and no unerring line.
>
> (ll. 151–52)

Pope even suggests that simple or unmixed (i.e., "equal") colors will not suit the problem; for only blended paints, implicitly less pure than the unmixed, can represent woman's evanescence and superficiality:

> For how should equal Colours do the knack?
> Chameleons who can paint in white and black?
>
> (ll. 155–56)

Within the paintings Pope makes further refinements. The pseudonymous women pose generally in costume or disguise, and not as themselves; and the costume is often of a mythological rather than historical figure: false names, false dress, false models. Or the sinners pose ironically as saints — Mary Magdalen, Cecilia. To such tokens of deception is linked the ancient contrast between naked truth and overdressed vice.

> Artists! who can paint or write,
> To draw the Naked is your true delight.
> That Robe of Quality so struts and swells,
> None see what Parts of Nature it conceals.
>
> (ll. 187–90)

Professor Hagstrum reminds us of Titian's *Sacred and Profane Love,* in which sacred love is naked and profane love clothed.[13] It is also obviously symbolic that the same woman should adopt contradictory roles in different paintings. The very syntax of such descriptions presses ambiguity upon us:

> Arcadia's Countess, here, in ermin'd pride,
> Is there, Pastora by a fountain side.
>
> (ll. 7–8)

The couplet seems deliberately paradoxical. Although she comes from Arcadia and should therefore be a shepherdess, she poses for one picture in the robes of a peeress; on the contrary, although her husband is presumably Earl of Pembroke and a great courtier, she disguises herself in the pendant picture as a country lass.

Finally, the metaphor of painting is borne out in the use of color imagery to contrast the Lady and the sinners. Gray and silver belong to her; red and gold to them; her scene is shaded; theirs is dazzling; she evokes the quiet moon, they the beaming sun. Since the Lady happens to be a spinster, the lunar tones appropriately suggest Diana and chastity.

*        *        *

If one were simply adhering to the principle of self-contained art, this point might well be the stopping place of criticism. The internal structure of Pope's poem has been, however hastily (I have not even mentioned the brilliant versification of the couplets leading up to the introduction of Mrs. Blount) set forth; his superiority to a rival (and mentor) has been indicated. Yet the power of the *Epistle* is obviously too great for one to feel right about leaving it so soon: the poem overflows, reaching beyond literature into reality. It is in the very structure of the *Epistle* that the overflowing occurs most beautifully, but the effect is evident as well

12. Hagstrum, *Sister Arts,* pp. 236–40.
13. *Ibid.*

in humbler ways that may be noticed first. There is, for example, a historical truth in the imagined situation. Pope had early experience of pictures like those he describes; he took painting lessons from Jervas; he was accustomed to thinking of poetry in pictorial terms; and he was accustomed to hearing an artist discuss painting in literary terms.[14] Though for him pictorial art was divided, in the curious categories of his age, between portraits and history painting, it was of portraits that he had the most experience; all his own efforts were in that category. He had, as it happens, seen pictures of some of the women to whom he alludes in the poem; he had himself copied one — the Duchess of Montagu — on canvas; and he had commissioned and owned at least two — Mrs. Blount herself and Lady Mary.[15] Since Mrs. Blount spent much time in his house, therefore, the setting of the poem is remarkably close to reality. Of course, Pope shields himself by the use of misleading details. To smother rumors and to protect the maiden Lady of his poem, he gives her a husband and a daughter; yet we all know she is drawn from the spinster Martha Blount.

As it was originally printed, the poem suffered enormous excisions, the most sensational characters being prudently omitted until Pope felt secure enough to face the consequences of releasing them — or else so near death that no consequence could touch him.[16] He would hardly have held back from publication the magnificent lines on Philomede, Atossa, Cloe, and Caroline if they were not allusions to the second Duchess of Marlborough, the Duchess of Buckinghamshire, the Countess of Suffolk, and the Queen. Sappho has universally been taken as a lampoon on Lady Mary Wortley Montagu. Arcadia's Countess is probably Margaret, first wife of the eighth earl of Pembroke. This employment of recognizable people and events is one persuasive ground of Pope's satirical appeal. Poetically, he keeps hinting, "These things have really happened." He does not mean that every name alludes to an existing person, or that every rumored scandal is true as represented. But since he claims that his insights are worth our attention, he must assume the wisdom of experience. By implying that he has observed at first hand the profusion of cases displayed in his argument, he encourages the reader to take him seriously. As a corollary, if the reader is to trust the obvious fables, he must recognize some facts. Just as Pope's didactic propositions shade from overt conventionalities to covert audacities, so his factual allusions shade from parables to direct reporting. The truisms serve to win the reader's faith so that he will respect the individual judgments; the facts season the legends so that the reader may credit the author as both an experienced and a faithful historian.

A more special effect is also felt because one never can be certain whether the poet has created an example or witnessed it. Once the reader thinks he can correctly name a pseudonymous character, he is bound to keep searching for new clues; and this search adds to Pope's late satires a vibrancy which deepens and strengthens their rhetoric. Young, in his satires, both sacrifices this special effect and weakens his general argument by dropping clues to a subject's name only when he is praising the person. His topical allusions are, as a careful scholar remarks, "not malicious," and individuals, if pointed out at all, are "generally mentioned in flattering terms."[17] Our curiosity is therefore dampened rather than aroused, and we infer that evil has less power than good.

The most brilliant allusion to reality, and the last effect I shall analyze in the poem, is central to the structure. This occurs at the negative climax and peripety, as Pope is completing and abandoning his collection of sinners; and it shows how a rhetorical order can be determined by facts external to a literary work. With the sequence of Atossa, Cloe, the Queen, and the Duchess of Queensberry, Pope seems to plot his path so as to reveal the sharpest contrast between the vicious and the good. He almost certainly intended the Duchess of Buckinghamshire to be recognized in Atossa. Katherine Darnley, Duchess of Buckinghamshire and Normandy, was the illegitimate daughter of James II. All her life, she exhibited a paranoid pride in her ancestry; she had a long feud with her husband's bastards, became famous for her megalomania, and ended up insane by any definition. "Cloe" almost certainly points to Henrietta Howard, Countess of Suffolk. She was at the same time both lady-in-waiting to the Queen and *maîtresse en titre* to the King. But although, as Prince of Wales, he had indeed made love to her, she was now superannuated, overweight, and deaf. It was years since he had shown her much tenderness. At court

14. On Pope's interest in painting and his connection with Jervas, see George Sherburn, *The Early Career of Alexander Pope* (Oxford, 1934). For the correspondence between Jervas and Pope, see the first volume of Sherburn's edition of Pope's *Correspondence* (Oxford, 1956). I refer particularly to *The Early Career*, pp. 69 and 102–3; the *Correspondence*, I, 189, 239, 315, 332.

15. See Mr. Bateson's note to I, 107; Pope's *Correspondence*, I, 189, and II, 21–22; and Pope's *Minor Poems*, Twickenham ed., VI, ed. John Butt, 211–12.

16. Bateson, ed., *Epistles to Several Persons*, pp. ix–xvi, 40–44.

17. Charlotte E. Crawford, "What Was Pope's Debt to Edward Young?" *ELH*, XIII (September 1946), 161.

she endured the contemptuous protection of the Queen, who did not wish her to be replaced by a less manageable instrument. The Countess of Suffolk was Pope's neighbor and friend.

Of course, the lines on Caroline are cautious. Pope discusses neither the Queen nor a painting of her. Instead, he ridicules the stereotype which always seems to be substituted for a description when a painter or author must represent the majesty of Britain. There is a parallel passage in Pope's version of Horace's *Satires*, II.i, addressed to Fortescue (ll. 21–32). No scholar seems to have observed that in both places the poet was probably alluding to Young's tinny tributes, in his satires, to the Queen and her eldest daughter.[18] It is such cliché praises and cliché poses that Pope pretends to be attacking, rather than the royal person. Because of these screens of nonsense, he says, one cannot look to the throne for a model of virtue.

As an alternative, however, he suggests, of all people, an avowed enemy of the court, whose title has a pun on "queen." Catherine Douglas, Duchess of Queensberry, was celebrated not only for her beauty and wit. She had bestowed the most liberal patronage on Pope's friend, Gay; and recently she had withdrawn from court because of a furious quarrel with the royal household over her grace's aggressive support of Gay's opera *Polly*. Nevertheless, says Pope, this duchess is too modest to act as a cynosure. He will therefore pass on to the general fact that humble persons are easier to see truly than the great; and the humble, therefore, will better provide us with examples. "If Queensberry to strip there's no compelling, / 'Tis from a handmaid we must take a Helen" (ll. 193–94).

In giving us a king's bastard, followed by a king's mistress, followed by the same king's queen, to whom the same mistress was lady-in-waiting, followed by a Duchess of Queensberry who had thrown over the whole court, I think Pope must be sounding a fanfare of innuendoes to draw attention to his theme and to announce his heroine.[19] Yet it is only by going outside the poem, to external facts, that we can establish the meaning of this sequence. We have touched the point of the social pyramid and found it the pinnacle of evil as well as of rank: the greatest vanity, the greatest lust, and the greatest power appear together; and since it is here alone that Pope uses proper names, we may also say this marks his most direct appeal to reality.[20]

Applying to Young the test that Pope meets so easily, one produces quite different results; for at several points Young may be described as defeated by reality. As a comprehensive principle the argument to which he tries to relate all the instances of vice or frivolity in his satires seems unpleasantly shallow: namely, that a desire for fame of one sort or another is the common source of foolish and vicious actions. Young may perhaps have flattered himself that he had a proposition to prove — and consequently more intellectual coherence than Pope in the *Epistle* — but the proposition is so weak and unconvincing as to disgrace its asserter. Even if it should be regarded not as a supposed truth but merely as a structural device, it fails, because many of the most effective passages in the poems cannot be related to the central theme — the denunciation of patron-hunters:

> Who'd be a *crutch* to prop a rotten peer;
> Or living *pendant*, dangling at his ear.[21]

The failure of the poems to cohere as a general argument would seem less offensive if Young allowed subordinate pleadings to move consistently with themselves. But repeatedly when he claims to fight for one doctrine, he wears the uniform of another. In his own person, for example, he reproaches venal authors and bemoans the willingness of poets to sacrifice truth to profit. Yet in the dedications, compliments, and apostrophes which intermit the satire, his quivering eagerness for mercenary advancement appears so openly that no reader can observe the reproaches without sneering. Furthermore, the portraits that seem to excite the poet's greatest energy do not exhibit threats to a real order of morality but reveal mere freaks or triflers, such as Brabantio, who is proud of a reputation for absentmindedness.[22] Normally, one has little sense that the characters are drawn from living people; they are too often governed by meaningless whimsies, and Young too willingly abandons the facts of human nature to satisfy his love of paradox — as in the character of Philander, who secretly loves his own charming wife but publicly keeps a mis-

18. Young, *Universal Passion*, satire V, p. 113; satire VI, pp. 155–56. Cf. Crawford, "Pope's Debt," p. 167. The ridicule of the stereotype-maker is also found in the *Epistle to Cobham*, ll, 87–92. The end of *To Augustus* is, I suppose, the last refinement of the theme.

19. The reference in l. 198 to "honest Mah'met," a servant to George II, seems intended to strengthen the innuendoes.

20. Cf. Mr. Bateson's comment, p. xlviii, on the accuracy of the poem. Pope's allusions to Martha Blount in his letters, and the contrast he draws between her and Lady Suffolk, are remarkably close to his language in the poem; see his *Correspondence*, III, 349, 434–35, 450, and IV, 187.

21. Young, *Universal Passion*, satire IV, p. 71.

22. *Ibid.*, satire III, p. 49.

tress to avoid an unfashionable reputation.[23] Young's supreme blunder, in a work supposed to advance virtue and ridicule vice, is to choose his objects of admiration from the irregular circles of political power. Several of his eulogies would, with no other change, become ironical insults if set in the frame of some lines by Pope. The fawning praise of Dodington, whom sober historians compare to a jackal, the exaltation of a pawn like Compton — "the *crown*'s asserter, and the *people*'s friend"! [24] — imply a contempt for the reality of British public life that vitiates Young's attack upon corrupt politicians.[25] As a final and wholly appropriate streamer to trail after his wobbling car, Young consecrates his closing "satire" to the climactic and wildly indecorous flattery of Walpole and the King.

✓　　✓　　✓

The two satires (V and VI) which Young allotted to women rise to a far higher level of art than the rest of the *Love of Fame* (or *Universal Passion*), but no judge has yet accused Young in these poems of an excess of craftsmanship. Probably the most brilliant piece of poetry between the works of Pope and the works of Blake is Gray's *The Bard*, against whose splendor the accusation might easily be brought. Once more, however, I think the astonishing internal, literary coherence of the poem has been insufficiently appreciated; and again I think the test of reality can bring out aspects of the poem which are fundamental to its value. The essential design of *The Bard* has a deep similarity to that of Pope's *Epistle*; for if we mark line 101 (two thirds of the way through) as the turning point, the ode comprises a long first part, aggressive and denunciatory, which is balanced by a shorter second part, affirmative and confident. Within this general contrast Gray, like Pope, establishes a set of symmetrical parallels. Thus the poem both opens and closes with a confrontation between Edward I and the last of the Welsh bards, on Mount Snowdon, with the Conway River running below. After cursing the king, the bard bemoans the deaths of his fellow poets, and then foretells the miseries of Edward's descendants as far as Richard III. At the peripety, the predictions of doom are symmetrically transformed into a paean of joy as the bard envisions the triumph of Welsh blood in the Tudor dynasty. This is symmetrically followed by a celebration of the Elizabethan literary renaissance, to match the lament over the singers murdered by Edward. Finally, in a gesture that reverses his opening challenge when he looked down from a beetling rock upon the descending army of invaders, the bard leaps triumphantly to his suicide in the "roaring tide" of the river.

In its general movement the poem opposes impetuosity to formal restraint. There is a boldness or extravagance in the action, imagery, and language which is met by a fixed complexity in the versification. The mountain landscape is deliberately sublime, anticipating the climactic scene of *The Prelude*.[26] Gushing under the peak, the river bears connotations suggestive of the creative flow of the poetic imagination as detailed in *The Progress of Poesy*. The bard poses in a style which recalls Raphael's representation of God appearing to Ezekiel, as Gray himself notes. It is therefore as an embodiment of the divinely creative principle that the bard stands higher than the king and the royal army. To intensify the terror that sublimity requires, Gray does not entrust the prophetic verses merely to the bard but rather gives them to a chorus of spirits — ghosts of the slaughtered poets — who are seen and heard by their living confrere. At the turning point, they complete their prophecy and vanish, to be replaced by the revelation to the bard of a visionary pageant that displays Tudor monarchs, courtiers, and poets, with Milton bringing up the rear.

Gray's boldly inventive vocabulary, his sudden shifts of point of view, the sensational choice of historical detail (including royal murders, civil wars, and infanticide), all strengthen the rushing violence that marks the poem. By exaggerating his normally rich use of expressive sound effects, Gray adds to the impetuosity of the movement. There is a quasi-onomatopoeia in a line like, "He wound with toilsome march his long array" (l. 12), or "Regardless of the sweeping whirlwind's sway" (l. 75). But the elaborate use of alliteration, assonance, chiasmus, internal rhyme, and similar devices seems dramatically appropriate as well, because Welsh poetry is characterized by such intricacies: notice, for example, the expressive contrast, before and after the caesura in line 71, of the same fricatives, sibilants, and liquids: "Fair laughs the morn, and soft the zephyr blows." On a modern ear the boldness of Gray's diction is dulled by the freedom that recent generations have exercised in altering old meanings and creat-

23. *Ibid.*, satire III, pp. 54–55.
24. *Ibid.*, satire IV, p. 63.
25. *Ibid.*, satire III, pp. 56–60.
26. Though Gray's influence on Wordsworth hardly wants demonstration — particularly in connection with his taste for mountains — I should like to call attention to the note, in the Selincourt-Darbishire ed. of *The Prelude* (Oxford, 1959), on Book V, ll. 581–601, of the 1805 text.

ing neologisms. Yet expressions like "lyon-port," "crested pride," and "hoary hair / Stream'd, like a meteor, to the troubled air" (ll. 117, 9, 19–20) still retain some of the shocking power that disgusted Johnson in spite of Gray's care to model his adjectival nouns and remote analogies upon authoritative example.

As a counter-vortex to the bursting richness of action, scene, and style, Gray imposes upon these elements the steady impulse of his formidable metrics and rhyme scheme. By refining on the form of the "true" Pindaric ode, he arrives at a triple-ternary structure, the whole work comprising three main units each of which in turn contains three stanzas: a paired strophe and antistrophe, and an epode. To tighten the already tight form, Gray requires not only that each antistrophe match its own strophe (an elaborate stanza form of his own invention), foot for foot and rhyme for rhyme, but also that precisely the same form be employed for all three pairs. Similarly, all three epodes possess a common, even more complicated stanzaic pattern. In order to clarify for the ear this articulated structure, Gray ends each stanza with an alexandrine preceded by a rhyming pentameter. To give a sense of burgeoning progression, he concentrates the short verses at the beginning of the stanza and makes the line-lengths expand near the end: thus each strophe and antistrophe opens with five tetrameter verses and closes with five pentameters before the alexandrine. Combining brevity with abruptness to give the effect of a sudden start ("Ruin seize thee, ruthless King!"), Gray omits the first syllable of the first line of each strophe and antistrophe, so that it sounds trochaic and is shorter than any other line except the fifth, which is heptasyllabic as well (I suppose, to regularize the effect). In the epodes each stanza begins with trimeters, has a heptasyllabic eighth line, and uses internal rhyme in the fifteenth and seventeenth lines (enriching the cadence of approaching conclusion). Although the stanzas are long, Gray breaks them up into distinct quatrains, sestets, and couplets. The strophes and antistrophes work out curiously like a Shakespearean sonnet; the epodes are composed of a sestet at either end, joined by two quatrains.

This whole, charted, subdivided apparatus of verses and rhymes is worked in counterpoint with the narrative of the poem. As in Pindar, the meaning often ignores the breaks between stanzas, and the pauses or transitions often occur at odd points within a stanza. The reader cannot help feeling the dancelike interplay of meaning and form, boldness and restraint, motion and fixity.

In spite of its manifest brilliance *The Bard* is widely acknowledged to be a failure. Why? I think the essential reason will be found in the weakness of the poem's appeal to reality. Unlike Pope, Gray, so far from inviting such a test, utterly evades it. This evasion appears in the very structure of the story. Indubitably, the poet asks us to treat the incident as fantasy. For all the vividness of the representation, for all the fullness of historical reference, the episode has no claim to authenticity. The text is largely devoted to the speech of the bard. Yet this speaker kills himself as soon as his monologue is over, and cannot, therefore, transmit his account to any reporter. On the English side no one is supposed to understand Welsh; and if anyone did, the details of events that have not yet occurred, and that are forecast with an obscurity hiding their meaning even from the bard, would be unintelligible. That Edward killed the Welsh singers might be known; what one of those singers prophesied alone, just before his death, and to an uncomprehending audience, could not possibly be preserved. The intellectual implications of the poem also remain as unreal today as they appear in Johnson's critique of *The Progress of Poesy*.[27] Contrary to Gray's argument, the true poet is not always patriotic; he does not necessarily defend freedom; if he lives in a "primitive" rural society, he will not write more "sublime" songs than a cultivated, urban poet (Milton and Caradoc make strange yoke-mates to draw Gray's "presumptuous car"); and finally, genius does not tend to flourish under a good government or to wither under despotism.

On the other hand, Gray's most successful poem has a positive bearing upon human life in general and the eighteenth century in particular. The *Elegy* possesses the subtle appeal of flattering the reader into separating himself from the redeemed, obscurely virtuous villagers and attaching himself to the toiling bearers of power. The ultimate ironic implication of the *Elegy*, that we gladly suffer the curse of greatness in order to enjoy its fruits, is no misleading account of human nature. In the vacuous lines of the *Ode for Music*, Gray was to destroy the power of this appeal by supplying only one, deadly conventional half of the dilemma:

> What is grandeur, what is power?
> Heavier toil, superior pain.

> (ll. 57–58)

Reality winces at the sound. But the theme of wasted virtue, merit un-

27. In the life of Gray.

rewarded, talents denied expression (at the center of the *Elegy*) echoes the cry of Swift, Fielding, and Johnson against their common society: we hear it in *Gulliver's Travels*, in *Tom Jones*, and in *London*.

There is nevertheless a sense in which *The Bard* does make a profound appeal to reality. In the final analysis Gray's contrast between impetuosity and restraint becomes identified with the meaning of the poem. The impetuous bard, making propaganda for liberty and justice, opposes the fixed, oppressive tyrant, who kills the imagination; the gushing torrent of creation streams beside the rocky, corpse-littered mountain; art confronts reality. Writing to Beattie (years after this ode appeared), and discussing the hero of *The Minstrel*, Gray recommended that when Edwin was driven to become a bard, he should perform some "great and singular service to his country." Such an action, said Gray, would constitute "the best panegyrick of our favourite and celestial science" (i.e., of poetry). There are several remarkable features in Gray's statement. One is that he cannot himself specify what the sublime service might be; another is that, according to Gray, simply creating poetry was not itself enough. Yet the deed must be one requiring the peculiar talents of a poet — "some great and singular service to his country? (what service I must leave to your invention) such as no general, no statesman, no moralist could do without the aid of music, inspiration, and poetry. This will not appear an improbability in those early times, and in a character then held sacred, and respected by all nations." [28] Without telling us much about Gray that Arnold does not intimate in his essay, these remarks do point at both the source of the energy the poet poured into the ode and the cause of its failure. "In those early times" the poet's character was truly sacred; in those times he could perform services in the power of no mere general, statesman, or moralist. But now such a character would appear too improbable to admit into the design of a serious literary work. If the life of his own time represented reality, Gray clearly felt that the poet's role in it was nugatory. This is why *The Bard* never reaches out beyond the limits of literature. Just how remote Gray thought that a true poet must be, in the middle of the eighteenth century, from any deep influence upon his fellow countrymen, just how far inferior he must remain to soldiers (on the eve of the Seven Years' War and Pitt's imperial victories), to politicians, and to priests, we may infer from the conclusion of this *chef d'oeuvre*: the "celestial science" means prophesying to those who cannot understand you, and then suffering martyrdom. Of course, during a regime in which devotion to literature is itself a heroic act (as in Baudelaire's France), this would be a significant relationship to one's time; but Gray's gesture belongs in a different class. The vision asserted by Collins in the *Ode on the Poetical Character*, the vision reinterpreted by Coleridge half a century later, was denied to Gray. For all its splendor *The Bard* is an assertion of its author's impotence.

✓    ✓    ✓

The slogan of the embattled critic-scholars of the 1930's was that form is meaning. But this cry becomes serviceable only when a degree of tautology is implied: significant form, effective structure, has a direct bearing on meaning. The corruption of the slogan by epigones produced the assumption, which underlies the vast, unwieldy bulk of academic critical analysis, that any discussion of formal structure is, by some mysterious action at a distance, a discussion of meaning and value. Johnson's Dick Minim the critic prides himself on every instance of expressive form that he can isolate. Yet the tendency disproves itself; for surely one cannot judge the expressiveness of a verse unless one grasps the meaning of the poem, and surely the meaning depends upon a relation to reality. To pretend that there are such things as self-contained aesthetic objects, or that poems are exquisite arrangements of the sounds and the lexical implications of separate words, is to deny the impulse that patently drives every great artist. He is always trying to say something of immense importance to him: this is what *he* (not the poem) means; this is his "intention"; this is what we must apprehend. In every age the supreme geniuses have wished to be measured against reality, against the truths of human nature, the facts of the social order. Wordsworth said he wished to trace, in the *Lyrical Ballads*, "the primary laws of our nature"; Coleridge said the merits of *The Three Graves* were "exclusively psychological." [29] When we narrow the grounds of their achievement and judge them by a simpler standard than they themselves proposed, when we reserve for Dostoevsky and Kafka the test of reality but limit the reference of the Augustans to terms of art, I suspect we may be not honoring the masters of our poetry but insulting them.

28. Letter of July 2, 1770 — the day Gray signed his will.
29. See the sixth paragraph of the 1800 preface and Coleridge's headnote to the poem.

❧ RALPH COHEN

# Thomson's Poetry of Space and Time

J AMES THOMSON'S *The Seasons* is a cyclical poem, dealing with the
changes of nature in space and time. In it, the seasons change, and their
changes are depicted in many places on earth and also in the heavens. Although the poetry of these changes was based on georgic conventions, it
frequently departed from precedent and sought new expressions for
space and time. To study these experiments and to probe their artistic effects is the intent of this essay.

If we begin with Thomson's view of nature, it will be apparent that
what he considers that "nature" exists in tripartite space. The following
example from *Summer* indicates the imagery he develops to convey it:

> Confessed from yonder slow-extinguished clouds,
> All ether softening, sober Evening takes
> Her wonted station in the middle air,
> A thousand shadows at her beck. First this
> She sends on earth; then that of deeper dye
> Steals soft behind; and then a deeper still,
> In circle following circle, gathers round
> To close the face of things.
>
> (*Summer*, ll. 1647–54)[1]

The passage distinguishes among "ether," "the middle air" and "earth":
"ether" is the purer air of clouds and heavens; "middle air" is the space
between earth and ether; and earth has the "lower" air that man breathes.
Thomson makes the same distinction in *Autumn*, calling the "middle air"
the "middle sky" (l. 709).

The image of "sober Evening" is a personification mixed with natural description. "Evening" takes her station and "softens" the ether. The act of sending shadows to earth begins as deliberate; but shadows of "deeper dye" steal behind and still others behind those. Not only is the image mixed; the personification shifts in time from active to passive in intensity of color, in diminution of space. Moving from the upper air, Evening casts shadows upon earth "in circle following circle" and in narrowing the circles reaches the total darkness which resembles the infinity of the upper air.

John Scott objected to this blending of natural description and personification.

Both would have been proper, and indeed beautiful, had they been kept asunder. The gradual vanishing or extinction of colour in the clouds, justly discriminates evening, considered as a point of time; but as such vanishing or extinction occasions darkness, it could not possibly render evening visible as a person. The prosopopoeia, however, is in itself just and noble; Evening stands a conspicuous figure in air.[2]

The mixture Scott rejected was a characteristic mode of Thomson's imagery. As the shadows fall, the evening grows darker, and the re-direction of the ether's brightness shows that temporal as well as spatial changes are taking place. Thomson's usage is not a confusion or an artistic failure but an innovation which makes man and nature two visible, separable parts of a whole universe, indicating the unshared as well as the shared qualities of the image. Other examples of this technique can be found; the fog in *Autumn*, the "black night" in *Winter*, are personified and naturalized:

> at last,
> Wreathed dun around, in deeper circles still
> Successive closing, sits the general fog
> Unbounded o'er the world, and, mingling thick,
> A formless grey confusion covers all.
> (*Autumn*, ll. 727–31)

> Through the black night that sits immense around,
> Lashed into foam, the fierce-conflicting brine
> Seems o'er a thousand raging waves to burn.
> (*Winter*, ll. 158–60)

1. Unless otherwise indicated, all quotations are from *The Complete Poetical Works of James Thomson*, ed. J. Logie Robertson (London, 1908). Line numbers are given in parentheses.
2. John Scott, *Critical Essays* (London, 1785), pp. 353–54.

The image in *Summer* depicts the fluidity of space, the spatial changes wrought by moments of time, and the infinity of darkness that night finally brings. The image of the last shadow gathering "round" to shut out the last bit of light is reduced to a cliché by "the face of things." But the personification when compared with the "general fog" reveals Thomson's varied uses of the same device. In the fog, it is the disorder, not the degrees of succession, that Thomson stresses. The fog is a wreath and its circles are deadly; they lead to a "general" fog without bounds; its dunness is a confused mingling; and it negates rather than establishes order. In *Summer*, order was observed in the sentence structure, "first . . . then . . . then." In *Autumn*, the fog is described in a densely involved sentence.

In *Winter*, Thomson uses the image unsuccessfully, for the spatiality of "immense" black night that "sits" is neither part of the violence of the storm nor of its contrast, although "sits" is contrasted with "lashed," "fierce-conflicting," "raging" — violent adjectives. The mixed personification and natural description — "that sits immense around" — fails here, because the image of position and size creates expectations about night and its blackness that are unfulfilled. The failure, it should be noted, is not in the mixture but in the neglect of its possibilities. There is a difference between "sits . . . unbounded" and "sits immense around": the first, in creating a resting posture, accepts confusion, a "mingling" and "confusion." The personification indicates bounds, because a sitting person is a defined form; "unbounded" and "immense," too, give nature an extension into infinity which the posture of the individual does not have. The black night, however, does not become involved with the environment; it remains an incidental description.

Each of these personifications becomes immobile, sitting or standing, whereas the natural description is highly active — the softening of the ether or the dun, mingling fog or the deep blackness of the night. The personified traits suggest human attitudes — ease, authority, disregard — implying that nature has a socially relevant as well as scientifically correct appearance.

Thomson is not without ironical awareness even of the burlesque aspect of nature, for sun and clouds can express, as in Swift, a comic view of behavior, sometimes even a grotesque one.

> When from the pallid sky the Sun descends,
> With many a spot, that o'er his glaring orb

Uncertain wanders, stained; red fiery streaks
Begin to flush around. The reeling clouds
Stagger with dizzy poise, as doubting yet
Which master to obey.

(*Winter*, ll. 118–23)

Burlesque tone also exists in the description in *Autumn* of the drunken sight of "double tapers," compared with the "wading" sun:

Before their maudlin eyes,
Seen dim and blue, the double tapers dance,
Like the sun wading through the misty sky.

(*Autumn*, ll. 554–57)

Such an interpretation of these mixed images reduces the possibility that Thomson was here imitating painting, because the images lack the precision and the detail of painting, and his poetic use of tripartite space is not identical with painting's foreground, middle ground, and background.

The conception of space as vertical division leaves the narrator capable of physical movement within only the middle space or the earth. There are no bird's-eye views in Thomson's poetry despite the "flights" of the narrator: heavens are seen from the earth or the mountain. This is understandable, for the heavens look down on man but it is beyond man to do more than worship God above him. The middle air and the earth, however, are places from which man views distance, and these form the prospect view and the local view. The prospect view conveys the sense of the merging of nature, of oneness amid variety; and the local view details the individuality of nature, of variety amid oneness.

In the following passage, for example, expansive nature is described in a distant (or prospect) view followed by a close view:

Snatched through the verdant maze, the hurried eye
Distracted wanders; now the bowery walk
Of covert close, where scarce a speck of day
Falls on the lengthened gloom, protracted sweeps;
Now meets the bending sky, the river now
Dimpling along, the breezy ruffled lake,
The forest darkening round, the glittering spire,
The ethereal mountain, and the distant main.
But why so far excursive? when at hand,
Along these blushing borders bright with dew,
And in yon mingled wilderness of flowers,

Fair-handed Spring unbosoms every grace —
Throws out the snow-drop and the crocus first,
The daisy, primrose, violet darkly blue,
And polyanthus of unnumbered dyes;
The yellow wall-flower, stained with iron brown.
And lavish stock, that scents the garden round:
From the soft wing of vernal breezes shed,
Anemones; auriculas, enriched
With shining meal o'er all their velvet leaves;
And full ranunculus of glowing red.
Then comes the tulip-race, where beauty plays
Her idle freaks: from family diffused
To family, as flies the father-dust,
The varied colours run; and, while they break
On the charmed eye, the exulting florist marks
With secret pride the wonders of his hand.
No gradual bloom is wanting — from the bud
First-born of Spring to Summer's musky tribes;
Nor hyacinths, of purest virgin white,
Low bent and blushing inward; nor jonquils,
Of potent fragrance; nor narcissus fair,
As o'er the fabled fountain hanging still;
Nor broad carnations, nor gay-spotted pinks;
Nor, showered from every bush, the damask-rose:
Infinite numbers, delicacies, smells,
With hues on hues expression cannot paint.
The breath of Nature, and her endless bloom.

(*Spring*, ll. 518–55)

The prospect view distracts the hurried eye by its variety, and the narrator is pulled in all directions at once by the astounding mixture in nature — "now," "now," "now." In a series of elliptical sentences, the speaker's "hurried eye," although understood as subject, is too hurried to complete the grammar. The sentence enacts the distractions, the eye "meeting" one extensive object after the other, each demanding a different response to the elements of nature — the "dimpling river" (smiling) or the "ruffled lake" (annoyed) — and the narrator realizes that such mixtures are not merely "far excursive" but also within reach of his hand:

at hand,
Along these blushing borders bright with dew,
And in yon mingled wilderness of flowers,
Fair-handed Spring unbosoms every grace.

(*Spring*, ll. 526–29)

Naming the flowers — crocus, polyanthus, anemones, auriculas — creates that sense of emergent power or fullness in nature which Thomson achieves through the use of Latinate terms in other contexts. In evoking simple colors and forms he creates rhetorical impressiveness, and with them creates a sense of derivation and analogy (of development): ranunculuses — flowers like frogs; anemones — sea and land flowers; the oxeye daisy, wallflowers, and others. If earlier (l. 504) the narrator had referred to the sight of "unnumbered flowers," now a single flower, the polyanthus ("many-flowers"), had "unnumbered dyes" (l. 532).

The effectiveness of Thomson's achievement goes beyond analogical floral names and evocations of the senses, beyond even the musical variety of the chosen names. It extends to the sentence structure, returning at the conclusion of the passage (ll. 544–55) to the elliptical structure of the prospect which expressed, in the immediacy of time, the distracting variety and mixture of space — heavenly with earthly. The concluding eleven-line sentence operates by negation, making a positive listing of spring's flowers while denying that the "gradual bloom" can be expressed fully. Beginning with the "bud/First-Born" (ll. 545–46) the passage concludes with the damask-rose, "showered from every bush" (l. 551), a reference to the descent of personified *Spring*, "veiled in a shower/Of shadowing roses" (ll. 3–4).

The "gradualness" the sentence conveys is not merely the spectrum from virgin white to sexual red, but the analogical qualities of the flowers. Thus, the innocent hyacinth, "low bent and blushing inward" is seen with the narcissus that over "the fabled fountain" hangs — neither modest nor blushing. And the "gradual bloom" describes the white hyacinth, the yellow jonquils, the white and yellow narcissus, the human-colored carnation, the "gay-spotted" pinks, and the deep red damask rose. The sentence moves to a climax of color and sensuality, the achievement of "bloom" that begins as "gradual" and comes to be seen as "endless" (l. 555) because it is an expression of God's presence, an ever-flowering spring, a harmony of color.

> With hues on hues expression cannot paint,
> The breath of Nature, and her endless bloom.
>
> (*Spring*, ll. 554–55)

The prospect view leads from the lengthened scene to infinity, a merging of sky and river, mountain and sky. It places man in infinite space,

makes him part of the circling world. The local view provides the details
of space that do not move in distance but in infinite variety, in allusive
recollection of changes in space, of the possibilities of future and the
actualities of past space. The sense of the past which critics have pointed
to in the Latinate derivations of Thomson's diction seems relevant here.
For the individual object and the language used to describe it convey
attitudes to time as well as to space.

The devices for unfolding time are extensive in *The Seasons*. One of
them is distinction through recurrence. Storms, sunrises, sunsets appear
and reappear in the poem, and are used for distinctions of place and
time. In *Summer*, for example, the sunrise is described in the temperate
zone and in the torrid zone.

> But yonder comes the powerful king of day
> Rejoicing in the east. The lessening cloud,
> The kindling azure, and the mountain's brow
> Illumed with fluid gold, his near approach
> Betoken glad. Lo! now, apparent all,
> Aslant the dew-bright earth and coloured air,
> He looks in boundless majesty abroad,
> And sheds the shining day, that burnished plays
> On rocks, and hills, and towers, and wandering streams
> High-gleaming from afar.
>
> . . . . . . . . . . . . . . . . . . . .
>
> See how at once the bright effulgent sun,
> Rising direct, swift chases from the sky
> The short-lived twilight, and with ardent blaze
> Looks gaily fierce o'er all the dazzling air!
> He mounts his throne; but kind before him sends,
> Issuing from out the portals of the morn,
> The general breeze to mitigate his fire
> And breathe refreshment on a fainting world.
>
> (*Summer*, ll. 81–90, 635–42)

The king of day "rejoices in the east" because the summer sun is the
richest of seasonal suns and its sumptuous golden quality is a form of
pleasure especially since, rising from the east, it brings its wealth and
brilliance to the temperate zone. In the temperate world, the description
deals with the illumination of power, the light of the sun which gilds,
burnishes, shines, and is reflected in gleamings. But the torrid sun moves
swiftly from the light image — "swift chases from the sky/ The short-
lived twilight" (ll. 636–37). The temperate sun "plays" on rocks, hills,

towers; the torrid sun expresses his kindness by sending forth the "general breeze to mitigate his fire" (l. 641). Although it is the same joyous sun that looks upon the different zones, seen in the same imagery of benevolent majesty, in the first passage the sun gilds and colors all nature, in the second it sends fire and the mitigating breeze: the sun is still "gay" but it is also "fierce." The repetition is an organizing device to treat physical distance as part of a varied whole, and the contrary qualities of the sun are seen as variations of a natural force. Although Thomson reveals differences in similar events in the same season, consistency is maintained in the interpretation of the sun: the summer sun is a power, sometimes benevolent, sometimes tyrannical. In the first, the sun (fire) "kindles" the azure (l. 83) and colors the air (l. 86), burnishes the earth (l. 86) and is reflected from the stream (ll. 89–90); there is a reflective interplay among all elements of nature — earth, air, fire, and water.

The temporal implication is the changing character of natural objects. In different places, the object becomes different; each object has both a momentary (cyclical) character and an absolute one, changes in space can result from changes in time. The implications are that, first, each moment is significantly different from others; second, each moment arises from a past cycle and becomes part of a present one; third, although space may merge with infinity, time exists most vividly in the present.

There is a considerable difference between the artistic quality of the two summer sunrises. Not only does the first have subtle distinctions within present mobile nature, but the participles, "burning" and "kindling," for example, that deal with present and continuing action, are distinguished from the past participle "illumined." The evanescent clouds and azure change; the mountain, however, only seems changed; the personified "brow" is gilded by sunlight. The description moves from the heavens to the middle air to the earth and streams, gleaming in return. In a phrase like "aslant the dew-bright earth and coloured air," "aslant" not only conveys the time of day and the spatial penetration, but also the elasticity of joy and the sense of power that everything is "apparent" even though obliquely observed.

No such organized tone, extensive reference, interrelatedness of position and space mark the second description. There is an excessive formalism to the sun of the torrid zone: "but kind before him sends,/ Issuing from out the portals of the morn." The sense of power and haste with which the passage begins is not pursued, and there is no properly developed sense of force and fire implied. The failure of imagery seems to be due to a difficulty in picturing the static and vivifying the formal. It is a difficulty which extends beyond the images studied here.

I have noted the difference between Thomson's sunrises within a season. The following sunrise from *Winter* permits comparison between seasons:

> the sun
> Scarce spreads o'er ether the dejected day.
> Faint are his gleams, and ineffectual shoot
> His struggling rays in horizontal lines
> Through the thick air.
>
> (ll. 44–48)

Movement involves time, and Thomson's time coexists with his emergent space. The sense of time is based, for example, on shifts described in place; the same place appears slightly different at different times. What Thomson achieves is a sense of the moment-by-moment transformation of nature, that, however slight, proves significant. By applying the theory of gradualness, or gradation, to nature, he creates a sense of process in the character of man and his environment. Critics have confused this deliberate technique with repetition and artistic ineptitude, but if one examines the three successive storm descriptions in *Winter* the differences in them become clear, as do some of the experiments with time:

> Then comes the father of the tempest forth,
> Wrapt in black glooms. First, joyless rains obscure
> Drive through the mingling skies with vapour foul,
> Dash on the mountains brow, and shake the woods
> That grumbling wave below.
>
> (ll. 72–76)

> Then issues forth the storm with sudden burst,
> And hurls the whole precipitated air
> Down in a torrent.
>
> (ll.153–55)

> The keener tempests come; and fuming dun
> From all the livid east or piercing north,
> Thick clouds ascend, in whose capacious womb
> A vapoury deluge lies, to snow congealed.
>
> (ll. 223–26)

Each storm exemplifies one aspect of winter's violence, yet the three storms, one following upon the other, convey the temper of the season. Showers and storms exist in each season, but in no season do they follow so frequently upon each other or with such force as in *Winter*. "Time" meaning "time of year" is thus distinguished by frequency of repetition as well as by the increasing intensity of the storms. The seasonal recurrence of storms establishes the cyclical quality of time: storms repeat themselves, just as the sun rises in each season. The function of this cyclical time is to place momentary change within the infinite revolutions of the seasons, the unending cycle of time.

But I have pointed out that *The Seasons* is dominated by present time, by the effective transformation of past into present, and, in some hints, of the present into future time. It is this sense of the present that Thomson achieves, technically, through tense and connectives, like "now," "then," "first." But the "presentness," the unfolding of time, is achieved within each storm which begins with foreshadowing gloom or foreboding signs, and continues to progress in intensity. Each *Winter* storm undergoes a progress in time, although all are aspects of violence and all continue into the night. The difference between the first and the second storms, for example, can be noted by comparing the effects upon the trees. In the first the rains "shake the woods/ That grumbling wave below" (ll. 75–76). In the second, the branches are torn and scattered:

> Low waves the rooted forest, vexed, and sheds
> What of its tarnished honours yet remain —
> Dashed down and scattered, by the tearing wind's
> Assiduous fury, its gigantic limbs.
>
> (ll. 181–84)

Paradoxically, the third storm — the snowstorm — called the "keener tempests" (l. 223) is beautiful as well as destructive. It creates "one wild dazzling waste, that buries wide/ The works of man" (ll. 239–40). The dreadful beauty creates a drifting nature that buries the shepherd in his own fields.

The meaning of these temporal distinctions is, among others, the particularly vivid and momentary changes that take place in nature. Since Thomson operates within the Christian convention of immortality, it is important to note how he converts it to his own use. By describing the effects of the storm upon man and other creatures as well as upon nature, he develops a pattern of simultaneous events, a sense of the simultaneity of occurrences. This awareness of associative time permits him to see positive as well as negative effects in a broad range of space. It also explains, from a temporal point of view, the reasons for the mixture of personification with natural description. By attributing certain human qualities to nature simultaneously with its nonhuman ones, he provides a religious justification for inanimate nature by analogy to man's place in the universe.

Thus when he writes "Then comes the father of the tempest forth" (l. 72) he gives a parental interpretation to the violence of the storm; the father is described in magisterial terms. The storm which wildly "issues forth" is the unconstrained descendant, and the violence has been freed from apology because it has been made part of the accepted view of God's powers. The resumption of detailed natural description permits a case for momentary action, a submersion in the moment that requires no excuse. One can attend to the moment because its place in the convention has been suggested. It is thus not unusual to discover ironic juxtapositions of infinite time with momentary experiences; an address to God to provide knowledge of "sacred, substantial, never-fading bliss" (l. 222) is followed immediately by the line, "The keener tempests come" (l. 223).

There are in *The Seasons* formal attempts in the historical catalogues to suggest the presence of past time, but these have neither the vividness nor the implications of the more successful temporal attitudes. For in addition to the techniques noted above, Thomson achieves a sense of present and changing time by the introduction of scientific phenomena and by the ingenuities of sentence structure. In *Autumn*, for example, the sunrise is first seen as gentle and calm; then suddenly it is changed into the refulgent summer sun.

> Attempered suns arise
> Sweet-beamed, and shedding oft through lucid clouds
> A pleasing calm; while broad and brown, below,
> Extensive harvests hang the heavy head.
> Rich, silent, deep they stand; for not a gale
> Rolls its light billows o'er the bending plain;
> A calm of plenty! till the ruffled air
> Falls from its poise, and gives the breeze to blow.
> Rent is the fleecy mantle of the sky;
> The clouds fly different; and the sudden sun
> By fits effulgent gilds the illumined field,
> And black by fits the shadows sweep along —

A gaily chequered, heart-expanding view,
Far as the circling eye can shoot around,
Unbounded tossing in a flood of corn.

(Autumn, ll. 28–42)

The "attempered suns" create a "pleasing calm" and between the adjective-noun constructions the balance is achieved by a characteristic construction — the past participle conjoined with a present participle — "sweet-beamed, and shedding." The past participle implies that suns have, repeatedly, now that summer is departing, been gentle. Johnson suggests that "attempered" is an example of a sun "weakened by mixture of something else" or "diluted" so that the autumn sun is without summer's "fierce effulgence" (l. 25) and with "beams" that please the senses. The phrase that follows it explains the kind of pleasure it gives (emotional, not visual), and the harvest, as well as man, reflects this.

The sentence structure creates a pause after "calm"; and the subordinate clause which follows it separates the action of the harvest from that of the heavens. For the sun's rays which calmly shine are compared with the equally calm but dependent heaviness of the harvest "below." The connectedness and calmness are maintained "Till the ruffled air/ Falls from its poise, and gives the breeze to blow" (ll. 34–35). The imbalance of the line lies in the monosyllables which throw it out of balance with the other lines in the passage and with the "equal scales" of Libra (l. 24). The awkward construction of "gives the breeze to blow," in which "gives" means a gift as well as an undeserved offering, is supplemented by the concluding infinitive which is the only (and uncalled for) rhyme in the entire passage.

The short noun clauses that follow are unbalanced by a long fragmentary exclamation at the end. The "attempered sun," with the strange use of an adjective of violent motion to modify "sun" which rotates in order, conveys just the kind of surprise sought "by fits." For although "By fits effulgent gilds the illumined field" appears redundant, because "effulgent" means both "gild" and "illumine," it makes significant discriminations. "Effulgent" alludes to the summer sun's "fierce effulgence" (l. 25). The "fit" abruptly brings back the quality of parting summer which had been replaced by the "serener blue" (l. 26) of autumn. The "illumined field" refers to the fact that the lucid clouds have been "rent," and the fields lit by the direct rays are not "enlivened" as in autumn, or balanced, but over-balanced, "gilded" — adorned by more than necessary color. And the sun hides as suddenly as it appears, with the large shadows of the clouds sweeping over the grain.

This imbalance, however, has its own value, for *Autumn* is the season of fruition and excess as well as of shadow and change. Thus the "pleasing color" of balanced autumn can be matched by the "heart-expanding view" of unbalanced nature, for "chequered" nature is "heart-expanding" because it suggests the infinite space of nature and nature's fruition. The eye "shoots" around at the scene, looking directly at each change as well as seeing them all. "Unbounded tossing" can modify "view" with tossing describing the view (in a "tossing" flood of corn); or "circling eye" can toss unbounded (in a circle) in the flood while shooting glances everywhere.

Josephine Miles has defined the sublime poem, of which *The Seasons* is an example, by its "cumulative sentence structure, its piling up of nouns and epithets, participles and compounds, and by its minimum of clausal subordinations and active verbs."[3] But the definition, while it may be statistically accurate, fails to note the important transformation going on in this poetry. For what happens in *The Seasons* is that the participles create active nouns. Although the verbs do not predominate, the objects and events in nature are active and in process. The temporal flux which Thomson achieved by this device can be seen from the following example.

> The uncurling floods, diffused
> In glassy breadth, seem through delusive lapse
> Forgetful of their course.
> (*Spring*, ll. 159–61)

"Uncurling" describes the vigorous untwisting of the waves and "diffused" their subsiding into motionlessness in which the present appears a continuation of a fixed past. The sentence imagery is contained in the participles, and they perform the function normally carried out by verbs.

The participles can contrast continuing actions with completed actions, and present time with past time, to establish either a contrast or a derivation.

> Still fondly forming in the farthest verge,
> Where the round ether mixes with the wave,
> Ships, dim-discovered, dropping from the clouds.
> (*Summer*, ll. 943–45)

The process of imagination catches two moments of time — the forma-

tion of the ships, the discovery, and dropping from the clouds — an act
in which the forming, although it precedes, actually follows the "discovered" ships.

When Thomson describes the green serpent as "forth-issuing" (*Summer*, l. 900), he inverts the verb to make it a participle in which "forth"
describes the darting of the head after which the serpent gathers up his
train "in orbs immense" (l. 901). I have quoted above the line from
*Winter*, "Then issues forth the storm with sudden burst" (l. 153) in
which the entire storm is seen in simultaneous eruption. The order of
terms indicates the order of events. And there is a clear distinction to be
drawn between "issuing forth" and "forth-issuing."

The attempt to make the language enact the movement is accomplished
by the present participle invoking continued action. But Thomson's use
of present participles is not exclusively a matter of the ongoing present;
it connects action accomplished with subsequent action to convey continuing time and shifting place: "drives them wide-dispersed,/ Wounded
and wheeling various down the wind" (*Autumn*, ll. 377–78). It is perhaps unnecessary to point out that the connection of these actions
is held together by the consonantal recurrence — "wide," "wounded,"
"wheeling," "wind" — although the action is a dispersal. The participial
construction is not merely a technique to relate past and present in a continuum; the frequency of participial constructions suggests that the varied actions, which in fragmentary ways form part of a continuum, are
part of an active universe. Some parts of this universe are beyond the
eye of man to see or the ear to hear. To suggest this, Thomson uses paradox as a way of expressing the invisible: "The unfruitful rock itself, im-
pregned by thee,/ In dark retirement forms the lucid stone" (*Summer*,
ll. 140–41). The rock seen in terms of "fruit" and birth, darkness bringing forth light — the recognition of solid space giving birth to new
forms — these are applications of traditional poetic devices to the implications of nature's transforming process. And in describing the insects
unseen and unheard by man, insects which form part of worlds beyond
man's senses, he writes:

> for, if the worlds
> In worlds inclosed should on his senses burst,
> From cates ambrosial and the nectared bowl

3. Josephine Miles, *Eras and Modes in English Poetry* (Berkeley and Los Angeles, 1964), pp. 56–57.

> He would abhorrent turn; and in dead night,
> When Silence sleeps o'er all, be stunned with noise.
>
> (*Summer*, ll. 313–17)

Here unseen insect life swarming in minute space is sufficient to drive man from his sensual pleasures, and the order of the world keeps man limited. The "worlds in worlds inclosed" prevent him from realizing that he is no god — for his "cates ambrosial" and "nectared bowl" can only be enjoyed in ignorance. Although night appears "dead" and silence seems to prevail, another world lives, and if man heard it, he would "be stunned with noise."

The revisions Thomson made amplify the techniques he used in the earlier versions of *The Seasons* regarding space and time, and a study of one of these will explain how even his use of science supported the process view of nature as a shifting space between ether and earth and a shifting time between past, present, and future. The shower passage in *Spring* was based on a distillation image of the relations between the sky and the earth — it originally read:

> But who would hold the Shade, while Heaven descends
> In universal Bounty, shedding Herbs,
> And Fruits, and Flowers, on Nature's ample Lap?
> Imagination fir'd prevents their Growth,
> And while the verdant Nutriment distills,
> Beholds the kindling Country colour round.[4]

The 1744 version read as follows:

> But who can hold the shade while Heaven descends
> In universal bounty, shedding herbs
> And fruits and flowers on Nature's ample lap?
> Swift fancy fired anticipates their growth;
> And, while the milky nutriment distils,
> Beholds the kindling country colour round.
>
> (*Spring*, ll. 180–85)

The revisions included "would" to "can," "imagination" to "swift fancy" and "verdant" to "milky." The first two changes stress present time and movement and confirm the stylistic traits I have defined. "Milky," however, represents a more subtle technique. At the time Thomson made these changes, he added one line to the bird passage of the shower; I italicize it:

> Hushed in short suspense
> The plumy people streak their wings with oil

*To throw the lucid moisture trickling off,*
And wait the approaching sign.
*(Spring,* ll. 164–67)

"Verdant" formed part of the original passage and was used to refer to the promised grass. It was part of the Psalmist's language of rain as "herbs/ And fruits and flowers." The addition of the scientific line established a close relation between it and the distillation image, for "to distil" meant, in eighteenth-century usage, "to trickle off." Thus the "trickling off" of the rain from the birds who did not use it was compared with the "distilled" rain upon the landscape, a rain fruitful with nourishment. "Lucid," therefore, was compared not with a color but with a nonlucid appearance, "milky," at the same time that removing "verdant" eliminated the repetition of "falling verdure" (164).

The scientific image combined religious with scientific language, and "milky nutriment" contributed to this combination of past with present. But the distillation image uses science to create an emergent space. The light of the fancy sees the rain dripping down ("distilled"), and this distillation is a "milky nutriment" which inflames ("kindles") the whole countryside. Thus the rain gives life, gives the fiery color of life. The fancy or imagination which is inspired ("fired") can be understood as distilling, by its fire, the falling rain, and, while distilling, also "beholds" it. The power of the imagination to anticipate nature becomes a fire, inspiration, color image. The scientific diction merges with the religious to reinterpret the process of nature. Science is used to support the religious interpretation and the merger coincides with Thomson's view of *Spring* as earth reflecting the fire of the sun in a burst of growth, color, and interaction of present with future.

The cycle of the seasons was, for Thomson, an emergent and vivid recurrence, and he developed techniques with which to express the temporal and spatial changes. There are, in the poem, recurrent events in nature within each season and from one season to another that become examples of the subtle differences in time and the responsiveness of one kind of nature to another. Man and nature are seen as part of one universe, and recurrence becomes a method for exploring the inevitable differences in it. In using the inherited techniques of paradox and irony, Thomson adapted them to new scientific ideas so that minute space con-

4. *Spring* A, ll. 205–10 in *Thomson's Seasons,* ed. Otto Zippel, *Palaestra,* LXVI (1908), 15.

tained worlds, and silence roared with noise. Within the accepted view of space, he saw a constant shifting and interrelating. To express this he developed a form of personification that was mixed with natural description and that permitted him to interpret nature as including man, yet extending beyond him. And he set up a sentence structure, composed of fragments or inversions, of appropriate clauses, to enact the view of nature he was developing.

This view was, of course, nature emergent in space and time, and the emergence placed a premium upon the active present. The very objects of nature were often being dizzily transformed and Thomson used a language heavily laden with present and past participles to convey action in objects. Nouns could be converted to verbs and verbs to adjectives to display the life force of inanimate objects. And to support this view he developed a language that incorporated biblical metaphor with scientific imagery. He was able, therefore, to create a poetry which moved within a religious tradition but which contained an exhilarating sense of the present.

❧ WILLIAM H. HALEWOOD

# "The Reach of Art" in Augustan Poetic Theory

WHAT in general the art of painting meant to neoclassical poets can be illustrated with Nahum Tate's lines of compliment to Thomas Flatman:

> Thy happy Pencills more than Pictures give,
> Thy Drafts are more than Representative,
> For, if we'll credit our own Eyes, they live.

Painting mirrored the external world and deserved praise in proportion as it seemed to "live." In this it was the "sister art" of poetry, explained with a theory which had been borrowed from poetry in the Renaissance[1] and equally bound by the classical necessity of "imitation" and the "Design and Intention . . . to move and affect the Passions, to teach and instruct, and lastly to please and divert Mankind."[2] The most obvious and best-studied of its reciprocal influences on poetry — exerted through the cherished doctrine of *ut pictura poesis* — was, as Meyer H. Abrams has said, to corroborate "the concept that poetry is a reflection of objects and events."[3]

1. See Rensselaer W. Lee, "*Ut Pictura Poesis*: The Humanistic Theory of Painting," *Art Bulletin*, XXII (1940), 197–269.
2. Charles Lamotte, *Essay upon Poetry and Painting* (London, 1730), p. 15. The formula is typical of one strain in neoclassical discussion of the sisterhood of the two arts in pressing Horace and Aristotle into the service of an essentially unclassical sensationalism. The order of objectives — giving priority to the "Design and Intention . . . to move and affect the Passions" — can be found in the art treatises.
3. *The Mirror and the Lamp* (New York, 1953), p. 34. The most complete dis-

An opposite influence can also be made out, however, and this essay will attempt to show that the analogy with painting had a clandestine usefulness to poetry in resisting its danger from a too narrowly understood mimetic purpose, in revising its conception of its nature and function, and, incidentally, in raising its self-esteem. In all of these things painting and art theory were, to be sure, secondary forces of uncertain dependability. Larger forces were also at work, of which some of the most urgent emanated from Boileau's translation of Longinus; and as Longinus in turn had an effect upon art theory, we cannot always be clear in individual treatises on art whether we have to do with positions indigenous to art theory or with assimilations from "the sublime." In the discussion that follows such doubtful cases have generally been decided in favor of indigenousness, and an attempt has been made to define a continuity, if not a tradition, of emphases and attitudes accessible to English neoclassical poetic theory in writings about art. The simplification does no great violence to the facts: on the points that will concern us, such later treatises as those of De Piles and Richardson, who knew Longinus, do not diverge significantly from Junius or Sanderson (or Leonardo) who, presumably, did not.

ɬ ɬ ɬ

Parallels (as distinct from influences) with Longinian emphases and attitudes are obvious, as Pope half hints in the suggestion that Longinus is "himself the great Sublime he *draws*." [4] (The reference, though perhaps not obvious, is not obscure: the art of painting, as explained in neoclassical theory, lay almost entirely in drawing or "design"; for even an ignorant "sign-post dawber," as one reads repeatedly, can be counted on to achieve agreeable effects of color.[5]) Whatever Pope intended, however, it would not have been eccentric in the first decades of the eighteenth century to regard Longinus as the literary proprietor of conceptions having some independent life in the history and theory of painting. Certainly Vasari and those who followed him held a variety of views in which Longinians could concur. They gave equal importance, for example, to the natural endowments of the great artist [6] — the great soul emphasized by Longinus being a faculty comparable, as will appear, to their "great genius" — and they were no less interested in the emotional impact of the work of art on its beholder, or in the creative *furor* which produced it. Thus Dennis, championing enthusiasm in poetry, would seem to have been aware that an argument parallel to his own existed in writings on art and cites the role of passion in painting as a "given" to which enthusiastic poetry might appeal:

Passion then, is the Characteristical Mark of Poetry, and, consequently, must be every where. . . . without Passion there can be no Poetry, no more than there can be Painting. And tho' the Poet and the Painter describe Action, they must describe it with Passion . . . and the more Passion there is, the better the Poetry and the Painting.[7]

cussion of the theoretic bases (and the history) of the poetry-painting analogy is Jean H. Hagstrum's *The Sister Arts: The Tradition of Literary Pictorialism and English Poetry from Dryden to Gray* (Chicago, 1958) which revives the term *enargeia* for the characteristics of pictorial vividness and particularity in poetry — the intended products of a poetic determined that poetry shall be "a reflection of objects and events." Another recent and valuable discussion of the sister arts concept is contained in William K. Wimsatt, Jr., and Cleanth Brooks, *Literary Criticism: A Short History* (New York, 1957), pp. 262–82.

4. Such a reading of this line has been expressly prohibited by Robert J. Allen ("Pope and the Sister Arts" in *Pope and His Contemporaries: Essays Presented to George Sherburn*, ed. James L. Clifford and Louis A. Landa [Oxford, 1949], p. 81). Allen considers the word "draws" to be "merely an equivalent of 'writes about,' having lost all metaphorical suggestiveness." It seems clearly "alive" as metaphor elsewhere in Pope, however (cf. "Now look thro' Fate! behold the scene she draws" — *Dunciad*, iii, 127; "Virtue confess'd in human shape he draws" — "Prologue to *Cato*," 17, where drawing is not less explicitly draftsmanly than in the reference to what "the faithful pencil has designed" in *Essay on Criticism*, 484.

5. Cf. Dryden on Dufresnoy: "Our author calls Colouring *lena sororis*; in plain English, the bawd of her sister, the design or drawing . . ." *Essays of John Dryden*, ed. W. P. Ker (Oxford, 1900), II, 147. This position was not uncontested, of course, and color ultimately emerged respectable from the *Conférences* of the French Academy.

6. The opening paragraph of Vasari's "Life" of Michelangelo was the prototype of many later examples: "While the most noble and industrious spirits were striving, by the light of the famous Giotto and of his followers, to give to the world a proof of the ability that the benign influence of the stars and the proportionate admixture of humours had given to their intellects, and while, desirous to imitate with the excellence of their art the grandeur of Nature in order to approach as near as possible to that supreme knowledge that many call understanding, they were universally toiling, although in vain, the most benign Ruler of Heaven in His clemency turned His eyes to the earth, and, having perceived the infinite vanity of all those labours, the ardent studies without any fruit, and the presumptuous self-sufficiency of men, which is even further removed from truth than is darkness from light, and desiring to deliver us from such great errors, became minded to send down to earth a spirit with universal ability in every art and every profession, who might be able, working by himself alone, to show what manner of thing is the perfection of the art of design. . . . He was pleased, in addition, to endow him with the true moral philosophy and with the ornament of sweet poesy, to the end that the world might choose him and admire him as its highest exemplar in the life, works, saintliness of character, and every action of human creatures, and that he might be acclaimed by us as a being rather divine than human." *Lives of the Most Eminent Painters, Sculptors and Architects*, trans. Gaston DuC. De Vere (London, 1915), IX, 3.

7. *Critical Works*, ed. Edward Niles Hooker (Baltimore, 1943), I, 215–16.

The effectiveness of painting in *moving* the passions was no less a commonplace, and one which would seem to have been drawn on as a sympathetic tradition when Longinus, "translated from Boileau's translation," taught the English appreciation of passages of "great and lofty thoughts [which] do not so truly persuade, as charm and throw us into a Rapture . . . a kind of Admiration made up of Extasy and Surprize . . . which ravishes away the hearer's soul against his consent." [8] Admiration, astonishment, suspension of the critical faculties were the standard effects of visual art on the properly constituted beholder. Chiaroscuro, drawing, foreshortening, when "justly express'd . . . *strike only with Admiration*," says a writer in the *Gentleman's Magazine* in 1735, "and this is one of the finest effects of the Magick of Painting." [9] Junius, writing almost a century earlier, described the power of painting to "sweetly enthrall and captivate the hearts of men with the lovely chain of due admiration and amazement." [10]

It is significant that for Junius and others the power of enthrallment in painting is associated with the power of sight. Amazed beholders of paintings all but surrender consciousness to their eyes, "their sense of seeing bereaving them of all other senses." [11] The idea of a union of emotional transport and seeing as principal elements in the "aesthetic transaction" (making it a kind of "vision") had, of course, a background in Neoplatonism and a culmination, as an artistic program, in the highly affective Baroque art of the seventeenth century. Such artists as Rubens and Bernini are determined to provide transport-by-spectacle and employ every virtuoso device to achieve it. The purposes of painting (as of poetry) became in some ways more modest in the latter half of the seventeenth century (particularly in England, where religious painting was feared as an instrument of popery and where, from very early — that is, well before Lely and Kneller — portraiture was the dominant mode); but the claims of art theory did not diminish at the same rate as those of painters, and in equal tension with the demand for "just and lively" representation (which, in fact, was not a call for Quattrocento literalism) and the exaggerated respect for laws and "law-givers" such as Leonardo and Poussin,[12] one finds the continuing insistence on transport and inner vision and the traditional celebration of the eye as the chief of sensory organs.

It would seem important to recognize that these conceptions, with their Platonic overtones, and the vocabulary in which they were traditionally treated were preserved in the theory of the visual arts during the period that saw the highest ascendancy, in poetics, of Aristotle, reason, and the decorum of the ideal. What is viable in one area of aesthetic endeavor at a given time, however, is usually accessible to others (and that "Painture near adjoining lay" was an article of faith to Mrs. Anne Killigrew's contemporaries), and there are indications that poetic theory succeeded, in ways direct and indirect, in refreshing itself with the headier ideas that passed current in commentary on the visual arts.

Joseph Addison was perhaps one of the most efficient agents of the transmission of these ideas into poetics. Other sources for Addison's concern in the papers on "The Pleasures of the Imagination" with "astonishment" and "amazement" as responses to works of art and literature, and with the eye as the sponsoring organ of these emotions, have been easier to detect because he made them so: Longinus and Locke, he makes us aware, are authorities who are never far behind him. But equally close are the writers who described the pleasures which the imagination could derive from the visual arts, and their influence on Addison's ideas would seem to have been more extensive than has been recognized.

If it is a true proposition that, as Addison wrote, "most of the observations that agree with descriptions [in poetry] are equally applicable to painting and statuary," [13] the reverse, clearly, is also true, and observations that had been made regarding painting and sculpture might be applied to descriptive poetry — or expanded, as in other parts of Addison's essay, into general aesthetic principles. Certainly Addison's first premise, that "Our sight is the most perfect and most delightful of all our senses," [14] echoes a standard assertion of the art treatises. And he

8. *An Essay upon the Sublime Translated from the Greek of Dionysius Longinus Cassius, the Rhetorician, Compared with the French of the Sieur Despreaux Boileau* (Oxford, 1698), p. 3.

9. *Gentleman's Magazine*, V (May 1735), 247.

10. Franciscus Junius, *The Painting of the Ancients in Three Books: Declaring by Historicall Observations and Examples, the Beginning, Progresse and Consummation of that Most Noble Art* . . . (London, 1638), p. 332.

11. *Ibid.*, p. 329.

12. Thus William Aglionby, in acknowledging Leonardo "the *Father* of the Third Age of *Painting*, which we call the *Modern*," includes among his merits that "he gave better *Rules*, more exact *Measures*, and was more profound in the Art than any before him." *Painting, Illustrated in Three Dialogues* (1685), p. 73.

13. *Spectator*, 416. Citations are to the edition of George A. Aitken (London, 1898).

14. *Spectator*, 411. Cf. Dennis's view that the eye "is a Sense that the Poet ought chiefly to entertain; because it contributes more than any other to the exciting of

appears no less in their debt when he undertakes a general definition of beauty: "This consists either in the gaiety or variety of colours, in the symmetry and proportion of parts, in the arrangement and disposition of bodies, or in a just mixture and concurrence of all together" (*Spectator*, 412). Similar painterly notions and painterly metaphors appear in his description of nature unimproved by the imagination: "but what a rough unsightly sketch of nature should we be entertained with, did all her colouring disappear and the several distinctions of light and shade vanish?" (*Spectator*, 413). And he would seem to have adopted from the same sources the view that the pleasures of the imagination are easy. Painting was celebrated in art treatises from the early Renaissance to the eighteenth century as a "universal language" whose meanings were accessible to all and required no special knowledge (as of ancient languages) or exertion of thought to come at. So the Addisonian imagination: "It is but opening the eye," says Addison, "and the scene enters." [15] The thought appears everywhere among the writers on art, but Charles Lamotte's phrasing is perhaps nearest Addison's: in a brief passage of dialogue a young man admiring a painting of Raphael's declares, "to have a true Relish for Virgil, one must have Language, Grammar, Learning and a true Taste for Poetry; whereas it is only having Eyes and Common Sense, to be ravished and transported at this." [16]

Addison, it is true, is a cautious champion of these views, who would resist the democratizing impulse implicit in the statement of Lamotte's young man (for one is to educate taste systematically, in the trust that "A man of a polite imagination is let into a great many pleasures that the vulgar are not capable of receiving") [17] and who seems easier with the notion of "conversing" [18] with pictures than with being ravished by them. There appears, in fact, to be a discontinuity between Addison's intended meaning and his language — the Platonizing, enthusiastic vocabulary of art commentary suggesting an intensity in imaginative pleasures and a kind of importance for them from which there is a noticeable tendency in his argument to withdraw. The response of the imagination to natural "greatness" ("where we are not struck with the novelty or beauty of the sight but with that rude kind of magnificence which appears in . . . stupendous works of nature") is described in terms of enthusiasm and ecstasy: "We are flung into a pleasing astonishment at such unbounded views, and feel a delightful stillness and amazement in the soul at the apprehension of them" (*Spectator*, 412). We seem hopelessly remote from such excitements, however, when imaginative pleasures are commended to us, as they are in the first paper of the series, for their harmlessness and efficacy in keeping people out of trouble.

There are, indeed, but very few who know how to be idle and innocent, or have a relish of any pleasures that are not criminal; every diversion they take is at the expense of some one virtue or another, and their very first step out of business is into vice or folly. A man should endeavour, therefore, to make the sphere of his innocent pleasures as wide as possible, that he may retire into them with safety, and find in them such a satisfaction as a wise man would not blush to take. Of this nature are those of the imagination, which do not require such a bent of thought as is necessary to our more serious employments, nor, at the same time, suffer the mind to sink into that negligence and remissness which are apt to accompany our more sensual delights, but, like a gentle exercise to the faculties, awaken them from sloth and idleness, without putting them upon any labour or difficulty.[19]

strong Passion." *The Advancement and Reformation of Modern Poetry, Critical Works,* I, 269.

15. That it enters as supposed in the art treatises is made clearer in Addison's next sentence: "The colours paint themselves on the fancy, with very little attention of thought or application of mind in the beholder." *Spectator,* 411.

16. Lamotte, *Essay upon Poetry and Painting,* p. 38.

17. *Spectator,* 411.

18. *Ibid.*

19. *Spectator,* 411. Despite its importance to the subsequent history of aesthetics, "The Pleasures of the Imagination" does not put a consistently high value on aesthetic experience — as in fact is hinted in its title. "Pleasure" is evidently to be distinguished, as in Aristotle (*Ethics,* 1095b–1103a; 1176a–1179a) from the "happiness" which is the "end" or "good" of man, and which is described by Addison in the third paper of the series in a Christianized echo of Aristotle: "The Supreme Author of our being has so formed the soul of man that nothing but Himself can be its last, adequate and proper happiness." For Aristotle there are better and worse to be distinguished among pleasures, but even the best are merely ancillary to the exercise of man's essential function, which is the exercise of reason (that "labor of the brain" which, in Addison's account, is distinguished absolutely from the processes of imagination). The fervor implicit in Addison's vocabulary of aesthetics has, certainly, its counterweight in condescension.

It can be claimed that the imagination has uses, in Addison's conception, as a means of grace — "reconciling man, with his spiritual needs and his desire to belong to a living universe of purpose and values, with a cosmos that begins to appear alien, impersonal, remote, menacing . . ." (Ernest Tuveson, *The Imagination as a Means of Grace* [Berkeley and Los Angeles, 1960], p. 97), but where he shows it thus employed (in the series of "speculations . . . upon infinitude and eternity": *Spectator,* 565, 571, 580, 590, 628) it is not occupied with works of art — which in any case he had judged in the earlier series to be less pleasurable than works of nature (414). Even his search into "final causes" fails to turn up a distinct role for art and literature, or a sufficient ground for appreciation. The distance is not so great as one could wish between Addison and Joseph Spence, who in his preface to *Polymetis* (1747) declared his intention to discuss ancient art and poetry with as

Despite Addison's deflations and contradictions of concepts which had been allowed larger development and suggestiveness in the art treatises, it seems clear that they contributed — somewhat randomly in a rather random work — to his aesthetic theory and his critical vocabulary (enriching the latter especially with what in Addison's hands became little more than hyperboles of appreciation: such formulas as "transporting," "ravishing," "delights the soul").[20]

*     *     *

Dryden offers in some ways a still more vivid example of the ambivalence of the neoclassical poetic theorist confronted with the exuberancies of neoclassical art theory. In the essay "A Parallel of Poetry and Painting," which prefaces his translation of Dufresnoy, Dryden includes a lengthy excerpt from Giovanni Pietro Bellori's *Vite di Pittori, Scultori et Architetti Moderni*, whose ambitious account of art as imitation of the idea of beauty he considers "cannot be unpleasing, at least to such who are conversant in the philosophy of Plato." [21] But Bellori is not altogether pleasing to Dryden himself, and he complains of "pompous expressions" and "smoke" — i.e., of such obscurities of enthusiasm as are contained in Bellori's celebration of the power of the artist's idea to excel nature:

From hence Phidias, Lysippus, and other noble sculptors, are still held in veneration; and Apelles, Zeuxis, Protogenes, and other admirable painters, though their works are perished, are and will be eternally admired; who all of them drew after the ideas of perfection, which are the miracles of nature, the providence of the understanding, the exemplars of the mind, the light of the fancy; the sun, which, from its rising, inspired the statue of Memnon, and the fire, which warmed into life the image of Prometheus. 'Tis this, which causes the Graces and the Loves to take up their habitations in the hardest marble, and to subsist in the emptiness of light and shadows.[22]

Dryden's objection, however, is chiefly to the extravagance of the style, for he "must needs say, there is somewhat in the matter," [23] and proceeds, once launched by Bellori, to make his most complete statement of idealist theory. His idealism is not, perhaps, of a kind that shows him to have been foremost among those "who are conversant in the philosophy of Plato," and indeed shows inevitably its provenance in Aristotle and Horace, to whom — with Longinus — Dryden confessed owing his lights. It is an idealism somewhat diminished, certainly, from Bellori's,[24] which, in fact, was hardly needed to lead Dryden to the perception that "there is scarcely a frailty to be left" in the heroes of epic poems or that "all perfections are not suitable to all subjects" (and that, therefore, characters of tragedy and comedy must be left with some of their frailties intact).

Doctrines of ideal form were, of course, sufficiently familiar in neoclassical poetic theory: *la belle Nature* was one of the first and most enduring of the exports of French critical theory received in England, and it was one of the principal theoretical bases — as firmly supporting as the contrary doctrine that poetry is a reflection of particular "objects and events" — for the conception denominated in the Horatian phrase *ut pictura poesis.*[25] It provided a footing on which the relation of poetry and painting as sister arts, the subject of Dryden's discourse, appeared obvious and secure.[26]

But Dryden's notion that Bellori's idealism is related to "the philosophy of Plato," would seem to suggest a difference from his own. The *idea* which Dryden commends to poets (as that which the presumably more congenial Dufresnoy commends to painters) is unequivocally the prod-

much "easiness" as possible, for "I have long thought it particularly misplaced and absurd, to put on a very grave face, in this kind of subjects: which after all that one can say for them, are certainly not of the highest importance to mankind; and if they are not entertaining, can have but very little else to recommend them."

20. One instance of a reflection on art made by Addison himself surviving to inform a famous phrase of his literary criticism (and turning him in a third direction — to the *expressing* artist, as distinct from the imitating work of art or the action of the work on its beholder) may have sufficient interest to record. In *Spectator*, 166, Addison had remarked on the impermanence of works of art: "Michael Angelo, Fontana, and Raphael, will hereafter be what Phidias, Vitruvius, and Apelles are at present; the names of great statuaries, architects and painters, whose works are lost. The several arts are expressed in mouldering materials; nature sinks under them, and is not able to support the ideas which are imprest upon it." It seems highly probable that Addison consulted this passage, or remembered it, when, five months later, he wrote of Milton that "Our language sunk under him and was unequal to that greatness of soul which furnished him with such glorious conceptions." *Spectator*, 297.

21. *Essays*, II, 117.

22. *Ibid.*, II, 122–23.

23. *Ibid.*, II, 123.

24. Bellori had a principal role in systematizing the concept of ideal form in classical art theory "which first developed the doctrine of the idea into a law of aesthetics." See Erwin Panofsky, *Idea, Ein Beitrag Begriffesgeschichte der älteren Kunsttheorie*, 2nd ed. (Berlin, 1960), p. 72.

25. See Hagstrum, *Sister Arts*, especially pp. 11–12; Wimsatt and Brooks, *Literary Criticism*, pp. 316–17.

26. It also had usefulness in a wider synthesis, as Charles Batteux was to show in his *Les Beaux Arts Réduits à un Même Principe* (1746), which found imitation of *la belle Nature* to be the single unifying principle of poetry, painting, sculpture, music and dance.

uct of the mind's own processes of abstraction, an eclectic idea assembled from elements found in nature. This conception of the idea — more Aristotelian than Platonic — is also present in Bellori, who represents it (as it had been represented repeatedly since the fifteenth century) with the legend of Zeuxis, who copied parts of the bodies of five beautiful virgins to produce a composite and perfect image of Helen.[27] But this is to consider the idea as aesthetic prescription only, which did not exhaust its interest for neoclassical art theory — in general less reluctant than contemporary poetic theory to go beyond aesthetic prescriptions to metaphysical explanations.[28] Bellori, at this level, is typically and thoroughly Platonist:

God Almighty, in the fabric of the Universe, first contemplated himself, and reflected on his own excellencies; from which he drew and constituted those first forms which are called ideas. So that every species which was afterwards expressed was produced from that first idea, forming that wonderful contexture of all created beings. But the celestial bodies above the moon being incorruptible, and not subject to change, remained forever fair, and in perpetual order; on the contrary, all things which are sublunary are subject to change, to deformity, and to decay. And though Nature always intends a consummate beauty in her productions, yet through the inequality of the matter the forms are altered; and in particular, human beauty suffers alteration for the worse, as we see to our mortification, in the deformities and disproportions which are in us. For which reason, the artful painter and the sculptor, imitating the Divine Maker, form to themselves, as well as they are able, a model of the superior beauties; and reflecting on them, endeavour to correct and amend the common nature, and to represent it as it was at first created, without fault, either in colour, or in lineament.[29]

Félibien is a theorist of equal scope:

Si vous voulez prendre la peine de faire réflexion sur les diverses parties de cet Art, vous avouerez qu'il fournit de grands sujets de méditer sur l'excellence de cette première Lumière, d'où l'esprit de l'homme tire toutes ces belles idées, et ces nobles inventions qu'il exprime ensuite dans ses Ouvrages. . . . Et enfin quand nous penserons que toutes ces merveilles de l'Art qui charment ici-bas nos yeux et surprennent nos esprits, ne sont rien en comparaison des idées qu'en avoient conceû ces maîtres qui les ont produites; combien aurons-nous sujet d'adorer cette Sagesse éternelle qui répand dans les Esprits la Lumière de tous les Arts . . .[30]

Dryden's scope was less, to be sure, but it is suggestive at least of sympathy with these larger conceptions, useful in exalting the artist's function, that he translated the passage of Bellori quoted above and included

it in his account of the ideal basis of the sisterhood of poetry and painting. It would seem to have been an advantage of that relation in the last
decades of the seventeenth century that the Platonizing art treatises could
assist in renewing the vision of the poet as one who "doth glance from
heaven to earth, from earth to heaven."

✓     ✓     ✓

For Dryden, certainly, it was an unfrenzied glance and involved no
real defection from the standard which led him to his "definition of poetical wit" as a "propriety of thoughts and words." He seems to have
sought, or expected, in Dufresnoy an art theorist with similarly correct
views: Dufresnoy had been commended to him, he says, as "one who perfectly understood the rules of painting; who gave the best and most con-
cise instructions for performance, and the surest to inform the judgment
of all who loved this noble art: that they who before were rather fond
of it, than knowingly admired it, might defend their inclination by their
reason." [31] *De Arte Graphica*, on the whole a meticulously reasonable
collection of precepts, of course fulfilled the promise. But even Dufresnoy, first founder of the laws of the French Academy, could employ the
language of Platonizing enthusiasm with an ease and fluency not seen in
English criticism after Sidney and Jonson (who made easy and fluent use
of it in *Timber*). Art and poetry, according to Dufresnoy, " 'that they
might advance the sacred honours of religion,' have raised themselves to
Heaven; and, having found a free admission into the palace of *Jove* himself, have enjoyed the Sight and Conversation of the Gods." And "from

27. The legend of Zeuxis, with variations, gave a common mythology to the
concept of the immanent ideal in art and poetry. Thus, in a gloss on Aristotle's
account of the "universal" in poetry, Samuel Wesley refers poets to the practice of
painters. "History, says Aristotle, treats of particular Things as they really are;
Poetry, as they ought to be; and therefore he prefers Poetry as the more grave and
more instructive; the Poets being forc'd to follow the same Methods with their
Kindred-Art, that of the Painters, and gather a great many Beauties together, out
of 'em all, to steal one Venus." *Essay on Heroic Poetry*, 2nd ed. (1697), Augustan
Reprint Society, Series II, no. 2 (Los Angeles, 1947), p. 4.

28. Louis Bredvold ·has said of the neoclassical champions of the ideal that "if
they were not Platonists in a strict philosophical sense, it was merely because in
their theorizing they stopped short of metaphysical problems; had they been metaphysicians, they would have been Platonists." "The Tendency toward Platonism
in Neo-Classical Esthetics," *ELH*, I (1934), 117.

29. Dryden's translation in "A Parallel of Poetry and Painting" in *Essays*, II,
117–18.

30. *Entretiens sur les Vies et sur les Ouvrages des plus Excellens Peintres Anciens
et Modernes* (Paris, 1705), I, 41.

31. *Essays*, II, 115.

Heaven they take their passage through the World; and 'with concurring Studies' collect whatsoever they find worthy of them." [32] "Invention" he describes as a "kind of Muse, which, being possessed of the other advantages common to her Sisters, and being warmed by the fire of Apollo, is raised higher than the rest and shines with a more glorious and brighter flame." [33] In a stanza urging the painter to cultivate "grace" and "nobleness," he suggests that this is "a most difficult undertaking; and a very rare present, which the artist receives rather from the hand of Heaven, than from his own industry and studies." [34]

There is some encouragement in this for boldness. And, while Dryden had evidenced a distaste for the mere regularity of a "flat design" [35] thirty years before translating Dufresnoy, his arguments for license frequently suggest understanding of the freedoms (theoretically) allowed the painter. His famous appreciation of Shakespeare in the "Essay of Dramatic Poesy," for example, turns on notions of subjectivism and inspired self-reliance and "grace" which had been conspicuous in Mannerist theory a century earlier. Shakespeare had a genius sufficient to itself, "he needed not the spectacles of books to read nature; he looked inwards and found her there." (For "books" read "mathematics," and the statement is identical with the doctrine of the Mannerists Zuccaro and Lomazzo, concerned to overthrow Renaissance rules of proportion in the name of the *disegno interno*, the inward drawing, or idea.[36]) Shakespeare, says Dryden, was "the man who of all modern, and perhaps ancient poets, had the largest and most comprehensive soul. All the images of Nature were still present to him, and he drew them, not laboriously, but luckily . . ." [37]

The distinction between luck and labor, made by Dryden in favor of luck and Shakespeare, exploited a formula which had become a commonplace of the art treatises in the century and a half since Vasari. Both luck and labor were recognized as indispensable to art, and a balance between them recommended by all authorities. There was a clear tendency, however, to associate luck with "genius," creative energy, and the "spirit which animates the whole," and to depreciate labor as a craftsmanly necessity, the effects of which should be concealed [38] — for "an unresolved and timorous lingerer doth . . . deface and utterly overthrow all the hope of Grace." [39] Labor was a vice if it led to too meticulous detail or to overfinishing, or if permitted to show, and the parable of Apelles's reproach to Protogenes for not staying his hand gave steady force to the notion that the painter must know when to leave well enough alone. Sir William Temple perhaps reflects its influence in literary criticism in deploring that "much application has been made to the smoothness of language or style, which has at the best but the beauty of colouring in a picture, and can never make a good one without spirit and strength." [40]

An important corollary of this attitude, in Vasari, was an emphasis on speed and "dash" in execution, a notion that luck consists in lack of cau-

32. *The Works of John Dryden*, ed. Walter Scott and George Saintsbury (London, 1892), XVII, 343–45. Roger De Piles's "Observation" on this passage, appended to Dryden's translation in 1695, maintains the parallel at an equal loftiness: the arts "follow the same bent, and suffer themselves to be rather carried away, than led by their secret inclinations, which are so many seeds of the Divinity." *Ibid.*, 397–98.

33. *Ibid.*, 349–51.      34. *Ibid.*, 363.

35. "An Essay of Dramatic Poesy," *Essays*, I, 77.

36. See Anthony Blunt, *Artistic Theory in Italy 1450–1600*, 2nd ed. (Oxford, 1956), pp. 137–59. The Mannerist treatises were known in England. Richard Haydocke's translation of Lomazzo's *Trattato dell' arte della Pittura, Scultura et Architettura*, the first book about art to be translated into English from Italian, was made available to English readers only fourteen years after its first publication in Italy (1584) and appears to have been used widely in the following one and a half centuries. A number of references to it have been noted by Frederick Hard in his article "Richard Haydocke and Alexander Browne: Two Half-Forgotten Writers on the Art of Painting," *PMLA*, LV (1940), 727–41. Vasari was a "basic text." See Luigi Salerno, "Seventeenth-Century English Literature on Painting," *Journal of the Warburg and Courtauld Institutes*, XIV (1951), 234–58.

37. *Essays*, I, 79–80. Painterly metaphors of boldness appear repeatedly in Dryden's attacks on the regularly dull. " 'Tis one thing," he says in the Preface to *Sylvae*, for a translating author "to draw the outlines true, the features like, the proportions exact, the colouring itself perhaps tolerable; and another thing to make all these graceful, by the posture, the shadowings, and, chiefly, by the spirit which animates the whole" (*Essays*, I, 252–53). Again, "the boldest strokes of poetry," he declares, "when they are managed artfully, are those which most delight the reader," and these include catachresis and hyperbole which can be used in poetry "as heightenings and shadows are in painting, to make the figure bolder, and cause it to stand off to sight" (*Essays*, I, 183–84).

38. Labor to achieve skill, as distinct from labor in employing it, was of course recommended. Limits to its effectiveness were recognized, however: De Piles, for example, would have it that "Genius is the first thing we must suppose in a Painter; 'tis a part of him that cannot be acquired by Study or Labour" ("Observation," p. 1). The example of Correggio was cited to show the irrelevance of all aids to genius: "Correge's Genius appears in all he has done, that wonderful Greatness of natural Genius, and fine Taste of Beauty, which was able without any assistance to rise to a most sublime pitch of Perfection. 'Tis no Wonder he was not altogether correct, not having any assistance from the Antique, nor indeed from any Master. . . . History hardly affords a greater Instance of Strength of Genius, than in this excellent Painter: For all his Sweetness and Greatness, considering his circumstances and Education, can be ascribed to nothing else but to a very rare natural Stock of these excellent qualities" (Turnbull, p. 162).

39. Junius, *Painting of the Ancients*, p. 326.

40. "Of Poetry" in *Five Miscellaneous Essays by Sir William Temple*, ed. Samuel Holt Monk (Ann Arbor, 1963), p. 197.

tion and that "grace" is to be taken by surprise.[41] Writers of later treatises, while turning strongly toward system and the restraints of reason, continued to insist on the role of happy accident in artistic creation and to tolerate, indeed applaud, the wrecking of the rules by the greatest accidents. There are energies which cannot be confined, and the errors to which they lead are to be preferred to mere correctness. Thus Rubens can be admired, although he "failed in what regards Taste of Beauty, and very often in Design; his lively great Mind not permitting him almost ever to mend or change what he had done: All the Errors he committed, he was transported into them by the Rapidity and Impetuousness of his Genius." [42]

The principle is stated everywhere in the treatises. Junius holds that free and forward spirits are not to be restrained within the compass of a narrow cariere, but that wee must rather give our Invention the full raines: for as mettled horses are best known by a spacious race; so must Artificers have an open field, as it were, to runne in, with a loose and unrestrained libertie, seeing that the forwardnesse of this same most generous Art is weakened and broke when a man goeth about to contain it within the limits and bounds of a straight running place.[43]

De Piles urges the painter not to content himself "with being exact and regular," for he should "in everything he does shew a *grand Gusto*, and above all things avoid what is mean and insipid." [44] William Sanderson joins forces with Francis Bacon and thrusts at the whole fabric of the rules:

There is no excellent *beauty* without some strangeness in the proportion, and both Apelles and Albert Durer, doe but trifles out the time and trouble us; the one to compose a personage by Geometrical proportion; and Apelles by collecting the best parts from several faces, to make one excellent. Indeed a *Painter* may make a better personage than ever was seen since the first Creation; which he does by a kind of felicity, not by *Rule*; as a Musitian doth his French Aires, not by true method of setting.[45]

There is a danger in collecting such passages of exaggerating the importance of the pressure for freedom, for the counterpressure of restraint was, of course, a dominant and defining characteristic of neoclassicism. Freedom, for most of its advocates, was not a universal prerogative: "There are none but great Genius's who are above the Rules," said De Piles.[46] But errant and transcendent genius had elaborate provisions made for it in the art treatises, and they gave a glamor to rulelessness.

This would seem to have followed, almost of necessity, from the nature of the materials of art history, which included a great deal of irregular genius for neoclassical theory to take account of. The "World's Wonder" Michelangelo [47] might be made, as he was, to yield pride of place to Raphael (until restored by Reynolds), but he could not be ignored; and what was seen in him was "a vast uncommon strength of Genius, something leaning toward the Savage and Furious . . . a masculine, daring, comprehensive Genius." [48] In lesser degrees Correggio, Caravaggio, Tintoretto, Rubens, and, of course, "Savage" Rosa all demanded appreciation in similar terms, placing very sizable obstacles in the way of an inflexible insistence on rules.

There was scant encouragement for a Rymer, it might be said, where there were so many Shakespeares, and it seems possible to suggest that these artists and the disposition they fostered in art theory may have helped to prevent the development of more Rymer-like positions in English critical theory. Certainly the example of the painter was an example of freedom for some Augustan authors and did some service against the rules of poetry. [49] Leonard Welsted intends an immediate application to

41. For a discussion of Vasari's concept of grace see Blunt, *Artistic Theory*, pp. 93–98. Blunt's view that Vasari first introduced this concept into aesthetic theory is corrected in Samuel Holt Monk's article "A Grace beyond the Reach of Art" (*Journal of the History of Ideas*, V [1944], 131–50) which traces it to Classical sources.

42. George Turnbull, *Treatise on Ancient Painting* (London, 1740), p. 164.

43. Junius, *Painting of the Ancients*, p. 226. Cf. Fréart on invention: "a particular talent, not to be acquired by study or labor; but is properly a certain ardor exciting the imagination, prompting and enabling it to act." Roland Fréart de Chambray, *An Idea of the Perfection of Painting*, trans. John Evelyn (London, 1688), p. 11.

44. Roger De Piles, *The Art of Painting* (London, 1706), pp. 1–2.

45. William Sanderson, *Graphice, The Use of the Pen and Pencil, or the Most Excellent Art of Painting* (London, 1658), p. 16. The passage is borrowed, with insignificant alterations, from Bacon's essay "Of Beauty." Dufresnoy himself disclaims any intention to "stifle the genius, by a jumbled heap of rules: nor [to] extinguish the fire of a vein which is lively and abundant."

46. De Piles, *The Art of Painting*, p. 40.

47. Sanderson, *Graphice*, p. 18.

48. Turnbull, *Ancient Painting*, p. 168.

49. It is significant that Temple, who was no friend to the rules, appears to have considered that he was using "painters terms" no less in praising Homer for "the most spirit, force, and life" than in praising Vergil for "the best design, the truest proportions, and the greatest grace" — an apportionment of virtues that would seem to exploit fully the contrasting values of restraint and freedom, imitation and inspiration, inherent in the analogy with painting ("Of Poetry," p. 181). It may be noted, however, that where Temple's argument is most "inspirational," his comparisons are with music (p. 179).

poetry when he asks "what advantage, think you . . . it would be to a young painter, if with a magisterial air one should document him in this manner? 'I will disclose to you the mysteries of your art and the laws that preside over it. Attend.'"[50] William Davenant, although not an uncompromised champion of poetic liberty, relayed its impulse directly to Pope in a metaphor of painting: "*Wit* is the laborious and the lucky resultances of thought, having towards its excellence, as we say of the strokes of Painting, as well a happinesse as care."[51] And Pope, anticipating slightly later developments, accepted the message but changed the metaphor to music:

> Some beauties yet no precepts can declare,
> For there's a happiness as well as care.
> Music resembles poetry; in each
> Are nameless graces which no methods teach.[52]

The analogy between poetry and painting had also a "public relations" aspect, and insistence on the sisterhood of the two arts (reversing the direction of dependence which had obtained during the Renaissance, when painting gained in public dignity and credit from sisterly association with an art secure in its humanistic pretensions)[53] was useful to poetry in enlarging its pretensions and dignifying its method. Among the Augustans, painting enjoyed immense prestige, which could be drawn upon to justify other departments of aesthetic enterprise.[54]

The basis of this prestige was, of course, the brilliance of the achievement of the painters of the Italian Renaissance, for which neoclassical critics could find no adequate parallel in other arts or in other (modern) times. The great figures of English poetry were scarcely admitted to competition.[55] Thus the young Addison, giving his "Account of the Greater English Poets" to Mr. H. S. in 1694, omits Shakespeare altogether, dismisses Spenser as "barbarous," and, while recognizing greatness in Milton's "unfettered" genius, finds occasion to deplore its republican bias. Seven years later, in "A Letter from Italy," Addison shows with how much more certain warmth the taste of the time responded to Renaissance painting, especially Raphael.

> Fain would I Raphael's godlike art rehearse,
> And show th' immortal labours in my verse,
> Where from the mingled strength of shade and light
> A new creation rises to my sight,

Such heavenly figures from his pencil flow,
So warm with life his blended colours glow . . .

The sudden glory of high Renaissance painting was near-miraculous —
"that . . . prodigy which happened at Rome," [56] and what most moved
the Augustans to admiration was that it seemed to have occurred, not as
an independent flowering of genius, but as a restoration. "In the year
1500 I conclude the Re-establishment of these Arts," wrote Pierre Monier,[57] and Lamotte, also, is typical in citing Michelangelo and Raphael as
"Restorers of Painting in Italy." [58] But the Renaissance masters did not

50. "A Dissertation concerning the Perfection of the English Language" (1724)
in *Eighteenth-Century Critical Essays*, ed. Scott Elledge (Ithaca, 1961), I, 331.

51. "Preface to *Gondibert*" in *Critical Essays of the Seventeenth Century*, ed.
Joel E. Spingarn (Oxford, 1907), II, 20. See Monk, "A Grace beyond the Reach
of Art," p. 148.

52. *Essay on Criticism*, pp. 141–44. Abrams and others have discussed the change
from the poetry/painting analogy to poetry/music as a sign of change from a
mimetic to an expressive poetics, Classical to Romantic. See *The Mirror and the
Lamp*, pp. 50–51, 93–94. The present essay, while arguing for certain expressive
meanings in poetry's appeal to painting, does so, on the whole, within the same
general framework of assumptions. A survey of the art treatises, however, would
suggest that this framework might be expanded to give a larger place to expressive
values in art theory. Fréart's *Idée de la Perfection de la Peinture*, for example, is a
treatise which, it has rightly been said, "from beginning to end treats painting as
an art of expression" (William Guild Howard, "*Ut Pictura Poesis*," *PMLA*, XXIV
[1909], 69).

53. See Lee, "*Ut Pictura Poesis*."

54. There is some evidence that painting was less sure than it might have been
of its place in public reputation; for the claims of the art treatises, while large, are
often defensive. Richardson, for example, in *The Theory of Painting* (1715), insists on the superiority of the painter in a way that recalls the Renaissance *paragoni*,
the contests of precedence in which the champions of painting and poetry engaged
at a time when painting sought acceptance as a liberal art: "To be an accomplished
painter, a man must possess more than one liberal art, which puts him on a level
with those that do that, and makes him superior to those that possess but one in
equal degree: he must also be a curious artificer, whereby he becomes superior
to one who equally possesses the other talents but wants that. A Raphaelle, therefore, is not only equal, but superior to a Virgil, or a Livy, a Thucydides or a
Homer" (*Works*, Strawberry Hill ed., 1792, p. 18). But all this is by way of objection to the fact, as Richardson sees it, that "the word painter does not carry
with it an idea equal to that we have of other professions, or employments not
superior to it" (p. 17).

55. The claims of English dramatic writing did not go unrecognized, however.
Cf. the early appreciations of Dryden and Temple.

56. Jean Baptiste Dubos, *Critical Reflections on Poetry, Painting and Music*,
trans. Thomas Nugent (London, 1748), II, 131.

57. Pierre Monier, *The History of Painting, Sculpture and Those Who Excelled
in Them* (London, 1699), Preface.

58. The paragraph in which this statement occurs is notable for the suggestion
that the Renaissance masters may have laid violent hands on the remains of the

merely restore the art of the ancients; they also vied with it, and, although loyalty to Apelles and Protogenes and other ancient painters continued strong through the first decades of the eighteenth century (despite the lack of examples of their art) there was widespread belief that their achievement had been fully equaled by the Italians, who seemed, indeed, to have met not only all past but all possible competition —"insomuch that there is little *Amendment* to be expected in *Painting*, after such Artists." [59] The neoclassical critic could find little in modern poetry that pleased him so well, or for reasons whose force he was so eager to admit. Joseph Warton's thumbnail reckoning in *The Adventurer* of Ancient and Modern credits and debits would have had the consent of many of his contemporaries: in epic poetry, Tasso, Ariosto, Camoëns, and Milton are less than Homer and Vergil;[60] in tragedy, Shakespeare, Racine, and Corneille are less than Aeschylus, Sophocles, and Euripides; but the case is different in painting. "I must own," says Warton (owning also that it is a "disputable point") that "if the moderns approach the ancients in any of the arts here in question, they approach them nearest in the art of painting. The human mind can with difficulty conceive any thing more exalted than 'The Last Judgment' of Michael Angelo and 'The Transfiguration' of Raphael." [61]

Raphael, of course, was the special darling of Neoclassicism, and there are innumerable testaments of its devotion: "*Raphael del Urbin* was the greatest Painter that ever was";[62] "It was Raphael d'Urbin, who raised Painting in the last Age to its highest degree of Perfection";[63] ". . . the great luminary of Painting . . . the undoubted head of the Roman school, and of the modern painters, Raphaelle Sanzio da Urbino." [64] The reasons for this devotion are, for the most part, familiar and are obviously related to the prevailing respect for the virtues of the antique. Raphael is constantly praised for simplicity, rationality, judgment, ease, truth to nature, exactness, and justness. The desperately banal author of *Epigrams on the Paintings of the Most Eminent Masters* (1700) notes unerringly that

> In Urbin's works nothing can be descry'd
> But what is most judiciously apply'd.[65]

Raphael was above all the painter of rule and reason, the supreme master of painting's "universal language," and the inventor of its most broadly intelligible dialect — a presiding figure of extraordinary attractive power in the "pictorial pantheon" [66] of a nation still capable of feeling in Pope's young manhood that it had never yet had a great poet who was correct.

But Raphael could also be admired for other qualities, and such as make clear his participation in a myth of the artist as great soul, which would seem to have been too strong for the taming impulses of Neoclassicism. His "grace," "strength of natural genius," "greatness of invention" (Turnbull), and "great *Gout*" (De Piles) are noticed in even the most conventional critiques and those most concerned to bring him into relation with the ancients. They suggest the endowments of genius in the modern sense of the word, and the inexplicability of great artistic achievement. The mold had been set by Vasari and succeeding biographers, who established the genius as the artist-type and inspiration and grace as a creative norm. They were perhaps responding to Renaissance poetic theorists such as Scaliger and Minturno who fervently revived, as did Milton later, the classical claims for the divine power of the poet; but, if so, the response, in duration at least, far overmatched the challenge.[67]

art which they "restored," in order to avoid unfavorable comparisons. "I am very apt to believe," says Lamotte, "that they made bold not only with *Basso Relievos*, but even with the Fresco Paintings, that were left of the Ancient Masters." *Essay upon Poetry and Painting*, p. 35.

59. Aglionby, *Three Dialogues*, pp. 124–25.

60. It is interesting that neoclassical discontent with the literary achievement of the moderns fastened most strongly on the shortcomings of the poets of the Italian Renaissance, who derived no advantage from the respectability of their painting countrymen. Shaftesbury's view is typical: "The Italian authors in particular . . . may be reckoned no better than the corrupters of true learning and erudition, and can indeed be relished by those alone whose education has unfortunately denied them the familiarity of the noble ancients, and the practice of a better and more natural taste." *Characteristics*, ed. J. M. Robertson (London, 1900), I, 216n. Cf. *Spectator*, 5, 62, 279, 297, 369.

61. *The Adventurer*, 127. Warton is in part responding to *Spectator*, 249, in which Addison joins the Battle of the Books on the side of the Ancients and does not make Warton's exceptions. Painting did not enter significantly into the issues of the *querelle*, as they were repeated in England. Temple almost ignored it in "An Essay upon the Ancient and Modern Learning." William Wotton, although himself a diffident champion of the modern achievement in the arts, quoted some fifteen pages of Modern apologetics from Perrault — who gave highest praise, not to the masters of the High Renaissance, but to Le Brun, Poussin, and Bernini. *Reflections upon Ancient and Modern Learning*, 3rd ed. (London, 1705), pp. 59–74.

62. Aglionby, *Three Dialogues*, p. 76.

63. Monier, *History*, p. 18.

64. Jonathan Richardson, "The Science of a Connoisseur" in *Works*, Strawberry Hill ed., p. 202.

65. . . . *by J[ohn] E[lsum]* (London, 1700), p. 102.

66. The term is borrowed from Hagstrum, *Sister Arts*; see especially pp. 108–12.

67. The myth is doubtless more complex than I suggest, and more remote and obscure in its origins (continued, rather than begun, by Renaissance biographers).

The mystery of art and its divine power received elaborate obeisances which the authors of the neoclassical treatises sometimes suggest were excessive. Much of their effort is devoted to opening a subject which has been understood only by those with special knowledge and which has been encumbered and obscured by philistine reverence and the "high Cant of Connoisseurs." [68] Aglionby, for example, states that his whole "Design is to make Painting Familiar and Easie to the Nobility and Gentry of this Nation, and to enter them so far in the Knowledge and Acquaintance of the *Italian Painters*, that they may converse with their Works, and Understand their different Characters." But a tradition of two centuries inhibited ease and familiarity with painting and served to imbue it with a high austerity which, for the Augustans, had its nearest parallels in poetry in the doctrines of Milton and Longinus. It is described, with some edge of skepticism, by Horace Walpole:

In Italy, where the art of painting has been carried to an amazing degree of perfection, the lives of the painters have been written in numberless volumes, alone sufficient to compose a little library. Every picture of every considerable master is minutely described. Those biographers treat of the works of Raphael and Correggio with as much importance as commentators speak of Horace or Virgil; and indulging themselves in the inflated style of their language, they talk of pictures as works almost of a divinity. [69]

I quote from one important psychoanalytic study of art: "The belief in the artist's magical power, and at the same time also the belief in the forbidden nature of his activity, is deeply rooted in the mind of man. For it was precisely those demigods of myth who had been rebellious and punished — the imprisoned Daedalus, the lame Wieland, the crippled Haephestus, and their great ancestor, the enchained Prometheus — whose heritage early biographers awarded to the artists." Ernst Kris, *Psychoanalytic Explorations in Art* (New York, 1952), p. 78.

68. *Gentleman's Magazine*, V (May 1735), 248. The same author complains (237) of the mystifications of authorities who attempt to give to "those that hear them so *abstruse an Idea* of the Art, that they dare not trust their own Eyes afterwards."

69. *Anecdotes of Painting*, 4th ed. (1786), I, i–ii.

WALTER J. HIPPLE, JR.

# Philosophical Language and the Theory of Beauty in the Eighteenth Century

PHILOSOPHERS have always, or at any rate often, divided the world of philosophic discourse into three provinces: the true, the good, and the beautiful. But it has been the fate of the third of these, the province of beauty, to receive both less, and less systematic, attention than is devoted to the truth of things or the nature of the good. Few thinkers until modern times have examined in any detail the nature of beauty. Indeed, one may say that the stream of aesthetic theory begins only in the eighteenth century, the theories of earlier ages being not part of a continuing discussion but only isolated and incomplete conjectures, usually very much subordinate to some more compelling interest in the theoretical or practical sciences. Beginning, then, with Addison and Hutcheson in England, and a little later with Baumgarten in Germany, the stream of aesthetic theory has never flowed very wide – nor, some would add, very deep. The shelves of books on beauty and taste are impoverished in comparison with those groaning under inquiries into the truth of nature and the nature of truth, or with examens of virtue and the good. One has the impression, too, that of these writers on beauty, some are only devising rationalizations for a taste which they wish to promote or an artistic practice which they wish to defend, while others, after their analyses of causality or justice, are only completing the symmetry of their thought by a perfunctory excursion into the province of aesthetics. And so the geography of that province remains largely uncharted; it is more a wilderness than a garden.

This neglect of aesthetic theory, both in common life and in the life of speculation, is altogether natural. The imperative demand of life is for guidance in action. A stranger and afraid in a world he never made, man looks less for the beauty of sunset than for the light of noonday. To understand the forces within and without him, to adjust to circumstances or make circumstances adjust to him, to conquer nature and avoid being conquered by his fellows, to transform the primitive urges of his soul into moral energies: these are first problems of life. The beauty of a coreopsis demands examination less urgently than do the laws of economics; and even the theory of relativity is more pressing than an account of mountain gloom and mountain glory.

In recent years, however, philosophers of the analytic sect have ceased to deplore the neglect of aesthetic theory, and have asserted with increasing vehemence that aesthetics in its traditional forms is only a pseudoscience, its principles either patent falsehoods or vacuous generalities, its practitioners more muddleheaded even than metaphysicians. Professor J. A. Passmore, in an utterance typical of his school, declares that

even if there are things which are worth saying about "literature" . . . and other things which are worth saying about music, about architecture, and so on, it still does not follow that there is such a thing as aesthetics, in distinction from literary theory, musical theory, etc.; it seems to me possible at least that the dullness of aesthetics arises from the attempt to construct a subject where there isn't one. . . . There is something suspect ("phony") about beauty.[1]

The remedy, he suggests, is "an intensive special study of the separate arts, carried out with no undue respect for anyone's 'aesthetic experiences,' but much respect for the real differences between the works of art themselves." [2] And Morris Weitz — to choose an example from the American branch of the school — declares that the main concern of aesthetics is the formulation of a definition of art, a definition grounded upon the essential properties of art. But he sets up this objective only to topple it: his *real* purpose is "to show that theory — in the requisite classical sense — is *never* forthcoming in aesthetics," [3] that "aesthetic theory is a logically vain attempt to define what cannot be defined, to state the necessary and sufficient properties of that which has no necessary and sufficient properties, to conceive the concept of art as closed when its very use reveals and demands its openness."[4]

It is odd that aestheticians, special pleaders or dabblers though many of them are, have never discovered that their problem is only a pseudo-problem. Not odd at all! the reply may come; metaphysicians have for millennia been grappling with pseudoproblems! Yes; but theology has demanded that philosophers produce suitable metaphysical and ethical rationalizations — hence the multiplication of puzzles about vacuum and plenum and action at a distance, about self-caused causes, about freedom of the will, and the like. There has been no such overmastering demand, however, for aesthetic theories; and it *is* odd that aestheticians should have voluntarily wandered into the mazes which have bewildered them, and which can be laid open only with the powerful tools newly devised by analytic philosophy. It it odd, too, that "beauty" and "beautiful" — so deeply ingrained in our talk about the aesthetic aspects of experience — should be terms quite hollow and futile.

I propose here to lay down some general conditions for a theory of beauty, to exhibit the extent to which some speculations of eighteenth-century British aestheticians met these conditions — and to suggest at the same time that such theorizing is neither false nor vacuous.

A theory of beauty cannot, in the first place, be confined to works of art, nor take the beauty of art as logically prior to that of nature. For not all beauty, nor most beauty, nor even the most striking beauties, are to be found in art. Even in the lives of the most sophisticated, the beauties of art are less pervasive than those of nature. And, I would add, less intense as well. None of the complicated effects of pictorial art yields a delight so spontaneous and gratifying as a sunset. He who finds Milton more sublime than mountains, or a statue more beautiful than a woman, requires psychotherapy rather than aesthetic theory. It

1. "The Dreariness of Aesthetics" in *Aesthetics and Language*, ed. William Elton (Oxford, 1954), pp. 49–50.

2. *Ibid.*, p. 55. D. H. Monro, in reviewing a book of mine on eighteenth-century aesthetic theories, is driven "to the trite conclusion that writers on aesthetics, in the eighteenth as in other centuries, are illuminating when they discuss the details of some particular art (heroic poetry or landscape gardening) but either vacuous or patently inaccurate when they frame general theories about 'the Beautiful'" (*Mind*, LXVIII [July 1959], 419).

3. "The Role of Theory in Aesthetics" in *Philosophy Looks at the Arts*, ed. Joseph Margolis (New York, 1962), p. 49. Weitz's essay is reprinted from the *Journal of Aesthetics and Art Criticism*, XV (September 1956), 27–35.

4. *Ibid.*, 52.

is of course true that the work of art is more *purely* aesthetic; the response it evokes is less mixed with practical anxieties and gratifications. I need not take cover from the bombs bursting in air when they burst only in a song. I can contemplate the picturesque disorder of the painted farmyard without feeling that it ought to be set right, and without the odor which might destroy my relish for the actual scene. It is true also that the object of art is more unified and coherently ordered than are most natural things. And in some arts devices are employed which are far more elaborate than their natural counterparts. The figures and rhythms of language enhance the beauty or sublimity of the thought and passion expressed; music creates an aesthetic province vastly more extensive than that of natural sounds, and one more independent of visual accompaniments.

But after all these concessions are made, it seems to me still true that the aesthetic gratifications of nature are more powerful than those of art. The storm of *Typhoon*, though created in words of matchless art, is still less thrilling aesthetically than such a storm itself. For although art may be purer and more orderly, and may employ devices not found in nature, nature is yet incomparably more vivid. The country walk, the battle, the love affair of actual experience are more moving (aesthetically as well as practically) than their counterparts in art; so too is the cardinal on my windowsill or the face glimpsed in a crowd.

Aesthetic value is found chiefly, and in its more fundamental forms, in nature. A corollary to this proposition is that beauty and other aesthetic modes should not be defined in terms of the circumscribed character of art. Even the most artful of aestheticians is likely to grant, in a footnote, that prospects as well as poems may be beautiful; and he will accordingly devise some extension of his terms so that we may legitimately say what is obviously true.[5] But I desire more than this: the primary meanings of the aesthetic vocabulary should be available for the bulk of aesthetic experience and pertain directly to nature.

But there is a further and independent point. A just philosophical method in aesthetics will be analytical; it will seek to resolve aesthetic objects into their constituent elements and relations. Now since nature is simpler than art, it is logically as well as chronologically prior to art. The beauty of art may comprise all the elements to be found in natural beauty and others besides — imitation, and the projection into the work of powers of the artist's mind; and just for this reason, aesthetic theory should deal first with natural beauty. Aesthetics is not the criticism of art, although it provides a part of the basis for such criticism. The corollary follows again that beauty and other aesthetic modes should not be defined in terms of art. To define beauty as "the characteristic excellence of a work of art" is to employ complex and derivative phenomena as the *definiens* of a fundamental term. It is as if, in dynamics, one were to define "force" in terms of the operation of internal combustion engines. This point stands even if my first generalization be denied; deny, if you will, that most aesthetic experience is to be found in nature — it would still be a point of procedure that the aesthetic modes should be analyzed in terms of simple and elementary, and therefore in terms of natural, phenomena.

The British aestheticians of the eighteenth century, from Addison at the beginning of the tradition to Stewart at the close, were never in any doubt about this point. "The works of nature more pleasant to the imagination than those of art," reads the summary head of Addison's fourth paper on "The Pleasures of the Imagination";[6] and his discussion moves from the aesthetic effects of natural things to those of architecture (which creates rather than imitates) to those afforded by the representative arts. Even the writers of the picturesque school find, in the picturesque, beauties originally natural and reflected back upon nature from the mirror of art. And such a theorist as Lord Kames, who has in view chiefly the problems of artistic, and especially literary, criticism, actually treats first the general causes of aesthetic experience, from which he advances by stages into the realms of art. The artistic effects which he analyzes are explained in terms of general aesthetic principles operating under the "boundary conditions" of the various artistic species; *Elements of Criticism* is thus a work of *philosophical* criticism, a treatise on aesthetics.

Most writers of the current analytic school who discuss aesthetic topics, however, make the nature of art, or of arts, or of works of art, their central inquiry, and thereby tacitly deny that natural phenomena

5. Professor Passmore accordingly acknowledges that "perhaps beauty has a stricter sense in the description of landscape than in any other context and could be reserved as a description of the 'natural'" ("Dreariness," 51n). Such a view, however, both in its radical distinction of each art from every other and of all the arts from nature, and in its restriction of "beauty" to nature or to the still narrower province of landscape, is so arbitrary as to be implausible.

6. *Spectator*, 414.

are important for aesthetics. Granted, moreover, the restriction to art, and the emphasis upon the distinctiveness of different arts, it at once follows that such aesthetic modes as beauty, which cut across these demarcations, will be neglected or condemned. But within the broad orthodoxy of the analytical method, many variant positions are of course possible; and it is easy to discover writers in this new tradition who are explicitly aware that aesthetic experience is not restricted to art. J. O. Urmson, for instance, writes that

it seems obvious that we also derive aesthetic satisfaction from artifacts that are not primarily works of art, from scenery, from natural objects and even from formal logic; it is at least reasonable also to allow an aesthetic satisfaction to the connoisseur of wines and to the gourmet. . . . We may take it, then, that we are not exclusively concerned with the philosophy of art, and that whatever the criteria of the aesthetic may be they cannot be found by trying to delimit a special class of objects.[7]

But although aesthetics does not confine itself to artificial phenomena, neither does it embrace (as the etymology of the name might suggest) all perception or even all pleasurable perception. Muscular exercise may be enjoyable, but it is not often aesthetic; the flavor of strawberries is delightful, but it is not beautiful. Whether one adopts an objective or a subjective view of beauty, it is true that beauty is objective in a sense in which the flavor of strawberries and the enjoyments of soccer are not. Whatever one's theory about beauty, one perceives the beauty as in the object. The pleasureful flavor of strawberries is in my mouth, whereas the beauty of a sunset is not in my eye but in the sky. The gratification of exercise is in me, but the beauty of a nocturne is in the music. This objective character of beauty may be an illusion; beauty, and the world entire, may be only my idea. But the point is that beauty always *seems* to be in the object, just as the secondary properties of matter seem to be objective.

This objective character of beauty is inseparably connected with another property: that beauty is originally confined to phenomena of eye and ear. For in these two senses there is no consciousness of organic sensation, and we have the illusion of being in direct contact with the object perceived. With touch and taste and smell we are too conscious of the local sensation, we feel too clearly that the pleasure is in the organs of sense, for the objectification of aesthetic feeling to occur. Peach Melba may be beautiful, but it is the color which is seen, not the flavor which is tasted, that makes it so. It is an error to say, as Urmson does, that "if I value the rose aesthetically the most obviously relevant grounds will be the way it looks . . . and the way it smells." [8] Most people sensitive to language would find it odd to call a fragrance "beautiful" (though it might be said to be "sweet," "delightful," even "lovely"); and this reluctance to call odors, flavors, and purely tactile sensations "beautiful" witnesses to a distinction in the kinds of feeling involved. If any disinterested and nonintellectual response is to be called aesthetic, then no doubt my appreciation of the rose's odor is an aesthetic experience. But as Socrates remarked, in our terminology as in carving a chicken, we should cut at the joints; and there is a very conspicuous joint separating the pleasurable responses of the lower senses from those of sight and hearing.[9] The pleasing odor of the rose becomes aesthetic only by association with the visual beauty of the flower.

All of the sensations of the lower senses, as also muscular feeling and other internal sensations, though not directly aesthetic can become so indirectly and by association. Grant, for instance, that a piece of polished wood affords more pleasure to the touch than one rough and jagged with splinters. This pleasure is not in itself aesthetic; but the visual appearance of the polished wood may acquire an aesthetic value. For the appearance is a sign of the potential pleasure to the touch, yet, being visual, is perceived as a trait of the object and not as an organic pleasure. Again, the polish of the wood may be construed as a sign of intention and of the exertion upon it of human effort; and both perception of the intention and recognition of the skill afford pleasure which, through association with the visual appearance, becomes aesthetic. Even if the wood had been scoured smooth by wind and sand, the pleasure from design and skill

7. "What Makes a Situation Aesthetic?" in *Philosophy Looks at the Arts*, p. 14. Urmson's essay is reprinted from *Proceedings of the Aristotelian Society*, Supplementary Volume, XXXI (1957), 75–92. I do not agree that experiences of the lower senses are aesthetic, except by association with visual or auditory experiences.

8. Urmson, "Aesthetic?," p. 23.

9. I recall encountering at the New Bauhaus an "odor symphony" consisting of a flaring horn into which one poked one's head while a fan wafted upwards combinations of fragrances selected by playing a "keyboard," and also a "feely" or board on which were mounted substances of various textures — woolly, sandy, scratchy, slick — over which one was to draw a hand, presumably exhaling a sigh of voluptuous satisfaction. Surely such objects, if aesthetic at all, are not beautiful but ridiculous. It is true that an artful dinner may have aesthetic character, but only (I should think) because the visual component of the experience is not negligible.

would remain, for we would consider that nature had worked as man would have done; the surprise might even heighten our appreciation.

The British aestheticians were agreed that the original objects of intellectual taste — aesthetic objects — are visual or audible. Addison had declared that "The pleasures of the imagination arise originally from sight," and he argued that the delights of other senses (including hearing) only enhance the visual beauties with which they are conjoined.[10] Gerard and Lord Kames distinguish a sense of harmony which, like the visual sense of beauty, provides original aesthetic pleasures; but the lower senses are not, unless by association, aesthetic. Stewart explains in detail how "beauty" radiates from an original delight in colors to other visual qualities, to phenomena of hearing, to moral and intellectual traits. Alison, who finds all beauty to consist in the expression of mind, of course finds mind expressed in visual and audible phenomena but not in the phenomena of the other senses. In one way or another, all the writers of this tradition concur in the judgment that only objects of sight, or of sight and hearing, are originally aesthetic.

I have intended to establish, incidentally to explaining the apparently objective character of beauty, that beauty in its various modes is a category narrower than perception or pleasurable perception. It must be noted too that beauty is also wider than perception — that is, that many things which are not perceptions are beautiful. We speak, for instance, of beautiful manners. And we apply such epithets also to the deeper springs of character. Unflinching courage, profundity of vision are sublime; humanity, modesty are beautiful. Marcus Aurelius and St. Francis, Joan of Arc and Abraham Lincoln are not only moral exemplars but shining objects of aesthetic value. Even things purely and abstractly rational may have aesthetic value; we admire the cogency of a proof, and the mathematician speaks of an "elegant" demonstration, the physicist of a "beautiful" experiment. To discover what is common to all these beautiful things — to colors, forms, and textures, to manners and morals, to the constructions of logic — this is a problem well fitted to baffle the ingenuity of philosophers.

But to state the problem just this way may be misleading, and many have in fact been misled. For there need not be some common essence of beauty pervading fuschias and frescoes, mathematics and magnanimity. A common name need not imply a common character. But the assumption that it does so has underlain most aesthetic systems. " 'Beautiful,' "

Diderot declared, "is a term which we apply to an infinity of things. But whatever differences there may be among these things, it is certain either that we make a false application of the term 'beautiful,' or that there is in all these things one quality which the term 'beautiful' signifies."[11] Although Diderot's statement is unusually explicit, the view which it presents is typical. But this assumption invariably leads to the erection of some one mode of beauty as the archetype, other modes being left outside the pale or else brought within only after some strange transmogrification. Every theory based on the principle that there is one beauty to be found in all things rightly called beautiful is either partial or is implausibly reductionist.

Correction of this philosophic error was one of the achievements of the eighteenth century; and a theory of language expounded first by Richard Payne Knight and then more fully by Dugald Stewart goes between the horns of the dilemma. I shall quote Stewart's account of the transitive meaning of terms:

I shall begin with supposing that the letters A, B, C, D, E, denote a series of objects; that A possesses some one quality in common with B; B a quality in common with C . . . [etc.]; — while, at the same time, no quality can be found which belongs in common to any *three* objects in the series. Is it not conceivable, that the affinity between A and B may produce a transference of the name of the first to the second; and that, in consequence of the other affinities which connect the remaining objects together, the same name may pass in succession from B to C; from C to D; and from D to E? In this manner, a common appellation will arise between A and E, although the two objects may, in their nature and properties, be so widely distant from each other, that no stretch of imagination can conceive how the thoughts were led from the former to the latter.[12]

This principle would convert the problem of aesthetics from that of finding a common essence among the things denoted by an aesthetic term to that of discovering the history of the term. Not that it would make aesthetics a branch of philology! For although one would be interested to study the actual uses of terms like "beauty," as history and lexicography have preserved them, one would soon discover both that the most im-

10. Summary head of the first paper on "The Pleasures of the Imagination," *Spectator*, 411. The observation about the pleasures of the other senses occurs at the end of the second paper (June 23, 1712).

11. "Beau," *Encyclopédie, Oeuvres*, XII (Paris, 1821), 460.

12. "On the Beautiful" in *Philosophical Essays* in *Works*, ed. Sir William Hamilton (Edinburgh, 1877), V, 195–96.

portant parts of the historical record are generally lost; and also that, even if the record were fully preserved, we would still need to discover the reasons for the transitions. Philology does not replace philosophy; it has only directed us to look not for one beauty but for a series of beauties, each related to some of the others, though not to all, yet all bearing the name which radiated from the more primitive members of the cluster. Reconstruction of the process of radiation is apt to be more an exercise in conjectural psychology than an actual historical inquiry.

Stewart developed this principle of transitive meanings as a major device of philosophical analysis, and John Stuart Mill borrowed it from him. But it was Payne Knight who first enunciated the principle; and Knight's major work in aesthetic theory exhibits the use he made of it. "The word Beauty," he observes, "is a general term of approbation . . . applied indiscriminately to almost every thing that is pleasing, either to the sense, the imagination, or the understanding; whatever the nature of it be, whether a material substance, a moral excellence, or an intellectual theorem." All of these applications of the term are, moreover, literal, notwithstanding that "all epithets, employed to distinguish qualities perceivable only by intellect, were originally applied to objects of sense . . . and are therefore applied *transitively*, though not always *figuratively*, to objects of intellect or imagination." Thus, "the word Beauty entirely changes its meaning . . . accordingly as it is applied to objects of the senses, the imagination, or the understanding; for, though these faculties are so mixed and compounded in their operations . . . that it is extremely difficult to discriminate them accurately; yet the pleasures of each, though mixed in their effects, are utterly distinct in their causes." [13] The three parts of the *Analytical Inquiry into the Principles of Taste* manifest this theory: devoted to sensation, to the association of ideas, and to the passions, these divisions are intended to disentangle the various causal strands in the fabric of beauty and to explain the transitions from one sense of the term to another. Consider Knight's doctrine of the picturesque. There is a picturesque dependent on the eye alone, consisting of "harmonious, but yet brilliant and contrasted combinations of light, shade, and colour; blended, but not confused; and broken, but not cut, into masses . . . intricacy of parts and variety of tint and surface." [14] This sensuous picturesque is indeed the primal beauty, the beauty of purely visual values. There is also, however, an imaginative picturesque involving association with the art of painting; picturesque objects "recall to mind the imitations, which skill, taste, and genius have produced; and these again recall to the mind the objects themselves, and show them through an improved medium — that of the feeling and discernment of a great artist." [15] It is of course this picturesque of the imagination which has supplied the name, since the art of painting (as it develops from Classic to Baroque, from the clear and linear to the painterly and unclear) has cultivated our sensibility to the purely visual values. The term "beautiful," in turn, radiates to those imaginative and intellectual properties which come to constitute the greater part of beauty; and the picturesque (which is a sensuous beauty) can thus stand in contrast with what is in a broader sense beautiful. A flayed beef, a ragged beggar, a rutted lane are not "beautiful," since all are offensive or inconvenient or suggestive of misery; but they are all "picturesque." The theory of transitive meanings, conjoined with Knight's faculty psychology, thus serves to explicate the subtle but important distinction between beautiful and picturesque.

But even before the notion of transitive meanings was formulated by Knight, it was implicitly employed by other theorists. Alexander Gerard, for instance, opens his discussion "Of the Sense or Taste of Beauty" by observing that "Beautiful objects are of different kinds, and produce pleasure by means of different principles of human nature." [16] He is thus at once freed from the necessity of finding a common essence in beautiful things, as Hutcheson had done in attempting to make uniformity in variety the one principle of beauty. "There is perhaps no term used in a looser sense than *beauty*, which is applied to almost every thing that pleases us," writes Gerard. "Though this usage is doubtless too indefinite, we may, without a faulty deviation from precision, apply this epithet to every pleasure which is conveyed by the eye, and which has not got a proper and peculiar name" — such as "sublimity," for example.[17] Gerard is conscious, moreover, that he should explain *why* one term can include pleasures which operate by different principles: why call a splendid color, an intricately composed figure, a well-adapted mechanism, a kind face, all *beautiful*? A moral virtue, for instance, would never be called "beautiful" if it did not manifest itself in the face, where it modifies the various

13. *An Analytical Inquiry into the Principles of Taste*, 3rd ed. (London, 1806), pp. 9, 11, 12–13.
14. *Ibid.*, p. 68.
15. *Ibid.*, pp. 152–53.
16. *An Essay on Taste*, ed. Walter J. Hipple, Jr. (Gainesville, Florida, 1963), p. 29.
17. *Ibid.*, p. 43.

visual beauties; we derive pleasure from the virtue, its appearance in the countenance blends inextricably with other beauties, and the term "beautiful" comes to be applied to a face that reveals conspicuous kindness or humanity. From the expression of the quality in the face, the term is further transferred to the quality itself, and we say that kindness is a beautiful trait of character.

Or again, why is a mathematical demonstration beautiful? It would not be, I suppose, if it did not have something in common with some visual property, or at least with some third entity which has something in common with a visual property. Let us take for granted that the term "beauty" is already rightly applied to visual proportions which possess a pleasing unity in variety. But there are also proportions which, although not especially pleasing for *this* reason, are the result of useful adaptations to some end that is desirable. We regard the means with pleasure because the end is pleasing; but the means involve certain figures and proportions, and we already have a name for pleasing figures and proportions. Thus, forms which express utility come to be so far beautiful. One conspicuous kind of utility is efficient design, in which each part plays its role with the greatest economy. But what is praised when a demonstration is called "elegant" is just this: an elegant proof is economical, involves a minimum number of steps and principles. Here is a resemblance between the relation of parts and whole in an intellectual object and the relation of parts and whole in a visual object — and we are already calling the visual object "beautiful" because of that very relation. Clearly, the aesthetic term will be extended to the intellectual instance. Sometimes, of course, a proof is "elegant" not because of economy but because of a resemblance to or symmetry with some other proof — but in this case another transition is obvious.

So with other enlargements of aesthetic terms. Gerard is neither so explicit nor so detailed as I have been; his attention is centered upon other aspects of the problem of beauty. But neither have I "read into" Gerard a kind of analysis which belongs only to later writers. He particularly notices some of these meanings of "beauty," and he is quite clear that "beauties" are either visual or are related to visual properties by some species of association. What Gerard does not do — what I have done for him in my examples — is to discover *chains* of transition or radiation. Not having formulated the principle of transitive meanings, Gerard does not recognize that C may be described by the same epithet as A not because there is a direct connection between C and A but because B serves as intermediate link. *This* discovery was reserved for Stewart, acting on a clue from Knight; and this discovery permits philosophical analysis of terms like "beauty" to be more complex, more subtle — and more plausible.

It would not be difficult to show that Hume too was quite aware of transitive meanings. Indeed, his categorizing beauty as a mode (not a simple quality) reflects his awareness that beauty is a set of related qualities — related, of course, by associations near or remote through which the same name comes to be applied to the entire set. But it is surely now supererogatory to show further that the error which the analytic philosophers sometimes term "essentialism" — supposing that a term like "beauty" is the name of some essence common to all beautiful things — was exploded two centuries ago, and moreover that some of the very devices of linguistic analysis now current were developed and applied by the British aestheticians.

Another conspicuous feature of the theories of the eighteenth-century aestheticians is their insistence upon a standard of taste. Although recognizing that beauty is not a simple quality, and in any case not a quality of objects, but instead a set of related reactions of the mind, they were one and all prepared to offer "reasons" for aesthetic judgments. Hogarth's title for his essay in aesthetic theory was *The Analysis of Beauty, Written with a View of Fixing the Fluctuating Ideas of Taste*; and his purpose was typical. The more sophisticated of these men were quite aware that aesthetic preferences are determined by culture, by one's place in the various subgroups of that culture, by individual temperament and experience; none would have been confounded to discover that an Australian blackfellow does not appreciate a picturesque view of a Dutch kitchen or that an American college student does not like Homer. For beauty is an emotion (though not *one* emotion) and the man who doesn't feel it when I feel it is not mistaken in the sense that he would be mistaken in thinking that Vermeer was Flemish or that Homer was one person. Still, all the British aestheticians recognized that there is a "standard of taste," and that aesthetic judgments can be erroneous, that taste may be good or bad, correct or incorrect. A man who feels the sentiment of beauty knows that he feels it and cannot easily be mistaken. But error can still enter in two ways. First, since the subordinate varieties of aesthetic feeling are not always sharply different, the man who is unaccustomed to distinguish these feelings accurately may misclassify his feeling. He is not likely to mistake beauty for sensory pleasure or for moral sentiment, but he may fail to perceive the differences between his responses to the Rhone glacier, a cherry orchard in bloom, and a rutted sand road under live-oak trees hung with Spanish moss. Instead of calling one sublime, one beautiful, and one picturesque, he may call them all "beautiful," the inadequacy of his terminology determining the poverty and imprecision of his response. Indeed, one of the great contributions of the eighteenth-century aestheticians was the distinction of different aesthetic modes.[18] It may be argued that they stopped too soon, with too few categories distinguished; but one would also wish to avoid the contrary extreme of making up a new category for each object, as if there were only differences and no resemblances. This, at any rate, is the first source of error: failure to discriminate feelings that are partly resemblant. But the second kind of error is both more frequent and more philosophical: it is to make an erroneous guess about the causes of the feelings.

For this is the principal province of aesthetic theory: to discover the causes of aesthetic emotion and the mechanisms through which these causes act. It is, moreover, through such causal analysis that the standard of taste is established. Everyone really believes in a standard of taste; and the skeptic has no sooner declared *De gustibus non est disputandum* than he discovers himself inwardly, and very probably overtly, condemning another's taste as insensitive, immature, or perverted. I do not think that a standard can be established by inductive arguments which generalize directly from widely admired works of art or widely appreciated objects in nature. For in truth there are no works of art or scenes of nature that are approved by more than a fraction of humanity. Homer no longer enthralls most readers even on that one continent where he once was popular; our taste for mountain scenery is not shared by the inhabitants of the Andes. The test of consensus always fails, whether applied to art or to nature, for there never is a consensus. Even if there were, and we could list the great works of art and the striking effects of nature which are admired always and everywhere, it would be a hopeless task to elicit from them the more general principles of taste. One might equally well expect to determine the laws of motion by observing a swarm of bees. The laws are presumably always present, but they are not easily to be elicited by direct induction. Rather, there must be simplifying assumptions, hypotheses and deductions from hypotheses, and some consilience between the deduced results and the imperfect empirical generalizations.

Unfortunately, the concepts and the deductive chains are not so clear in aesthetics as in dynamics; nor are the empirical phenomena, even in the simplest cases, so easily made conformable to the theoretical results. But what progress can be made will be made this way; and it is in this way that the correctness of aesthetic judgment will best be determined. That is, those traits of things which are fitted to affect men, in the absence of obstructing causes, will be isolated; factors universally operative will be distinguished from those that affect only people of a particular culture, sex, age, epoch, or profession; and these in turn from the influences which affect only individuals. The standard of taste is, in the last analysis, the set of preferences which would result from the more general factors when the influence of the less general is reduced.

As the eighteenth century advanced, efforts to ground a standard of taste on the consensus of ages and nations were replaced by reasonings drawn from general principles of human nature. The shift can be seen in miniature in Johnson's Preface to Shakespeare, where the initial argument from consensus ("no other test can be applied than length of duration and continuance of esteem") gives way to the principle that "Nothing can please many and please long, but just representations of general nature." And in more philosophical writers like Gerard,[19] these psychological and causal principles are far more fully elaborated. A strong contrast emerges here between the British aestheticians of the eighteenth century and those of the twentieth: for our contemporaries of the analytic school do not consider causal analysis part of the province of philosophy. The philosopher, it will be held, ought to investigate what it is to make a causal analysis — but actually making it is the business of the physicist or the economist or —. Who (we may ask) *ought* to be making causal analyses of aesthetic reactions? Not critics, surely, for they are usually much too concerned with particulars, and much too unfamiliar with both psychology and philosophical method. Not sociologists and anthropologists, for they are generally too little conversant with the arts, and too little familiar with aesthetic theory, to make accurate distinctions or penetrating analyses. Not experimental psychologists, for their chief service (until

18. I have given a succinct account of sources and causes of these distinctions in my introduction to Gerard's *Essay on Taste*, pp. xii–xiv, and shall not repeat it here.

19. Gerard's argument on the standard of taste, added as Part IV to the third edition (1780) of his *Essay on Taste*, it is the most acute of the century in its perception of the logic of the problem.

now, at least) is to restrain the wilder guesses of philosophers who venture imprudently into physiological hypotheses. Who, then? The British aestheticians of the eighteenth century (as I see it) were right: introspective psychology is a field in which the philosopher is better trained than anyone else, and aesthetics is a branch of introspective psychology. The function of the philosophical aesthetician is not a merely *critical* role of clarifying the "logic" of his subject; his is the task of exploration and discovery as well. The *logical* examination of aesthetic terms and judgments depends upon the *psychological* investigation of aesthetic response.

Let me recapitulate the general points which I have made about the character of any just aesthetic theory. Such a theory will be concerned originally and primarily with natural beauty, which is both logically prior to the beauty of art and more important in the economy of life. The method will be analytical, endeavoring to discover the least elements and relations to which there is aesthetic response, and then synthetical, attempting to account for more complex problems in terms of combinations of such elements and relations. Three problems will be addressed: to distinguish the various aesthetic emotions, to discover the properties in things which evoke them, and to determine the causal mechanisms. It will not be supposed that there is some common character in all the things to which such a name as "beauty" is rightly applied. And the aesthetician will recognize his responsibility to distinguish the different causes and levels of aesthetic response, and thereby to form and regulate taste.

The British aestheticians, in different fashions and in varying degrees, theorized in accordance with these principles; and these are the virtues which adorn that tradition. Current philosophical concern with analysis of philosophical language justifies especial stress upon the achievement of the British aestheticians in tracing the transitive meanings of aesthetic terms. This achievement was of course possible only because they discovered much of the psychology of aesthetic response; for it is only the tracing of the roots of aesthetic feeling which permits explication of the ramifications of aesthetic language. For a final illustration of this method, a method both logical and psychological, I shall take the problem of sublimity. This aesthetic mode has the advantage, for purposes of illustration, of being both more circumscribed and more unified than beauty, whether "beauty" be taken in the comprehensive sense of serious positive aesthetic value (in which case sublimity is a species of it) or in the narrow sense of a particular aesthetic mode which contrasts with sublimity.[20]

There is general agreement about the things to which the term "sublime" should be applied. In natural scenery, the Alps; the ocean, especially in a storm; the heavens with a multitude of stars. In human nature, the heroism of Alexander, or the scientific genius of Newton. In letters, the Bible's "Let there be light, and there was light," or Corneille's "Qu'il mourut," or *Paradise Lost* almost anywhere; in painting, the Sistine ceiling; in architecture, a Gothic cathedral; in music, Beethoven's last symphony, or the close of the *Götterdämmerung*. (My list is deliberately hackneyed, since I aim to clarify sublimity, not to achieve it.) A fair measure of agreement obtains also about the emotion these things evoke. The first response to a sublime object is a sense of being dwarfed and intimidated; one is awed, astonished, overwhelmed; Burke's celebrated phrase, "tranquillity tinged with terror," though flamboyant, is not inaccurate. But the mind rebounds, successfully contemplating the sublime object, and feels, as Longinus originally put it, "a glorying and sense of inward greatness."

The emotions produced by these different classes of sublime objects, though somewhat resemblant, are yet quite various; and we must ask how the term "sublime," originally applicable to some one of these phenomena, comes to be progressively applied to the rest. We must ask, too, how far the common term, by associating more closely the phenomena it names, reacts upon them to make the evoked emotions more similar.

In its primitive sense, the word "sublime" is applicable to height. Altitude evokes the typical sublime emotion: ascent, since it opposes gravity, requires effort and struggle; great and steep ascent is daunting, but conceived as surmounted, exhilarating. Now height is so inseparably associated with depth that depth shares this original sublimity; and one of the most characteristic features of sublime emotion has its origin in depth. For depths are terrifying, and fear — if only suggested and not an actual and humiliating passion — is often conspicuous in the thrill of sublimity. Granted that height is sublime, moreover, horizontal extent becomes so, if only from the obvious association that a great height commands a wide prospect.

By these easy transitions, all spatial extension has become susceptible of sublimity, although less markedly so in the horizontal dimension than in

20. For the most part I follow Stewart, "On the Sublime" in *Philosophical Essays* in *Works*, V. But I have woven in without distinction observations of other writers and conjectures of my own.

the vertical. But extent of time, both the remoteness of the past and the distance of futurity, is also sublime. It seems to me unlikely that this transition of the term occurs through the connection of time with space in motion. But the action of the mind in traversing time is very like its action in traversing space, and this resemblance of feeling is reflected in the regular use of spatial terms and diagrams to represent time. In a very similar way, vastness of quantity and greatness of number become sublime.

Another extension of the term "sublime" radiates from the original sublimity of height in a different direction. Height is associated with power, partly because power is required to attain a height; partly because one most easily exerts power from above, whether subduing an enemy or packing a steamer trunk; partly because the great astronomical and meteorological agents which govern our lives are above us. For these reasons, supernatural powers are generally conceived as above us; this superiority is to a primitive mind quite literal, and remains indelible in metaphors in the language of the most sophisticated, as the very word "superiority" sufficiently displays. All the moral and intellectual perfections of supernatural powers are accordingly conceived as above us, and are duly called "sublime." Of course, other causes cooperate in leading us to call such traits sublime; in our own growth from infancy, increasing height is accompanied by increasing intelligence and perhaps by increasing virtue; and one may even wonder whether mental qualities would be sublime if our heads chanced not to be on top. The notions of mental excellence, as of power, success, and glory, are unavoidably conceived as the high reward of upward struggle: *Ad astra per aspera*. The analogy of the progress of life with the revolutions above us of the sun and stars is so obvious that no people has failed to remark it; and it provides a further connection between the physical and the mental applications of sublimity: "As the heavens are high above the earth," says Jehovah, "so are my thoughts above your thoughts, and my ways above your ways."

The sublimity of sound may depend upon several connections with these other sublimities. An obvious and universal instance of sublime sound is thunder, from which the very word "astonishment" is derived; thunder is terrifying and it comes from above, directly associated with conspicuous visual displays of natural or supernatural power. The roar of wind likewise; and the crashing of breakers is so closely connected with the wind by resemblance and causation that the feeling and the name would naturally extend over it too. The voices of animals, and the inarticulate human voice, may be sublime if loud — or even when soft, if the sign of menace. The significance of the metaphor "to raise one's voice," as in anger, is not lost upon us.

These transitions and extensions do not occur, it is clear, in a simple linear pattern, or even as a simple branching tree, but as a complicated web of intertwining reinforcements. I have not attempted to do more in this illustration than to suggest the way the pattern forms. A term accompanies the association of ideas and feelings along links formed by resemblances and causal connections. Indeed, once the word is established as the name of a cluster of phenomena, the word itself becomes a powerful associating link, cements the bonds between the phenomena, and unifies the feelings to which they give rise. Any one of the phenomena thus acquires the power of evoking a feeling to the formation of which all the others have contributed.

Contemporary philosophical analysis has directed our attention particularly to this aspect of the work of the British aestheticians; but exploration of the transitive meanings of terms was only one virtue of an aesthetic method literal, empirical, atomistic, psychological. It is because these eighteenth-century writers explored as far as they did the possibilities of such a method that they are not only the object of a scholarly and historical interest but remain real and vital contributors to our own thought on matters aesthetic.

# Hume's "Of Criticism"

DAVID HUME never wrote a book entitled "Of Criticism." Most moderns associate him with philosophy and some few with history, yet the leading statement of his brief autobiography runs, "I . . . was seized very early with a passion for literature, which has been the ruling passion of my life and the great source of my enjoyments." Granting the all-embracing connotations of "literature" in the Age of Enlightenment, we cannot reduce this supreme man of letters to the mere philosopher and historian. During his last illness, at the age of sixty-five, he was reading three books just off the press and commenting on them: Gibbon's *Decline and Fall of the Roman Empire*, Adam Smith's *Wealth of Nations*, and George Campbell's *Philosophy of Rhetoric*. The scope of his mind included all aspects of the "science of man" which, he maintained, is the only solid foundation for the other sciences.

Although Hume's contemporaries took considerable notice of his views on aesthetics and criticism, both in praise and in blame, later historians and students have seldom given full recognition to his accomplishments in those subjects. This is partly, though inadvertently, his own fault. When he published in 1739 the first two books of *A Treatise of Human Nature*: "Of the Understanding" and "of the Passions," he was, as the "Advertisement" stated, trying the taste of the public. "If I have the good fortune to meet with success," he observed, "I shall proceed to the examination of Morals, Politics, and Criticism; which will compleat this Treatise of Human Nature." He did not meet with success because the public was unprepared for a Newtonian revolution in philosophy; nevertheless, the comment in *My Own Life* that the *Treatise* "fell *dead-born from the press*" is an exaggeration. In 1740 he did bring out "Of Morals," which had already been in an advanced state of composition, but the projected fourth and fifth books never appeared and more than likely were never composed.

Hume's original intention in presenting *A Treatise of Human Nature: Being an Attempt to Introduce the Experimental Method of Reasoning into Moral Subjects* as "a compleat system of the sciences" founded on the "science of human nature" may have been thwarted by lack of public interest, but he did not capitulate. He proceeded to salvage what he could by turning into the more popular essay form both those books of the *Treatise* already published and those only projected. This piecemeal presentation has not made it easy for the student of Hume, especially respecting the promised "examination of . . . Politics, and Criticism."

Passing references in the *Treatise*, the *Enquiry concerning Human Understanding* (1748), and the *Enquiry concerning the Principles of Morals* (1751) provide the groundwork for the theoretical reconstruction of the missing "Of Politics." Yet the gist of what Hume had to say about "politics," that is, in eighteenth-century terminology, government, economics, commerce, and history, is to be found in certain of the *Essays Moral and Political* (1741, 1742, 1748) and, above all, in the *Political Discourses* (1752), together with a few essays of later years. The *History of England* (1754–1762) and the political comments scattered throughout his letters complete the practical, as distinct from the philosophical, treatment of "politics."

The same procedure has to be followed in the theoretical reconstruction of the missing "Of Criticism," but the task is rendered more difficult and complex because there is no work analogous to the *Political Discourses*. The nearest approach is *Four Dissertations* (1757), which contains "Of Tragedy" and "Of the Standard of Taste," his only essays entirely devoted to aesthetics and criticism. The difficulty of reconstruction is indicated by the relative paucity of writings on these subjects as contrasted with the profusion on his politics. Modern treatments consist of a single book, a few chapters and numerous passing references in other books, and a few articles. The book, though a valiant and praiseworthy effort, is neither comprehensive nor conclusive; and most of the other publications, restricted as they are to single essays by Hume, are vitiated because the writers have failed to study all of his works. Notable for their awareness of the whole Humean "science of man," however, are two unpublished doctoral dissertations.[1] What has yet to be achieved in a book certainly cannot be achieved in the present essay, which pretends to do no more than survey the field with the hope of inducing some qualified scholar to make a full study. No attempt will be made here to criticize Hume's concepts, to treat of his antecedents, or to trace his influence on his successors. This essay will be based on Hume's own writings and he will be allowed to speak for himself whenever possible.

As a philosopher Hume is remarkably consistent — though by no means perfectly so, especially in the meanings of key words. Had he proceeded with "Of Criticism" he would have been compelled to reconcile the real and apparent inconsistencies both in diction and thought and produce a systematic inquiry into the working of the human mind when confronted with an aesthetic experience. As his thinking on the nature of beauty and deformity is based upon or, rather, actually is an integral part of his philosophy, it will be necessary to examine briefly his philosophical assumptions.

First, he held that philosophy and criticism were inseparable. Writing a highly important letter of self-scrutiny in 1734, some five years before the publication of the *Treatise*, the twenty-three-year-old Hume relates how he entered into a "new Scene of Thought." "Every one, who is acquainted either with the Philosophers or Critics, knows that there is nothing yet establisht in either of these two Sciences [i.e., philosophy and criticism], & that they contain little more than endless Disputes, even in the most fundamental Articles." The youthful philosopher continues: "Upon Examination of these ['endless Disputes'], I found a certain Boldness of Temper, growing in me, which . . . led me to seek out some new Medium, by which Truth might be establisht." [2] In other words, Hume began by being puzzled about certain endless disputes in philosophy and criticism, and thus was led to seek out a new method; and it was this search which precipitated the "new Scene of Thought." Criticism, in fact, was one of his original starting points.

Second, for Hume, philosophy begins and ends with human nature. Human nature, however, cannot be known a priori but solely, and then inadequately, by experience. Certainty is achievable only in the realm of the relations of ideas, that is, in the highly restricted areas of pure logic and pure mathematics, which rest on the proposition: "That is demonstrably true whose opposite contains a contradiction." In the realm of matter of fact, demonstration cannot be reached. There is no logical fallacy in denying the existence of any fact, because "Whatever *is*, may *not be*." Likewise, whatever is conceivable is possible, no matter how patently preposterous it may seem. Consequently, while reason governs the relations of ideas, it plays only an intellectual and subordinate role in the realm of real existence and matter of fact. There are, in effect, two types of reason: abstract reasoning, concerning number and quantity, which yields certainty; and empirical reasoning, concerning matter of fact, which yields probability. In the science of man only probable reasoning is pertinent. And Hume insists that "all probable reasoning is nothing but a species of sensation. 'Tis not solely in poetry and music, we must follow our taste and sentiment, but likewise in philosophy."

A fig for the long-held Socratic-Platonic tradition, says Hume, in effect: "Reason is, and ought only to be the slave of the passions, and can never pretend to any other office than to serve and obey them." Man, upon careful empirical investigation, is found to be less a thinking than a sentient animal. We feel before we ratiocinate. In the ordinary affairs of life we *believe* although we do not have absolute knowledge. This natural propensity to believe is based upon experience: the sun will rise in the morning, we believe, because so far as we know, it always has. Laws of nature are not abstract a priori concepts but generalizations based on experience and experimentation. We believe in cause and effect, not by reason but by experience; consequently, custom or experience is the great guide of life. With his fundamental reliance on experience, Hume has no patience with those poets who, in all ages, have laid claim to divine inspiration. "There is not . . . any thing supernatural in the case. Their fire is not kindled from heaven. It only runs along the earth; is caught from one breast to another; and burns brightest, where the materials are

1. The book is by Teddy Brunius, *David Hume on Criticism* (Stockholm, 1952). The two unpublished doctoral dissertations are of 1950 and 1952: Charles Noyes, "Aesthetic Theory and Literary Criticism in the Works of David Hume" (University of Texas) and Ralph Cohen, "The Critical Theory of David Hume" (Columbia University). .Cohen has revised and published two chapters: "David Hume's Experimental Method and the Theory of Taste," *ELH*, XXV (1958), 270–89, and "The Transformation of Passion: A Study of Hume's Theories of Tragedy," *PQ*, XLI (1962), 450–64. To both Noyes and Cohen I am much indebted. I also wish to thank R. L. C. Lorimer, of the Editorial Board of Oliver & Boyd, Ltd., Edinburgh, and Professor Ian S. Ross, of the University of British Columbia, for helpful suggestions.

2. *The Letters of David Hume*, ed. J. Y. T. Greig (Oxford, 1932), I, 13; hereafter cited as HL.

best prepared, and most happily disposed." [3] Far from being divine, the poet's "inspiration" is psychological, social, and influenced by a particular climate of opinion.

Perceptions of the mind — that is, its contents — are classified by Hume as impressions or ideas. Sense impressions are the ultimate source of all ideas. The view of a sunset is an impression, the recollection of the view, an idea. Impressions are stronger than ideas, which are fainter copies of them in the memory and the imagination. Ideas in the memory are based upon direct experience, those in the imagination occur by volition. Secondary impressions of reflection may proceed directly from original ones of sensation or by the imposition of its ideas. Passions and other emotions are secondary impressions and may be either calm or violent. Through the association of ideas (the relations of causality, contiguity in time or place, and resemblance), the imagination can create complex ideas with or without reference to reality. While reason is powerless to stimulate action, that being the function of the passions, imagination is active and creative, indeed, the most important faculty possessed by man. "Nothing is more free than the imagination of man; and though it cannot exceed that original stock of ideas, furnished by the internal and external senses, it has unlimited power of mixing, compounding, separating, and dividing these ideas, to all the varieties of fiction and vision" (IV, 40).

Sympathy, along with imagination, constitutes man's creative power through the conversion of ideas, which are weaker, into impressions, which are stronger and more vivid. Our relations with others as social beings arouse sympathy, by which we share their feelings. Under certain circumstances this sharing with others may bring about a "disagreeable" sympathy; but "agreeable" sympathy, the more prevalent form, is a powerful principle in human nature, not only in the judging of morals, but also in our sense of external beauty. In both cases the principle of utility or functionalism or convenience may also enter. In morality the useful qualities of mind are deemed virtuous because of their social utility, and utility may also enhance our appreciation of external beauty. Our judgments of approbation or disapprobation in both morality and aesthetics, that is, our value judgments, are nonrational in origin, although among the more sophisticated, reason enters at a later stage.

To proceed to "Of Criticism," it is clear that this term has for Hume two meanings: the study of beauty (aesthetics) and the study of beauty in art (criticism in modern usage). In deposing reason for the passions and in exalting the creative role of the imagination, it is manifest that Hume is moving away from the rationalistic principles implicit in Neoclassicism. In moving from the general to the particular, from the objective to the subjective, in emphasizing individual feelings, he is adumbrating the philosophical bases of a different, more "romantic," and more "modern" aesthetics. That value judgments are nonrational provides the foundation upon which his aesthetics is constructed. The principle is stated in various places and in various forms but perhaps the best known and the most forceful is the following: "Beauty is no quality in things themselves: It exists merely in the mind which contemplates them; and each mind perceives a different beauty. One person may even perceive deformity, where another is sensible of beauty; and every individual ought to acquiesce in his own sentiment, without pretending to regulate those of others" (III, 268–69).

As all sentiment is right simply because it is real, we are presented with the seeming impossibility of ever attaining anything resembling a standard or general rule of taste. Yet critical nihilism is out of the question as no one is actually willing to grant that the taste of all individuals is on an equal footing. The opinions of an untutored child or those of an untutored adult about, say, the epics of Homer or Milton are scarcely worthy of consideration by the more cultivated. How, then, does Hume reason his way out of the dilemma in which he finds himself? Like natural laws, rules of composition and criticism are not known a priori but by experience. Certain procedures have been found to please generally, others to displease generally. Granted; but there still exists considerable disagreement. Why is this so?

Hume's answer to this question is one of his major contributions to aesthetics. Clearly the taste of some people is more refined and delicate than that of others. This refined and delicate taste is present where the endowments of a man are so fine and exacting as to be able to perceive all the qualities of the object or composition. A delicacy of wit or beauty is desirable because it is the source of innocent pleasure and enjoyment. But such exquisite taste is necessarily as rare as men who are sage and women who are beautiful. The point is illustrated by a story from *Don*

3. *The Philosophical Works of David Hume*, ed. T. H. Green and T. H. Grose (London, 1875), III, 177; hereafter cited in the text by placing volume number and page reference within parentheses.

*Quixote*. Sancho tells of two of his kinsmen who were widely ridiculed when they gave their judgment of a hogshead of wine. While both agreed that the wine was good, one detected a taste of leather in it and the other a taste of iron. When the hogshead was emptied both were vindicated as a key with a leathern thong tied to it was found on the bottom. The moral of the story is that while the onlookers were totally lacking in delicacy of taste, each of Sancho's kinsmen had developed an individual delicacy but neither had achieved perfection (III, 272). Delicacy of taste is not innate but demands self-cultivation in the form of freedom from prejudice derived from the realization of a point of view and a sense of historical change. In this respect, reason, though no original part of taste, can assist in recognizing and eliminating prejudice, in determining the end or purpose of the work of art, and in analyzing the relations of parts to each other and to the whole. Necessary also is continued experience, the repeated examination of the work of art under all possible circumstances in order to develop the intensity of the response. "In a word, the same address and dexterity, which practice gives to the execution of any work, is also acquired by the same means, in the judging of it" (III, 275).

Even among those rare critics who have been able to achieve a delicacy of taste, personal likes and dislikes may result in different opinions, all of which are justifiable. "One person is more pleased with the sublime; another with the tender; a third with raillery." Some prefer simplicity and some ornament. Age and maturity may enter into the picture: "At twenty, Ovid may be the favourite author; Horace at forty; and perhaps Tacitus at fifty" (III, 281). There are even partisans of different genres, such as comedy, tragedy, satire, odes. These natural predilections cannot be avoided, but what can and must be avoided at all costs is the approbation of the favorite genre at the expense and the condemnation of all others. Our own age or country is not to be preferred to the exclusion of other ages or countries, since there is a continual revolution in manners and customs. But, wherever found, immorality in art is not to be praised, because immorality causes pain, not pleasure; it offends the perceiver and disfigures the art. So morality, for Hume, may legitimately enter into the critical judgment of art, a point to be resumed later in connection with his practical criticism.

Delicacy of passion in an excessive degree, Hume warns, may be a grievous disadvantage. Rousseau was to provide the prime illustration of such an excess during Hume's lifetime. "He has only felt, during the whole Course of his life," noted Hume before the outbreak of the famous quarrel, "and in this Respect, his Sensibility rises to a Pitch beyond what I have seen any Example of: But it still gives him a more acute Feeling of Pain than of Pleasure." And Hume concludes: "He is like a Man who were stript not only of his Cloaths but of his Skin, and turn'd out in that Situation to combat with the rude and boisterous Elements, such as perpetually disturb this lower World" (HL, II, 29). Delicacy of taste, on the contrary, is always to be cultivated. The beauties of poetry, eloquence, music, or painting excite emotions that are soft and tender. "They draw off the mind from the hurry of business and interest; cherish reflection; dispose to tranquillity; and produce an agreeable melancholy, which, of all dispositions of the mind, is the best suited to love and friendship" (III, 93). But as this delicacy of taste is achievable only by a few, it leads those few to be happy and content only in a select society wherein the opportunities to refine taste ever further are presented through the stimulation of sympathy.

So Hume proposes a method of critical judgment, one which is purely empirical and based upon repeated observation. As such it discerns a set of rules which are not, as has mistakenly been held by many commentators, the rules of Neoclassicism. Those are a priori, prescriptive rules, which Hume's never are. Hume does not refer to an absolute and invariable standard in the evaluation of beauty any more than in any other aspect of the world of real existence. "To seek the real beauty, or real deformity, is as fruitless an enquiry, as to pretend to ascertain the real sweet or real bitter. According to the disposition of the organs, the same object may be both sweet and bitter; and the proverb has justly determined it to be fruitless to dispute concerning tastes" (III, 269). Beauty and deformity, causing pleasure and pain respectively in the person perceiving them, are qualities not in the object perceived but sentiments in the person himself. Hume's "true" values arise from the observation of the creations of artistic genius by the critic who has developed an intensified response. To produce these general rules or avowed patterns of composition is like finding the "key with a leathern thong." [4]

At this point, Hume summarizes his argument: "Strong sense, united to delicate sentiment, improved by practice, perfected by comparison,

4. See Redding S. Sugg, Jr., "Hume's Search for the Key with the Leather Thong," *Journal of Aesthetics and Art Criticism*, XVI (1957), 96–102.

and cleared of all prejudice, can alone entitle critics to this valuable character [of a 'true' judge]; and the joint verdict of such, wherever they are to be found, is the true standard of taste and beauty" (III, 278–79). In short, Hume is a relativist holding a position antithetical to that of the neoclassical concept of "general nature." Particular ideas are always clearer and more lively than general or abstract ideas; hence the more variety the better, as affording more pleasures to be enjoyed and cultivated. The artistic imagination has to be under some discipline, however, to be truly creative; otherwise it may become wild, uncontrolled, delirious, and in consequence not truly artistic.

Discrimination, to Hume, is the very essence of taste, and there is nothing absolute about the taste of even the best of critics. The unique effect of art has to be recognized. The problems of art are not the same as the problems of society or metaphysics and require, therefore, different methods. There is a poetical system, rules of art, discovered by the poet either by genius or observation. Art is not a weak or false imitation of nature, because art is not life. The rules of tragedy, for instance, like all rules of art, are not arbitrary or based on authority. They do not include, so far as Hume is concerned, the three neoclassical unities of action, time, and place. The only unity he accepts is that of action, which requires a well-knit and believable plot unembellished by unnecessary and distracting subplots.

Now a complication arises: while aesthetic responses derive originally from the sentiment of the perceiver, "there are certain qualities in objects, which are fitted by nature to produce those particular feelings" of beauty and deformity (III, 273). If Hume is vague and hesitant in identifying those certain qualities in objects, he has much to say about one, and that is utility. For example, " 'Tis certain that a considerable part of the beauty of men, as well as of other animals, consists in such a conformation of members as we find by experience to be attended with strength and agility, and to capacitate the creature for any action or exercise" (II, 369). As for inanimate objects: "A ship appears more beautiful to an artist, or one moderately skilled in navigation, where its prow is wide and swelling beyond its poop, than if it were framed with a precise geometrical regularity, in contradiction to all the laws of mechanics." Knowledge of the useful purpose of the ship adds to its beauty in the eyes of the trained viewer. On the contrary, all deformity displeases: "A building, whose doors and windows were exact squares, would hurt the eye by that very proportion; as ill adapted to the figure of a human creature, for whose service the fabric was intended" (II, 202). As to nature: "I know not but a plain, overgrown with furze and broom, may be, in itself, as beautiful as a hill cover'd with vines or olive-trees; tho' it will never appear so to one, who is acquainted with the value of each. But this is a beauty merely of imagination, and has no foundation in what appears to the senses." So utility indirectly makes the vines or olive trees seem more beautiful to those who know their value. The utility that is not useful to any particular viewer may yet be perceived through the principle of sympathy by which the viewer senses the feelings of others. Such is the case of the nonowner of the vines or olive trees. Similarly, household furniture may be beautiful to the owner because of its utility, "nor is there any thing but sympathy, which can interest the spectator" (II, 151).

Occasionally, Hume has been rashly accused of maintaining that all beauty is based on convenience, function, or utility. For instance, in an interesting and entertaining fictional dialogue written by his good friend, Adam Ferguson, that has only recently come to light and been published, the extreme utilitarian position is pushed to a *reductio ad absurdum*.[5] Ferguson taunts Hume: "Utility wherever found should have the same Effect, And a Dunghill be more admired than the Pantheon of Agrippa or the Dome of St Peters." Abashedly Hume is made to concede: "I grant you that Utility without art or Design, especially if it offend our other Senses, is not admitted for Beauty." Yet a careful reading of Hume himself reveals such a passage as this: "the beauty of all visible objects causes a pleasure pretty much the same, tho' it be sometimes deriv'd from the mere *species* and appearance of the objects; sometimes from sympathy, and an idea of their utility" (II, 371). And from the passages cited above it is evident that to Hume the principle of beauty founded on utility is preceded by the impression of beauty itself.

Hume's position that art is not the falsification of life (Plato's "lie" or Mencken's "the melodious assertion of the patently not true"), but exists as a separate and independent realm, is used to good advantage in his analysis of the age-old paradox that the spectators of a well-written tragedy can derive pleasure from disagreeable emotions. "They are

5. See my "Adam Ferguson's 'Dialogue on a Highland Jaunt,' with Robert Adam, William Cleghorn, David Hume, and William Wilkie" in *Restoration and Eighteenth-Century Literature*, Essays in Honor of Alan Dugald McKillop, ed. Carroll Camden (Chicago, 1963), p. 304.

pleased in proportion as they are afflicted, and never are so happy as when they employ tears, sobs, and cries to give vent to their sorrow, and relieve their heart, swoln with the tenderest sympathy and compassion" (III, 258–59). Previous theories on this topic are rejected by Hume in whole or in part: catharsis of whatever variety, rousing the passions from indolence, recognizing the fictional nature of the play, empathy or the identification of spectators with actors. The pleasure of imitation which Hume does acknowledge is not, however, that of representation but rather that of sympathy.

Hume's original contribution to the problem is a theory of emotional conversion. The melancholy scene inspires disagreeable emotions in the spectator which constitute, at first, the predominant movement, whereas the art of the playwright is the subordinate movement. When the art is so truly beautiful as to attract and hold the attention of the spectator, the melancholy or disagreeable passions are gradually converted into pleasurable ones. The subordinate movement has then been converted into the predominant. The ideal spectator is thus one who is capable of a full emotional response to the art as art and not as reality. To achieve this full emotional response he must be disinterested, sensitive, and highly attentive. He must, in effect, have the previously listed qualities of the ideal critic. And, just as there are few such critics, there are few spectators of the tragedy capable of converting the subordinate movement into the predominant: fit audience though few.

Longinus had long been favorite reading of Hume, as is evidenced in his first extant letter written at the age of sixteen, which is ecstatic about Longinus's rules of rhetoric or elevation of style (HL, I, 11). But Hume was to move away from this early eighteenth-century use of the term. As the distinguished author of *The Sublime: A Study of Critical Theories in XVIII-Century England* concluded thirty years ago: "Hume it was who gave the signal that the time had come to adopt a psychological method, and this step once taken, the sublime came into the sphere of the aesthetic" (p. 112). The rigid distinction drawn by Burke between the sublime and the beautiful was unacceptable to Hume. The Burkean dualism seemed quite unnecessary to the philosopher who viewed "greatness" or the "sublime" as merely the intensification of beauty. Nor was he impressed by Burke's curious physiological, in addition to psychological, treatment of the sublime. Furthermore, there is no indication that he accepted Burke's insistence that terror is a prime requisite for the sublime. Hume was too astute a thinker to be led into the aesthetic blind alley of the sublime *and* the beautiful.

As theorist Hume restricted himself largely to literature, and as practical critic even more so. "Such a superiority do the pursuits of literature possess above every other occupation," he professed in the *History of England*, "that even he who attains but a mediocrity in them, merits the pre-eminence above those that excel the most in the common and vulgar professions." [6] And in the last year of his life while he was desperately ill he forcefully reiterated his precepts of discrimination, practice, taste, and the pleasure of full emotional response to imaginative literature. In a letter to his favorite nephew, David, brilliant student of law at Glasgow University, Hume counseled: "I cou'd wish to see you mix the Volumes of Taste and Imagination with more serious Reading" of the legal treatises of "Voet, Vinnius, and Grotius. I did not observe you to be very fond of the Poets," he admonished, "and surely one may pass through Life, though not so agreeably, without such Companions: But the Familiarity with them gives Taste to Prose Reading and Compositions; and one wou'd not allow so agreeable a Vein to dry up entirely for Want of Exercise." [7]

There is a natural propensity to pit the theorist against the practitioner and determine to what degree they are reconcilable. In this respect Hume has been harshly dealt with not only by those who know little or nothing of his aesthetics and who have little sense of historicity but also by others who say that in practice he does not live up to his principles. Wordsworth is an example of the former type, and many moderns of the latter. Had Wordsworth known something of Hume's aesthetics (as apparently Coleridge did) he would have found much to agree with. He might even have tempered his prejudices, as when he pronounced "Adam Smith, the worst critic, David Hume not excepted, that Scotland, a soil to which this sort of weed seems natural, has produced." [8]

It is the judgment of the second group, however, those who grant that Hume's theory was not neoclassical but that his practical criticism was,

6. VI, 197, in edition of Edinburgh, 1792; hereafter cited in the text as *Hist.*
7. "Dawida Hume'A Nieznane Listy W Zbiorach Muzeum Czartoryskich (Polska)," ed. Tadeusz Kozanecki, *Archiwum Historii Filozofii I Mysli Spolecznej*, IX (1963), 138.
8. "Essay Supplementary to the Preface to the Poems of 1815," in *Poetry and the Poets*, ed. R. Brimley Johnson (London, 1926), p. 238.

which warrants investigation. But before doing so, let us glance at two incidents in his life that afford insights into his personality, temperament, and literary preferences. Upon first meeting the blind and indigent Scottish poet, Thomas Blacklock, in 1742, Hume was impressed with his "very delicate taste." Consequently, says Hume, "I repeated to him Mr Pope's Elegy to the Memory of an unfortunate Lady, which I happened to have by heart: and though I be a very bad reciter," he admits, "I saw it affected him extremely. His eyes, indeed, the great index of the mind, could express no passion: but his whole body was thrown into agitation. That poem was equally qualified to touch the delicacy of his taste, and the tenderness of his feelings." (HL, I, 200.) Note well that Hume just "happened to have by heart" the eighty-two lines of Pope's most "romantic" or emotional poem, that he recognized a delicacy of taste in Blacklock, and that he himself displayed a high degree of sensibility. No doubt his later patronage of Blacklock was influenced by the "prejudices" of country and of compassion for blindness and indigence; yet his original incentive was the intensity of his own feelings and sympathy for those of another in responding to a work of art.

An instance of failure to recognize Hume's intensity of emotion in art is found in a remark of Rousseau in the letter of eighteen folio pages of July 10, 1766, specifying all the paranoiac grievances that he held against *le bon David.* One of these, in a footnote, charges that Hume always kept a copy of *La Nouvelle Héloïse* on his table, "Comme si je ne connoissois pas assez le gout de M. Hume," complains Rousseau bitterly, "pour être assuré que, de tous les Livres qui existent, l'Héloïse doit être pour lui le plus ennuyeux" (HL, II, 389). The truth of the matter is quite the contrary. Hume had first eagerly read the novel in French shortly after publication and, before receiving Rousseau's bill of complaints, had informed an intimate friend that, "I think this Work his Master-piece; tho' he himself told me, that he valu'd most his *Contrat sociale*; which is as preposterous a Judgement as that of Milton, who preferd the Paradise regaind to all his other Performances." [9] The highly keyed emotionalism of the novel was preferred by Hume to the more sober treatise on political science.

How well did Hume live up to the high standards that he had posited for the "true" critic? Freedom from prejudice is a cardinal point. No man can free himself entirely from prejudice, as Hume was willing to concede; and he himself is no exception. He was a man of deep devotion to his friends. He was a patriotic Scot seeking to encourage literary talent in his countrymen. Nevertheless, not all the Scots are praised nor all the English damned. Hume's attempt to foster literature in Scotland is laudable, though his methods have been questioned. Speaking Lowland Scots all his life, he aimed at writing acceptable Southern English and labored mightily to eradicate Scotticisms. In addition to setting this powerful linguistic example, he patronized other Scots who wrote in English. His reasons are fully understandable. He wished to be cosmopolitan and international and to avoid any imputation of parochialism and regionalism. He had a vision of English becoming the major world language (HL, II, 171). Presumably such views are responsible for his ignoring the writers in Scotland who were keeping alive, and enriching, native literary traditions in both Lowland Scots and Gaelic. Our modern sense of what is truly vital in the literary creations of Hume's contemporaries leads us to complain that he did nothing, apparently, to publicize the work of those true servants of the vernacular muse, Allan Ramsay and Robert Fergusson, and, perhaps more excusably, since he had no Gaelic, the work of the two greatest poets in that tongue, Alexander Macdonald and Duncan Ban McIntyre. Hume, of course, died ten years before the appearance of *Poems, Chiefly in the Scottish Dialect* of 1786. How he would have reacted to Burns is a matter of conjecture; but many friends who held convictions and aspirations similar to his passed that test with flying colors. The muse in "hamely attire" touched the heart of the literati and the lowly alike. Humean critical principles, at least, were vindicated, even if the linguistic ones went by the board.

Much ridicule has been heaped upon Hume by succeeding generations for his preference of Addison to Bunyan. Yet this is an instance of the historical, relativist point of view. To say that the entire eighteenth century agreed with Hume would be an exaggeration, although the great majority did. And certainly there are numerous of the well-read in the twentieth century who show little enthusiasm for reading Bunyan a second time. More important than the fluctuations of taste concerning Bunyan is another question: How well did Hume live up to the historical point of view that he advocated? He was, on the one hand, capable of excusing what he actually considered immorality in ancient literature because of cultural changes, but, on the other hand, he was opposed to

9. See my "New Hume Letters to Lord Elibank, 1748–1776," *Texas Studies in Language and Literature*, IV (1962), 450, and HL, II, 28.

the immorality of the Restoration stage. Thus to Hume the pain caused by immorality in a distant and different culture may be condoned, though not approved, while the pain caused by immorality in one's native modern culture must be condemned. Yet moral deformities of the ancients, though condoned, are not approved: "I cannot, nor is it proper I should, enter into such sentiments; and however I may excuse the poet, on account of the manners of his age, I never can relish the composition." And he drives the point home: "The want of humanity and of decency, so conspicuous in the characters drawn by several of the ancient poets, even sometimes by Homer and the Greek tragedians, diminishes considerably the merit of their noble performances, and gives modern authors an advantage over them" (III, 282–83). Judgment of art on a moralistic basis is generally unacceptable to the twentieth century, yet Hume, moralist as well as critic, is consistent within his own system whether we like it today or not.

Some of the literary criticism found in Hume's *History of England* (and he was the first British historian to include such material) certainly does not live up to the historical point of view: all ages prior to the Augustan Age are prone to be regarded as semibarbarous or at least lacking in refinement. Spenser, for instance, is praised for his high poetical standards but his subject matter is deemed tedious: "the affectations, and conceits, and fopperies of chivalry, . . . appear ridiculous as soon as they lose the recommendation of the mode" (*Hist.* V, 491–92). Shakespeare is praised for his poetical genius but damned for the many irregularities "and even absurdities [which] so frequently disfigure the animated and passionate scenes intermixed with them" (*Hist.* VI, 191). This theme is taken up in a letter in which an intimate friend is admonished: "For God's sake, read Shakespeare, but get Racine and Sophocles by heart" (HL, I, 215). Milton, though one of the "fanatics," that is, the Puritans, comes off remarkably well. "It is certain that this author, when in a happy mood, and employed on a noble subject, is the most wonderfully sublime of any poet in any language; Homer and Lucretius and Tasso not excepted" (*Hist.* VII, 343–45). Elsewhere, Milton is "that divine Poet" and "the great poet" (III, 379; II, 436).

Hume's two published examples of practical criticism of literature merit a few words of comment. That both are somewhat prejudiced because of friendship and patriotism is undeniable. Nevertheless, two works — John Home's tragedy of *Douglas* and William Wilkie's epic, *The Epi-*

*goniad* — are praised for embodying Hume's cardinal principle of criticism, that intense emotion should be converted into art. It is on this basis, and not for meeting the neoclassical rules, that *Douglas* is endorsed by Hume in the "Dedication" to his *Four Dissertations* (1757) which he addressed to the author of the tragedy. Incontestable proofs of "true theatric genius" are to be found in "the unfeigned tears which flowed from every eye, in the numerous representations which were made of it in this theatre; the unparalleled command, which you appeared to have over every effusion of the human heart" (IV, 440). Writing to the *Critical Review* some two years later, Hume praised Wilkie's epic in similar terms, singling out not the story, "the least essential part" of a poem, but "the force of the versification, the vivacity of the images, the justness of the descriptions, the natural play of the passions" (IV, 433).

The unpublished essay "Of the Poems of Ossian" [10] is a much more trenchant piece of criticism, providing as it does an excellent example of Hume's use of the historical point of view and his mastery of the comparative approach. The critique was instigated by the attack of Dr. Johnson in the *Journey to the Western Islands of Scotland* (1775) not merely on the character and integrity of Macpherson but on the character and integrity of all Scots: "A Scotchman must be a very sturdy moralist, who does not love Scotland better than truth: he will always love it better than inquiry; and if falsehood flatters his vanity, will not be very diligent to detect it." [11] Aside from his indignation at this unwarranted aspersion upon the integrity of his countrymen, Hume agreed with Johnson about the fraudulence of Macpherson's epics, but on a higher critical level. Johnson was content simply to demand more and more evidence of the authenticity of the works. Hume made the perfectly valid historical point that two long epics have never been and never could be handed down totally uncorrupted, over the course of fifteen centuries, through the sole agency of oral tradition. He went on to contrast ballads of many countries and Lapland and Runic odes, which have "a savage rudeness, and sometimes grandeur," with Macpherson's "insipid correctness, and regularity, and uniformity, which betrays a man without genius, that has been acquainted with the productions of civilized nations, and had his imagination so limited to that tract, that it was impossible for him even to mimic the character which he pretended to assume" (IV, 417). The

10. Incorrectly entitled "Of the Authenticity of Ossian's Poems," IV, 415.
11. P. 108 in R. W. Chapman's London ed., 1934.

pity is that such a vigorous display of critical acumen did not see print, probably because Hume did not wish to embarrass his friend, the Reverend Hugh Blair, Professor of Rhetoric and Belles Lettres in the University of Edinburgh, whose international fame rested on the promotion and defense of Ossian.[12]

In conclusion, two questions may be asked. First: Was Hume a distinguished practical critic? No; but he was certainly not so poor a critic as has often been alleged. After all, most of the great works he knew had been composed according to classical principles and, as an empiricist, he necessarily observed those principles in action. Nevertheless, he does attempt to bring his own principles into play and to criticize a work of art from a historical, relativist point of view and on its own terms. Which leads to the second question: Was Hume a distinguished aesthetician and theoretical critic? Here the answer has to be put in more guarded terms. Pregnant hints and fruitful ideas are scattered throughout his works, but he never developed and synthesized them. Even so, had these elements of distinction been more widely known, they would certainly have added to his reputation and influence. It is, therefore, both fitting and proper to end the essay as it began, though with sufficient reason now to deplore this matter of fact: David Hume never wrote a book entitled "Of Criticism."

12. Hume urged Blair to inquire empirically into the authenticity of Macpherson's *Ossian* (HL, I, 398–401). The procedure outlined in this letter was adopted by the Highland Society of Scotland (see their committee's *Report . . . [on] the Nature and Authenticity of the Poems of Ossian*, 3 vols. [Edinburgh, 1805]) and by the modern scholar Derick S. Thomson in *The Gaelic Sources of Macpherson's "Ossian"* (Edinburgh, 1952). The evidence collected suggests that Macpherson made use of some fourteen or fifteen ballads in Gaelic but no epics.

❦ ROBERT M. RYLEY

# William Warburton as "New Critic"

W ILLIAM WARBURTON was an execrable critic, but he was sometimes execrable in an almost twentieth-century way. I intend to
argue, in fact, that his criticism bears certain superficial but nonetheless
interesting similarities to what we call the New Criticism. Whether my
thesis has any significance for the eighteenth century or for the twentieth
I hesitate to say. I do not know whom Warburton influenced, though I
think I know who influenced him; and I do not know whether his criticism illuminates our contemporaries' or not. I think, though, that he
deserves some recognition as a pioneer, even if he left no trail for those
who came after him, and even if they settled the territory without ever
knowing that he had been there.

⚡     ⚡     ⚡

Close reading is the *sine qua non* of the New Criticism, and I need
hardly point out that Warburton practiced it. His *Vindication of Mr.
Pope's Essay on Man* was, at the time of its publication in 1739, the most
elaborate study of a poem to have appeared in English criticism. The only
precedent for it was the Richardsons' book on *Paradise Lost*,[1] and as a
precedent even this was dubious, for it is merely a collection of notes on
separate lines. The *Vindication*, on the other hand, containing more quotations than will, I think, be found in any other eighteenth-century critical essay, is a coherent, almost line-by-line analysis of an entire poem.

1. Jonathan Richardson, father and son, *Explanatory Notes and Remarks on
Milton's Paradise Lost* (London, 1734).

No wonder Pope called Warburton "the greatest general critic I ever knew." [2] Thanks to Warburton, he became the first living poet to see his work publicly honored by so close and so sympathetic a reading.

Warburton said himself, however, that the *Vindication* was not intended as a study of the poem as a poem,[3] and it is not in this work that we see him at his most New Critical. The criticism that I am concerned with is based on reading just as close as that in the *Vindication*, but flashes only occasionally from the drab notes in Warburton's edition of Pope's works.[4] This criticism takes three forms: holistic interpretation of imagery, semantic analysis, and what I shall call the search for complexity. In each of these forms, it seems to me, Warburton's criticism is primitively modern.

Discussing "The Organic Nature of Poetry" in their textbook *Understanding Poetry*, Cleanth Brooks and Robert Penn Warren praise a metaphor because "there is not only the application, as it were, of the general idea in a concrete image that can be seen as a picture, but also an application appropriate to the special situation." [5] A similar theory of metaphor (or of Popean metaphor, at least) is implied by Warburton's assertion that "the *Similitudes* in [Pope's] didactic poems, of which he is not sparing, and which are highly poetical, are always chosen with such exquisite discernment of Nature, as not only to illustrate the particular point he is upon, but to establish the general principle he would inforce." [6] Now I do not want to exaggerate the significance of what Warburton says here. He obviously assumes that Pope's metaphors are "highly poetical" in addition to being functional, whereas Brooks and Warren would insist that the beauty of a metaphor is inseparable from its function.[7] And though elsewhere Warburton says that Pope "hath the Art of converting Poetical Ornaments into Philosophic Reasoning," [8] he generally assumes not that metaphor is in itself a mode of thought, but that it is something added to thought. In spite of these heresies, however, Warburton's view of metaphor is closer to the modern than, say, Johnson's, in which figures of speech are treated as ennobling or illustrative contributions to the immediate context alone. Moreover, in its application to specific poems, Warburton's theory implicitly demands of the critic an alertness to the relation of part to whole such as Brooks and Warren explicitly recommend.[9]

When in fact Warburton applies his theory, the results are sometimes fantastic, but in accordance with the theory he tries to point out relationships in a poem that the casual reader would certainly have missed. To illustrate the general statement quoted above, for example, Warburton cites Pope's line "Chameleons who can paint in white and black" (*Epistle to a Lady*, l. 156). Pope uses the chameleon image, Warburton says, for the obvious purpose of illustrating female inconsistency. But, he continues,

'tis nevertheless the great principle of this poem to shew that the general Characteristic of the Sex, as to the Ruling Passion, which they all have, is more uniform than that in Man: Now for this purpose all Nature could not have supplied such another illustration as this of the Chameleon, for tho it instantaneously assumes much of the colour of every subject on which it chances to be placed, yet, as the most accurate *Virtuosi* have observed, it has two native colours of its own, which amidst all these changes are never totally discharged, but, tho often discoloured by the neighborhood of adventitious ones, still make the foundation, and give a tincture to all those which, from thence, it occasionally assumes.[10]

The chameleon image, in other words, implies the idea made explicit in lines 207–10:

> In Men, we various Ruling Passions find;
> In Women, two almost divide the kind;
> Those, only fix'd, they first or last obey,
> The Love of Pleasure, and the Love of Sway.

The "adventitious" colors of the chameleon correspond to the superficial inconsistency of women, and the "two native colours" correspond to the two Ruling Passions. In a similar way, the line "Comets are regular, and Wharton plain" (*Epistle to Cobham*, l. 209) "has an exquisite beauty" arising from the fact that

the appearance of irregularity, in a Comet's motion, is occasioned by the greatness of the *force* which pushes it round a very eccentric orb; [just

2. Joseph Spence, *Anecdotes, Observations, and Characters, of Books and Men*, ed. S. W. Singer (London, 1820), p. 337.

3. *A Critical and Philosophical Commentary on Mr. Pope's Essay on Man* (London, 1742), p. 2, hereafter cited as *Commentary*.

4. *The Works of Alexander Pope, Esq.*, 9 vols. (London, 1751), hereafter cited as *Works*. Citations from Pope are to this edition.

5. 3rd ed. (New York, 1960), pp. 19–20.

6. *Works*, III, 204n.

7. "The poetic effect depends not on the things themselves but on the kind of use the poet makes of them," p. 16.

8. *Commentary*, p. 137.

9. *Understanding Poetry*, p. 271.

10. *Works*, III, 204n.

as] the *violence* of the Ruling Passion, that, impatient for its object, in the impetuosity of its course towards it, is frequently hurried to an immense distance from it, . . . occasions all that puzzling inconsistency of conduct we observe in it.[11]

The parallel between comets and Wharton, Warburton argues, implies a parallel between the "force" that moves comets and the Ruling Passions that move men. And by means of this parallel, Pope is able to imply the essential consistency in the apparent inconsistency of human behavior, an idea central to the meaning of the poem. Thus does Warburton read from parts to wholes and find subtle beauties in coherence unperceived.

Sometimes, however, Warburton's interpretations of images are so brief as to conceal the holistic analysis on which they are based. For instance, of Pope's couplet "A Wild, where weeds and flow'rs promiscuous shoot / Or Garden, tempting with forbidden fruit" (*Essay on Man*, I, 7–8), he remarks, "The *Wild* relates to the human *passions*, productive (as he explains in the second epistle) both of good and evil. The *Garden*, to human *reason*, so often *tempting* us to transgress the bounds God has set to it, and wander in fruitless enquiries." [12] Since there is nothing in the immediate context about either passion or reason, this reading of the wild and garden metaphors seems on the face of it mechanical and arbitrary. The truth is, however, that Warburton has related the metaphors to other parts of the poem, so that we have to reconstruct his reasoning to find out what he is driving at. First of all, some justification for believing that Pope associates the passions with the wild is provided by another metaphor in Epistle II, to which Warburton directs us in the note:

> As fruits, ungrateful to the planter's care,
> On Savage stocks inserted, learn to bear;
> The surest Virtues thus from Passions shoot,
> Wild Nature's vigor working at the root.
> What crops of wit and honesty appear
> From spleen, from obstinacy, hate, or fear.
>
> (ll. 181–86)

This metaphor not only associates the wild with the passions, but suggests that the wild is productive of both good and evil — hence Warburton's reading of "weeds and flow'rs." Furthermore, the couplet in question implies a contrast paralleled by the passion-reason contrast in Epistle II, lines 53–54: "Two principles in human nature reign, / Self-love, to urge, and Reason, to restrain." If the wild (disordered, unrestrained) stands for the passions, the garden (ordered, restrained) can quite appropriately stand for reason. And since reason is not without its temptations — "In Pride, in reas'ning Pride, our error lies" (I, 123) — Warburton can read "forbidden fruit" as "the bounds God has set to it." I will not pretend that this reading is entirely satisfactory.[13] My point, however, is not that Warburton's conclusions are correct, but that his means of reaching these conclusions are modern.

Warburton's holistic method of interpretation can be further illuminated by comparing Warburtonian and nineteenth-century readings of the same line. In Epistle IV of the *Essay on Man*, Pope writes, rather obscurely, that happiness is "O'er-look'd, seen double, by the fool, and wise" (l. 6). Elwin suggests that the line means "Overlooked in the things that would yield [happiness], and in other things magnified by the imagination." [14] This reading is plausible enough to have earned a place in the Twickenham Edition,[15] but it is surely questionable. How, one wonders, did Elwin derive "magnified by the imagination" from "seen double," which we should normally expect to signify "mistakenly seen in two places at once"? His reasoning, I suspect, went something like this: Since happiness consists in many things, it is to be expected that men will see it in two places at once. Pope, therefore, could not have meant "seen double" in its common acceptation, which would suggest that men who see happiness in two places at once are having hallucinations. But Pope mentions wise men and fools, and wise men, of course, have more imagination than fools. If fools overlook happiness, perhaps wise men imagine it to be more important than in fact it is: i.e., it is "magnified by the imagination." The trouble with this reasoning, however, is that, since Pope states explicitly that "Virtue alone is Happiness below" (l. 310) and that "Virtue only makes our Bliss below" (l. 397), happiness as it is defined in the poem consists not in "things," but in one thing only. Elwin, in other words, rips the line from its context and interprets it according to his own notions about the sources of happiness. Warburton, on the other hand, takes the rest of the poem into account. Happiness is overlooked,

11. *Works*, III, 188n.
12. *Works*, III, 3n.
13. Warburton fails to explain how the passions and reason relate to "the scene of man," the topic of this passage.
14. Whitwell Elwin and William John Courthope, ed., *The Works of Alexander Pope* (London, 1871–1889), II, 429n.
15. The Twickenham ed. of the poems of Alexander Pope, *An Essay on Man*, ed. Maynard Mack (London and New Haven, 1950), p. 128n.

he writes, "by those who place Happiness in any thing exclusive of Virtue; *seen double* by those who admit any thing else to have a share with Virtue in procuring Happiness." [16] This reading makes as much sense as Elwin's, is consistent with the definition of happiness stated elsewhere in the poem, and preserves the idiomatic meaning of "seen double." More importantly, it shows that Warburton's approach to interpretation is closer to the New-Critical ideal than that of his Victorian successor. "The student in reading any poem," write Brooks and Warren, "should be on the alert for the implications of the imagery and for the relation of the imagery to the full meaning of the poem." [17] In his own heavy-handed way, Warburton was following that advice about two hundred years before it was written.

But Warburton is also New Critical in his approach to poetic diction. Diction, of course, is a frequent topic of discussion in eighteenth-century criticism. But whereas the neoclassical critic normally asks whether a word is plain or fancy, high or low, Warburton anticipates the semantic interests of twentieth-century critics by trying to determine precisely the meaning of a word or phrase in its special context. Without using the word "connotation," he often suggests that the connotation of a word or phrase accounts for its peculiar effectiveness. Thus he praises the precision of "tincture" and "discolour'd" in Pope's couplet "All Manners take a tincture from our own; / Or come discolour'd thro our Passions shown" (*Epistle to Cobham*, ll. 33–34). Whereas "tincture," he writes, suggests "a weak colour given by degrees" and thus implies the gradual, almost imperceptible effect of manners, "discolour'd" suggests "a quicker change and by a deeper dye" and thus implies the deeper and more lasting effect of the passions.[18] He comments favorably on the word "trim" in Pope's line "Gave alms at Easter, in a Christian trim" (*Epistle to a Lady*, l. 57), because it implies that Narcissa's "very charity was as much an exterior of Religion, as the ceremonies of the season." [19] He praises the aptness of expression in Pope's line "And Nero's Terraces desert their walls" (*Epistle to Burlington*, l. 72). Had Pope said that Nero's walls desert their terraces, "this would have given us the image of a destruction effected by time only." But Pope's purpose is to expose the results of "unsupported taste." Thus "it is with great propriety that the *Terraces desert their walls*, which implies purpose and violence in their subversion." [20] But perhaps Warburton's keenest observation is on the line "And desp'rate Misery lays hold on Dover" (*The Sixth Epistle of the First*

*Book of Horace*, l. 57). He calls attention quite correctly to a "prettiness in this expression" consisting in the fact that the verb "lays hold" attributes to the quack Dover the slipperiness of the quicksilver for which he was notorious.[21]

The modernity of Warburton's interest in diction, however, is most fully exemplified by his almost Empsonian references to poetic ambiguity. Unfortunately, Warburton sometimes finds ambiguity where the context clearly rules it out. He scandalized Joseph Warton,[22] for instance, by suggesting a "pleasantry" in Pope's "Bards triumphant" (*Essay on Criticism*, l. 189) that "alludes to the state of *warfare* that all true Genius must undergo while here upon earth." [23] And probably he scandalizes everybody by insisting that "*Virtue . . . is an empty boast*" (*Epilogue to the Satires*, I, 113) can mean "either that those *starve who have it*, or that those who *boast of it, have it not.*" [24] On the other hand, he often finds ambiguity where it can reasonably be said to exist. He remarks of "observant" in "Great Nature spoke; observant Men obey'd" (*Essay on Man*, III, 199) that it implies "both obedience to the voice of Nature, and attention to the lessons of the animal creation." [25] He praises "the happy ambiguity of the word *loosely*" [26] in "The stage how loosely does Astraea tread" (*The First Epistle of the Second Book of Horace*, l. 290), evidently because it implies that Mrs. Behn's plays are both badly constructed and immoral. He finds "a peculiar elegance" in Pope's placing Swift in "Rab'lais' easy chair" (*Dunciad*, I, 22). The phrase, he says, contains an "equivoque" that simultaneously suggests Swift's age, his character, and his position as "the heir and successor of that original genius." [27] He finds an "elegant and satiric ambiguity" [28] at work in "the Court see nothing in't" (*Epilogue to the Satires*, I, 2), which he reads, evidently, both as "the court of the King sees nothing of interest in it" and as "the

16. *Works*, III, 112n.
17. *Understanding Poetry*, p. 271.
18. *Works*, III, 169–70n.
19. *Works*, III, 198n.
20. *Works*, III, 276n.
21. *Works*, IV, 131n.
22. *An Essay on the Genius and Writings of Pope*, 5th ed. (London, 1806), I, 133–34.
23. *Works*, I, 160n.
24. *Works*, IV, 310n.
25. *Works*, III, 91n.
26. *Works*, IV, 186n.
27. *Works*, V, 71n.
28. *Works*, IV, 299n.

court of law sees nothing actionable in it." But however real or imaginary the ambiguities that Warburton discovers in Pope's verse, his honorific use of the term "ambiguity" and his alertness to the possibilities of intentional or unintentional equivocation represent a curious foreshadowing of twentieth-century thought.

The last of Warburton's New-Critical methods is what I have called the search for complexity. According to Wimsatt and Brooks, some New Critics "would seem to demand a certain complexity as the desideratum of any 'good' poem." [29] So would Warburton, if his critical assumptions can be inferred from his practice, for he takes great delight in seeking out depth and richness in apparent simplicity. One of the complexities he looks for, for example, is a heretofore undiscovered pattern of images in Pope's verse. One such pattern, Warburton insists, Pope develops through the use of personification in the *Epistle to Burlington*:

> Consult the Genius of the Place in all;
> That tells the Waters or to rise, or fall;
> Or helps th'ambitious Hill the heav'ns to scale,
> Or scoops in circling theatres the Vale;
> Calls in the Country, catches op'ning glades,
> Joins willing woods, and varies shades from shades;
> Now breaks or now directs, th'intending Lines;
> Paints as you plant, and, as you work, designs.
>
> (ll. 57–64)

This passage, according to Warburton, is "one of the noblest and most sublime descriptions of *Design*, that poetry could express." Pope has managed the personification of "the Genius of the place" so as gradually to increase the reader's estimation of its importance:

First, the *Genius* of the place *tells the waters*, or only simply gives directions: Then he *helps* th' *ambitious hill*, or is a fellow-labourer: Then again he *scoops the circling Theatre*, or works alone, or in chief. Afterwards, rising fast in our idea of dignity, he *calls in the country*, alluding to the orders of princes in their progress, when accustomed to display all their state and magnificence: His Character then grows sacred, he *joins willing woods*, a metaphor taken from the office of the priesthood, in the administration of one of its holy rites; till at length, he becomes a Divinity, and creates and presides over the whole. . . . Much in the same manner as *plastic Nature* is supposed to do, in the work of human generation.[30]

In lines 73–100 of Book IV of *The Dunciad* (a passage too long to be quoted here), Warburton finds a different kind of pattern, in which Dulness is seen as a planet and her three classes of worshippers are seen as satellites in a recurring Newtonian metaphor:

The *first* [class of worshippers], drawn only by the strong and *simple impulse of Attraction*, are represented as falling directly down into her; as conglobed into her substance, and resting in her centre,

> — *all their centre found,*
> *Hung to the Goddess, and coher'd around.*

The *second*, tho' within the sphere of her *attraction*, yet having at the same time a *projectile* motion, they are carried, by the composition of these two, in *planetary revolutions* round her centre, some nearer to it, some further off:

> *Who gently drawn, and struggling less and less,*
> *Roll in her Vortex, and her pow'r confess.*

The *third* are properly *excentrical*, and no constant members of her state or system: sometimes at an immense distance from her influence, and sometimes again almost on the surface of her *broad effulgence*. Their use in their Perihelion, or nearest approach to Dulness, is the same in the moral World, as that of *Comets* in the natural, namely to refresh and recreate the dryness and decays of the system. . . .[31]

Both of these readings are incredible, of course. Since whatever "tells the Waters or to rise, or fall" has as much power as what "Now breaks or now directs, th'intending Lines," Pope's personification is as high in "our idea of dignity" at the beginning of the passage as it is at the end. And since the planetary metaphor fails to appear in the last fifteen lines of the *Dunciad* passage, the last class of worshipers is not treated as a part of any system, Newtonian or other. In principle, however, the search for a pattern of images is not so absurd as Warburton's egregious notes would suggest. And surely the assumption that a poem can be more complex than thousands of readers have ever realized and that it is the critic's task to discover that complexity is congenial to New-Critical theory.

Some such assumption also underlies Warburton's analyses of single metaphors. He often argues, for instance, that Pope's metaphors are effective because they are based on a sound knowledge of natural phenomena and implies that a reader must have the same knowledge in order fully

29. William K. Wimsatt, Jr., and Cleanth Brooks, *Literary Criticism: A Short History* (New York, 1957), p. 648. This demand for complexity, however, is based on a sophisticated aesthetic of which, needless to say, there is no trace in Warburton's thinking.
30. *Works*, III, 273–74n.
31. *Works*, V, 234–35n.

to appreciate them. (We have already seen something of this in Warburton's comments on the chameleon and comet metaphors discussed above.) Thus of Pope's simile comparing false eloquence with a prism (*Essay on Criticism*, ll. 311–17) he remarks,

This simile is beautiful. For the false colouring, given to objects by the prismatic glass, is owing to its untwisting, by its *obliquities*, those threads of light, which Nature had put together in order to spread over its works an ingenuous *candor*. . . . And *false Eloquence* is nothing else but the straining and *divaricating* the parts of *true expression*. . . .[32]

Warburton also praises some of Pope's metaphors for being analogically exact and discusses them as if they were telescoped metaphysical conceits that must be extended if the reader is to understand their full significance. For example, he praises the spider metaphor in the following lines from the *Epistle to Dr. Arbuthnot*:

> Who shames a Scribler? break one cobweb thro',
> He spins the slight, self-pleasing thread anew:
> Destroy his fib or sophistry, in vain,
> The creature's at his dirty work again,
> Thron'd in the centre of his thin designs,
> Proud of a vast extent of flimsy lines.
>
> (ll. 89–94)

This metaphor is successful, Warburton says, because "every thing concurs." The scribler and the spider "both *spin*; not from the *head* [reason], but from the *guts* [passions and prejudices] and such a *thread* that can entangle none but creatures weaker than themselves."[33] Obviously Pope himself does not develop these "similarities" or even imply them. Warburton simply extends the analogy as Pope might have done if he had had a mind to and discovers in Pope's relative simplicity a complex, almost Donnean metaphor.

But if Warburton's search for complexity seems generally futile, in one instance, at least, it pays off handsomely, and we may fittingly conclude this part of our discussion with what is probably Warburton's most interesting critical discovery. Pope writes in the *Essay on Criticism*:

> 'Tis with our judgments, as our watches, none
> Go just alike, yet each believes his own.
> In Poets as true genius is but rare,
> True Taste as seldom is the Critic's share;
> Both must alike from Heav'n derive their light,
> These born to judge, as well as those to write.
>
> (ll. 9–14)

Here, Warburton remarks, Pope

inquires . . . into the necessary *Qualities* of a true *Critic*: And observes
first, that JUDGMENT, simply and alone, is not sufficient to constitute this
character, because *Judgment*, like the *artificial measures of Time*, goes
different, and yet each relies upon his own. The reason is conclusive,
and the similitude extremely just. For *Judgment*, when alone, is always
regulated, or at least much influenced by custom, fashion, and habit,
and never certain and constant but when founded upon TASTE: which
is the same in the *Critic*, as GENIUS in the *Poet*: both are derived from
Heaven, and like the Sun (the *natural measure of Time*) always constant
and equal.[34]

Warburton's dogmatic pronouncements on the difference between
judgment and taste are annoying, but it seems to me that he has correctly
drawn out the implications of Pope's "watch" simile. The "light" from
"Heav'n" does suggest the sun. And since the sun is the measure of time,
the "watch" simile, apparently dropped after two lines, can be seen to
function covertly as part of an extended analogy. Is this overingenious?
Possibly. But John Crowe Ransom once wrote of certain contributors
to the *Kenyon Review* that they "judge well because they are professionally sensitive to what is latent in the work, therefore likely to be
difficult, and will not content themselves with what is manifest and for
everybody to see." [35] Unfortunately, it cannot be said of Warburton that
he judges well. But surely it can be said that he is professionally sensitive
to what is latent in the work, therefore likely to be difficult, and will not
content himself with what is manifest and for everybody to see.

⚹ ⚹ ⚹

If the criticism that I have examined is, in fact, primitively New Critical, a question arises as to whether it is merely aberrant or indicative of
a critical tendency of the age. The answer is that it is probably both.
For no doubt much of what Warburton wrote is the product of inex-
plicable eccentricity and of a raging vanity that led him to prefer ingenuity to common sense. On the other hand, there are ways and ways
of being ingenious. And it seems to me that Warburton would not have
chosen *his* way if the age had not provided him with a critical method
that made it easy for him to do so.

32. *Works*, I, 174–75n.
33. *Works*, IV, 15n.
34. *Works*, I, 138–39.
35. *The Kenyon Critics* (Cleveland and New York, 1951), p. viii.

The truth is that a rationale for Warburton's critical practice and a kind of criticism similar to his had been developed seventeen years before the edition of Pope in the Richardsons' *Explanatory Notes and Remarks on Milton's Paradise Lost*, which I have already mentioned as a vague precedent for Warburton's *Vindication*. Although the announced intention of the book was to help "the General Eye in Contemplating this Noble Luminary," [36] it was, in effect, a reply to Bentley's edition of the poem, which had appeared two years earlier. Bentley, of course, had pretended to believe that Milton had had an incompetent amanuensis who had made errors in spelling and punctuation, and a perfidious friend who, in seeing the poem through the press, had ignored typographical errors and added to the text some of his own verses.[37] Proceeding on this assumption, Bentley was able to justify the application of his emendatory method to a text that nobody had thought was corrupt. His audacity, however, seems to have infuriated the Richardsons, for they took issue with him at almost every turn. For example, the notion that all texts of *Paradise Lost* were corrupt, they declared, was "Presumption, Folly, or Something Worse," [38] and they devoted thirteen pages to proving it. "I leave the reader to judge," they concluded, ". . . Whether this Book affords any Pretense or Excuse to a New Editor, who shall Dare to Change though it were with the Utmost Deliberation, and Taste. He may indeed Honestly Say Thus and Thus the Author Should have Thought or Said, but let him not Palm Himself upon us as a Genuine *Milton*." [39] Moreover, they implicitly contrasted their own editorial methods with Bentley's, declaring, "We have Reverenc'd our Text, have handled it as Something which it would be a Sort of Prophaneness, as well as a Ridiculous Presumption in Us to Aim at Improving, by Adding or Diminishing." [40] An indication of the extent of their quarrel with Bentley is the fact that thirty-three of their notes on Book I alone, implicitly take issue with Bentley's notes on the same lines.

What is important for our purposes, however, is that in challenging Bentley the Richardsons had to adapt Bentley's critical method to their own ends. One scholar has remarked that, for all his faults, Bentley "applied to the *Paradise Lost*, for the first time that this had been done with any English poem, the standards of scientific scholarship and of classical quality, testing it by these standards line by line and word by word." [41] The Richardsons also had to test the poem line by line and word by word, not because the text was corrupt, but because, they said, Milton

"Expresses himself So Concisely, Employs Words So Sparingly, that whoever will Possess His Ideas must Dig for them, and Oftentimes pretty far below the Surface." [42] Nor was this kind of reading, they insisted, tedious or pedantic. On the contrary, it increased the reader's enjoyment of the poem:

Besides the Pleasure we have in These Particulars [the beauties of poetry] 'tis Some Addition to it when we Reflect, (as Self-Love will teach us) on our Own Ability to Discover, and lift up our Selves to the Perception of the Brilliant of these Beauties; and Thus, as it were, become Sharers in the Honour of them. [43]

Moreover, the purpose of this approach to the poem was simply to give Milton his due — perhaps more than his due:

In Expounding Him, we have Therefore Always given, as well as we were Enabled, a Poetic Sense, either as what was found in Other Great Poets whence it Seem'd Himself had receiv'd it. . . . Or where the Thoughts seem'd to be his Own, *we have Understood him in the Noblest Sense we could Attain to, as believing That to be most Probably His.* [44] (My italics.)

In short, what the Richardsons did was, first, by treating obscurity as a virtue, to justify close reading for other than textual purposes, and second, by assuming that the poet can always be understood "in the Noblest Sense," to justify the search for complexities that may never have entered the poet's mind. And in thus developing a rationale for their own criticism, they seem also to have developed a perfect rationale for the kind of criticism that Warburton himself was to write in the edition of Pope.

The Richardsons' criticism, moreover, has some of the characteristics of Warburton's. One example will make my point. Bentley had questioned Milton's phrase "darkness visible" because "*Darkness visible* will not serve to *discover Sights of Woe* through it, but to cover and hide

36. Richardson and Richardson, *Explanatory Notes*, p. clxxxi.
37. Richard Bentley, ed., *Milton's Paradise Lost* (London, 1732). The Preface, in which these notions are stated, is unpaginated.
38. Richardson and Richardson, *Explanatory Notes*, p. cxxii.
39. *Ibid.*, p. cxxxv.
40. *Ibid.*, p. clxxiii.
41. J. W. Mackail, *Bentley's Milton*, Warton Lecture on English Poetry, XV, *Proceedings of the British Academy*, XI (n.d.), 17.
42. Richardson and Richardson, *Explanatory Notes*, p. cxliv.
43. *Ibid.*, p. clvii.
44. *Ibid.*, p. clxxiii.

them." What Milton probably wrote, Bentley suggested, was "a tran-spicuous gloom." [45] To this matter the Richardsons devote almost four pages. They argue that

no doubt when Milton was describing Hell as all in Flames, he found This took away the Idea of Darkness, Utter Darkness! Essential to Hell; he must therefore Reconcile these, which he does by imagining This Fire has not the Property of Light, as Ours, but instead emanates Darkness. Yet the Damn'd must no more have the Comfort of One than of the Other: This Darkness must then serve to discover Horrid Objects, and be Visible it self as One of them; 'tis Greatly and Poetically imagined.

Moreover, they continue, there may exist a fire that gives no light and a visible darkness, and things may be seen in such a darkness if "their Tincts are Inherent, and not owing to what is Foreign to them as Light is to us." [46] Surely this note is as fantastic as any of Warburton's. At excessive length it attributes to Milton an intention that he probably never had and tries unnecessarily to justify the idea expressed by the phrase as scien-tifically plausible. If we forget for a moment that Bentley had made a defense of the phrase necessary, we can read the note as a typical War-burtonian analysis of what does not need to be analyzed.

In pointing out a similarity between the Richardsons' criticism and Warburton's, however, I do not mean to suggest that the one directly influenced the other. Warburton, in fact, was openly contemptuous of the Richardsons' book. [47] What I am suggesting is that, as the Richardsons had done, Warburton adapted the methods of textual criticism to his own purposes. Certainly he was conscious of the problems posed by the application of Bentley's method to modern texts, for he was intimately concerned in the composition of Theobald's preface to his edition of Shakespeare and probably wrote the passage in which Bentley's and Theobald's methods are distinguished. [48] Moreover, by 1741, when Pope made Warburton his official commentator, [49] Warburton had been prac-ticing textual criticism possibly for as long as fourteen years, and it is reasonable to suppose that when he began to edit Pope he carried over to the task some of the habits he had formed while working on the text of Shakespeare. We know, in fact, that he had the temerity to suggest emendations to Pope. "Your partiality to me," Pope wrote to him on November 15, 1743, "is every way so great, that I am not surprized to find you take it for granted, that I observe more Method, & write more correctly, than I do. Indeed in one of your Conjectures you are right, as I see by casting my eye on the Original Copy; but in the other, no such matter, the Emendation is wholly your own." [50] Since Warburton's letter is not extant, we cannot know what excuse he used to justify his attempt at emendation. But it is evident from the attempt itself that he had shifted his attention from Shakespeare to Pope without bothering to adjust his critical focus.[51]

But some adjustment had to be made, obviously, for although Warburton could emend Pope in private, he could hardly do so in print. Even if he had wanted to, the terms of Pope's will prevented him from making changes in the texts of the poems. Of what use, then, was the method of searching for corruptions that he had practiced so assiduously for more than a decade? It could be of use only if, as the Richardsons had done, he turned the method upside down and used it to search for hidden beauties.

And in the rhetoric of Warburton's notes one can sense this method being applied. For Warburton often argues against what seem to be imaginary objections to words or lines, as if, accustomed to exposing alleged corruptions, he must first attack before he can defend,[52] or, to put it another way, as if he were Bentley and the Richardsons rolled into one. Thus of Pope's "Court-virtues bear, like Gems, the highest rate" (*Epistle to Cobham*, l. 141), he writes,

A man dispos'd to cavil would fancy the similitude not exact; for that

45. *Ibid.*, p. 4.
46. *Ibid.*, pp. 12–14.
47. John Nichols, *Illustrations of the Literary History of the Eighteenth Century*, II (London, 1817), 32–33, 81.
48. D. Nichol Smith, ed., *Eighteenth Century Essays on Shakespeare*, 2nd ed. (Oxford, 1963), pp. xlvii–xlviii, and Lewis Theobald, *Preface to the Works of Shakespeare*, ed. Hugh G. Dick, Augustan Reprint Society, no. 20 (Los Angeles, 1949), pp. xxxix–xl.
49. *The Correspondence of Alexander Pope*, ed. George Sherburn (Oxford, 1956), IV, 361.
50. *Correspondence*, IV, 480.
51. Delmore Schwartz has noticed a similarity between textual criticism and the criticism of R. P. Blackmur. See "The Critical Method of R. P. Blackmur," *Poetry*, LIII (October 1938), 28–29.
52. Cf. Helen Gardner's tart comment on the New Critics: "It is a part of the game of 'explication,' as it has developed, to begin by expressing complete bafflement, as if the critic had never met a metaphor in his life. Then after every kind of obtuseness has been exhibited and all possible interpretations and misinterpretations have been considered, the true explication rises like the sun out of foggy mists." *The Business of Criticism* (Oxford, 1959), p. 54n.

principal reason of our preferring the Gem for its durability. But does he not see it is equally for its rarity; and that when once a Court-virtue rises and comes in the way of such a lover of it as our poet, it seldom sets again, but bids fair for being immortal? [53]

Here is a cavil that one doubts ever got caviled — except by a textual critic who is in the habit of raising just such objections as this one. Similarly, in the 1748 edition of the *Essay on Man*, he writes of line 12, Epistle III, "*Form'd* and *impell'd* are not words of a loose, undistinguishable meaning, thrown in to fill up the verse. This is not our author's way; they are full of sense, and of the most philosophical precision." [54] No doubt. But who ever said that the words are "of a loose, undistinguishable meaning?" Nobody but Warburton, who reads Pope as an emendor, but explicates him as a friend.

✦    ✦    ✦

It is easy enough to make fun of Warburton. Arbitrary, dogmatic, and arrogant, he wrote a great deal of nonsense at unconscionable length. But to write his nonsense, it was at least necessary, as Johnson said of the metaphysical poets, to read and think. Moreover, if I am correct about Warburton's adapting the methods of textual criticism to new ends, a certain amount of nonsense was to be expected. For close reading is no critical open-sesame. It cannot be undertaken profitably without a relevant critical hypothesis to give it purpose and direction. Empson, for instance, did not devise a theory of ambiguity as a result of reading closely. He began to read closely to test a theory of ambiguity that had been suggested to him by Laura Riding and Robert Graves. [55] Critical theories are no doubt modified by what close reading turns up, but close reading would probably turn up nothing if there were no theory in the first place: Empty minds find empty poems.

But where in the eighteenth century was Warburton to find a critical hypothesis that would guide his reading? Perspicuity, consistent use of metaphor, aptness of diction — these were the terms in which eighteenth-century critics thought when they turned their attention to the text of a specific poem. And if the Richardsons provided a rationale for digging below the surface, they could suggest only that the critic dig for something called "Ideas." Thus when Warburton began to examine the text of Pope as minutely as he had examined the text of Shakespeare, he was rather like the first man to use a microscope. There was nobody to tell him what to look for. The wonder is, perhaps, not that he saw so much that was not there, but that he saw so much that later critics, trained in the use of microscopes, were to imagine they were seeing for the first time.

53. *Works*, III, 181n.
54. P. 30n.
55. I. A. Richards, as quoted by Stanley Edgar Hyman in *The Armed Vision* (New York, 1948), p. 294.

# The Naked Science of Language, 1747-1786

IN THE conclusion to his *Plan for an English Dictionary* (1747), Dr. Johnson compared himself with the soldiers of Caesar about to invade Britain. He said he looked on the English language as a "new world which it [was] almost madness to invade." Still, he said, if he could not hope to complete the conquest, he might "at least discover the coast, civilize some part of the inhabitants, and make it easy for some other adventurer to proceed further, to reduce them wholly to subjection, and settle them under laws." [1] Clearly the analogy was not meant to include the users of English: *coast* and *inhabitants* both refer to language, one aspect of which is mappable, and the other, dynamic, alive, in need of governing or ordering. Like Caesar the *discoverer*, Johnson would *describe* the territory; but also like Caesar, he would try to introduce law.

It was not a very happy analogy, since he had already made it clear that he hoped to *find* the laws that described the operations of language, rather than to *dictate* them. And he had made it clear that language was most like men in that it was born, it developed, and it declined according to the inexorable laws of its own nature. But the analogy is interesting because its imperfection suggests the dilemma, the uncomfortable tension, Johnson felt between his role as discoverer ("adventurer") and his role as lawgiver ("civilizer").

The structure of the *Plan* is straightforward and clear, consisting of an introduction, a conclusion, and eight topics: (1) Principles for the choice of words to be included, (2) Spelling, (3) Pronunciation, (4) Etymology, (5) Morphology, (6) Syntax, (7) Definitions, (8) Classification. In the introduction, the inconsistency or incompatibility of the two roles appears almost at once, for Johnson describes the popular concept of the work of the lexicographer as that of a drudge requiring "neither the light of learning nor the activity of genius," and then refers to the patrons of French and Italian dictionaries as men "solicitous for the perpetuity of their language" and interested in promoting the eloquence of that language — implying that lexicographers enhance their language as one would not expect drudges without learning or genius to be able to do. The introductory remarks were addressed to Lord Chesterfield, to whom Johnson dedicated the *Plan*; they were meant to be more polite than expository and should not be taken very seriously. Nor does Johnson say that these views are his views. Still, in this introductory gesture are implied two contrasting ideas of the work of lexicographers — as low, safe, innocent, useful, and unenviable, and as contributing to the perpetuity and the eloquence of their language.

The counterpoint between lexicographer as discoverer, describer, observer, or recorder (passive) and lexicographer as civilizer, animadverter, guardian, purifier, fixer, or perpetuator (active) runs throughout the eight sections. The intention to "preserve purity" is balanced by the intent to "ascertain meaning." Both the preserving and ascertaining can be done by *considering* usage in speech and in writing. The lexicographer simply studies and explains how foreign words become naturalized; and he simply ascertains the component sound of words. But he *settles* accents. In the section on principles of selection of words Johnson's emphasis is on the function of observation and recording, just as it is in the second section, on spelling, where the lexicographer is seen setting up the alternatives of customary spelling and reasonable spelling, or the alternatives supplied by two differing authorities. In choosing between them, to be sure, he acts upon the language. And in the third section, on pronunciation, he is much more a civilizer than a discoverer. Since "one great end . . . is to *fix* the English language," it will be necessary to *fix* the pronunciation, to "*guard* . . . against the danger of . . . variation," as in Italy no modern poet is *suffered* to create a new variant pronunciation (V, 8–9). Except perhaps for the last section of the *Plan*, the discussion

1. *Works* (Oxford, 1825), V, 21. Subsequent references are included parenthetically in the text by volume and page numbers.

of pronunciation is the only one where the prevailing concern is pre-scriptive. The discussions of etymology and morphology (topics four and five) are full of such verbs as *distinguish, attain, inquire, search, conjecture, discover, examine,* and *note.* In an aside on what he says his critics may consider his capricious conjectures, Johnson makes the first of a series of comments on the relation between the imperfections of language and the imperfections of mankind: "what is so much in the power of men as language, will very often be capriciously conducted." But the section concludes with a sentence much less philosophical in which the diction is not that of an explorer but that of a missionary: "We shall secure our language from being overrun with cant, from being crowded with low terms, the spawn of folly or affectation, which arise from no just principles of speech, and of which, therefore, no legitimate derivation can be shown" (V, 11). And the last sentence of the section on morphology sounds a similarly discordant note: "neglect of [the differences between transitive and intransitive verbs] has already introduced some barbarities in our conversation, which, if not obviated by just animadversions, may in time creep into our writings" (V, 12).

At this point, however, before turning to the second class of topics (syntax, definition, and classification), Johnson summarizes or looks back in a more scientific way and speaks like an investigator, with a rhetoric that seems to undercut all the pretenses of the civilizer:

Thus, my Lord, will our language be laid down, distinct in its minutest subdivisions, and resolved into its elemental principles. And who upon this survey can forbear to wish, that these fundamental atoms of our speech might obtain the firmness and immutability of the primogenial and constituent particles of matter, that they might retain their substance while they alter their appearance, and be varied and compounded, yet not destroyed?

But this is a privilege which words are scarcely to expect: for, like their author, when they are not gaining strength, they are generally losing it. Though art may sometimes prolong their duration, it will rarely give them perpetuity; and their changes will be almost always informing us, that language is the work of a man, of a being from whom permanence and stability cannot be derived. (V, 12)

By its position (at the mid-point of the essay) and by its authentically Johnsonian tone and movement this passage attracts our special attention. It sharpens the conflict between the notion that the dictionary should have an effect on the language and Johnson's apparently strong conviction that the laws of the life of a language are stronger than any human lawmaker. And the comparison of the lexicographer with the physician seems to carry deep melancholic certainty of the mutability of all the works of men, in contrast with the immutability of God-made atoms or other "primogenial and constituent particles of matter."

The two sections following this interlude, those on syntax and on definitions, emphasize the role of discoverer. Johnson says English syntax "is too inconstant to be reduced to rules" and can be taught only by "special precedents." We must "examine," "remark," and "consider." The long section on definitions, consisting of three topics—the arrangement or ordering of various meanings of a word, the discriminating between synonyms, and the tracing of the changes in meaning of a word—may be said to concern the work of a civilizer insofar as Johnson says he will try to discriminate among words "generally accounted synonymous"; still the prevailing metaphor makes the lexicographer not a legislator but a judge whose endeavor will be "to collect the testimonies on both sides and . . . to discover and promulgate the decrees of custom, who has so long possessed, whether by right or by usurpation, the sovereignty of words" (V, 16).

In the last of the eight main parts of the *Plan*, Johnson discusses what he calls "that part of lexicography which is strictly critical," by which he means not "loosely popular," but of scholarly or perhaps scientific or linguistic interest. It consists of labeling words according to whether they are words of general use, words found "chiefly in poetry," obsolete words, and the like. It is clearly a job of exploring and describing, or to make the metaphor a little more specifically scientific, a job of collecting and classifying. The tone is free from suggestions of civilizing. The last class, however, consists of "barbarous, or impure words and expressions" which "will be branded with some note of infamy, as they are carefully to be eradicated wherever they are found." In only one other place in the essay—the passage, quoted above, about "cant . . . and low terms, the spawn of folly or affectation," lacking "legitimate derivation" (and being therefore bastards)—only in that one other place does Johnson sound more like the prosecutor than the judge.

In the conclusion Johnson opposed, or arranged, the prescriptive-descriptive functions in this way:

This, my Lord, is my idea of an English dictionary; a dictionary by which the pronunciation of our language may be fixed, and its attainment facilitated; by which its purity may be preserved, its use ascertained, and its duration lengthened. And though, perhaps, to correct the language of nations by books of grammar, and amend their manners by discourses of morality, may be tasks equally difficult, yet, as it is unavoidable to wish, it is natural likewise to hope. . . . (V, 20–21)

In this opposition there is no literal or logical inconsistency, perhaps, but Johnson comes close to suggesting that though he aims to *fix*, nothing will stay fixed; though he aims to *purify*, nothing will stay purified; though he aims to *perpetuate*, he can only hope to lengthen the duration of the language.

We are reminded of Imlac's remark that "inconsistencies cannot both be right, but, imputed to man, they may both be true." Johnson *knew* perfection was impossible, but he thought there was something humanly right in striving for perfection. The only bit of Johnsonian humor in the *Plan* occurs in the discussion of "difference of signification in words," where he says:

the strict and critical meaning ought to be distinguished from that which is loose and popular; as in the word *perfection*, which, though in its philosophical [scientific or logical] and exact sense it can be of little use among human beings, is often so much degraded from its original signification, that the academicians have inserted in their work, *the perfection of a language*, and, with a little more licentiousness, might have prevailed on themselves to have added *the perfection of a dictionary*. (V, 16)

No modern linguist has a more sophisticated general concept of language or linguistics than Johnson seems, in places at any rate, to have had before he began to work on the *Dictionary*.

One of the clues to Johnson's understanding of the relation between explorer and civilizer is a sentence in the *Plan* that refers to a somewhat different question: "In lexicography, as in other arts, naked science is too delicate for the purposes of life" (V, 3). It is a great Johnsonian axiom — a principle that informs Johnson's criticism. In the *Rambler* (208) he ranked criticism "among the subordinate and instrumental arts"; and though he said that its task was "to establish principles" and "to improve opinions into knowledge" and that it "reduces those regions of literature under the dominion of science which have hitherto known only the anarchy of ignorance," still at the beginning of the Preface to Shakespeare he distinguishes the art of criticism from the sciences: "Demonstration immediately displays its power, and has nothing to hope or fear from the flux of years; but works tentative and experimental must be estimated by their proportion to the general and collective ability of man" (V, 104). Here Johnson was speaking of works of art "not raised upon principles demonstrative and scientific, but appealing wholly to observation and experience," and was emphasizing the human, imperfect, inexact, nonscientific character of literature. And throughout his criticism we are reminded of Johnson's preeminent concern with the human uses of literature, and the "purpose of life": "That book is good in vain which the reader throws away" (VII, 337); "The only end of writing is to enable the reader better to enjoy life, or better to endure it" (X, 245); "I rejoice to concur with the common reader" (VIII, 487) — and so on. Johnson's concern in making the *Dictionary* concurred with the interests of the booksellers who promoted it — that is with its usefulness, not to the English language, but to the users of the language: "The value of a work must be estimated by its use: it is not enough that a dictionary delights the critick, unless, at the same time, it instructs the learner" (V, 3).

In the selection of words, Johnson would rather be overinclusive, because "they that take a dictionary into their hands, have been accustomed to expect from it a solution of almost every difficulty" (V, 3) and because he must consider the needs of "them that only read" as well as "those that write." Some foreign words must be included "because the purchasers of the Dictionary will expect to find them" (V, 5). The users are referred to in two of the aims listed in the conclusion: to "facilitate the attainment" of the language and to "ascertain" its use. The majority of his "readers," he thought, would be not writers and linguists, but Englishmen who wished to know the meaning of words they had read or heard, the spelling of words heard, or the pronunciation of words read. Then, as now, they were by and large men who sought information of immediate use to them, "the solution of a difficulty." In his effort to fill the need for such a book, Johnson would have to be prescriptive, no matter what he thought about the higher, more interesting, more scholarly approaches to the study of language. Even if the *Dictionary* had not been a commercial venture, Johnson would have thought of his "common readers," and would have done his best to warn them about the status of some words, the use of which might make undesirable impressions on their audiences, and to tell them how to avoid similar embarrassments produced by misspelling and mispronunciation. He thought of students, of men in the process of educating themselves — and he

thought of foreigners and translators, whose needs were not much different from those of any Englishman who wished to "attain" the language
and "ascertain" its use.

One other group of users much in Johnson's mind were the generations to come who wished to read the great works in English literature.
Swift and Pope were, of course, not the only men who regretted the fate
of Chaucer, whose works could no longer be fully enjoyed because modern English was not Middle English. Many of Johnson's contemporaries
(especially writers, presumably) believed that a good dictionary would
prolong the life and fame of Augustan literature by fixing the English
language in its present perfect state. Swift, in what Johnson called his
"petty treatise," had called for an academy to fix it *forever*. But it is
interesting that when Johnson comes to this subject in his *Plan*, he ne-
glects the easy opportunity to agree with the "fixers" and suggests instead
that his dictionary will prolong the life of English literature, *not* by
preventing changes in the language, but by supplying aftertimes with
the means of reading eighteenth-century English. Notice how the argument goes:

Closely connected with orthography is pronunciation, the stability of
which is of great importance to the duration of a language, because the
first change will naturally begin by corruptions in the living speech. The
want of certain rules for the pronunciation of former ages, has made us
wholly ignorant of the metrical art of our ancient poets; and since those
who study their sentiments regret the loss of their numbers, it is surely
time to provide that the harmony of the moderns may be more permanent. (V, 8)

Johnson does not say, as the argument of the fixers would make us expect, that want of uniformity and rules for pronunciation allowed earlier
English to change and therefore make Chaucer's harmonies inaudible,
but rather that want of a record of the rules of pronunciation of Chaucer's English prevented later ages from knowing how to read Chaucer
"correctly." Later, in the Preface to the *Dictionary* (1755) this is clearly
Johnson's line:

In hope of giving longevity to that which its own nature forbids to be
immortal, I have devoted this book. . . . The chief glory of every people arises from its authors. . . . I shall not think my employment useless
or ignoble if, by my assistance, foreign nations, and distant ages, gain
access to the propagators of knowledge, and understand the teachers of

truth; if my labours afford light to the repositories of science and add celebrity to Bacon, to Hooker, to Milton, and to Boyle. (V, 49–50)

This use of the *Dictionary* was, it seems, more interesting to Johnson than any immediate use it would be put to by schoolboys, foreigners, or others who sought solutions to difficulties. And his scholarly concept of the value of the dictionary was never very congenial with the notions of Chesterfield and others who did indeed think that the language should be purified and fixed. Johnson knew better than to consider language as something a dictator could control (Chesterfield, in his unlucky letter to the *World* (November 28, 1754), said that the times required a dictator in English usage and that he would vote for "Mr. Johnson to fill that great and arduous post.") His own experience as a reader, writer, and scholar would have told him; but in fact we may surmise from his quoting Quintilian that he had recently read a classical warning on the subject. In the section of the *Plan* about analogy, Johnson said, "To our language may be with great justness applied the observation of Quintilian, that speech was not formed by an analogy sent from heaven."

The part of the *Institutes* Johnson refers to is in Book I, Chapters v and vii, on correctness and on language, a *locus classicus* that probably every important writer on language in the eighteenth century was well aware of. Quintilian's warnings about dogmatic and prescriptive efforts to fix the language were, to be sure, directed not at lexicographers but at teachers of composition; but otherwise Quintilian's subject, his analogies, and his ideas were those appropriate to a philologist, and a glance at the context of the passage Johnson refers to will suggest that he found Quintilian's ideas congenial. At the beginning of the chapter on language Quintilian says, "Language is based [*sermo constat*] on reason, antiquity, authority, and usage," by which he means that the question of what words or idioms or constructions are correct or acceptable may be answered by reference to one or more of these four criteria. He then shows how each of the first three are abused by "fat fools" and obstinate pedants, and it is in the course of his warnings about reason (i.e., analogy and etymology) that he points out that analogy was not sent down from heaven: It "was discovered after [men] began to speak. . . . It is therefore based not on reason but on example, nor is it a law of language, but rather a practice which is observed, being in fact the offspring of usage. Some scholars, however, are . . . perverse and obstinate in their passion for analogy." [2] And a few lines further on he says that though we should "resist all tendencies to change," only perversity and pedantry try to retain "forms long obsolete and extinct." Of the four criteria, usage is "the surest pilot," he says, and adds that "we should treat language as currency minted with the public stamp" (I.vi.1–3).

Quintilian's definition of usage would not have offended Johnson nor would it have seemed unscholarly, as it has to some twentieth-century linguists, for Quintilian, linking language and humanity just as Johnson the moralist did, said that usage is "the agreed practice of educated men, just as where our way of life is concerned I should define it as the agreed practice of all good men" (I.vi.45). Johnson's respect for the taste of the common reader was not respect for democratic majorities who might at times be as vicious as Quintilian's Roman majorities who practiced depilation and "drinking to excess in the baths." Johnson mistrusted all critics who arrived at their judgments by slavish following of system ("Naked science is too delicate"); and establishing usage on a simple statistical basis would be as foolish as relying simply on analogy, or etymology, or history, or authority — certainly as foolish as setting up a dictator, as Chesterfield has suggested.

Johnson's role of civilizer may have been thrust upon him by Chesterfield. Sledd and Kolb have made clear nearly all that the data will reveal about the history of the *Plan* and Lord Chesterfield's part in it,[3] but we still do not know to what extent Johnson was influenced by a desire to please his patron or, indeed, by the force of Chesterfield's arguments. What we do know, or what we can reasonably infer from a study of the documents (i.e., the manuscript "A Short Scheme for Compiling a New Dictionary of the English Language," the fair copy of "The Plan of an English Dictionary," and the printed *Plan*), seems to suggest that from the beginning Johnson's desire to explore was at odds with Chesterfield's desire to civilize.

First, Sledd and Kolb point out that in the manuscript "Scheme," when Johnson spoke of orthography, he said it "was long very vague and uncertain but is now more settled and settled with such propriety that it may be generally received, at least the Word is always to be ranged according to the Spelling in present use." But this sentence was revised before the *Plan* was published to read "was long very vague and uncertain, was at last in many cases settled, and by accident, and in which *your Lordship observes* that there is still great uncertainty among the best writers." Chesterfield thought there was more need for fixing than Johnson did, and at every point in the *Plan* where Johnson addresses Chesterfield there seems to be this difference of opinion. Of the six references to his Lordship two are in the introduction and the conclusion, added between the writing of the "Scheme" and the draft of the "Plan" from which the fair copy was made. In the introduction perhaps the most interesting sentence is "I here lay before your Lordship the Plan of my undertaking, that more may not be demanded than I intend" (V, 16). And in the conclusion it is the qualification that follows the summary of aims (fix and facilitate the attainment of pronunciation, preserve purity, ascertain use, lengthen duration) that carries the rhetorical emphasis: "Though, perhaps, to correct the language of nations . . . by books of grammar, and amend their manners by discourses of morality, may be tasks equally difficult, . . . it is . . . natural . . . to hope that your Lordship's patronage may not be wholly lost" (V, 21).

Of the other direct addresses to Chesterfield, one (already quoted) regards spelling, and one comes at the end of a brief discussion of Johnson's plan to give semantic information where appropriate. Here I think we can hear the echo of a basic disagreement between Johnson and Chesterfield; and remembering Johnson's characteristic dialectical method, I find it interesting that Johnson addresses his patron when he states the opinion he wishes to disagree with or correct. He says he knows how trifling these excursions in semantics may seem to "sportive idleness" or "arrogant stupidity," but he will pay no attention to the opinions of those who "know not the difficulty or importance of philological studies." Certainly he did not mean to imply that Chesterfield was among those so ignorant, but Johnson is, nevertheless, defending his concern for exploration against the criticism of those who would simply civilize and subjugate.

In the other two places the case for disagreement is stronger, for in them the problem of prescription is fully confronted; Johnson meets the questions of what is unacceptable and who says so. In both he sounds like a man defending his own ideas and criticizing his opponent's. The first passage was cited earlier; it introduces the art-versus-nature metaphor in a comparison linking *words* and *men*, whose life may be prolonged

2. I.vi.16–18, trans. H. E. Butler, in the Loeb Classical Library ed. (New York, 1920), I, 119.

3. James Sledd and Gwin J. Kolb, *Dr. Johnson's Dictionary: Essays in the Biography of a Book* (Chicago, 1955), pp. 85ff.

but not perpetuated — that basic metaphor that underlies Johnson's concept of language, linguistics, and lexicography. The second, especially, has been insufficiently noticed by historians of linguistics:

With regard to questions of purity or propriety, I was once in doubt whether I should not attribute too much to myself, in attempting to decide them, and whether my province was to extend beyond the proposition of the question and the display of the suffrages on each side; but I have since been determined, by your Lordship's opinion, to interpose my own judgment . . . And I may hope, my Lord, that since you, whose authority in our language is so generally acknowledged, have commissioned me to declare my own opinion, I shall be considered as expressing a kind of vicarious jurisdiction, and that the power which might have been denied to my own claim, will be readily allowed me as the delegate of your Lordship. (V, 19)

Without using the word Johnson is here speaking of taste, and that leads him in the next paragraph to the question of authority: Whose taste? or, as Johnson puts it, "Who shall judge the judges?" With what seems now like great subtlety, Johnson exposes the dilemma in Chesterfield's position by simply saying that as for the examples, the citations to support the judgments in the dictionary, "many of the writers whose testimonies will be alledged were selected by Mr. Pope," referring to Pope's well-known plan for an English dictionary.

Chesterfield's almost compulsive interest in correctness has been thoroughly documented by J. H. Neumann, who shows how often in the letters to his son Chesterfield spoke of the importance of proper pronunciation, idiom, and spelling. In a letter to Mason (April 17, 1744) Walpole speaks of being amused to find irregularities in the speech of Chesterfield, "who thought of nothing so much as the purity of his language." [4] That was ten years before Chesterfield wrote his famous essay for the *World* praising the forthcoming *Dictionary*; and the remark of Walpole's illuminates the essay. Having no doubt reviewed the *Plan*, dedicated to him and published some years earlier, and with an eye on Johnson's conclusion about authorities, Pope, and soldiers of Caesar, Chesterfield wrote:

Our language is, at present, in a state of anarchy . . . The time for discrimination seems to be now come. Toleration, adoption, and naturalization, have run their lengths. Good order and authority are now necessary. But where shall we find them, and at the same time, the obedience due to them? We must have recourse to the old Roman expedient in times of confusion, and choose a dictator. Upon this principle, I give my vote for Mr. Johnson . . . and . . . surrender all my right and privileges in the English language . . . Nay, more, I will not only obey him like an old Roman, as my dictator, but, like a modern Roman, I will implicitly believe in him as my Pope, and hold him infallible while in the chair, but no longer. (*World*, November 28, 1754)

If we remember that in the *Plan* Johnson's most convincing metaphors compared the lexicographer not to Caesar as dictator but Caesar as discoverer, not as a god with the gift of immortality, but as a physician able perhaps to prolong life, not as a lawmaker but as a judge who reviewed the evidence and in the light of precedents made a decision, not as a physical scientist dealing with mathematical certainties but as a humanist dealing with the behavior of men — if we remember this, we may imagine how this passage in Chesterfield's letter may have exacerbated Johnson's resentment of his "patron," for Chesterfield here reminded Johnson of their basic disagreement about language. Johnson may have suffered for not telling Chesterfield right at the start that his own "dreams of a poet" were at variance with his lordship's understanding of the task of a lexicographer. If there was something not quite honest in accepting the support of Chesterfield and the booksellers, it was no more dishonest than the little compromises that often must be made to gain the support of patrons. And, what is more, and what is often forgotten by modern critics who smile at the notion of fixing the language, Johnson knew that relatively speaking, a good, widely-used dictionary would in fact tend to fix the language, would have some effect on usage, would retard the rate of change, just as even the most nonprescriptive dictionary tends to normalize usage. Johnson was "scientific" enough to know that in the very act of observing a phenomenon he would affect it, or at least that in publishing the results of his observations he would influence the language itself.

✓   ✓   ✓

The notion that Johnson set out to fix the language persists, partly because of our natural tendency to assume that the "neoclassical" age in its confidence in reason had many foolish notions that the Romantic poets and modern science have freed us from. In a recent review a distinguished linguist says that "it was only the long and arduous labor, the

4. J. H. Neumann, "Chesterfield and the Standard of Usage in English," *MLQ*, VII (1946), 475.

constant observation of linguistic facts, that led [Dr. Johnson] to change his mind" about the possibility of arresting all change in English by simply "ascertaining" the language. And the editors of an anthology of essays on language, prepared for the use of college freshmen, say:

Even the normally clear-headed and realistic Dr. Johnson . . . felt it was his duty, as chief lexicographer of his age, to "correct or proscribe" the "improprieties and absurdities" of the language. . . . [The "rules" for the elimination of "undesirable" or "barbaric" locutions] were based either on tradition or logic. Dr. Johnson, for example, selected the English of the Elizabethan period as his standard and urged his readers to adjust their language accordingly.

Both statements about Johnson are misleading. In the section of the Preface on spelling, Johnson said:

Every language has its anomalies, which, though inconvenient, and in themselves once unnecessary, must be tolerated among the imperfections of human things; and which require only to be registered, that they may not be increased, and ascertained, that they may not be confounded; but every language has likewise its improprieties and absurdities, which it is the duty of the lexicographer to correct or proscribe.

That sounds like the normally clearheaded and realistic Dr. Johnson addressing himself to both linguists and common users of a dictionary. The editors' second remark is more faulty, for in both *Plan* and Preface Johnson explains that his "examples and authorities" come from works written between 1558 and 1660; these he regarded as "the wells of English undefiled" (using Spenser's phrase about Chaucer) because since the Restoration

our language . . . has . . . been . . . deviating towards a Gallick structure and phraseology, from which it ought to be our endeavor to recall it, by making our ancient volumes the ground-work of style, admitting among the additions of later times only such as may supply real deficiencies, such as are readily adopted by the genius of our tongue, and incorporate easily with our native idioms (V, 39).

His notion of what ought to be our endeavor may seem naïve to modern students of linguistics, but it is not so silly as "urging his reader to adjust their language" to the idioms of the Elizabethan period. Johnson did not go back before 1558 because he did not want to include obsolete words and, except in a few cases, he did not go beyond 1660 because he did not wish to "admit testimony of living authors" lest he be "misled by partiality" or give any of his contemporaries reason to complain. And in the preceding paragraph he had said that some of the examples had been taken from undistinguished writers because "words must be sought where they are used. . . . Many quotations serve no other purpose than that of proving the bare existence of words" (V, 39).

In another widely-read freshman anthology of essays on language is a piece written originally for a popular magazine by a well-known professor, who represents Johnson as seriously ignorant about the nature of language when he undertook to write the *Dictionary*: "Eight years of 'sluggishly treading the track of the alphabet' . . . taught Johnson that the hopes of 'fixing' the language and preserving its 'purity' were but the 'dreams of a poet doomed at last to wake a lexicographer.'" But that is grossly misleading: what Johnson said in fact emphasizes how much, in the beginning, he aspired not to fixing or purifying but simply to *discovering*:

When first I engaged in this work, I resolved to leave neither words nor things unexamined, and pleased myself with a prospect of the hours which I should revel away in feasts of literature, the obscure recesses of northern learning which I should enter and ransack, the treasures with which I expected every search into those neglected mines to reward my labour, and the triumph with which I should display my acquisitions to mankind. When I had thus inquired into the original of words, I resolved to show likewise my attention to things; to pierce deep into every science, to inquire the nature of every substance of which I inserted the name, to limit every idea by a definition strictly logical, and exhibit every reproduction of art or nature in an accurate description, that my book might be in place of all other dictionaries, whether appellative or technical. But these were the dreams of a poet, doomed at last to wake a lexicographer. (V, 42)

The same essayist says a little later on that Johnson "entered on his task a medieval pedant," and "emerged from it a modern scientist." But I hope I have demonstrated that Johnson entered on his task in a spirit of scientific inquiry, anxious to discover and describe, and that in carrying out the task he could not forget that "naked science is too delicate for the purposes of life." He was never a medieval pedant or a modern scientist.

✦     ✦     ✦

Johnson is not the only eighteenth-century scholar whose ideas about language have been misrepresented by modern linguists turned literary historians. In a third anthology of essays on language widely used in college courses, it is said that the philosophy of the eighteenth century was "inimical to scientific research in language" and that "the prevailing conceptions of language were (1) that language is a divine institution, originally perfect, but debased by man; (2) that English is a corrupt and degenerate offspring of Latin and Greek." These generalizations are false. Other misleading statements about the theory of language in the eighteenth century are common in the writings of the twentieth-century linguistic enlightenment, but these examples will serve. Indeed it might not seem necessary to notice any of these bits of careless history if one of the chief sources for them had not been revived by the recent reprinting of Sterling Leonard's *The Doctrine of Correctness in English Usage 1700–1800* (Madison, 1929), a book full of interesting data and false conclusions. It is one of those works whose pre-emption of the field has prevented a second attempt, and for that reason the reprinting seems an especially discouraging sign. Rather than summarizing Leonard's misunderstandings, I should like to correct some of his generalizations by reviewing briefly a few of the eighteenth-century works that contributed most to the naked science of language.

1    1    1

The year 1786 is a convenient point to mark the beginning of modern philology. In that year Sir William Jones, in his lecture *On the Hindus*, made explicit what had only heretofore been hinted at, namely that Greek, Latin, Gothic, and Celtic all had the same origin with Sanskrit. But during the thirty-five years between 1751 and 1786 at least six important and influential works, in addition to Johnson's *Dictionary* and its Preface, contributed to the development of attitudes and concepts necessary to the scientific study of language. These were James Harris's *Hermes* (1751), *Joseph Priestley's Lectures on the Theory of Language and Universal Grammar* (1762), Adam Smith's "Considerations concerning the First Formation of Languages" (published as an appendix to the third edition of his *Theory of Moral Sentiments* in 1767), Lord Monboddo's *Of the Origin and Progress of Language* (1773–1792), George Campbell's *Philosophy of Rhetoric* (1776), and Hugh Blair's *Lectures on Rhetoric* (1783). All these were by men whose learning we cannot afford to condescend to, and all contributed to the growing interest in the nature of language. To be sure, they were imperfect by present standards, but none was prescriptive, none was primarily aimed at purifying the language, and all were informed by their author's desire to arrive at scientific truth by the process of generalizing from observation.

Aristotle and Quintilian and Horace had for centuries been teaching some things about language that were true enough; Bacon and Locke had recently stirred men's interest in the nature of words; many writers and critics, in discussing style, had discussed language. But not until the middle of the eighteenth century did anyone set himself to the task listed among Bacon's desiderata in *De Augmentis Scientiarum* (VI, 1), that is, a study of philosophical, rational universal grammar. For *philosophical* we should, of course, not read *metaphysical*, or *logical*, or *ethical*, but *scholarly* and *scientific*; and for *universal grammar* not a grammar to control all languages, but rather what we call linguistics — the discovery of the laws (generalizations) that govern (function in) language.

No one who will spend an hour or two with *Hermes: A Philosophical Inquiry concerning Universal Grammar* can fail to discover why the book was popular (by 1806 it had been through six editions). Nor is a careful reader likely to understand why Sterling Leonard so misread it.

What is most noticeable from the beginning is Harris's concern for method. He intends to be scientific and he is proud to think of the study of language as having no immediate end or purpose, but as being just as "liberal" a study as mathematics or chemistry — pursuits suitable to the dignity of the human intellect. In his defense of his extensive use of ancient writers, he gibes at moderns who think "all Philosophy to be the Invention of their own Age," and who "look no higher than to *experimental Amusements*, deeming nothing *Demonstration*, if it be not made *ocular*." But Harris considers his science to be "the study of mind, intellection, and intelligent principles," which like arithmetic and geometry do not depend upon experiment. The modern philosopher errs in thinking that the "criterion of all truth is an Alembic or an Air-pump" and that "what cannot be proved by experiment" is "no better than *mere Hypothesis*."

His method, to be sure, was limited by the insufficiency of his data, but he built his work on observation: "Those things which are *first to Nature* are not *first to Man*. *Nature* begins from *Causes*, and thence descends to *Effects*. *Human Perceptions* first open upon *Effects*, and thence by slow degrees ascend to *Causes*." His reading of Bacon had been effective, and his effort to make linguistics a science was in itself more important than the errors he made. His elaborate effort to find a law explaining gender might have been aborted if he had known that in German *die Sonne* is feminine. His admiration for Greek blinded him to some of his own assumptions. He was capable of saying such things as: "It is perhaps owing to the imperfect manner in which the Article *a* defines, that the Greeks have no Article corresponding to it." Still, in his own ideas and in those of his authorities (particularly Ammonius, the fifth-century commentator on Aristotle's *De Interpretatione* and on Porphyry's *Five Predicables*) Harris taught a generation to look at languages in ways that would eventually bring important discoveries.

First, he considered his subject as *speech*. He said that the more "sublime" part of the study of language comprised the synthetic aspects, the use of language considered under logic, rhetoric, and poetics. He intended, however, to investigate the less sublime, the "analysis" of language. Much in this "analysis" is conventional or of little interest, but Harris's central ideas were noteworthy.

In Book III he defines language as sounds differing from other sounds in having meaning; the meaningful sounds of language differ from other meaningful sounds (cries of animals) in that the meanings in language derive not from nature but from compact. Harris nowhere mentions Locke's name, in a treatise full of reference to scores of authorities ancient and modern; in a long aside Harris argues against Locke's theory of ideas; but he does not speak of language as a gift of God, and he builds his definition on the assumption that men in the process of inventing language gave meaning arbitrarily and *by Compact*.

The sounds of language Harris considers first physiologically, noting that some of the sounds of the human voice are produced before they reach the mouth ("mere primary and single Voices") and that others consist of both voice and articulation, effected by teeth, tongue, and lips. After discussing these mechanics, Harris makes another step in his definition of language. He can now say that a word is a "*Voice articulate and significant by Compact*" and that language may be defined as "*a System of such Voices, so significant.*" In other words, there is no question that Harris recognized what modern linguists call the "primacy of the spoken language," and that he wished to proceed in a scientific way from observations to generalizations. He did, it is true, think language had deteriorated since the time of the Greeks, but he did not think that language was a gift of God or a mysterious entity.

One of Harris's important recognitions was that words stand not for things but for ideas of things. From Aristotle and Ammonius he took the important distinction between symbol and imitation and shows why language had to become symbolic. Long before von Humboldt, Harris suggested that national differences are reflected in languages. And, finally, in his discussion of verbs Harris recognized some of the epistemological problems involved in any speculation about the origin of language, namely the concepts of time and space. It was, he says, man's power to "differentiate the objects of the world, both in their distribution in Space and their succession in Time" that forced man to find a language more elaborate than a few natural cries or sounds.

The eighteenth-century interest in universal grammar sprang not from religious, metaphysical, or Neoplatonic impulses in such men as Harris and those who followed him; it came from Bacon's notion that "Philosophic" (i.e., scientific) grammar should be distinguished from "Simple and Literary" grammar (i.e., rhetoric and poetics). "The noblest species of grammar, as I think, would be this: if some one well seen in a great number of tongues, learned as well as vulgar, would handle the various properties of *languages*." And in the same place (*De Augmentis*, VI, 1) Bacon said this grammar should "diligently inquire . . . [into] the analogy between words and things, or reason; not going so far however as that interpretation which belongs to Logic." Harris's sympathies were partly with the ancients, to be sure, but he was, like other eighteenth-century thinkers, attracted by the possibilities of the attitudes and methods that Bacon had recommended. And *Hermes* is interesting and important in the history of linguistics if for no other reason than the intelligence with which Harris managed to blend Bacon and Locke.

✦   ✦   ✦

Joseph Priestley's *Rudiments of English Grammar Adapted to the Use of Schools* (1762) was not so popular a work as Bishop Lowth's *Grammar* (1762): Priestley's work was in its eighth edition in 1800, Lowth's in its twenty-second. But the commonplace that Lowth was in the long run more influential is misleading. The most influential grammar in nineteenth-century America was that of Noah Webster, who made perfectly clear his sympathy with and debt to Priestley; and Lindley Murray's famous grammar, first published in York in 1795, was much more "scientific" and much less "prescriptive" than it is generally said to be — thanks to the influence of Priestley. In a recent article, Redding S. Sugg, Jr., has done all that should be necessary to correct the common notion that eighteenth-century grammars were unusually prescriptive and were also the source of the benighted, unscientific concepts of language from which modern linguists have freed us.[5] It is an important and excellent article, especially in showing why Lowth's grammar, in its scholarly spirit and its general conceptions, is not very different from the best twentieth-century work; but it is not, I think, quite fair to the most famous and most widely read of all school grammars (two hundred editions before 1850), that of Lindley Murray. In his Preface Murray acknowledged his debt equally to Harris, Johnson, Lowth, Priestley, and Blair, but it was Priestley more than anyone else who showed him how to adapt the naked science to the purposes of life.

In the Introduction to *Rudiments of Grammar* Priestley opened with a strong protest against the use of Latin terms in English grammar; they were, he said, "awkward and superfluous." Murray, time and time again, reminds his students of his agreement with Priestley.

From Grammarians, who form their ideas, and make their decisions respecting this part of English Grammar, on the principles and construction of languages, which, in these points, do not suit the peculiar nature of our own, but differ considerably from it, we may naturally expect grammatical schemes that are not very perspicuous nor perfectly consistent, and which will tend more to perplex than inform the learner. (Section 4 in "Etymology")

The Latinizing of English grammar not only did not come from the eighteenth century, it persisted in spite of the eighteenth century.

Again, in the Introduction to his *Rudiments* Priestley had said that the business of the grammarian was not to try to fix the language, but to "exhibit its actual structure and the varieties with which it is used." A year before, in his *Course of Lectures on the Theory of Language and Universal Grammar* (1761), he had elaborated this point by saying that "literary critics" must not be used as authorities; their opinions should be "left to recommend themselves by their own right," but when their decisions "have the sanction of any authority," then usages are likely to be established which later ages will wish to correct. "Undue influence," he said, "may keep a language much longer in an imperfect state than it otherwise would have been." Now compare Murray on the same subject:

With respect to anomalies and variations of language, thus established, it is the grammarian's business to submit, not to remonstrate. In pertinaciously opposing the decision of proper authority, and contending for absolute modes of expression, he may, indeed, display learning and critical sagacity; and, in some degree, obscure points that are sufficiently clear and decided; but he cannot reasonably hope either to succeed in his aims, or to assist the learner, in discovering and respecting the true standard and principles of language. ("Syntax")

In dubious cases the grammarian may "reason and remonstrate," "but when authority speaks out and decides the point, it were perpetually to unsettle the language, to admit of cavil and debate. Anomalies then, under the limitation mentioned, become the law, as clearly as the plainest analogies." That some prescriptive theories of grammar survived in the nineteenth century cannot be blamed on the eighteenth-century grammarians or that maligned eclectic, Murray.

There are many other signs in Murray of the scientific theory and spirit of Priestley; the most interesting of them all are Murray's definitions of parts of speech:

A Substantive may, in general, be distinguished by its taking an article before it, or by its making sense of itself; as, a *book*, the *sun*, an *apple*; *temperance, industry, chastity*.

An Adjective may be known by its making sense with the addition of the word *thing*: as, a *good* thing: a *bad* thing: or of any particular substantive; as, a *sweet* apple, a *pleasant* prospect, a *lively* boy.

A Verb may generally be distinguished by its making sense with any of the personal pronouns: or the word *to* before it: as, I *walk*, he *plays*, they *write*: or, to *walk*, to *play*, to *write*.

Now thirty-four years before, another young schoolteacher had recognized the value of this essential point in structural or descriptive linguistics. Near the end of his *Course of Lectures*, in a discussion of the advantages of the diversity of languages, Priestley says that a knowledge of more than one language can free a man "from many prejudices and errors which arise from *verbal* associations and analogues," for it is people who know only one language that "perpetually confound the ideas of words with the ideas of things." And he goes on to praise the liberal or humanistic value of the study of language:

Let the experiment be tried upon a person of good understanding, and it will be found . . . that he can learn to distinguish the most obviously distinct parts as *substantives, adjectives*, and *verbs*: and perhaps he will

5. "The Mood of Eighteenth-Century English Grammar," *PQ*, XLIII (1964), 239–52.

distinguish them, at last, rather by their circumstances and adjuncts, than by an attention to the nature of the ideas they present to his mind. For instance, he will distinguish an *adjective* by admitting *man* or *thing* after it; a *substantive*, by its taking *good* or *bad* before it; and a *verb*, by its being preceded by the personal pronouns *I, those, he* &c, and not by considering that a substantive is a name of a thing.

*The Course of Lectures on the Theory of Language and Universal Grammar* was printed by Priestley in Warrington for his students in the Academy there; it was, he later said, "never published." [6] But all subsequent writers on language in English in the eighteenth century seem to have known the work. Priestley's most important points (in the Grammar and the Lectures) can be summarized. "The custom of speaking is the original and only just standard of any language," and the real nature of the language cannot be learned by a study of Addison, Swift, and other "classical" writers. "In *modern* and *living* languages it is absurd to pretend to set up the composition of any person or persons whatsoever as the standard of writing." Since all the sciences seem to be making progress, we can hope that the science of language, on which the art is based, can also progress to a point where it can acquire "a more fixed and established character" as the result of a general consensus based on all the data ascertained by the linguists. "Grammar may be compared to a treatise of Natural Philosophy; the one consisting of observations on the various changes, combinations, and mutual affection of words; and the other on those of the parts of nature." But the languages of men are not so uniform as works of nature. He thought alphabets too imperfect to be of divine origin; and he believed that the confusion of tongues after Babel was brought about by God "through natural means." In his method he incorporates two means of studying development of language. One is stated in this awkward sentence: "The method of learning and using a language that is formed, must be analogous to the method of its formation" (i.e., phylogeny recapitulates ontogeny). The other was comparative linguistics. Priestley knew Latin, Greek, French, German, Italian, Hebrew, and "the rudiments of Chaldee, Syriac, and Arabic." In the notes to the lectures he refers to words or idioms in Middle English, Malayan, Brazilian, Welsh, "Algonkine," and "the Poconchi tongue, spoken in some parts of the *Honduras*."

The mind and method of a scientist mark these lectures, and though Priestley was capable of speculation that may now seem naïve, his attitude was clearly that of a man interested in collecting the facts. "Before we can improve upon *nature*, by an artificial combination of its powers, the laws of nature must be understood; and they are only to be understood by a careful observation of what doth in fact take place in consequence of them." So, we are inclined, or should be inclined, to forget that Priestley thought that the great number of inflections in Latin and Greek must have made it impossible for the common people of Greece and Rome to speak their languages "in their full extent and purity." And we do well to notice that Priestley concluded his lectures by saying that if he "had had the good fortune to meet with more books (which are probably extant)" like Hadrian Reland's *De Linguis Insularum Quarundam Orientalium* and *De Linguis Americanis*, books which "treat of the peculiarities of foreign tongues," he could have made his lectures more valuable. "If any person into whose hands this performance may fall, would direct [me] to such books, [I] will thankfully acknowledge the favour."

⁊ ⁊ ⁊

The essential idea of Adam Smith's essay "Considerations concerning the First Formation of Languages" may have been expressed as early as 1748, the year Smith gave his first lectures in rhetoric and belles lettres at Edinburgh. What is now known is that it was the subject of one of the lectures Smith gave in his course in Glasgow in the winter of 1763–1764.[7] It seems safe to assume that Smith's theories were known before Priestley published his lectures, even though the essay (in an expanded form) was not published until 1767, when it appeared as an appendix to the third edition of the *Theory of Moral Sentiments*. Priestley speculated about the progress of languages from a highly-inflected to a less-inflected form; he thought that mixture of languages, incident to conquests of one nation by another, would tend to simplify the surviving languages; and he thought composition by means of inflection rather than by means of auxiliary verbs and prepositions was the earliest form because it was the most natural. But if Smith worked out his notions along those lines before Priestley did, it is little matter; for in fact both men may have got the suggestion for this interesting theory from Bacon, who was, I think, the

6. It was reprinted in 1824, in Vol. XXIII of his *Theological and Miscellaneous Works*, ed. J. T. Rutt.

7. See Smith's *Lectures on Rhetoric and Belles Lettres*, ed. John M. Lothian (London, 1963).

first to suggest it. As an illustration of the kind of observations his new scientific grammarians might make (*De Augmentis*, VI, 1) Bacon says:

And is it not a fact worthy of observation (though it may be a little shock to the spirits of our moderns) that the ancient languages were full of declensions, cases, conjugations, tenses, and the like, while the moderns are nearly stripped of them and perform most of their work lazily by prepositions and verbs auxiliary? Surely a man may easily conjecture (how well so ever we think ourselves) that the wits of the early ages were much acuter and subtler than our own.

In the exploration of this observation Smith made his contribution to modern linguistic theory by hypothesizing that primitive languages are in general more complex than the languages of highly-cultivated societies. He assumed that men developed their languages slowly, going from those elements which required the least generalization to those that required more. The names for specific things would be the first words invented. Each of the succeeding steps must have required "a considerable degree of abstraction and generalization," a phrase Smith uses to discuss (1) the jump from words for specific, individual things to words for classes of things — e.g., from a word for the particular cave a particular man lives in to a word for all caves, (2) the invention of "nouns adjective," (3) the invention of prepositions, probably the last group of words invented — "*of* is the most metaphysical of all prepositions," (4) the invention of "number, considered in general, without relation to any particular set of objects numbered." Now because of the great difficulty of forming abstract and general terms, Smith thought, the earliest declensions and conjugations must have been very complex. That is, just as early man had different words for each tree but no word for all trees, so he would have different words (or different *forms* of the same word) for every different relationship the word could be used in. The process of simplification may have begun when an influx of foreigners eager to learn the language of the natives bypassed some of the difficulty by using prepositions and auxiliary verbs instead of inflections. Smith's central metaphor is a mechanical engine. All machines are very complex when first invented, but as it is discovered that three or four different parts of the engine can in fact be replaced by one standard, uniform part, the machine becomes simple. In language it was discovered that four or five prepositions and half a dozen auxiliary verbs "were capable of answering the end of all the declensions and of all the conjugations of the ancient languages." Latin, a mixture of Greek and ancient Tuscan, is less complex than Greek — "the number of infinitives and participles is much smaller in Latin than in Greek." Italian is more simple in declensions and conjugations than Latin. However, Smith said, Italian "composition" is more complex than Latin. He thought that although machines become more perfect as they become simpler, languages do not. Modern languages with their lack of inflection permit less variety in composition because position is such an important part of syntactical structure, and also because modern languages are more prolix: "What a Roman expressed by . . . *amavissem* an Englishman is obliged to express by four different words, *I should have loved.*"

Whatever we may think of Smith's criteria for language and his sense of Western man's decline, we should recognize the importance in the development of linguistics of the hypothesis that the typical progress of a language is from complex to simple — even if it was expressed in a context of eighteenth-century admiration for Hellenism or for primitivism.

*✻ ✻ ✻*

*Of the Origin and Progress of Language*, by James Burnett, Lord Monboddo, was published anonymously in six volumes successively from 1773 to 1792. The first volume, of most interest to the present study, was revised, augmented, and republished in 1774. On the tour of the Hebrides, Boswell was delighted at the success of his efforts to get Johnson to visit Monboddo, whom Johnson had met some years before in London and had taken a dislike to. Not only was Johnson polite to Monboddo, he seemed to be won over to some personal affection, even if he continued to be contemptuous of Monboddo's pre-Darwinian theories of the origin of man. Boswell reports that Johnson was reading the first volume of the *Origin of Languages* on September 19, 1773, though five weeks earlier Johnson had said "it was a pity to see Lord Monboddo publish such notions as he has done, a man of sense and of so much elegant learning. . . . Other people . . . have strange notions, but conceal them. If they have tails, they hide them." During the famous interview Monboddo "showed Mr. Johnson *Hermes*, as the work of a living author for whom he had great respect. Mr. Johnson said nothing. He afterwards told me that Harris was a coxcomb." There is reason to think better of both *Hermes* and Monboddo than Johnson did. "Readers of this generation," the author of the article on Monboddo in the ninth edition of the *Encyclopaedia Britannica* says,

are more likely to be surprised by the scientific character of his method and the acuteness of his conclusions, than amused by his eccentricity. . . . His idea of studying man as one of the animals, and of collecting facts about savage tribes to throw light on the problems of civilization bring him into contact with [Darwinism].

Volumes II–VI of his work on language are not so interesting, because not so original, as Volume I, but they are not dull and they reflect always a lively mind, a widely-read humanist with a "scientific" curiosity. In Volumes IV–VI, for example, Monboddo shows that he is aware of the importance of Jones's hypothesis about the Indo-European languages. In Volume I he makes clear his debt to earlier writers, particularly to Harris, Priestley, and Smith — as well as his awareness of Rousseau, Condillac, and other continental writers on the subject.[8] Monboddo had the advantage of some books on the languages and customs of primitive tribes that Priestley had regretted the lack of.

The most "modern" of his ideas was the one that Johnson resisted and perhaps misunderstood: that the behavior of animals might teach us something about man. Priestley had said we might learn something about how language develops by studying children; Monboddo said we might learn from studying orangutans as well as the language of primitive peoples. He argued that the difference between animals and human beings might be the possession not of a language but rather of the power to generalize, that the power to reason might have developed before the power to communicate, and that orangutans might be men "in a state of nature," reasonable but inarticulate. He was pleased to believe that in an important sense "man is the work of man," and that language was one of his contributions to his own humanity. The first language must, he thought, have been rude and artless; but by means of it men achieved a level of sophistication on which they were able to create a second language founded on rules of art. In Greek, for example, he thought the root words, or stems, had been chosen for reasons of art, and that classical Greek could not have been produced by the common people. He was an enthusiastic Hellenist and at times sounded like another eighteenth-century primitivist — convinced as he was that men and their languages have been constantly deteriorating since an early age of perfection.

All such amusing speculations, however, should not detract from the contributions Monboddo made to the scientific study of language. First, his interest was in the spoken language: "Language spoken may be said to be *living language*, compared with *written language*, which may be called the *dead letter*, being altogether *inanimate*, and nothing more than the marks or signs of language" (IV, 170). His aim was to be scientific: in his Introduction he says his style will be "plain and didactic" as befits a scientific treatise, and in Volume IV, after comparing Greek, Latin, English, French, and Italian, he says, "In short, by this comparison, we are led to know, and to know scientifically, what is most perfect in [the art of language]." He made use of published accounts of the "barbarous languages" of the "Huron, Galibi, and Caribee," to show that in primitive languages the words are long and full of vowels and to illustrate the complexity of primitive languages that results from inadequate ability to generalize. He thought of language as process — not as a static set of conventions; and it was change that fascinated him most. Among primitive languages he saw signs of constant improvement — in "accounts of languages that are not barbarous spoken by Barbarous Nations; — such as that of the Garani, — of the Algonkins, — of the Goths, — of the Laplanders, — of the Albinaquois." Of Gothic he says it was "a language of much greater art than any of its descendants, such as German, Swedish, or English." And he quotes Thomas Falkner, "a Jesuit of Paraguay," who said that the language of Patagonia was "a language of great art." Perhaps his emphasis on the possible help anthropology could lend linguistics was his greatest contribution.

✓    ✓    ✓

Two other works on language, published before Jones's lecture *On the Hindus*, need only brief notice. *The Philosophy of Rhetoric* (1775), by George Campbell, D.D., F.R.S. Edinburgh, Principal of Marischal College in Aberdeen, colleague and friend of Thomas Reid, Alexander Gerard, and James Beattie, did not add any new ideas about the study of language. Although it was not nearly so widely read nor so frequently reissued as Blair's *Rhetoric*, it was perhaps the most philosophical, the most distinguished, the most respected of the Scottish rhetorics. The first three

8. Monboddo apparently did not know Herder's *Über den Ursprung der Sprache* (1772), written to disprove the thesis of Johann Süssmilch (1766) that language was the gift of God. Herder's argument was not quite like Monboddo's, but both men were convinced that man had invented language and that the development of language paralleled the development of man's reasoning power.

chapters of Book II, on usage, reflect the modern, liberal, "scientific" attitudes towards the "laws" of language:

Language is purely a species of fashion (for this holds equally of every tongue), in which, by the general but tacit consent of the people of a particular state or country, certain sounds come to be appropriated to certain things as their signs, and certain ways of inflecting and combining those sounds come to be established as denoting the relations which subsist among the things signified.

It is not the business of grammar, as some critics seem preposterously to imagine, to give law to the fashions which regulate our speech. . . . The grammar of any language . . . is no other than a collection of general observations methodically digested . . . Nor does this truth concern only those more comprehensive analogies or rules which affect whole classes of words . . . but it concerns every individual word, in the inflecting or the combining of which a particular mode hath prevailed. Every single anomaly . . . [or exception] stands on the same basis on which the rules of the tongue are founded, custom having prescribed for it a separate rule. (II, i)

In his discussion of usage, to be sure, he follows the classical criteria of "reputable, national, and current" use, and he defines reputable, or "general," use as "whatever modes of speech are authorized as good by the writings of a great number, if not the majority, of celebrated [not necessarily the best] authors [of the present time]." Most of this section of his work is an essay in establishing "canons of use" by means of which men can choose between alternate or among various uses. Campbell does not write about the theory of language nor is he interested in speech; and it is no wonder that he disappoints such modern historians as Leonard. But as a student of written language Campbell does show the good effects of the liberating, inquisitive, scholarly approach of Priestley.

The Lectures on Rhetoric (1783), by Hugh Blair, the first occupant of the chair of Rhetoric and Belles Lettres in the University of Edinburgh, were "read in the University for twenty-four years" before their publication. Some of Blair's contemporaries are said to have felt that he did not sufficiently acknowledge his indebtedness to Adam Smith, whose lectures on rhetoric and belles lettres he had attended sometime about 1750 and who had later lent Blair the manuscript of his lectures. Now that we can examine Smith's lectures,[9] we can agree with those who think Blair's debt to Smith was inconsiderable. But the virtue of the work is its eclecticism. At the beginning of the first of the four chapters devoted to language Blair refers his readers to Smith's "Considerations concerning the First Formation of Languages," Monboddo's *Of the Origin and Progress of Language*, Harris's *Hermes*, Condillac's *Essai sur l'Origine des Connoissances Humaines*, Rousseau's *Discours sur l'Inégalité parmi les Hommes*, as well as works by le président de Brosses, Marsais, Beauzée, Batteux, l'Abbé Girard, and others; and during the course of the lectures he refers to Priestley and Campbell, as well as to Cadwallader Colden's *History of the Five Indian Nations*. Blair's *Rhetoric* was the most widely-read rhetoric in the world for about a century, and it is interesting that it should have been a work that so well summarized the new ideas and attitudes about the study of language. For our present purpose it has one other point of interest. Hugh Blair, the champion of Ossian, was interested in "that seeming paradox, that Poetry is more ancient than Prose," and in the possibility that all language was "originally poetical." Blair found in Ossian the true sublime, which he characterized in an earlier lecture as "great things in a few and plain words." We shall return in just a moment to the connection between the eighteenth-century interests in the sublime and in language.

✓ ✓ ✓

One of the "classics" of modern linguistic study, Leonard Bloomfield's *Language* (New York, 1933), says this about "what eighteenth-century scholars knew about language":

They stated the grammatical features of language in philosophical terms and took no account of the structural difference between languages, but obscured it by forcing their descriptions into the scheme of Latin grammar. They had not observed the sounds of speech, and confused them with the written symbols of the alphabet. This failure to distinguish between actual speech and the use of writing distorted also their notions about the history of language. They saw that in medieval and modern times highly cultivated persons wrote (and even spoke) good Latin, while less educated or careless scribes made many mistakes: failing to see that this Latin-writing was an artificial and academic exercise, they concluded that languages are preserved by the usage of educated and careful people and changed by the corruptions of the vulgar. In the case of modern languages like English, they believed, accordingly, that the speech-forms of books and upper-class conversation represented an older and purer level, from which the "vulgarisms" of the common people had branched off as "corruptions" by a process of "linguistic decay." The grammarians felt

9. In the edition of Lothian; see note 7, *supra*.

free, therefore, to prescribe fanciful rules which they derived from consideration of logic.

These misconceptions prevented scholars from making use of the data that were at hand: the modern languages and dialects, the records of ancient languages, the reports about exotic languages, and, above all, the documents which show us successive stages of one and the same language, as for instance of Anglo-Saxon (Old English) and modern English, or of Latin and the modern Romance languages.

In this Bloomfield seems to have relied on Sterling Leonard, whose conclusion was that "the eighteenth century made no real beginning of scientific historical study of languages (p. 135)." Three things vitiated the results of Leonard's study. One was his failure to evaluate his evidence: *any* grammar or *any* essay on language written in the eighteenth century seemed to him just as significant as any other. He did not even make the elementary distinction between a grammar written for schoolboys to help them learn to write and sound like educated men, and grammars written to advance humane learning. Second, he was so swamped by his materials that he could not make good generalizations; he had none of the gifts of a good historian. He said, for example, that

the eighteenth-century grammarians and rhetoricians were mainly clergymen, retired gentlemen, and amateur philosophers like the elder Shandy, with an immense distaste for Locke's dangerous and subversive doctrines. . . . They built in general upon the neo-Platonic notion of a divinely instituted language, perfectly mirroring actuality but debased by man. . . . (p. 13)

That is a rather misleading generalization if it refers to James Harris, whom Johnson called "a sound, sullen scholar"; Joseph Priestley, the amateur chemist; Adam Smith, the literary critic and amateur economist; Professors Campbell and Blair; or Judge Burnett, Lord Monboddo, an excellent scholar. It does not do justice even to Bishop Lowth, the Professor of Poetry at Oxford and distinguished student of Hebrew poetry. But Leonard's greatest weakness may have been his preconceptions about the eighteenth century — those Romantic and Victorian views which scholars in the last forty years have done much to revise.

One of Samuel Holt Monk's most important contributions to that revision was his study of Longinus in the eighteenth century, which showed how pervasive was the influence of the doctrine of the Sublime in a century that was supposed to have been bounded by the prescriptions of rules and reason, and held rigid by respect of "correctness." Even in the study of language Longinus may have had some influence (Thomas Sheridan the rhetorician was enthusiastic about the "rhetoric" of Longinus, and Blair's two chapters on the sublime precede his chapters on language). At any rate, Priestley's concept of language as a natural phenomenon that could be scientifically observed and analyzed just like other aspects of nature was not different from Longinus's interesting suggestion near the end of his treatise that "In *art* the utmost exactitude is admired; in the *works of nature*, grandeur; and . . . it is by nature that man is a being gifted with speech" (XXXVI, 3).

This identification of language with nature was congenial to all writers who sought to snatch a grace beyond the reach of art, and it was implied, at least, in some of the most important of the eighteenth-century pioneers in the science of language.

# Imlac and the Business of a Poet

THE FOLLOWING passage from the tenth chapter of *Rasselas* is the first half of Imlac's account of his apprenticeship as a poet, and of what a poet should be:

"I was desirous to add my name to this illustrious fraternity. I read all the poets of Persia and Arabia, and was able to repeat by memory the volumes that are suspended in the mosque of Mecca. But I soon found that no man was ever great by imitation. My desire of excellence impelled me to transfer my attention to nature and to life. Nature was to be my subject, and men to be my auditors; I could never describe what I had not seen: I could not hope to move those with delight or terrour, whose interests and opinions I did not understand.

"Being now resolved to be a poet, I saw every thing with a new purpose; my sphere of attention was suddenly magnified: no kind of knowledge was to be overlooked. I ranged the mountains and deserts for images and resemblances, and pictured upon my mind every tree of the forest and flower of the valley. I observed with equal care the crags of the rock and the pinnacles of the palace. Sometimes I wandered along the mazes of the rivulet, and sometimes watched the changes of the summer clouds. To a poet nothing can be useless. Whatever is beautiful, and whatever is dreadful, must be familiar to his imagination: he must be conversant with all that is awfully vast or elegantly little. The plants of the garden, the animals of the wood, the minerals of the earth, and meteors of the sky, must all concur to store his mind with inexhaustible variety: for every idea is useful for the inforcement or decoration of moral or religious truth; and he, who knows most, will have most power of diversifying his scenes, and of gratifying his reader with remote allusions and unexpected instruction.

"All the appearances of nature I was therefore careful to study, and every country which I have surveyed has contributed something to my poetical powers."

Whereupon Rasselas breaks in:

"In so wide a survey, said the prince, you must surely have left much unobserved. I have lived, till now, within the circuit of these mountains, and yet cannot walk abroad without the sight of something which I had never beheld before, or never heeded."

"The business of a poet, said Imlac, is to examine, not the individual, but the species; to remark general properties and large appearances: he does not number the streaks of the tulip, or describe the different shades in the verdure of the forest. He is to exhibit in his portraits of nature such prominent and striking features, as recal the original to every mind; and must neglect the minuter discriminations, which one may have remarked, and another have neglected, for those characteristicks which are alike obvious to vigilance and carelessness." [1]

And so on to the second half of the chapter, which concerns the poet's business with men and language, a passage with which I am not now concerned.

✓     ✓     ✓

When we read Imlac's speech we know how to take it, because Imlac is a personage in a tale. That being so, anything he says will be an expression of his fictitious character. Moreover, on this occasion we see that what he says is, to begin with at least, complicated by his feeling — that he is gently mocking at himself because he had begun this part of his career by assuming that literary genius can be acquired voluntarily. He was "desirous" and "resolved to be a poet." Johnson, also, is mocking at Imlac, as six months later he was to mock at Dick Minim, the pseudo-critic. In his little way and as far as this mistake goes, Minim is another Imlac. Like him, "being now at liberty to follow his genius," that is, his bent, Minim "resolved to be a man of wit and humour." Minim also undergoes the same apprenticeship as Imlac, though it is a slender and comic version of it. For him (*Idler*, 60), the process is Imlac's in reverse, in that reading supersedes living (in coffeehouses):

That he might be properly initiated in his new character, he frequented the coffee-houses near the theatres, where he listened very diligently day, after day, to those who talked of language and sentiments, and unities and catastrophes, till by slow degrees he began to think that he understood something of the stage, and hoped in time to talk himself.

1. *Rasselas*, ed. R. W. Chapman (Oxford, 1927), pp. 48–50.

But he did not trust so much to natural sagacity, as wholly to neglect the help of books. When the theatres were shut, he retired to Richmond with a few select writers, whose opinions he impressed upon his memory by unwearied diligence. . . .

Imlac, as I say, is one of Johnson's personages, but as everybody knows, there is something of Johnson in him, and that makes all the difference between Imlac and Minim. Imlac's conception of the poet — a conception that he could not himself fulfill — is in all essentials that of Johnson himself. It represents the beau ideal of the poet as Johnson sees it. There is no smile over this, only over Imlac's finding it too difficult for him.

First we note that the ideal poet is universally learned — and learning for Imlac, and Johnson, consists in book learning (though books are rejected as models) and knowledge of nature human and external. This is the learning that Johnson expects of any man, if he is a man of "vigorous intellect." *Rambler*, 103, from which that phrase is taken, concerns "curiosity": Johnson sees man as impelled to learn:

We are eager to see and hear, without intention of referring our observations to a further end; we climb a mountain for a prospect of the plain; we run to the strand in a storm, that we may contemplate the agitation of the water; we range from city to city, though we profess neither architecture nor fortification; we cross seas only to view nature in nakedness, or magnificence in ruins; we are equally allured by novelty of every kind, by a desert or a palace, a cataract or a cavern, by every thing rude and every thing polished, every thing great and every thing little; we do not see a thicket but with some temptation to enter it, nor remark an insect flying before us but with an inclination to pursue it.

The poet, on the other hand, has a purpose in learning: Imlac "saw every thing with a new purpose." And in the Life of Milton Johnson was to indicate how learning develops into poetry:

Poetry is the art of uniting pleasure with truth, by calling imagination to the help of reason. Epick poetry undertakes to teach the most important truths by the most pleasing precepts, and therefore relates some great event in the most affecting manner. History must supply the writer with the rudiments of narration, which he must improve and exalt by a nobler art, must animate by dramatick energy, and diversify by retrospection and anticipation; morality must teach him the exact bounds and different shades of vice and virtue; from policy and the practice of life he has to learn the discriminations of character and the tendency of the passions, either single or combined; and physiology must supply him with illustrations and images. To put these materials to poetical use is required an imagination capable of painting nature and realizing fiction. Nor is he yet

a poet till he has attained the whole extension of his language, distinguished all the delicacies of phrase, and all the colours of words, and
learned to adjust their different sounds to all the varieties of metrical
modulation.[2]

This brings in the technical requirement that Imlac deals with in a section
of this tenth chapter that I am not here concerned with. As usual, Johnson's thinking is found to be consistent with itself — those who see him as
replete with contradictions have not looked at him long and well enough.

His insistence that the poet should be universally learned came at a
time when that ideal showed some signs of slipping. Pope's learning had
been universal, but Collins was attempting no such feat. Universal learning was coming to seem no height for a poet to scale. After Collins came
Keats, who made his thrush sing: "O fret not after knowledge — I have
none,/And yet the evening listens. . . ."[3] The belief that poets did not
need to have very much knowledge was a consequence of the lyric's oust-
ing the epic and coming to be regarded as poetry par excellence. After the
mid-eighteenth century poets felt they had a choice between learning
and comparative ignorance — ignorance of what a learned man would
know — without detriment to their status. In earlier ages a poet knew that
without learning he could never hope to be a major poet. But in the mid-
nineteenth century, Hopkins, to take the supreme instance, was not a
learned poet *in his poems*: nor Rossetti, nor Meredith, nor Hardy (apart
from *The Dynasts*), though Tennyson and Browning were. When in the
nineteenth century we do get an echo of Imlac it is when Henry James
counsels the novelist to "Try to be one of the people on whom nothing
is lost"[4] (though of course he did not include book learning in his knowledge, except as it overlapped what the novelist could learn from his observation of people); and when Newman surveys the curriculum of a
university:

Among the objects of human enterprise, — I may say it surely without
extravagance, Gentlemen, — none higher or nobler can be named, than
that which is contemplated in the erection of a University. To set on foot
and to maintain in life and vigour a real University, is confessedly, as
soon as the word "University" is understood, one of those greatest works,
great in their difficulty and their importance, on which are deservedly
expended the rarest intellects and the most varied endowments. For, first
of all, it professes to teach whatever has to be taught in any whatever de-

2. *Lives of the Poets*, ed. G. Birkbeck Hill (Oxford, 1905), I, 170f.
3. "What the thrush said," ll. 11ff.
4. "The Art of Fiction," *Longman's Magazine*, IV (1884), 510.

partment of human knowledge, and it embraces in its scope the loftiest subjects of human thought, and the richest fields of human inquiry. Nothing is too vast, nothing too subtle, nothing too distant, nothing too minute, nothing too discursive, nothing too exact, to engage its attention.[5]

✦    ✦    ✦

My second point is a gloss on the following sentence in Imlac's speech: "Whatever is beautiful, and whatever is dreadful, must be familiar to his imagination: he must be conversant with all that is awfully vast or elegantly little." When we meet the word *beautiful* here we expect it to be followed by some such word as *ugly*, the logical principle being one of contrast. We should have expected *pleasing* instead of *beautiful* when *dreadful* followed. Readers of 1759, on the other hand, having encountered *beautiful* must have expected *sublime*, because two years earlier Burke had published his *Philosophical Enquiry into our Ideas of the Sublime and the Beautiful*. This book we know Johnson had read and admired: ten years later he praised it as an instance of "true criticism." [6] Here in *Rasselas*, though, he pointedly avoids making a plain reference to one of Burke's two categories. That he has the sublime, however, in mind is plain from his phrase "awfully vast," which is an obvious paraphrase of *sublime*; and indeed also from his word *dreadful*, since it had been a characteristic of Burke's understanding of the sublime that it is "based on terror." [7] It may well be that if Burke's book had not appeared Johnson would have written his sentence differently. The parallel phrase in the *Rambler* I have quoted is "every thing great and every thing little," which suggests the sublime only faintly, if at all. Professor Monk was surely right when he suggested that in writing this sentence Johnson "is thinking of the *Enquiry*." [8]

The sublime, I suggest, was not a category that Johnson was altogether happy about, for reasons I shall hazard later on. In the *Dictionary*, two years before Burke's *Enquiry* was published, he had given definitions of the term which were grossly conservative:

SUBLI'ME, *adj.* [*sublimis, Lat.*]
1. High in place; exalted aloft.
    They sum'd their pens, and soaring th' air *sublime*
With clang despis'd the ground.            MILTON
    *Sublime* on these a tow'r of steel is rear'd,
And dire Tisiphone there keeps the ward.     DRYDEN
2. High in excellence; exalted by nature.
    My earthly strained to the height

In that celestial colloquy *sublime*.　　　　　　　　　　MILTON
　　Can it be, that souls *sublime*
Return to visit our terrestrial clime;
And that the gen'rous mind releas'd by death,
Can cover lazy limbs?　　　　　　　　　　　　　　　　DRYDEN
3. High in stile or sentiment; lofty; grand.
　　Easy in stile, thy work in sense *sublime*.　　　　　PRIOR
4. Elevated by joy.
　　All yet left of that revolted rout,
Heav'n-fall'n, in station stood or just array,
*Sublime* with expectation.　　　　　　　　　　　　　MILTON
　　Their hearts were jocund and *sublime*,
Drunk with idolatry, drunk with wine.　　　　　　　　MILTON
5. Haughty; proud.
　　He was *sublime*, and almost tumorous in his looks and gestures.
　　　　　　　　　　　　　　　　　　　　　　　　WOTTON

I transcribe from a copy of the first edition in the British Museum, which was owned by Burke, who made no protest! He might well have done, for in 1755 *sublime* meant for Johnson scarcely more than *sublimis* meant for the Romans. To limit the content of the word as these illustrations do, all of which are from the seventeenth century (with the possible exception of the one from Prior), was not to allow even for the sense that Boileau had given the word, let alone the English writers after him. And there was surely some distaste expressed in Johnson's entry under *sublime* as a noun, though he speaks purely as a lexicographer:

SUBLI′ME, *n.s.* The grand or lofty stile.
*The Sublime* is a Gallicism, but now naturalized.

Now naturalized, forsooth. It had been used by Addison and Pope, as his illustrations show, which was naturalization indeed. When Johnson comes to define *sublimity* he is more cordial toward it, but only because that form of the noun was grounded in the Latin *sublimitas*.[9]

5. "Christianity and Scientific Investigation" in *On the Scope and Nature of University Education*, Everyman's Library (London, 1915), p. 209.
6. Boswell's *Life*, ed. G. Birkbeck Hill and L. F. Powell (Oxford, 1934–1950), II, 90.
7. Samuel Holt Monk, *The Sublime: A Study of Critical Theories in XVIII-Century England* (New York, 1935), p. 88.
8. *Ibid.*, p. 100, note 47.
9. Johnson himself does not, I think, use "the sublime" as a term except (1) for comic purposes — "the true sublime" is one of the items in Dick Minim's armoury of clichés; and (2) when, after discussing the absence of the "pathetick" from the poems of the Metaphysicals, he writes: "Nor was the sublime more within their reach . . ." (*Lives of the Poets*, I, 20). Here he was virtually quoting Joseph War-

Johnson's definitions distinguish sublimity as it exists in things (air, a tower of steel, a "celestial colloquy," souls, and so on), and as it exists in writing (in a style). But they are behind the times, and that because they pay no attention to sublimity as it exists in the things in which Johnson's contemporaries were increasingly finding it — in things like stupendous precipices and storm-shattered mountains. And yet in the rest of the *Dictionary* Johnson showed well enough that he apprehended this Burkean quality of sublimity in the sort of place where Burke was to find it most abundantly. Under *vast* we get the following:

VAST, *adj.* [*vaste*, Fr. *vastus*, Lat.]
1. Large; great. [Illustrations from Clarendon, Watts (". . . an ample and capacious mind that takes in *vast* and sublime ideas without pain"), and Thomson.]
2. Viciously great; enormously extensive or capacious. [Illustrations from Ben Jonson ("The vicious language is *vast*, and gaping . . ."), Milton ("They viewed the *vast* immeasurable abyss").]

VAST, *n.s.* [*vastum*, Lat.] An empty waste.
[Illustrations from Shakespeare ("They shook hands, as over a *vast*"), Milton ("Through the *vast* of heaven it sounded"), and Pope ("The wat'ry *vast*, Secure of storms, your royal brother past").]

We note that in the quotation from Watts *vast* is actually coupled with *sublime*. And of course Johnson was well aware of sublimity as a thing represented in Milton: in his *Dictionary* under *sublimity*, he quoted Addison's splendid remark that "Milton's distinguishing excellence lies in the sublimity of his thoughts, in the greatness of which he triumphs over all the poets, modern and ancient, Homer only excepted." More important still, Johnson had showed in *The Vanity of Human Wishes* that he could create the sublime style for himself, the style corresponding to his conception of sublime things as Burke was to see them:

> For why did Wolsey, near the steeps of fate,
> On weak foundations rear th' enormous weight?
> Why but to sink beneath misfortune's blow
> With louder ruin to the gulphs below.
>
> (ll. 125–28)

> But few there are whom hours like these await,
> Who set unclouded in the gulphs of fate.
>
> (ll. 311–12)

> Must helpless man, in ignorance sedate,
> Roll darkling down the torrent of his fate?
>
> (ll. 345–46)

Johnson, then, was sufficiently aware of the thing as Burke was to see it. Though he was aware of it, however, he did not show this in the place that most mattered, in his definition of *sublime*. And he had, I think, his reasons for his lack of cordiality toward it. He was loath to encourage men to go after sublimity, and authors especially. That of *Paradise Lost* he found wearying, and we know how unfairly he was to treat Gray's "Bard," which appeared four years after the *Enquiry*, finding that it promoted no "truth" either "moral or political." [10] The sublime he saw as a temptation for authors to neglect the "proper" matter for poetry, the normal stuff of man, the full tide of humanity that he found endlessly fascinating at Charing Cross. He also recoiled from it as a thing that asked man to surrender his godlike reason. When you are half dizzy on the brink of a black abyss you are least a man, and most an animal, and this was no recommendation to Johnson.

And yet, as if Burke's *Enquiry* had tilted a balance in his mind, he proceeded to face the new sorts of sublimity with his usual gusto. He was ready with the best to demonstrate his grip on the theory of the thing in the manner Burke himself had practiced, so much so that he achieved, as we shall see, the most overwhelming description of a sublime object that can be found anywhere in our literature.

ton, who used these categories as a stick to beat a poet Johnson revered as great: "The Sublime and the Pathetic are the two chief nerves of all genuine poesy. What is there very sublime or very pathetic in POPE?" (*An Essay on the Genius and Writings of Pope* [London, 1756], I, x); and cf. p. 280: "But shall I be pardoned for suspecting, that POPE would not have succeeded in this design [of writing an epic]; that so DIDACTIC a genius would have been deficient in that SUBLIME and PATHETIC, which are the main nerves of the epopea. . . ." After using "the sublime" as a virtual transcription from Warton, Johnson proceeds to show a preference for the word *sublimity*: "for they never attempted that comprehension and expanse of thought which at once fills the whole mind, and of which the first effect is sudden astonishment, and the second rational admiration. Sublimity is produced by aggregation, and littleness by dispersion. Great thoughts are always general, and consist in positions not limited by exceptions, and in descriptions not descending to minuteness. It is with great propriety that subtlety, which in its original import means exility [i.e., thinness, meagreness] of particles, is taken in its metaphorical meaning for nicety of distinction. Those writers who lay on the watch for novelty could have little hope of greatness; for great things cannot have escaped former observation. Their attempts were always analytick: they broke every image into fragments, and could no more represent by their slender conceits and laboured particularities the prospects of nature or the scenes of life, than he who dissects a sunbeam with a prism can exhibit the wide effulgence of a summer noon." (*Lives of the Poets*, I, 20f.) The word *aggregation* here need not give us pause, for Johnson's second definition of it in his *Dictionary* is "the collection, or act of collecting many particulars into one whole." For Johnson, as I shall show, sublimity depends on unbroken wholeness, whatever the substance — air, space, matter, mental image.

10. *Lives of the Poets*, III, 438.

His most interesting discussions of sublimity as a thing, not as a style, were to be prompted by passages in Congreve and Shakespeare. In the Life of Congreve comes this astonishing passage:

He has in these little pieces neither elevation of fancy, selection of language, nor skill in versification; yet, if I were required to select from the whole mass of English poetry the most poetical paragraph, I know not what I could prefer to an exclamation in *The Mourning Bride*:

"ALMERIA.
It was a fancy'd noise; for all is hush'd.
LEONORA.
It bore the accent of a human voice.
ALMERIA.
It was thy fear, or else some transient wind
Whistling thro' hollows of this vaulted isle [aisle]:
We'll listen.
LEONORA.
Hark!
ALMERIA.
No, all is hush'd, and still as death. — 'Tis dreadful!
How reverend is the face of this tall pile;
Whose ancient pillars rear their marble heads,
To bear aloft its arch'd and ponderous roof,
By its own weight made stedfast and immoveable,
Looking tranquillity! It strikes an awe
And terror on my aching sight; the tombs
And monumental caves of death look cold,
And shoot a chilness to my trembling heart.
Give me thy hand, and let me hear thy voice;
Nay, quickly speak to me, and let me hear
Thy voice — my own affrights me with its echoes."

He who reads those lines enjoys for a moment the powers of a poet: he feels what he remembers to have felt before, but he feels it with great increase of sensibility; he recognizes a familiar image, but meets it again amplified and expanded, embellished with beauty, and enlarged with majesty.[11]

And there is the following passage from Boswell, which serves as a gloss (we note, by the way, that Johnson is still avoiding the word *sublime*):

. . . 16th of October [1769] . . . Johnson said, that the description of the temple, in "The Mourning Bride," was the finest poetical passage he had ever read; he recollected none in Shakspeare equal to it. — "But, (said Garrick, all alarmed for 'the god of his idolatry,') we know not the extent and variety of his powers. We are to suppose there are such passages in his works. Shakspeare must not suffer from the badness of our memories." Johnson, diverted by this enthusiastick jealousy, went on with greater ardour: "No, Sir; Congreve has *nature*;" (smiling on the tragick eagerness of Garrick;) but composing himself, he added, "Sir, this is not comparing Congreve on the whole, with Shakspeare on the whole; but only maintaining that Congreve has one finer passage than any that can be found in Shakspeare. Sir, a man may have no more than ten guineas in the world, but he may have those ten guineas in one piece; and so may have a finer piece than a man who has ten thousand pounds: but then he has only one ten-guinea piece. — What I mean is, that you can shew me no passage where there is simply a description of material objects, without any intermixture of moral notions, which produces such an effect." Mr. Murphy mentioned Shakspeare's description of the night before the battle of Agincourt; but it was observed, it had *men* in it. Mr. Davies suggested the speech of Juliet, in which she figures herself awakeing in the tomb of her ancestors. Some one mentioned the description of Dover Cliff. JOHNSON. 'No, Sir; it should be all precipice, — all vacuum. The crows impede your fall.[12] The diminished appearance of the boats, and other circumstances, are all very good description; but do not impress the mind at once with the horrible idea of immense height.

11. *Lives of the Poets*, II, 229f. I have called this passage "astonishing" for the obvious reason that for us those lines of Congreve's pale before hundreds of other passages in English poetry. We may note, however, that Johnson does not accord the passage an absolute superlative: his words suggest that there are strong competitors. And, in the second place, part of the comparative weakness of the lines for us is the result of intervening poetry. We now dislike poetry that says "I feel," though of course for Almeria to say it is quite in order, since she is a personage in a play; we prefer poets to create what they are feeling in the minds of their readers, which they can least well do by saying that they are feeling. If, however, we cut out from Almeria's lines those that directly describe feeling, the rest is not so deplorable as in our astonishment we might first think: "reverend" is good, so is "marble heads," and also "By its own weight made stedfast and immoveable." ("Looking tranquillity" would also be good if we did not recognize it as imitated from Shakespeare.) Moreover we may note that Pope complimented the phrase "aching sight" by adopting it for his *Temple of Fame*. Again, the psychology implied in the last three lines is sound and new. Altogether, Johnson has a slightly better case than we might first be inclined to admit. And we have to bear in mind that to some extent, Shakespeare and Milton, who existed prior to the blessed revolution in the late seventeenth century, were distressingly *barbarous* poets for Johnson.

Clearly the passage is important in telling us what Johnson expected of the best poetry as distinct from what he expected of writing in other categories.

His comments about "increase of sensibility" no doubt suggested Wordsworth's distinction between the man and the poet in the 1802 preface to the *Lyrical Ballads*. Much of early nineteenth-century criticism has its roots in Johnson: for an example, see below, pp. 312–13.

12. Cf. Burke, *Enquiry*, ed. J. T. Boulton (London, 1958), p. 72 (pt. II, sec. vii): "I am apt to imagine . . . that height is less grand than depth; and that we are more struck at looking down from a precipice, than at looking up at an object of equal height. . . ." Burke ought to have linked this sensation with fear because we can fall from a precipice but not fall up it. As Monk notes (*The Sublime*, p. 93) depth for Burke is "the most powerful source of the sublime."

Passage from George Frederick Handel's *The Sublime Oratorio of the
Messiah.* Courtesy of the Trustees of the British Museum.

The impression is divided; you pass on by computation, from one stage of the tremendous space to another. Had the girl in "The Mourning Bride" said, she could not cast her shoe to the top of one of the pillars in the temple, it would not have aided the idea, but weakened it. . . . In the description of night in Macbeth, the beetle and the bat detract from the general idea of darkness, — inspissated gloom.' [13]

We can see that this idea of the sublime thing as huge and homogeneous would appeal readily to Johnson. Those couplets from *The Vanity of Human Wishes* well show his sense of size along with unbroken sameness, absence of parts and of details. He must have attended to Burke's remarks on "PRIVATION" (Part I, Section vi), where he read that "All *general* privations are great, because they are terrible; *Vacuity, Darkness, Solitude* and *Silence;*" and in Part IV, Section x, entitled "UNITY why requisite to vastness," we find phrases like "great uniform objects" and "one, simple and entire." We recall that Johnson's definition of *vast* (noun) in the *Dictionary* was "An empty waste." And to turn aside for an instance from music, there was Handel's setting in *The Sublime Oratorio of the Messiah* (to give it the enlarged title George Walker gave it in his edition of 1813, or soon after) of the words: "The People that walked in darkness have seen a great light": Handel matches the sublimity of these words, their "empty" vastness, by giving them an ungainly, stalking, an almost staggering tune, and denying it harmonization (opposite page).[14]

We may note how inevitably the love of magnitude along with unbroken sameness followed from the eighteenth-century love of generality cum simplicity. Johnson achieved the fine phrases "the grandeur of generality" [15] and "simplicity of grandeur." [16] Gray had looked forward to visiting Italy because he could there see "those grand and simple

13. Boswell's *Life*, II, 85–90.
14. It is an interesting comment on changing taste that when Mozart revised the work, he added to the very sparse harmony of Handel beautiful orchestral enrichment — *beautiful* is the word, in Burke's contrasted sense. Sublimity returns with Beethoven, though it is obvious that Mozart, like Pope, could produce it when he needed to, as in the masses and in the Jupiter; showing, again like Pope, that exquisiteness need not be fatal to it. The sublimity achieved by Beethoven seemed to John Henry Newman to be achieved as the sublime was for Burke and Johnson: "For myself, I like an extensive view, with tracts bold and barren in it, such as Beethoven's music seems to represent" (*Letters and Diaries*, ed. C. S. Dessain [London and New York, 1962], XII, 82).
15. *Lives of the Poets*, I, 45.
16. *Rambler*, 37.

works of Art, that are to amaze one, and whose sight one is to be the better for." [17]

The remark on the night piece in *Henry V* calls for comment. Whoever is speaking here thinks that its sublimity would have been improved if there had been nothing but emptiness in it — but he also feels, I think, that it suffers from having men in it. The sublime exists as detached from man as possible. An instance, therefore, of it at its completest is that verse of Genesis, which was a favorite exhibit during the eighteenth century: "God said Let there be light and there was light." Man is wholly outside this, because, when that event took place, he had not even been created! For Johnson Shakespeare's account of Dover Cliff was less sublime than it might have been because among its distracting details was a man — a man so unconcerned with his "dreadful" trade of gathering samphire as to be continuing to gather it. It was the picturesque that welcomed man, not the sublime — as I have said elsewhere, "almost all [eighteenth-century landscape pictures] have their shepherds or girls or house or bridge or spire." [18] If man is represented actually present on the edge or in the midst of the sublime, he must be properly cowering. It is unthinkable that he should be behaving as Johnson fancies Almeria behaving when he amusingly makes her shatter the sublime by throwing her shoe up a pillar of the temple.

Finally it is ironical that Johnson who, to say the least, took a long time to warm up to the sublime, should in the event figure as the writer who brings the eighteenth-century idea of it home to us as no one else did. He achieves this great, this sublime, feat when he describes Dover Cliff in his notes on *Lear*:

The description is certainly not mean, but I am far from thinking it wrought to the utmost excellence of poetry. He that looks from a precipice finds himself assailed by one great and dreadful image of irresistible destruction. But this overwhelming idea is dissipated and enfeebled from the instant that the mind can restore itself to the observation of particulars, and diffuse its attention to distinct objects. The enumeration of the choughs and crows, the samphire-man and the fishers, counteracts the great effect of the prospect, as it peoples the desert of intermediate vacuity, and stops the mind in the rapidity of its descent through emptiness and horrour.

Surely there is nothing in Milton, let alone Burke, to compare with this for physical horrification, for giving a sensation of horror in the pit of the stomach. It could create a soul under the ribs of death, and is enough of itself to attest Johnson's power of imagination.

✦ ✦ ✦

Johnson's opposition of "elegantly little" to the sublime will not keep us long. In that phrase both words are important: the little must not be so little as to cease to be elegant. In the *Dictionary* the word *elegant* and its cognates are defined as follows:

> ELE'GANCE, ELEGA'NCY, *n.s.* [*el*[*e*]*gantia*, Lat.] Beauty of art; rather soothing than striking; beauty without grandeur. [Illustrations from Raleigh (prose), Burnet, and the *Spectator*.]
> ELE'GANT. *adj.* [*elegans*, Lat.]
> 1. Pleasing with minuter beauties. [Illustrations from Pope and Johnson's own *London*.]
> 2. Nice; not coarse; not gross. [Illustration from Pope.]
> E'LEGANTLY, *adv.* [from *elegant*.]
> 1. In such a manner as to please without elevation. [No illustration.]
> 2. Neatly; nicely; with minute beauty. [Illustration from notes to Pope's *Odyssey*.] [19]

Johnson agrees with Burke as to the nature of the beautiful, and especially with III, xiii, "Beautiful objects small," which is not too long to quote in full:

> The most obvious point that presents itself to us in examining any object, is its extent or quantity. And what degree of extent prevails in bodies, that are held beautiful, may be gathered from the usual manner of expression concerning it. I am told that in most languages, the objects of love are spoken of under diminutive epithets. It is so in all the languages of which I have any knowledge. In Greek the ἰσγ, and other diminutive terms, are almost always the terms of affection and tenderness. These diminutives were commonly added by the Greeks to the names of persons with whom they conversed on terms of friendship and familiarity. Though the Romans were a people of less quick and delicate

---

17. Letter of November 16, 1739.
18. *Augustan Studies* (London, 1961), p. 186.
19. I have retained the accents of the first edition of the *Dictionary*. When not placed on the first syllable they are erroneous. Miss Janet Bately has reminded me that in his remarks on stress in the grammar section of his prefatory matter Johnson says that "Trisyllables ending in *ce*, *ent*, and *ate* accent the first syllable," and happens to give as an example the form *e'legant*. Accordingly one would expect also *e'legance*. Miss Bately notes that the 1756 *Dictionary*, "abstracted from the folio edition," has the entries *e'legance*, *e'legancy*, *e'legant*, *e'legantly*, with stress as in modern English, and so corrects the first edition, and that the accent is placed in this way in John Minsheu's *Guide into Tongues*, London, 1617, and Nathan Bailey's *Universal Etymological Dictionary*, London, 1721.

feelings, yet they naturally slid into the lessening termination upon the same occasions. Anciently in the English language the diminishing *ling* was added to the names of persons and things that were the objects of love. Some we retain still, as darling, (or little dear) and a few others. But to this day in ordinary conversation, it is usual to add the endearing name of *little* to every thing we love; the French and Italians make use of these affectionate diminutives even more than we. In the animal creation, out of our own species, it is the small we are inclined to be fond of; little birds, and some of the smaller kinds of beasts. A great beautiful thing, is a manner of expression scarcely ever used; but that of a great ugly thing, is very common. There is a wide difference between admiration and love. The sublime, which is the cause of the former, always dwells on great objects, and terrible; the latter on small ones, and pleasing; we submit to what we admire, but we love what submits to us; in one case we are forced, in the other we are flattered into compliance. In short, the ideas of the sublime and the beautiful stand on foundations so different, that it is hard, I had almost said impossible, to think of reconciling them in the same subject, without considerably lessening the effect of the one or the other upon the passions. So that attending to their quantity, beautiful objects are comparatively small.

And more to the same general effect comes at III, xxiv, "Concerning SMALLNESS." For Johnson there is something endearing in the "elegantly little," as there is when English people use the Scottish word *wee*, or as when Shakespeare refers to "the darling buds of May" or Tennyson to "the little speedwell's darling blue." Instances of things "elegantly little" would be kittens or ducklings. Poets — Johnson is saying — should not put in their poems things that can only be seen by those who screw up their eyes and peer. Rather they should put in such things as are "alike obvious to vigilance and carelessness." There is no pleasure in peering, and the little will cease to be elegant if it has to be peered at. Where poetry is concerned, Johnson is willing to let the slowest walker set the pace. The poet must use those items from external nature that have been observed by man at his worst as an observer. We see how differently Coleridge and Wordsworth were to proceed. They hoped to create the taste by which they were enjoyed. Wordsworth rises to the glowing lines: "What we have loved,/ Others will love, and we will teach them how." [20] And in accordance with this elation he mentions such things as "the star-shaped shadow" that the daisy throws across "the naked stone." The poet, Johnson would say, has no right to use examples of his own ocular triumphs in this way. Ocular triumphs are for men who for the nonce have become specialists — the last thing a poet should become. Johnson achieved them when he was peering at his chemicals during his experiments in natural philosophy. A botanist achieves them when he numbers the streaks of a tulip. But an ordinary man — the man poetry is about, and to whom it is addressed — stays where he has "carelessly" noted that on the tulip, if it happens to be a streaked tulip, streaks exist. The emphatic word is the verb, *number*, and the line is drawn between a striped tulip and the number of its stripes, its stripes in detail. The proper interests of man are served — to take an example — by Pope, when he writes in his second Moral Essay, "On the Characters of Women":

> Ladies, like variegated Tulips, show,
> 'Tis to their Changes that their charms they owe;
> Their happy Spots the nice admirer take,
> Fine by defect, and delicately weak.
>
> (ll. 41–44)

Johnson's *Dictionary* defines *variegate* as "To diversify; to stain with different colours," and Pope's four lines are quoted in illustration. Pope's lines show also the right literary use for streaked tulips, because they exist to illustrate a moral truth. Everybody knows the nature of women; everybody has seen streaked tulips — when Pope wrote, tulips had recently come in from Holland, and were all the rage. And everybody, when he reads these lines, has a new sense of the differences between women, because he has been made to recall variegated tulips in all their brilliant diversity and fragility. Johnson's logic is unchallengeable. When items of the external world are used for "the inforcement or decoration of moral or religious truth" they must not be items that darken counsel. Johnson might have taken as his examples Shakespeare's "Shall I compare thee to a summer's day?," Pope's "The calm sunset of thy various day," and Gray's "Full many a flower is born to blush unseen." All these lines use items of the external world to make more vivid the moral truth concerned — for we must remember that until the late nineteenth century "moral" included the psychological that has since been separated off from it. What would be the point of a poet's attempting to make an idea more vivid by referring it to something of which the normal reader had no experience? Imlac says that "he who knows most, will have most power of diversifying his scenes and of gratifying his reader with remote allusions and unexpected instruction," but he cannot do so unless he uses as the material for his comparisons allusions that, however remotely

20. *The Prelude*, xiv, 446ff.

fetched, are within the knowledge of the normal reader. Johnson complained subsequently of the Metaphysical poets because they "sought out remote resemblances," but here it is the "seeking out" that is blamed. The Metaphysicals' use of imagery struck Johnson, who represented the common reader, as too ingeniously collected, as not having "occurred" to the poet unsought. Those that he pillories do not so much illustrate a moral or religious truth as set up a rival picture, their minor term claiming more attention than their major. If he had not feared to be profane, Johnson would have applauded the practice of Jesus, who compared moral and religious truth to things like masters and servants, talents and lilies of the field. He would also have approved Job when he said that "man is born to sorrow as the sparks fly upward." Johnson is not averse to the poet's knowing everything. Indeed he requires him to do so as he is a man, a man of "vigorous intellect," but he wishes him as a poet to use only such matter as everybody else is acquainted with. The desideration that knowledge should be complete ensures that the poet finds the best image, but within what other men also know. Johnson himself knows that there are such flowers as tulips, that some tulips are streaked, and that the botanist may examine the number of the streaks. Johnson knows everything, but he does not want the poet, who also knows everything, to use such knowledge as he has acquired as a botanist. As he was to say in the Life of Milton, we are all moralists, but are geometricians (or botanists) only by chance. Being an amateur chemist, Johnson got closer to certain things than common men do, but you would not gather his interest in chemistry from *The Vanity of Human Wishes.*

Because Johnson's is an eminently reasoning mind, we feel that his reasoning would change if the materials on which it proceeded changed. The poet must neglect "those minuter discriminations" because "one may have remarked and another neglected [them]." If such a time were to come when mankind's curiosity about external nature improved in closeness, then the poet himself would be able to refer to external nature more closely. Johnson, we feel, would have seen the force of Wordsworth's idea that

The knowledge both of the Poet and the Man of Science is pleasure; but the knowledge of the one cleaves to us as a necessary part of our existence, our natural and unalienable inheritance; the other is a personal and individual acquisition, slow to come to us, and by no habitual and direct sympathy connecting us with our fellow-beings. . . . If the labours of men of Science should ever create any material revolution, direct or indirect, in our condition, and in the impressions which we habitually receive, the Poet will sleep then no more than at present, but he will be ready to follow the steps of the Man of Science, not only in those general indirect effects, but he will be at his side, carrying sensation into the midst of the objects of the Science itself. The remotest [21] discoveries of the Chemist, the Botanist, or Mineralogist, will be as proper objects of the Poet's art as any upon which it can be employed, if the time should ever come when these things shall be familiar to us, and the relations under which they are contemplated by the followers of these respective Sciences shall be manifestly and palpably material to us as enjoying and suffering beings.[22]

After Wordsworth, as closely observant as a botanist, had discovered the star-shaped shadow of a daisy on a stone, mankind was willing to be pleased too — the thing was manifestly and palpably material to mankind as "enjoying" beings. Johnson would also have seen the human interest in Rossetti's poem "The Woodspurge":

> The wind flapped loose, the wind was still,
> Shaken out dead from tree and hill:
> I had walked on at the wind's will, —
> I sat now, for the wind was still.
>
> Between my knees my forehead was, —
> My lips, drawn in, said not Alas!
> My hair was over in the grass,
> My naked ears heard the day pass.
>
> My eyes, wide open, had the run
> Of some ten weeds to fix upon;
> Among those few, out of the sun,
> The woodspurge flowered, three cups in one.
>
> From perfect grief there need not be
> Wisdom or even memory:
> One thing then learnt remains to me, —
> The woodspurge has a cup of three.

Grief has been experienced by everybody, and so a particular experience of it can be counted on to be generally interesting. "The Woodspurge" merely shows the inversion of the usual scheme — a moral or psycho-

21. The use of this word shows a detailed debt to Johnson, as the whole preface in which it occurs obviously shows a general debt to him.
22. Preface to the *Lyrical Ballads* (London, 1802), para. 19 (pp. 253-54 in R. L. Brett and A. R. Jones ed. (New York, 1963).

logical truth is here illustrating a readily accessible item of the external world. The experience of Rossetti on this occasion comes home to man as a "suffering" being.

Johnson's principle surely holds for all great poetry. Dante's imagery is the reverse of esoteric. Donne's compasses are things alike obvious to vigilance and carelessness, even though Johnson was not quite at liberty to see this.

IAN WATT

# The Comic Syntax of TRISTRAM SHANDY

LAURENCE STERNE received no notice in the annual bibliography of the *Philological Quarterly* for 1953. Since then there has been a rapid increase in published studies, but there are, as yet, few signs of converging perspectives in our view of *Tristram Shandy*. There are, of course, many things that recent studies have enabled us to see more clearly—its philosophical and literary traditions, the details of sources or of characterization; but these approaches hardly resolve the elementary problems which the reader faces as he tries to come to grips with the text. One of these problems, which persists even after many readings, concerns the unity of *Tristram Shandy*. A good deal has been done to demonstrate unity of plot and character, using the criteria that are traditional in dealing with the novel; what follows explores a very different, though not necessarily contradictory, approach to the problem.[1]

NOTE: Parts of this essay are from my introduction to an edition of *Tristram Shandy* in Riverside Editions (Houghton Mifflin).

1. See, for example and in addition to works cited later, Robert Curtis Brown, "Laurence Sterne and Virginia Woolf: A Study in Literary Continuity," *University of Kansas Review*, XXVI (1959), 153–59; Sigurd Burckhart, "*Tristram Shandy's* Law of Gravity," *English Literary History*, XXVIII (1961), 70–88; Henri Fluchère, *Laurence Sterne, de l'Homme à l'Oeuvre* (Paris, 1961); Charles Parrish, "The Nature of Mr. Tristram Shandy, Author," *Boston University Studies in English*, V (1961), 74–90; W. B. Piper, "Tristram Shandy's Digressive Artistry," *SEL*, I (1961), 65–76; J. M. Stedmond, "Genre and *Tristram Shandy*," PQ, XXXVIII (1959), 37–51; "Style and *Tristram Shandy*," MLQ, XX (1959), 243–51; and "Satire and *Tristram Shandy*," *SEL*, I (1961), 53–63; Gerald Weales, "Tristram Shandy's Anti-Book" in *Twelve Original Essays on Great English Novels*, ed. Charles Shapiro (Detroit, 1960). The James A. Work edition of *Tristram Shandy* (New York, 1940) has been used throughout.

We can probably recognize a passage taken at random from *Tristram Shandy* more quickly than one from any other book. The tone, the style, the attitude toward the reader, and the events, all are quite special; and they don't vary substantially from page to page or from beginning to end. One thing that is consistent in *Tristram Shandy* is its narrative voice.

Consider, for example, the opening paragraph:

I wish either my father or my mother, or indeed both of them, as they were in duty both equally bound to it, had minded what they were about when they begot me; had they duly considered how much depended upon what they were then doing; —— that not only the production of a rational Being was concerned in it, but that possibly the happy formation and temperature of his body, perhaps his genius and the very cast of his mind; —— and, for aught they knew to the contrary, even the fortunes of his whole house might take their turn from the humours and dispositions which were then uppermost; —— Had they duly weighed and considered all this, and proceeded accordingly, —— I am verily persuaded I should have made a quite different figure in the world, from that in which the reader is likely to see me. (I, i)

Taking notice of the promise of the title, we see that in a sense we are getting what we expect in this first chapter — the hero's begetting. It is whimsically done, to be sure, if only because we are unaccustomed to thinking about this particular action from the point of view of the end product; but after all, we may reflect, the author is only taking the conventions of autobiographical fiction with unprecedented literalness, and, with a vengeance, beginning at the beginning. Such a view of the text, which would still see it primarily as a novel, would continue to find some support from the ostensive narrative subject of the next six books; they proceed from Tristram's conception to his parturition, baptism, and breeching. But, of course, Sterne's main interest doesn't really lie with the traumatic consequences of these no doubt important events in his hero's life, as we can see from the way that none of them plays any part later except as a topic of jest, and, more important, that virtually nothing else about Tristram's life emerges.

At this point, if not before, we must take account of Sterne's epigraph, from Epictetus: "It is not things themselves that disturb men, but their judgments about these things." What matters, Sterne is telling us, is not particular actions, but the reflective consideration of them in the judging mind. In the passage quoted, for instance, even the grammar makes the action subordinate to reflection about it: we have to get through the first two lines — "I wish either my father or my mother, or indeed both of them, as they were in duty both equally bound to it, had minded what they were about" before we know the cause of the speaker's impatience; and when it is specified it comes in a subordinate clause: "when they begot me."

There is a further departure from the usual fictional emphasis on narrative event when Tristram proceeds:

—— Believe me, good folks, this is not so inconsiderable a thing as many of you may think it; —— you have all, I dare say, heard of the animal spirits, as how they are transfused from father to son, etc. etc. —— and a great deal to that purpose: —— Well, you may take my word, that nine parts in ten of a man's sense or his nonsense, his successes and miscarriages in this world depend upon their motions and activity, and the different tracts and trains you put them into, so that when they are once set a-going, whether right or wrong, 'tis not a halfpenny matter, —— away they go cluttering like hey-go mad; and by treading the same steps over and over again, they presently make a road of it, as plain and as smooth as a garden-walk, which, when they are once used to, the Devil himself sometimes shall not be able to drive them off it. (I, i)

Here Tristram seems to be thinking less of the event than of his auditors as he anticipates their derisive incredulity that, even after some forty years, he should still be so disgruntled at the thought of parental irresponsibility. "Believe me, good folks, this is not so inconsiderable a thing as many of you may think it; —— you have all, I dare say, heard of the animal spirits." "And if you haven't, you peasants, cringe," implies Tristram's lofty "I dare say"; and the paragraph continues to focus our attention so completely on Tristram's present claim on our commiseration and on the dangers of not granting it that we have almost forgotten Mr. and Mrs. Shandy.

They reappear for the final brief paragraph of the first chapter, but in a way that continues their subordination to Tristram's directing mind in at least three respects:

Pray, my Dear, quoth my mother, have you not forgot to wind up the clock? Good G —— ! cried my father, making an exclamation, but taking care to moderate his voice at the same time, —— Did ever woman, since the creation of the world, interrupt a man with such a silly question? Pray, what was your father saying? —— Nothing. (I, i)

Again, the narrative event is merely an occasion for talking. This time, however, the talk isn't soliloquy but conversation: first, conversation between the characters; and second, between the narrator and his audience. It's out of the combination of these two elements that the humor and suspense of the chapter arise; and these in turn ultimately depend upon Tristram's presence, more specifically on his withholding from his audience the narrative information required to understand the scene until it is needed for his comic climax: obviously all the connubial converse about the clock, and Tristram's reflections about it, remain fairly obscure until the reader's oscillation between bewilderment and understanding is finally resolved through Tristram's answer to the question interposed by his imaginary reader. " 'Pray, what was your father saying?' " —— " 'Nothing.' "

The design of the first chapter as a whole, then, reveals that Tristram's primary emphasis is rhetorical rather than narrative; we have to wait another three chapters before we fully understand Mrs. Shandy's question about winding the clock, but the chapter has perfect formal completeness in its own rhetorical terms, since the reader's questions in the first paragraph begin to be answered in the second, and are fully disposed of by the final clinching implication of the word "Nothing." Narrative as such is not autonomous or primary; it is merely the initial fictional pretext for a complex pattern of conversations: conversation between characters, in the first place; and, more important, conversation between Tristram and his readers. It is essentially the completion of this interplay, rather than that of a narrative episode, which determines Sterne's organization of his basic compositional unit, the chapter.

As we go on, indeed, it becomes apparent that the same rhetorical imperatives govern the interrelationship between chapters. Thus if we turn to the climax of the other main plot of *Tristram Shandy*, the courtship of Uncle Toby and the Widow Wadman in the last two books, we find exactly the same subordination of narrative development to the autonomous demands of rhetorical effect. In Book VIII, for example, when, at long last, the Widow Wadman trains upon Uncle Toby the full firepower of her amorous eye, under the pretense that there's a speck of dirt in it which he must remove: "—— I am half distracted, Captain *Shandy*, said Mrs. *Wadman*, holding up her cambric handkerchief to her left eye, as she approached the door of my Uncle *Toby's* sentry-box —— a mote —— or sand —— or something —— I know not what, has got into this eye of mine —— do look into it —— it is not in the white ——" (VIII, xxiv)

Up to now this is straightforward comic narrative, but there follows a long commentary by Tristram, who concludes Chapter 24 with the adjuration: "If thou lookest, uncle *Toby*, in search of this mote one moment longer — thou art undone."

In Chapter 25, after Tristram's long military simile, "An eye is for all the world exactly like a cannon," has reminded us of the parallel between the wars of love and those of Uncle Toby, we are finally taken back to the fictional scene:

I protest, Madam, said my uncle *Toby*, I can see nothing whatever in your eye.

It is not in the white; said Mrs. *Wadman*: my uncle *Toby* looked with might and main into the pupil ——

Once again the comedy of misunderstanding is interrupted by the narrator's bravura description of the eye's message, and the chapter ends when he finally interrupts himself with the reflection:

But I shall be in love with it myself, if I say another word about it. —— It did my uncle *Toby's* business.

That the interlocking of chapters is conceived primarily in rhetorical rather than fictional terms is clear enough: here a single narrative incident is related in two separate chapters, each with a parallel compositional structure, emphasized by the choric repetition of their closing phrase: "thou art un*done*"; and, "It *did* my uncle Toby's business."

The narrative event — Toby's falling in love — is a momentous one that has long been heralded; but Tristram does not use it for a full descriptive or psychological presentation of the event in its own right. Of the three main comic climaxes, for instance, only one, Mrs. Wadman's repetition of "It is not in the white," belongs within the fictional framework; the other two depend either on byplay with an imaginary reader — "it was not, Madam, a rolling eye" — or on Tristram's sudden transition from his own imaginary reaction to the widow's left eye to his confidential anticipation of poor Toby's doom: "It did my uncle Toby's business."

✦   ✦   ✦

The structure of Sterne's larger compositional units, then, is based on the rhetorical patterns arising out of the complex tripartite pattern of conversation between the narrator, his fictional characters, and his auditors. Exactly the same can be said of the smaller compositional units, from the clause to the paragraph; *Tristram Shandy* has at least one kind of unity, unity of style; and behind the style there is, of course, the man and his view of life.

"Writing, when properly managed, (as you may be sure I think mine is) is but a different name for conversation," Tristram himself tells us. His prose reflects the brilliance and ease of a great age of conversation whose most splendid historical record is Boswell's *Life of Johnson*. Sterne's style retains some elements of the careful parallelism and balance of sound, syntax, and meaning that we think of as typical of the Augustans. In the opening sentence, for instance, there is the balanced pattern of consonantal stops, "b," "d," and "t," which gives a certain sense of order to the petulant impression of the sounds themselves: "I wish either *my father* or *my mother*, or indeed *both* of *t*hem, as *t*hey were in *d*uty *both* equally *bound* to it, ha*d* min*d*ed what they were a*b*out when they *b*egot me . . ." The symmetry, however, is largely concealed by the tone of conversational abandon, most evident in the colloquialism ("minded what they were about"); the reader at once feels that he is being directly addressed in an easy and unbuttoned way, and that the units of meaning are being strung together in the most spontaneous way.

The most obvious indication of this conversational style is the punctuation, and especially the use of the dash. In the short chapter about Widow Wadman's eye (VIII, xxv), for example, there are more dashes — eighteen — than any other mark of punctuation; and even though the proportion is rarely as high elsewhere, there must be very few pages of *Tristram Shandy* which do not have many more dashes than is usual in any but the most amateurish writing.

The reasons for this great reliance on the dash go deep into the nature of Sterne's creative strategy. The dash is virtually proscribed in expository prose, presumably because it flouts the standard requirement that the verbal components of a sentence should be articulated into a coherent syntactical structure, a structure in which the subordination and superordination of all the parts should express the unity and direction of the sentence as a whole. Sterne's affront to conventional syntax is essential to establishing the qualities he required for Tristram's voice; Sterne didn't want unity or coherence or defined direction, at least in any conventional sense; he wanted multiplicity, not unity; he wanted free association of ideas, not subordination of them; he wanted to go backwards or forwards or sideways, not in straight linear paths.

We are, of course, quite used to these kinds of discontinuity in ordinary colloquial conversation. In the Widow Wadman's speech, for instance ("A mote — or sand — or something — I know not what, has got into this eye of mine — do look into it — it is not in the white") the dash is used as much to mark pauses as anything else; whatever meaning may be left obscure by the syntax is clarified by the implied situations and gestures; and it is the dashes which force the reader to imagine them. Elsewhere the dash is used merely for aggregating units, as in the dazzling series of descriptive phrases about the Widow Wadman's left eye; and here we observe the usefulness of the dash in Sterne's characteristic exploitation of the rhetorical expectations aroused by any extended verbal series. But the most important strategic function of the dash, both in these passages and in general, is to serve Tristram as a non-logical junction between different kinds of discourse: between past and present; between narrative event and authorial address to the reader; between one train of thought and another in Tristram's mind.

Sterne needed a much looser and less directed junction between units of meaning than normal syntax allows, for his psychology, for his narrative mode, for his manipulation of the reader, and for expressing his view of life. Dashes were invaluable for enacting the drama of inhibited impulse, of the sudden interruptions and oscillations of thought and feeling, which characterize Tristram both as a person and as a narrator. One obvious example of the latter occurs when there is an abrupt and unheralded shift in the point of view of the narration. Consider, for example, in the chapter cited above, the passage where the narrator comments: "there never was an eye of them all, so fitted to rob my uncle *Toby* of his repose, as the very eye, at which he was looking — it was not, Madam, a rolling eye . . ." Here the dash enables Tristram to turn suddenly from Toby to reprove an imaginary female interlocutor for her licentious ocular deportment. Similarly the rhetorical finality of the close of the chapter depends upon the dash on which hinges Tristram's sudden temporal transition from his own present attitude toward the eye to its devastating effect, nearly two generations ago, on Captain Shandy: "It did my uncle Toby's business."

Tristram's prose style, then, embodies the multiplicity of his narrative point of view; it is idiosyncratic because it serves a unique, and often puzzling, combination of functions. One of these, at least, demands further attention here, since it is both important in itself, and closely related to some of the main differences of interpretation to which *Tristram Shandy* has given rise.

✓　　✓　　✓

Tristram's voice, as we have seen, is uniquely adapted to rapid transitions, and they are an essential element in his humor. Kant wrote that "laughter arises from the sudden transformation of a strained expectation into nothing"; Sterne is a master at such transformations, undermining the expectation that has been built up by suddenly making Tristram change his point of view. The end of Le Fever's life, for example, offers a famous example: we are at the deathbed:

The blood and spirits of *Le Fever*, which were waxing cold and slow within him, and were retreating to their last citadel, the heart — rallied back, — the film forsook his eyes for a moment, — he looked up wishfully in my uncle *Toby's* face, — then cast a look upon his boy, — and that *ligament*, fine as it was, — was never broken. — 
Nature instantly ebbed again, — the film returned to its place, — the pulse fluttered — stopped — went on — throbbed — stopped again — moved — stopped — shall I go on? — No. [VI,x]

Here, of course, the humor arises out of the abrupt transition from narration to a direct address to the reader, which suddenly relieves the reader just at the moment when his suffering from the pathos of Le Fever's death has become unendurable; and the relief is easily achieved because only a dash is needed to switch us from the world where fiction seems real (as is typical in the novel) to the world where Tristram can jog the reader's elbow to remind him that his fiction is, after all, only fiction.

Tristram's attitude to his audience is in part that of the ventriloquist and in part that of the jester. Where he is recounting the actions and dialogues of the Shandy household, multiple impersonation is called for; and Tristram is as expert in vocal mimicry as in the external description of the dialogues between his characters. It is interesting, in this connection, to note Sterne's admiration of the famous Parisian preacher Père Clement, who, he wrote, converted his pulpit into a stage, so that "the variety of his tones [made] you imagine there were no less than five or six actors on it together." [2]

But the main dialogue which Tristram carries on is with the reader; at least half of *Tristram Shandy* is taken up not with narrative but with direct address to the audience by Tristram, often about matters only tangentially related to the story.

For this dialogue, the first need is for Tristram to ensure that his readers never lose themselves so completely in the story that they forget the monologist behind the footlights. One way of reminding the readers of his presence is for Tristram to break down the cold impersonality of print, whose impassive objectivity encourages us in most novels to forget the literary mirror in which the fictional world is reflected. The typographical tricks, the short or blank or misnumbered chapters, the squiggles, the black or marbled pages, the index fingers, though they may not always amuse us, at least serve to remind us that the image reflected in the mirror is less real than the mirror itself: that the mirror, not the reflections in it, has priority of status.

Many of Sterne's other typographical usages also serve to call us back from the show to the showman. Italics, for example, enact the actor's emphasis — the raised voice, the confidential whisper, or the wink; while capitals and Gothic letters supply heavier emphasis for a moral reflection, a scholarly reference, or a tear. Asterisks and blank spaces similarly provoke our active response, and lead us to ask what they stand for, or to supply something for ourselves, whether correctly or not we often don't quite know; they are the graphic equivalents of the figure of aposiopesis — rhetorically intentional hiatus — which Tristram so often employs. Faint but pursuing, we do our best to puzzle out the asterisks and fill up the gaps; and we are occasionally given the ostentatiously grudging reward which the professional stage performer usually bestows on the unfortunate amateur from the audience who has offered his cooperation. For instance, when Walter and Toby have been left halfway down stairs, and Tristram wants to start the next scene with Walter back in bed, he turns to us with patronizing indulgence: "—— So then, friend! You have got my father and my uncle *Toby* off the stairs, and seen them to bed? —— And how did you manage it? —— You dropped a curtain at the stair-foot —— I thought you had no other way for it —— Here's a crown for your trouble." (IV, xiii.)

As to the particular roles Tristram assumes in his address to the reader, they are as varied as his moods. He often seeks to excite pathos, but in different ways: as a Shandy baby he invites commiseration for the early catastrophes of his life; his appeal is more deeply felt and less ironic when he shares with us his mature recollections of his father and his uncle; and there are other times when the Shandy story is forgotten and he implores

2. *Letters of Laurence Sterne*, ed. L. P. Curtis (Oxford, 1935), p. 155.

our pity merely as an author who has just been battered by critics and reviewers. But of course pathos is only one of Tristram's moods, and it usually ends with a smile as he asks us: "Pray reach me my fool's cap" and reassumes his favorite pose — the jester's.[3]

As regards his psychological relationship to his audience, Tristram has many tricks for provoking an active and emotionally-charged participation, besides his various ways of keeping us guessing. His main gambit is the traditional one of divide and rule. The audience is imagined to comprise various groups of which the most vocal are a miscellaneous collection of unsympathetic auditors against whom, in mere self-defense, Tristram has to mobilize the rest of his hearers. There are the great Lords who demand submission and dedications; there are solemn critics, pedants, Dutch commentators, church dignitaries, and men of civic substance, who are usually addressed with mock deference as "Your Worships" or "Your Reverences." Equally hostile, and even more threatening, are the censorious prudes; always on the lookout for scandal and obscenity, they are usually addressed as "Madam"; and the appellation nearly always serves as a signal to the reader that there is some dubious imputation in the air. The only morally unobjectionable way of drawing our attention to such bawdy, of course, is to deny it with obtrusive indignation. Thus, for instance, when Tristram has mentioned Jenny as "his friend," he at once has "Madam" challenge his description of the relationship:

Friend! —— My friend. —— Surely, Madam, a friendship between the two sexes may subsist, and be supported without —— Fy! Mr. *Shandy:* —— Without any thing, Madam, but that tender and delicious sentiment, which ever mixes in friendship, where there is a difference of sex. Let me intreat you to study the pure and sentimental parts of the best *French* Romances; —— It will really, Madam, astonish you to see with what a variety of chaste expressions this delicious sentiment, which I have the honour to speak of, is dressed out. (I, xviii)

In this passage we also have an example of the exploitation of imaginary differences between different parts of the audience; for if there are insufferably dull and hostile characters around, there are also a few close friends, some of them imaginary, like Jenny, others real, like Eugenius and Garrick; and the reader, alarmed at the possibility that he might be numbered among the priggish and the pretentious, strives his utmost to achieve the perfect sympathetic understanding which will allow him to be enrolled in the charmed circle of Mr. Shandy's friends, a circle where, as a bonus, he will be on nodding terms with the great Mr. Pitt, and even join in Tristram's patronizing rejoinders to St. Thomas Aquinas and "Mr. Horace."

Among this ideal audience benevolence and good humor reign; and compelling the reader to adopt this mood was half Sterne's battle in achieving other literary effects. Aristotle pointed out that people don't normally laugh when they are alone, as readers usually are; so it is an essential prerequisite of Sterne's humor that he should create the sense of an active and friendly relation between himself and his audience, especially the unprudish and benevolent members of it; they must be brought to strain every nerve to achieve that *dies praeclarum* when they will be accepted as close friends by Mr. Shandy. For reasons further clarified by a remark in the pseudo-Aristotelian *Problemata*: "Why are people less able to restrain their laughter in the presence of friends? Is it because, when anything is especially elated, it is easier set into motion? Now benevolence causes elation, so that laughter more easily moves us (950. a. 18)."

For Sterne and his readers, benevolence meant, above all, a readiness to shed a sympathetic tear. The Le Fever passage may be taken as an illustration of how the flow of feeling also helps Tristram's humorous designs; it also, of course, raises the oft-mooted question of whether the climactic comic twists Sterne habitually gives to sentimental episodes means that he is really attacking or ridiculing the pathetic and benevolent feelings he so often arouses and indeed seems to applaud.

In the passage about Le Fever's death, for example, reader and author were deeply united in the fellowship of suffering before they pulled back to smile at the unexpected reality which their joint imaginings had momentarily assumed: "Shall I go on? — No." Community in commiseration is a precondition of community in merriment, Sterne seems to affirm. Our age tends to a circumspect gravity as well about life as about literature, which probably makes it difficult to fully appreciate Sterne's attitude. But we must remember that the eighteenth century's growing approval of humor runs exactly parallel to the growth of its cult of sentiment and benevolence. And not only chronologically: Shaftesbury [4] and Hutcheson [5] were the great precursors of both trends; and we can now

3. See E. N. Dilworth in *The Unsentimental Journey of Laurence Sterne* (New York, 1948), and A. E. Dyson's brilliant essay "Sterne: The Novelist as Jester," *Critical Quarterly*, IV (1962), 309–20.

4. In, especially, *Sensus Communis: An Essay on the Freedom of Wit and Humor* (1709).

5. Francis Hutcheson, *Thoughts on Laughter* (1725–1727).

see that the growing approval of laughter, and of emotional responsive-ness in general, may be regarded as parallel manifestations of the de-thronement of reason as the primary human faculty.[6]

Sterne's humor, it may be said, largely depends upon the force of this dual exploitation of man's sympathetic and risible faculties. In Restora-tion comedy, or in Swift and Pope, we think not so much of humor as of wit; behind the epigrammatic brilliance we sense a mocking rejection of the objects satirized; and if emotions are aroused, they are the negative ones — scorn, distrust, hatred. This was in keeping both with Hobbes's view of the aggressive function of laughter, and with the neoclassical critical theory whereby the aim of satire was to mobilize the reader's feelings against illusion, affectation, and vice.

But in *Tristram Shandy* there is no vice; illusion and affectation are there, of course, but they are fantastic, amusing, and even, in their way, necessary: as with Walter and Toby, for instance, they are merely hobby-horses. It's relevant here to observe that "hobby," in the sense of a favor-ite pastime, acquired its modern approbative sense only in the nineteenth century; originally it was a hobbyhorse, or an imitation horse, such as was used in the mummers' dance or as a child's toy; so a concern with hobbyhorses in an adult had, to an earlier generation, seemed a frivolous derogation of man's stature as a rational animal. But Sterne welcomed all such toys; he was willing to approve "an uncle Toby's siege —— or an *any thing*, which a man makes a shift to get a-stride on, to canter it away from the cares and solicitudes of life."

A special stylistic strategy was required to express the coexistence of humor and sentiment, and indeed of a very large diversity of attitudes, in a context that did not impose or imply a rationally-ordered hierarchy of values. This can perhaps be best illustrated by comparison. The typi-cal epigram, like the typical sentence, goes in one direction. When the Lincolnshire lady was ill-advised enough to show Dr. Johnson her un-derground grotto, and then inquired "if he did not think it would be a pretty convenient habitation?", Dr. Johnson retorted: "I think it would, Madam, for a toad." Either you're for houses or you're for grottoes; Johnson's wit directs our attention to the incompatibility between the categories. Sterne's outlook, on the other hand, is much more pluralist, and so is his style. His ostentatiously permissive syntax allows each cate-gory its own independent existence; the dash makes no assertion of rela-tion, but allows the sense to flow forwards and backwards between the phrases which it conjoins, very much at the reader's pleasure; the emphasis is up to us, and if there is exclusion, it is we who make it. Tristram, we feel, would have answered the Lincolnshire lady's query so as to leave open all the diverse possibilities on both sides; perhaps by saying "I *think* it would, Madam — for us — or — for a toad."

This sort of intentional leaving of the final evaluative attitude up to the audience is a very common technique in the stage comic; Mort Sahl is only the most extreme example of a style which depends entirely on the unstructured, parenthetic conjunction of diverse propositions and attitudes. At a much more highly controlled and complex level, we get an equally free choice in *Tristram Shandy*. Shakespeare's Yorick was a jester in a tragedy. Sterne's Yorick affirms a more programmatic kind of coexistence: sentiment and humor — and much else — should be regarded, however illogically, as somehow mutually consistent categories; we reject at our peril the exclusive claims either of the heart or of the head, or, for that matter, of the imagination, even if they seem to be in conflict.

At this point it is perhaps worth insisting that this open-ended mode of writing is very different in aim from such modern manipulations of point of view as "interior monologue" or "stream of consciousness." For "stream of consciousness" is normally supposed to be the expression of the unconscious and inarticulate flow of impressions, whereas Tristram is surely highly self-conscious and obtrusively articulate. Sterne would seem to agree with Locke that an unconscious idea is a contradiction in terms,[7] and deals mainly with conscious, and indeed rationally-conceptualized, matters. In addition Tristram's thoughts are quite overtly addressed to an audience, whereas stream of consciousness pretends that the reader does not exist. The stream of consciousness, in fact, takes the inner world of the individual character to the extreme limit of subjective realism; while Tristram's rhetoric is largely devoted to subverting the literal reality of fiction so that the reader's attention shall be focused on the reality not of the narrative but of the narrator.

Some critics, it is true, have seen the total of Tristram's reminiscences — that is, the whole book — as constituting a subjective individual portrait, much as Joyce and Proust portray their characters by presenting their inner thoughts. But although there is nothing exactly out of character

6. See Stuart M. Tave, *The Amiable Humorist* (Chicago, 1960).
7. *Essay concerning Human Understanding*, II, i, 1–4.

in Tristram's thoughts, they surely don't seem aimed at indirect character portrayal. Rather, the apparently rather random association of thoughts in Tristram's discourse surely reflects a comic exploration of the extremely varied possibilities of Locke's view of pathological mental processes. Faced with the observation that "There is scarce any one that does not observe something that seems odd to him, and is in itself really extravagant, in the opinions, reasonings, and actions of other men," [8] Locke explained that such failures of the human understanding result from the irrational association of ideas.

In the opening passage, we have a classical example of Mrs. Shandy's association of ideas between the dual monthly routines of Mr. Shandy in his timekeeping and his connubial roles. But there is nothing very unconscious about this in the modern sense; Pavlov's dog, had it the gift of tongues, would, under similar circumstances, have echoed Mrs. Shandy's words. In any case Sterne's emphasis is not on exploring the preconscious or unconscious mind of Mrs. Shandy so much as on using a logically inappropriate conjunction of ideas for comic purposes; and these comic purposes depend upon the reader's being keenly alive to the rational and conscious level of discourse from which Mrs. Shandy deviates.

Tristram's voice is by no means an irrational one, but a rational instrument for the revelation of human irrationality. Belonging to the Age of Reason helped Sterne to see and demonstrate that human behavior is not based on reason; in the end Locke had taught him, not so much that the human mind is a blank tablet, as that philosophical attempts to transcend ordinary human experience end up in a blind alley.

On the other hand, Sterne is as far from the intellectual satire of Swift as he is from the stream of consciousness, because his account of the nonrational aspects of human behavior does not condemn them. Sterne is as committed to the realities of the feelings and of the senses as he is to the life of the mind; he doesn't commit himself to the prior claims of reason and order, as wit and satire usually tend to do.

Here we can find abundant support in recent scholarship, in John Traugott's *Tristram Shandy's World* (Berkeley and Los Angeles, 1954) for instance, or in Ernest Tuveson's *The Imagination as a Means of Grace* (Berkeley and Los Angeles, 1960), for seeing *Tristram Shandy* as the most inclusive literary expression of a movement whose greatest philosophical representative is David Hume. Faced by the apparent failure of man to live up to his alleged nature as a rational animal, and forced to be dubious about the probability of success in Locke's effort to tidy matters up, this movement turned its attention to the complexities of actual human behavior and to the mysteries of psychological identification between individuals. Tristram's personal "Essay concerning Human Understanding" showed that understanding, if it came at all, came not through the rational faculty, nor through ordinary verbal communication, but through the operation of sympathy and imagination — the two faculties which were beginning to replace the traditional duality of passion and reason as the primary elements in man's understanding of his nature. Tristram's voice, if we attend to it, does not merely direct our attention to the traditional subject of comedy — human folly; it also suggests that we must go beyond the premature exclusions to which the rational mind's awareness of irrationality is always prompting us, and enlarge the area of our imaginative sympathy.

Consider, for example, Trim's great harangue on mortality, in which Tristram's directing presence deftly combines humor and pathos, and defies us to reject any of the human inconsistencies involved. Susannah the chambermaid, Jonathan the coachman, Obadiah the outdoor servant, the unnamed cookmaid, and the foolish fat scullion, are all gathered in the kitchen after hearing the news of the death of Bobby, Tristram's elder brother. Jonathan has just remarked that Bobby "was alive last Whitsuntide":

—— O *Jonathan*! 'twould make a good-natured man's heart bleed, to consider, continued the corporal (standing perpendicularly), how low many a brave and upright fellow has been laid since that time! —— And trust me, *Susy*, added the corporal, turning to *Susannah*, whose eyes were swimming in water, —— before that time comes round again, —— many a bright-eye will be dim. —— *Susannah* placed it to the right side of the page —— she wept —— but she court'sied too. —— Are we not, continued *Trim*, looking still at *Susannah* —— are we not like a flower of the field —— a tear of pride stole in betwixt every two tears of humiliation —— else no tongue could have described *Susannah's* affliction —— is not all flesh grass? —— 'Tis clay, —— 'tis dirt. —— They all looked directly at the scullion, —— the scullion had just been scouring a fish-kettle. —— It was not fair. ——

—— What is the finest face that ever man looked at! —— I could hear *Trim* talk so for ever, cried *Susannah*, —— what is it! (*Susannah* laid her hand upon *Trim's* shoulder) —— but corruption? —— *Susannah* took it off.

8. *Ibid.*, II, xxxiii, 1.

330 · STUDIES IN CRITICISM AND AESTHETICS

Now I love you for this —— and 'tis this delicious mixture within you which makes you dear creatures what you are —— and he who hates you for it —— all I can say of the matter is —— That he has either a pumpkin for his head —— or a pippin for his heart, —— and whenever he is dissected 'twill be found so. (V, ix)

*   *   *

We find it difficult to decide what are the appropriate criteria for the indeterminate literary genres, the kinds of writing where the total literary structure is an aggregate rather than an organic whole. Formally, as Northrop Frye has suggested,[9] *Tristram Shandy* may be regarded as a hybrid between the novel and the Menippean satire, or, as he prefers to call the genre, an Anatomy, like the works of two of Sterne's great forebears, Rabelais and Burton.

But if we must decide not so much the fictional category, as the primary principle of unity, of *Tristram Shandy*, it must surely be Tristram's voice. Through it Sterne discovered a principle of order which resides not so much in linear development in time as in a kind of timeless consistency of texture; it is this which has primary autonomy, and which controls every narrative element, from the phrase to the paragraph, the chapter, and the book. So, by "the comic syntax of *Tristram Shandy*," I mean only that the syntax, "the orderly or systematic arrangements of parts or elements" as the *Oxford Dictionary* defines it, of *Tristram Shandy*, is essentially a complex but consistent mode of comic speech which unites all its parts and attitudes, loosely no doubt, but with perfect appropriateness (this mode of speech is perhaps strictly speaking more humorous than comic, but my title defers to the trochaic rhythm of Sterne's). In any case it is this voice which joins the novelistic to the more miscellaneous elements of the book; which unites the pathetic and the laughable, the intellectual and the emotional; and which, above all, engages the author and the reader in so living a conversation that one no longer asks, as one does of a novel, for an ending.

Yeats called art "the social act of a solitary man." Sterne was a solitary; but toward the end of his life he found a way of talking which created its own society. The members of this society, comprising both the fictional characters in the book, its circle of readers, and its narrator, all have a very special literary quality; their voices are attuned to the endless dialogue within, which is so much more inconsequential, indecent, and above all — shall we face it — trivial, than the public dialogues we can hear going on around us, or that we find recorded in most of literature; Sterne's sad recognition of this enabled him to create a mode of speech which compels what he most desired — our acknowledgment of intimate kinship. And once the Shandean laughter has punctured the authorized hyperboles which make it so difficult for us to recognize our real identity, the remembering mind can sometimes go on beyond this to discover in and through Tristram's comic syntax that real feeling and a kind of logic somehow subsist and trace a shadowy coherence upon the muddled and miscellaneous indignities of our personal lot.

9. *Anatomy of Criticism* (Princeton, 1957), pp. 302, 308–12.

❈ ROBERT E. MOORE

# Reynolds and the Art of Characterization

BY DINT of hard application and altogether unique talent, Joshua Reynolds by the year 1761 had managed to establish himself as London's foremost portrait painter. Toward the end of that year he produced an unusual work combining portraiture with allegory entitled *Garrick between Comedy and Tragedy* (following page). When it was exhibited the next year the picture caused considerable talk, including an interesting comment from Horace Walpole: "The former [Tragedy] exhorts him to follow her exalted vocation, but Comedy drags him away, and he seems to yield willingly, though endeavouring to excuse himself, and pleading that he is forced. Tragedy is a good antique figure, but wants more dignity in the expression of her face. Comedy is a beautiful and winning girl — but Garrick's face is distorted and burlesque." [1] The picture is a useful one for the critic because it illustrates so clearly the aesthetic of much mid-century portraiture, while Walpole's remarks reveal a good deal about cultivated contemporary criticism. Reynolds based his picture on a famous classical motif, Hercules at the Crossroads between Virtue and Vice, that had been used by Rubens and Annibale Carracci, but by turning it into a modern parody he achieved something especially attractive to the age, something that Walpole himself described as wit. [2] It is a clever form of quotation. Reynolds's handling of tone is characteristic and notable — I use "tone" not in reference to color but in the literary sense — for the classical reminiscence serves a double

1. Walpole's *Anecdotes of Painting in England, 1760–1795,* ed. Frederick W. Hilles and Philip B. Daghlian (New Haven, 1937), p. 61.
2. See below, p. 347.

Sir Joshua Reynolds, *Garrick between Comedy and Tragedy*. Courtesy
of the Trustees of the British Museum

function: it compliments Garrick and elevates the subject, but at the same time, since Garrick is no Hercules, it is an amusing recognition of the difference between the contemporary world and that of the epic. As so often during the century, we are reminded that the popularity of the mock-epic form is owing to more than its utility in satire; or better, that, tastefully handled, a certain degree of irony can be complimentary.

Classical reminiscence is but one element in Reynolds's conception. He has not only turned a portrait into a subject-picture, and a subject with the appeal of personified abstraction as well, but in painting Tragedy after the manner of Guido Reni and Comedy in the style of Correggio, he has also recalled two of the favorite pictorial tastes of the mid-century connoisseur. In Walpole's commentary we can sense his love of *jeu d'esprit* and his admiration of Reynolds's ingenuity, but the most interesting thing about the comment is that he altogether misses the true brilliance of the picture and the essence of Reynolds's originality. The triumph of the canvas is surely not in the stagey emptiness of Tragedy nor in the oversweet Comedy but in the delineation of personality and character in Garrick himself. Here is the living man who, with an ingratiating shrug, grins at the spectator mischievously, and seems to be saying: "How happy could I be with either, Were t'other dear charmer away!" Capturing that force of expression which made Garrick unique is what makes Reynolds unique. One need merely glance at Hogarth's rather static portrait of Garrick painted four years earlier, in which his wife leans over his shoulder and draws away the pen from his hand, to see the enormous difference. There the actor is a staid elegantly-dressed gentleman of no particular individuality. In contrast Reynolds creates a powerful personality whose smiling complacency — he knows he is the master of both ladies — indicates that complete yet winning self-assurance which the painter regards as the key to Garrick's character. Finally, Walpole's commentary inadvertently shows just how original Reynolds must have seemed in 1762. Comedy and Tragedy were the usual thing, but Garrick, a true "speaking likeness," exhibits a forceful informality that was new, and Walpole was not ready for it.

This painting, early as it is, reveals that it is in Reynolds's achievement as a psychologist that his genius lies. Even Walpole, though not understanding the extent of it, later wrote in the *Anecdotes of Painting* that Reynolds had "ransomed portrait-painting from insipidity."[3] Before Reynolds's immediate predecessors, Hogarth and Allan Ramsay, characterization is a negligible quantity in British portraiture. A rather cold transcription of mere features is about all we get in Kneller, and often not even that in such of his successors as Jervas, Hudson, Knapton, Jonathan Richardson, and the rest. Although Richardson was a cultivated man who between 1715 and 1722 wrote four books which helped to raise the status of the painter, and later made a profound impression on the young Reynolds, his two ideals of "Grace" and "Greatness," to be cultivated by studying the Italian masters, were quite beyond his own grasp. Indeed these painters as a usual thing could not even boast the lower skill of copying natural appearances for which Richardson commended the Dutch school (who "servilely followed common nature").[4] The air of awkward amateurishness lying so heavily upon these stiff portraits damages their worth even as mere likenesses, and makes any question of character analysis irrelevant. Later we shall speak of Hogarth and Ramsay, who made great strides forward in naturalness and simplicity; but they do not go very far in the probing of character.

A brief look at the conception of character in the literature of the period may make clear the nature of the problem that faced Reynolds in portraiture, and may give some indication of his inventiveness and originality in solving it. Until *Clarissa* in the middle of the century, psychological analysis is virtually absent from literary characterization. To particularize was to circumscribe. "Proper names," Hobbes had said, "bring to mind one thing only; universals recall any one of many." By way of both the stage and the essay, type character was ingrained through influences reaching back to medieval drama, Ben Jonson, the character book, and so on, not to speak of Greek and Roman models. When Hogarth comes to create his moral histories it is as natural that he should think of types like Tom Rakewell, Moll Hackabout, and Francis Goodchild as it is for Addison and Steele, or for Defoe and Richardson. They all reflect one of the great classical traditions, the moral obligation of literature. To divide human nature into types as the most convenient short cut to getting it under control is eminently characteristic of the neoclassical point of view. The aim is always toward Nature, the general and universal rather than the particular and local, even though put in a familiar setting. The portraits to be sure are built of details, but details

3. *Anecdotes of Painting in England*, ed. Ralph N. Wornum (London, 1876), II, 317.
4. Richardson, "On the Art of Painting," *Works* (London, 1773), p. 93.

rigidly categorized and unified. Characterization is thus simplified in the interests of ethical instruction: after human folly is codified and exposed, we can hope that it will be eradicated.

Concurrently another influence deriving from classical example, most strongly from Plato, worked toward simplifying characterization: the cult of the ideal. Both these elements, the typical and the ideal, we can see in the popular metaphor of the mirror held up to nature, nature being both the way things are and the way they ought to be. In the *Dictionary* Dr. Johnson defined "mirror" in both ways: (1) a "looking-glass; anything which exhibits objects by reflection"; and (2) "a pattern; that on which the eye ought to be fixed; an exemplar; an archetype." [5] In its first meaning we hold the mirror up to nature to discover our flaws, to discern the cracks in the varnish; in its second meaning "mirror" points to a generalized rendition of archetypical nature, or to some kind of artistic idealization of the actual.

Concerning Johnson's first definition, "a looking-glass," there is some ambiguity because type characterization is in truth highly artificial; actuality has been rearranged by art in such a way that it is not at all what one would see in a looking glass. Such a distinction possibly would not worry so thorough a classicist as Johnson, who would merely reply that it is nature still but nature methodized. But this distinction does bring up another element in the development of literary characterization, the growth of realism. Increasing concern with actual place and time and with lifelike appearance, all fairly foreign to Renaissance and neoclassical theory, leads directly to the creation of the novel, where a new kind of character gradually emerges.

All this inevitably points to one of the central aesthetic problems of the age, a problem as crucial to Reynolds as to the writer: how can characterization combine a sense of the type and the ideal with a faithful adherence to realism? How can the artist be general and specific simultaneously?

That Reynolds had a singular talent for combining the familiar with the ideal has always been recognized; and he is singular too in being able to bring it off not just occasionally but repeatedly. He could capture that individual quality of personality in a familiar or relaxed manner which has been the despair of the portraitist in every age, and he could at the same time elevate his subject and suggest a universal type as well. Although urbane to a degree, he maintained a purity of spirit sufficient to convince him that most people have an innate nobility which it is the special province of the artist and poet to discover. In this sense the portrait can act as a moral force, for it holds people up to an ideal expressive of their best selves, their highest capabilities. His critics have called this gross flattery of his subjects, seeing in Reynolds a superbly commercial cynicism, but the censure in the majority of cases is by no means just. Even Romney, to whom Sir Joshua would be the most formidable rival, said that we see in his pictures what we have not seen in other painters but have seen often enough in nature.[6]

Before inquiring into the methods he employed, it may be useful as an illustration of what we will be discussing to recall to the reader one of the best known and most successful examples, that of Sarah Siddons as the Tragic Muse (following page). The face and body are unmistakably Siddons, but Reynolds has idealized his conception by making use of personification. The design, inspired by two of Michelangelo's prophets in the Sistine Chapel, portrays the seated actress as Melpomene surrounded by the attendant furies of Pity and Terror. In contrast, Gainsborough's famous portrait of Siddons in the National Gallery is merely an elegant woman of fashion. The picture for all its loveliness lacks the grandeur, the nobility of Reynolds, which many people may feel is no lack; but, more important, it also lacks Reynolds's truth. The significant thing about Mrs. Siddons is not that she looked splendid with powdered frizzed hair and a plumed hat, but that she was the Queen of Tragedy. Sir Joshua is supposed to have asked that he might go down to posterity by inscribing his name on the hem of her garment, but of course the honors were reversed, since neither the accounts of her acting nor any other of her numerous portraits have bestowed upon her the immortality that Reynolds did.

Unlike the Siddons, manifestly the product of considered intellectual effort, some of Reynolds's best paintings give the impression of an easy unstudied improvisation. The impression is deceptive. Indeed it is because he is a prime example of an intellectual painter whose principal interest is the analysis of character, and who has also written extensively on the art, that his work can be studied in a literary connection. "The

5. This example was brought to my attention by Jean H. Hagstrum, *The Sister Arts: The Tradition of Literary Pictorialism and English Poetry from Dryden to Gray* (Chicago, 1958), p. 135.

6. William Hazlitt, *Conversations of James Northcote, Esq., R.A.* (London, 1949), p. 35.

Sir Joshua Reynolds, *Sarah Siddons as the Tragic Muse*. Courtesy
of the Trustees of the British Museum

value and rank of every art," he said in the Fourth Discourse, "is in proportion to the mental labor employed in it, or the mental pleasure produced by it." Throughout the Discourses he is seeking to establish a tradition of both painting and criticism, an aim that in part accounts for his assiduousness in seeking out artists in other fields, particularly in literature; it was he, we remember, who founded the Literary Club. The artist "enlarges the sphere of his understanding by a variety of knowledge, and warms his imagination with the best productions of ancient and modern poetry." [7] Furthermore, "what such partial and desultory reading cannot afford may be supplied by the conversation of learned and ingenious men, which is the best of all substitutes for those who have not the means or opportunities of deep study." [8]

From the beginning he was interested in what his pupil James Northcote, long a lodger in Reynolds's house, calls "the mental part" of the art, which of course means not theory alone but the application of theory. This is what first stimulated him in Jonathan Richardson's writings, and later led him to break away from his uninspiring master, Hudson. He told his father that "he would rather be an apothecary than an *ordinary* painter." [9] When he went to Rome in 1750 it was not to learn facile and mechanical tricks of the profession — he paid little attention to contemporary Italian favorites — but to wrest from the supreme masters the sources of their inspiration and their vision. Though an ideal quest which could end only with his death, it is also a notable combination of philosophical and practical interests. The profound effect on his art is neatly illustrated by Northcote's remarks on a fairly obvious contrast, Sir Thomas Lawrence, whose pictures were "mirrors for personal vanity to contemplate itself in (as you looked in the glass to see how you were dressed), but . . . it was a mistake to suppose they would interest anyone else or were addressed to the world at large. They were private, not public property." [10] Simply face painting, it is neither character nor great art; on the other hand, Reynolds's portraits live "from their answering to a feeling in the mind," even when they are deficient (as they often are) as literal representations of external nature. Idea and interpretation

7. Third Discourse.
8. Seventh Discourse.
9. Ellis K. Waterhouse, *Reynolds* (London, 1941), p. 3. The authoritative work on Reynolds, this book contains the largest collection of plates (well over three hundred) plus an annotated bibliography and catalogue.
10. Hazlitt, *Conversations*, p. 116.

of character are their distinguishing qualities; in fact at the end of the Ninth Discourse Reynolds defined Beauty as "an idea residing in the breast of the artist." If such a statement seems to lose sight of all but the Platonic side of the art, two facts must be remembered: first, Reynolds's imagination was stimulated not by poetical ideas in the abstract like Poussin's, say, or Rubens's, but by concrete objects before his eyes; and second, the *Discourses*, wide though their range is in painting and even in other arts, are directed above all else at the grand ideal of history painting, which Reynolds regretfully but sensibly recognized was not his métier. Notwithstanding, in dozens of his best portraits Reynolds, by catching the prevailing look and character, can take a considerable stride toward the history painter. "His portraits," said Northcote, "had always that determined air and character that you know what to think of them as if you had seen them engaged in the most decided action." [11] This is character.

To find out how he did it may ultimately evade analysis, but a comment Reynolds made on the nature of his own mind seems to me enlightening. In actual fact he is here speaking of Shakespeare as a writer of tragicomedy, but it describes his own mental habit of generalizing and particularizing simultaneously:

The mind appears to me of that nature and construction that it requires being employed on two things in order that it may do one thing well. Perhaps this disposition proceeds from the mind having always been accustomed to do many things at once, as in reading and writing, in which, from long habit, the operation of the mind comes to be no operation, or at least not perceptible. This double operation, what it has been so long accustomed to, begins at last to be a thing necessary, and required even, in affairs where a man would wish the whole powers of his mind to concentrate. . . . If I was to judge from my own experience, the mind always desires to double, to entertain two objects at a time.[12]

This is a remarkable passage, not only for what it actually states, though that is sufficiently unusual, but for what it suggests about Reynolds as a worker, namely, that all his effects are consciously achieved. Thus to speak of him as a psychologist is more than impressionistic criticism; psychology is part of his craft. His effects are never accidental. In the Fourth Discourse he states that the painter "cannot make his hero talk like a great man; he must make him look like one. For which reason he ought to be well studied in the analysis of those circumstances which constitute dignity of appearance in real life." Undoubtedly his deafness, forcing upon him a certain detachment, strengthened his powers of observation. If trapped by bores "he was still hard of hearing," says Goldsmith; "He shifted his trumpet and only took snuff."

In theories of characterization Reynolds's closest parallel is Fielding. Although this may not be immediately obvious, it is clear enough when we study the preface to *Joseph Andrews* with any care that when Fielding speaks of "the exactest copying of nature" he means what the Augustans had meant, and what Reynolds means: nature rearranged by art. There is a surface appearance of realism about Fielding's novels, we say that his settings and his people are "like life," but in truth his art is infinitely contrived and manipulated. Like Swift and Pope only slightly before him, he was rooted in neoclassical literary tradition and saw the contemporary taste as vulgarized and anarchical. Just as those writers had detested the ruthless assertiveness of Defoe's world, which must have seemed to them like some monstrous wave of the future that could bury civilization in universal darkness, so Fielding scorned the triviality and vulgarity of the kind of mind that could produce *Pamela* and the *Familiar Letters*, and he looked with dismay upon the resounding commercial success of those books. Having been turned out of the theater, which had not even begun to tap his real powers anyway, he set out to raise the standards of the novel-reading public in a number of ways that need no discussion here, such as employing an epic model modified by Cervantes, and writing the series of exploratory essays on the art of fiction that interlard the narrative in *Tom Jones* (an obvious parallel, on a smaller scale, to Reynolds's *Discourses on Art*). These run directly counter to the realistic stream of Defoe and Richardson, and like the poetical satires and epistles of his grand predecessors, proclaim the work of art as an artifact, something "made," not something which "is."

It is Fielding's analysis of characterization that is most interesting to study in relation to Reynolds. In a famous passage he explains what he means by a "just imitation of nature" by distinguishing between character and caricature in painting, illustrated by a flattering reference to Hogarth. (Reynolds — at that date a youth of eighteen — would in some ways have been a better choice, for his conception, like Fielding's, is intellectual and philosophical, whereas Hogarth's is in the main instinctive and emotional.) Fielding compares caricature to burlesque, character

11. *Ibid.*, p. 12.
12. *Portraits*, ed. Frederick W. Hilles (New Haven, 1952), p. 135.

to the comic. His objections to the former are clear enough — "its aim is to exhibit monsters, not men; and all distortions and exaggerations whatever are within its proper province." Hogarth, he says, is not a caricaturist but "a comic history painter" whose accomplishment it is "to express the affections of men on canvas." Reynolds shares the strictures on caricature — his only experiments in this vein had been for the amusement of himself and certain British visitors during his residence in Rome, but he soon abandoned it as being the worst possible recommendation for an aspiring portraitist — and he admires Hogarth, though with reservations.

Both men feel the limitations of caricature in serious art: whereas the function of satire is to arouse the conscience of the public, overexaggeration stimulates only amusement or disgust. It is difficult to believe that Fielding ever regarded Smollett, for instance, as much of an artist, or indeed as anything more than a ferociously high-spirited entertainer. In this connection Reynolds made a very revealing remark about Goldsmith consistent with his comments on caricature generally: "He is very sparing of epithets, which though they give a richness destroy simplicity, which I think is the peculiar characteristic of his poetry." [13] He saw caricature, lacking simplicity, as the great distorter of eighteenth-century drama and fiction. Goldsmith had the literary taste always to avoid it.

Character presents a more complicated problem. Though they would doubtless hold divergent opinions on matters of detail, Fielding and Reynolds are strongly united by their belief that depiction of character is an intellectual thing — that is, the interpretation, the vision of the artist. When Fielding says that he describes "not an individual but a species," the implication could hardly be clearer. Though "everything is copied from the book of nature," one does not see the species walking about the streets; the artist alone can see it in his mind's eye. Fielding's analysis of the Ridiculous — that its source is affectation stemming from either vanity or hypocrisy — is a patently man-made theory and is tantamount to saying that nature is actuality rearranged, or discovered, by the artist. 'Tis nature still, but nature methodized. To such a view Defoe or Richardson obviously would never subscribe. For them it would be neither realistic nor truthful; yet their tricks of illusion Fielding would call sham. To pretend that the work of art is anything but man-made and artificial is nonsense. But it is equally erroneous to think that it can have very great value unless it involves meticulous observation of all manners of men in real life. Arcadia is nowhere.

In the *Discourses* Reynolds often iterates that the physical world is the source from which all knowledge of beauty is derived. "This great ideal perfection and beauty are not to be sought in the heavens, but upon the earth." The artist by long experience can distinguish the accidents and deformities of nature and will learn "to design naturally by drawing his figures unlike to any one object." [14] He thus becomes the instructor of mankind. Fielding in the same role had prayed that he might see mankind more clearly than they could see themselves. The ultimate moral function of art Reynolds describes in his definition of Beauty already in part quoted: it is "an idea residing in the mind of the artist," which, by conducting the thoughts through successive stages of excellence, eventually leads from Taste to Virtue.

In attempting to paint the species through a scrutiny of men's characters and personalities, Fielding, as we should expect from one so affirmative, makes extensive use of type-characterization. The most manageable way of depicting manners, it provides a solid foundation for a complex plot structure and an equally complex view of society. Specific instances from *Joseph Andrews* and *Tom Jones* are too numerous and familiar to name. But what is unique in Fielding is the new slant we get on the old types, not so much from what they do or say but from what he says in his own person about them. His stage comedies, as distinguished from several of the dramatic burlesques, are poor things, and the blame must rest largely on the failure of his dialogue to animate the stereotypes of Jonsonian and Restoration comedy. In the two great novels many of the same figures turn up again, but they leap into life by means of the obbligato of wit and wisdom provided by the impresario. It is often said that Fielding excels in the externalization of character in action, but this is true only in the special sense of including the author himself in the process. The recent widely successful film version of *Tom Jones* provides the plainest possible illustration. Though the film is very funny indeed, the comedy is not at all like that of the novel. What is actually said is not very remarkable — imagine hearing the sound track without seeing the images, or imagine a radio adaptation — nor can there be more than the sketchiest substitution for Fielding's own commentary. (To be

13. *Ibid.*, p. 58.
14. Third Discourse.

sure an attempt is made in the occasional intrusion of a narrator's voice, or a sudden startling gesture hurled straight at the audience by one of the principals.) Instead we have a visual and musical composition based on Fielding's breathless plot and vividly etched character types. Even the poorest actor by sheer physical presence will suggest more than a mere type. Seeing the actor must be our substitute for hearing the author. The film is complementary to the novel perhaps, but a very different thing.

All this is saying that Fielding is nonrealistic and arbitrary, but so rich is the commentary of the showman that his performance reminds us of life itself. He aimed at an imitation, said Coleridge, not a copy of reality. The richness owes much to Fielding's sympathetic treatment of humors as opposed to wit, the harder and more rigid form of the comic visible in the character types of Restoration drama.[15] Parson Adams is of course the prime example, a character Fielding himself implies is unrealistic: "designed a character of perfect simplicity," "the most glaring in the whole," "not to be found in any book now extant." Calling him the absent-minded benevolent, a familiar enough type-character, would be true but not true enough. With Adams we sense that Fielding comes to recognize humor as an aesthetic experience enjoyable for its own sake and only incidentally concerned with didacticism. For artistic autonomy and sophistication this would seem considerably more advanced than Defoe or Richardson, as well as in opposition to the general realistic movement of contemporary fiction. Of course Richardson is quite as self-conscious a portrayer of character as Fielding — witness Lovelace calculatedly using the stock expressions of the stage hero of both tragedy and comedy — but he will never abandon the pretense that his creation is historical truth.

In moving to specific examples that will illustrate Reynolds's great range in modes of characterization, we should keep in mind the distinction between character and characters.[16] It is precisely the ability to suggest human nature in its essence and generality at the same time that he is displaying characters in their singularity and diversity that puts him far ahead of any other British portrait painter. The style which he was to bring to perfection, a more intimate and informal manner than that of Kneller and company, had already been created by Hogarth and was being quietly explored by Allan Ramsay. The great Hogarth portrait of Captain Coram, painted in 1740 for the Foundling Hospital, was one of the most important influences on the young Reynolds.[17] Its manner is both familiar and monumental, showing the middle-class philanthropist seated in great dignity at a table, the seal of the royal charter clasped in his right hand, a globe at his side; yet his direct gaze and genial benevolence prevent any suggestion of pompousness. The pretensions of this work — its scale, its accouterments, its air — are much beyond Hogarth's usual rather plain portrait manner, and one is not surprised to learn that he deliberately modeled it on Rigaud's portrait of Samuel Bernard (known to him through Drevet's engraving),[18] but in toning down its baroque panoply he has managed to wed the grand European manner with native truth. From this painting, and a comparable one by Ramsay to be discussed presently, Reynolds's greatest works may be said to have taken their direction.

If Hogarth showed the way in which the grand style can be introduced into native English portraiture, it is Reynolds who, through his fertile and inventive imagination and constant experimentation, really established the style. Hogarth never again attempted anything in this manner and Ramsey very rarely.[19] From the beginning Reynolds was determined to raise portrait painting to a status as near to that of history painting as he possibly could. The central problem he states bluntly enough in the Fourth Discourse: "A history painter paints a man in general; a portrait painter a particular man, and consequently a defective model." If it be asked what "a man in general" is, and what such a man could have to do with a particular portrait, another remark from the same Discourse suggests the answer: "A painter of portraits retains the individual likeness; a painter of history shows the man by showing his actions." In his Coram portrait Hogarth managed to hint at the man in action by showing the globe, the sea, and the solid strength of the sitter's pose as he grasps the royal seal so firmly. Reynolds goes further, and it is characteristic that he proceeds from a deliberately formulated theory. The mind "should be kept unembarrassed with whatever may any way serve to divide the attention of the spectator," for example, "the minute peculiarities of the

15. I draw here on the illuminating study by A. D. McKillop in *The Early Masters of English Fiction* (Lawrence, Kansas, 1956), p. 104.

16. These terms E. A. Baker substitutes for Johnson's famous distinction between characters of nature and characters of manners (*History of the English Novel* [London, 1930]), IV, 72-73.

17. For this and other information on the remaining pages I am indebted to Ellis K. Waterhouse, *Painting in Britain, 1530 to 1790* (London, 1953).

18. Frederick Antal, *Hogarth and his Place in European Art* (London, 1962), pp. 45-46.

19. Alastair Smart, *The Life and Art of Allan Ramsay* (London, 1952), p. 52.

dress, furniture, or scene of action." The important thing is always character and personality.

This principle sets him apart not only from the Hogarth of the narrative series, who relies on specific place, time, and appearance as an essential part of his art, but also from the Hogarth of the portraits, who never
removes his sitter from a very palpable contemporary world. So accustomed are we to seeing eighteenth-century ladies in Reynolds's portraits
that it is hard to realize how boldly he deviated from contemporary fashion.[20] Occasionally the clothing of his sitters in garments that never existed becomes somewhat ridiculous, but dozens of pictures are made
memorable from this very circumstance: the superb full-length of Omai
dressed in loose white folds which make him an archetype of the magical
noble savage prince; or the lovely sylvan picture of Mrs. Lloyd carving
her lover's name on a tree, her vaguely classical robe blending with the
chequered shade of the glen in a highly poetic conception that an attention to fashion would utterly destroy.

This picture can lead us into the most important and most variable of
Reynolds's modes of exploring character and individualizing portraiture,
his appropriation of some pose or fiction from either literature or art that
will simultaneously illustrate something about the sitter and lend something dramatic or imaginative to the painting. The Mrs. Lloyd is called
a "fancy painting" from Shakespeare, which means that the painter has
invented a bit of fiction suggested by *As You Like It*. The pose, besides
being beautiful in itself, indicates at the same time her literary cultivation, her love of nature, and her devotion to her husband. The lightness
of touch so necessary for these things to come off successfully is illustrated best of all in his numerous "fancy" pictures of children: Master
Crewe as Henry VIII, for example, a terribly pleased four-year-old got
up in the famous Holbein costume and pose, but with the important addition of a puppy sniffing at his feet to indicate the lighthearted spirit in
which we are to take the picture; or Lady Caroline Scott as Winter, a
miniature enchantress bundled up in cloak and muff and set into a wintry
landscape to rule as goddess of the season. Their wit and unexpectedness
preserve them from the sentimentality into which Gainsborough and
Romney usually fall with their children.

One of his greatest skills lies in the way he borrows or adapts gestures
and attitudes from earlier masters. It is probably the principal method of
his constant experiments in abstracting the general idea of nature from

the particular. In the Third Discourse he recommended "the diligent study of the works of our great predecessors" not with the view of copying but rather of stimulating the imagination. We have already observed two very different examples in the Siddons portrait adapted from Michelangelo, and the Garrick derived from Carracci. To call this plagiarism is to misunderstand the neoclassical attitude toward public utterance explained plainly enough in the *Essay on Criticism*, itself a prime example of quotation from earlier masters. Blake's failure to understand this principle led him to say of Reynolds, "This man was hired to depress art," though Blake himself is a constant borrower from Michelangelo. (It is doubtless a different thing if one is directed by spirits.) Walpole's vigorous defense of Reynolds on this score says all that we need to know:

Sir J. Reynolds has been accused of plagiarism for having borrowed attitudes from ancient masters. Not only candour but criticism must deny the force of the charge. When a single posture is imitated from an historic picture and applied to a portrait in a different dress and with new attributes, this is not plagiarism, but quotation: and a quotation from a great author, with a novel application of the sense, has always been allowed to be an instance of parts and taste; and may have more merit than the original. . . . The exuberance of his invention will be the grammar of future painters of portrait.[21]

Even the pugnaciously independent Hogarth did not scorn to draw upon Rigaud (to mention no further borrowings). Similarly, the three volumes of *Vitruvius Britannicus* are only the most elaborate and public illustration of the practice among architects of keeping books of prints upon which they constantly drew without the slightest sense of plagiarism. Shaftesbury truly remarked that the invention of the print was to English culture in the eighteenth century what printing had been earlier to literature.[22]

During his Italian years Reynolds had filled his sketchbooks with examples from which he drew for the rest of his life. His famous portrait of Sterne was modeled after a Bronzino in the Corsini Palace, Mrs. Crewe as St. Genevieve from a picture in the Pitti, and Jacob Bouverie from a Salimbeni self-portrait in the Annunziata, to note only a very few.[23] As

20. Roger Fry in his edition of the *Discourses* (London, 1905), pp. 435–36.
21. Wornum, ed., *Anecdotes of Painting in England*, I, xvii.
22. *Second Characters; or, The Language of Forms* (Cambridge, Eng., 1914), p. 121.
23. See Charles Mitchell, "Three Phases of Reynolds's Method," *Burlington Magazine*, LXXX (1942), 35ff.

early as 1751 he began experimenting with self-portraits adapted from Rembrandt. By such means lesser artists than Reynolds would draw up a sketchbook of stock attitudes or "typical poses" from which a patron presumably could choose one that suited him. Interpretation of character does not enter into it. Kneller was particularly prone to this method, and since usually he painted only the heads, employing a studio of assistants each to execute whatever part of the portrait was his specialty, the results can be stiff and unharmonious. It is curiously related to an aspect of Burlington's architecture which Wittkower has called *staccato*, an emphasis upon each individual feature in such a way as to give a jerky and abrupt effect to the elevations, an effect that one might compare with caricature.[24] While Burlington's formula-loving mind visualized each motif separately, Reynolds's harmonization of his motifs is usually felicitous. In his "fancy" of the Child St. John the Baptist it can be shown that he used three separate Raphael attitudes to give coherent form to the figure.[25]

Great as Reynolds's superiority is to Kneller in tonal and rhythmic unity, of most interest to us is the care with which he chose the design or attitude to bring out the particular personality of the sitter. His first elaborate essay in the grand manner, Viscount Keppel, though familiar to students of Allan Ramsay, is too important to neglect here, for while it shows that Reynolds had been anticipated in his wedding of classical models to British portraiture, the great advance in drama and imaginative coloring over his predecessors even at so early a stage in his career (1753) makes the style his own. Ramsay's sole excursion into a dramatic and nonstatic design is the 1748 painting of Norman, the twenty-second Chief of Macleod, walking by the seashore in a pose taken from the Apollo Belvedere in reverse. Rocks are at the left, the sea at the right, the laird sharply silhouetted against a calm sky. Appropriating the design, Reynolds utterly transformed it. In Professor Waterhouse's words, "He . . . took a classical theme which had been arranged by Ramsay for chamber music and showed what he could make of it by scoring it for a full orchestra."[26] The coloring is darkened, the sea made tempestuous, the amount of silhouette much reduced in order to tie the figure into the landscape, while the gesture of the right arm, in Ramsay one of friendly welcome, becomes a command. The changes are a part of Reynolds's character portrayal; Keppel, recently shipwrecked, had heroically survived. Reynolds gets both the event and the man. Ramsay's seashore had been a conventional reference to the island home of the Macleods; in Reynolds the warring elements are an essential part of the meaning, an interpretation of character. It is doltish to call this plagiarism.

A better-known model than the Apollo Belvedere would be hard to find, but what we are likely to forget is that literally hundreds of more obscure works were fairly widely known owing to the enormous traffic in prints and engravings. Classical statuary, for example, was far more familiar to the cultivated European then than it is now. The seemingly endless catalogue of prints after Reynolds's own paintings gives us an idea of what the phrase "public artist" means in the eighteenth century. The point to be made here is that, far from wishing to conceal his debts to former masters, Reynolds in many works expects them to be known; Walpole's comment shows that the wit consists in our appreciating to what new use the artist has put his source. They are quotations wittily applied or manipulated. The delight of recognition is of course central to neoclassical culture, but Reynolds's employment of this kind of quotation is an earnest of the future, indeed is one of the reasons that he continues to grow as an artist; I refer to his emphasis on association as a primary element of aesthetic response. Throughout the *Discourses* he had repeated a concept found in Plato, that as the mind is determined by the nature of what it contemplates, we must take care that it not be narrowed by accident or fashion. But from here he moves to contemporary associationalist psychology, doubtless influenced by his friendship with Burke. Beauty and sublimity act directly upon the nervous system through sense impressions, and taste becomes a matter of associated ideas. The importance of choice in his borrowed attitude or model is thus crucial not only to what it suggests to Reynolds himself about the personality of the sitter, but what it may suggest to others as a portrait. It is the same with Fielding, a name not usually connected with associationism or Hartley, in his use of epical theory and practice in general and of Cervantes in particular as he writes *Joseph Andrews*, and with Pope and Johnson in their imitations of Horace and Juvenal. Fielding's Preface speaks of burlesque diction in places "not necessary to be pointed out to the classical reader for whose entertainment those parodies or burlesque

24. Cited by John Summerson, *Architecture in Britain, 1530–1830* (London and Baltimore, 1953), p. 203.
25. Mitchell, "Three Phases," pp. 38–39.
26. Waterhouse, *Painting in Britain*, p. 166.

imitations are chiefly calculated," and in the epical overtones he is hoping to claim for the novel the dignity of the highest narrative art. Likewise the verse imitations do not merely say what they state, but also manage to evoke venerable and august associations.

A simple example in Reynolds is a portrait of Mrs. Bouverie and Mrs. Crewe entitled *Et in Arcadia Ego*. The two young matrons are pictured gazing at the Countess of Coventry's tomb, and are touched with a most affecting reverie and tenderness. Reynolds could have painted exactly the same expressions and left out the tomb, but the impression would be quite different because of associations too obvious to explain. The associations are tied up with his interpretation of their characters. Many of his mother-and-child portraits are adaptations of madonna motifs which, though seldom calling attention to themselves, elevate the subject and temper the sweetness. When, in one of the loveliest of all the madonna pictures, the Nelly O'Brien now in the Wallace Collection, he substitutes a Pekingese for the infant, one is equally surprised at his audacity and delighted at his humor. (Nelly was a very expensive courtesan.) Another variation also celebrated is the exuberant Duchess of Devonshire and daughter (at Chatsworth) who seem to be playing pat-a-cake. It is both a flattering and a penetrating analysis of motherhood.

That these pictures make us smile or sometimes even laugh is important to remember as we move to another method of Reynolds's character study, the invented allegory or mythology. His paintings in this mode have been handled roughly even by Professor Waterhouse, who describes *Lady Sarah Bunbury Sacrificing to the Graces* as in a "somewhat unfortunate portrait style. . . . high-minded and doctrinaire." His other comment, however, points to Reynolds's originality: "It was a deliberate innovation of his own, for it does not correspond to any contemporary European fashion nor to a perceptible reaction towards classicism apparent in British society.") [27] The picture, influenced by Guido Reni, shows the lady pouring a libation upon a smoking altar before a statue of the three graces. An inferior priestess kneels behind her making ready a second offering. That the painting is intended to be taken with solemnity I am not convinced. The parallel with Belinda at the dressing table in the *Rape of the Lock* could hardly have escaped Sir Joshua's notice. Naturally he does not mean to satirize Lady Sarah — he does not share Fielding's low opinion of high life — but he is complimenting her with enough exaggeration that both she and everyone else are expected to smile. The tone is exactly right for saying something about the *femme savante*. The age knew it was not epical, but never tired in all sorts of amusing and partly self-deprecatory ways to show how admiring they were of that quality. Even the much grander picture of Mrs. Siddons as the Tragic Muse, the most serious of all Reynolds's invented allegories, is not to be viewed in awestruck silence. The key to the tone, as I have said earlier, is in the many delightful pictures of children in this mode. Northcote said that Reynolds learned grace from watching children;[28] the comment is enlightening here.

Pictorially the most elaborate of these allegories is the enormous painting in the National Gallery of the three Montgomery sisters as *Three Graces Adorning the Term of Hymen*. Its compositional history is extremely complicated, involving designs from Poussin, Rubens, an anonymous Rape of Proserpina, plus an earlier picture of his own of Lady Elizabeth Keppel.[29] The composition is bound together by the long chain of flowers held by each of the three girls who, in their flowing drapery which forms an enchanting rhythmic line with the background, look both alike and different. In scale and composition as well as theme it is as successful an approach to history painting (with the Montgomery sisters as models) as Reynolds feels comfortable with. Though more than a touch of the baroque can be seen in his handling of these allegories, their lightness of touch aerates them. When he tries the same thing in straight history painting he nearly always fails, for the tone is wrong. Of course he had his disasters in this lesser vein as well, Lady Blake as *Juno Receiving the Cestus from Venus* being a particularly depressing instance. Either the painter could discover no character to be interpreted, or he aimed too high. Though Reynolds may have given her Juno's ox eyes, Lady Blake remains a gangling nonentity. Such complete failures are rare, but in the works of a painter whose output is around a thousand it is not surprising that many do not rise above competence merely. For the most part I am concerned with those paintings suggesting some element of drama, which usually show him at his best.

The recital of still different modes of character portrayal with plentiful examples could go on almost indefinitely, but I shall end with two related methods in which Reynolds stands quite alone. The first might be

27. *Ibid.*, p. 168.
28. Hazlitt, *Conversations*, p. 179.
29. E. H. Gombrich, "Reynolds's Theory and Practice of Imitation," *Burlington Magazine*, LXXX (1942), 40–45.

Sir Joshua Reynolds, *Colonel Tarleton*. Courtesy of the
Trustees of the British Museum

described as portraiture in which a strongly delineated individual is translated into the representative of a type without losing any of his individuality. The Siddons allegorical portrait has something of this quality, as do the simpler complementary pieces, Mrs. Abington as the Comic Muse (the pixie face is wedded to something more generalized in the piquant attitude and by the comic mask which she holds in her hand), and that of the singer Mrs. Bilington as St. Cecilia, who, standing motionless herself, is surrounded by swirls of motion in clouds and singing *putti*, the whole suggesting the Spirit of Music amidst a flood of celestial sound.

These are partial allegories, however, and are thus less surprising than the portraits which set out to be simply the man himself. I choose three military heroes to add to the early Commodore Keppel already described. Two are of young men in whom Reynolds has miraculously caught contrasting aspects of the Romantic Warrior by the special combination of facial expression, stance, and background accouterments. The National Gallery portrait of Colonel Tarleton (opposite page) is the epitome of Byronic daring, dash, and grandiosity. Bending to adjust his sword, he is caught in the midst of battle, cannons to the right, left, and indeed below him (he is standing on one), while a horse rears behind. The Waddesdon portrait of Colonel St. Leger, equally romantic, is the antithesis of Tarleton. He is standing on a barren strand against a dark stormy sky, which would seem melodramatic did not his sadly pensive expression raise the picture into a mood of poetry and wistful melancholy. In each case the individual is indelibly impressed upon the imagination, and so is the universal. More famous and quite different is the magnificent portrait of the governor of Gibraltar, Lord Heathfield, posed against a cannon and lowering clouds and holding his great key. Through the rugged, very individual countenance of the old soldier, Reynolds has managed to suggest both a type-character and an allegorical figure, the Guardian of the State, Britannicus Nobilissimus. Not an individual but a species, said Fielding, yet in Parson Adams contriving to create both; both an individual and a species, Reynolds would say, offering example after example to show how it could be done.

The last category involves again the individual portrait translated into a higher sphere, but instead of capturing a character-type or a profession it is rather some human quality in the abstract. Professor Wimsatt's definition of the concrete universal,[30] in which he analyzes "The Age of

30. In *The Verbal Icon* (Lexington, Kentucky, 1954), pp. 75–76.

Sir Joshua Reynolds, *Dr. Johnson*. Courtesy of the
Trustees of the British Museum

Innocence," is the kind of thing I have in mind, but a more subtle because less obviously deliberate effort seems to me illustrated in a pair of paintings of Dr. Johnson. In the great final portrait, familiar to everyone, realism has reached its ultimate limit, yet what makes the picture so moving is that it has caught a kind of abstraction of human suffering. The man Johnson is there, but so is the tragic sense of life. The earlier idealized portrait of Johnson in a habit suggesting an antique Roman (now at Knole) shows him in profile without his wig and holding a scroll which was subsequently painted out (opposite page). Though again the severity of the visage suggests suffering, Reynolds emphasizes that side of Johnson which made him an object of reverence, his grave moral force and nobility of intellect. Reynolds saw Johnson as a great soul. Analysis of personality is made manifest on canvas. Finally there is the one great portrait of Sterne, the only adequate likeness anywhere, in an attitude borrowed from Bronzino, but with an expression never dreamed of in that master's philosophy. What emerges almost uncannily is a personification of satanic glee. These portraits like most of his best work impress us with the fact that Reynolds sees character as both the analysis of personality and as an aesthetic experience. Pictorial values and human values strengthen each other in his harmonization.

In the end it is this combination of human with pictorial values that makes Reynolds such a slippery figure to analyze. In some of the sheer mechanics of painting, "the grammatical part of the art," he was often deficient — look at the awkwardly drawn hand in his great Johnson portrait, or see what his experiments in pigmentation have sometimes done to his colors — and in his high ambitions for elevating portraiture to the level of history he can climb into the laughable. Yet he achieved history, though not in quite the way he was seeking; our knowledge of the great English society of the second half of the eighteenth century in all its rich full range has been permanently influenced by Reynolds. If he is not a history painter, he is a historian.

In this connection comparing him with Gainsborough is as inevitable as it is useful. As a sheer poet in paints Gainsborough is alone, but his world turns ever more inward as he becomes entranced with the glitter and sheen of fabrics and with a gossamer vision of a landscape that never was. It has been well observed that the later portraits, from which all "the grosser qualities of human personality" have been purged, depict celestial beings that "hardly belong to the history of portraiture so much as to the world of . . . 'fancy-pictures.'" [31] It is all but a dream world. Professor Waterhouse cites a letter of May 24, 1787, written by Lavinia, Countess Spencer, to her husband about a portrait to be painted for his college which makes a telling comparison: "she cannot bear anyone having a Sir Joshua of him but herself, but . . . she thinks 'a daub by Gainsborough' would do well enough for his College." [32] The difference is between an impressionistic sketch and the completely realized psychological portrait.

Gainsborough's individuality is obviously the thing we most value in him, but what I have been endeavoring to show is that the individuality of Reynolds has wider significance in various directions — psychological, literary, aesthetic. Northcote pointed out in the comparison with Lawrence quoted earlier that with Reynolds the face was only a part of the likeness, that the interpretation, the "mental part," was more important. We are more interested in the artist than the subject, or at least are interested in the subject principally because of the artist. Fielding's practice seems to me a very close parallel. It is surely significant that when in *Amelia* he lets his characters tell their own stories in flashbacks he loses the advantage of his own presence as controlling narrator, and consequently loses as well the greater part of his distinction. The kind of realism that demands the invisibility of the artist is irrelevant if only our imaginations are stirred. However emotional the appeal of art, the art itself remains a rational and intellectual pursuit. More than most artists, Reynolds and Fielding bring this truth home to us, since they are themselves so strongly before us in their works.

As an old man Northcote often talked about his revered master in a series of brilliant conversations with Hazlitt. I should like to give him the last word, for much that I have been saying can be seen through his tribute:

If I was to compare him with Vandyke and Titian, I should say that Vandyke's portraits are like pictures . . . Sir Joshua's like the reflection in a looking-glass, and Titian's like the real people. There is an atmosphere of light and shade about Sir Joshua's, which neither of the others have in the same degree, together with a vagueness that gives them a visionary and romantic character, and makes them seem like dreams or vivid recollections of persons we have seen. I never could mistake Vandyke's for any thing but pictures, and I go up to them to examine them as such; when I see a fine Sir Joshua, I can neither suppose it to be a mere picture nor a man; and I almost involuntarily turn back to ascertain if it is not some one behind me reflected in the glass: when I see a Titian, I am riveted to it, and I can no more take my eye off from it, than if it were the very individual in the room.[33]

Though this is a very personal and impressionistic observation, it suggests something incontrovertible about Reynolds. He combined character with a certain sweetness, so that, while he is assuredly the greatest classical master of British portraiture, his appeal remains largely romantic. The sitter is there before us, but there is also something beyond, which is Reynolds himself. As Northcote says, "You come to this at last — what you find in any one that you can get nowhere else. If you have this about you, you need not be afraid of time."

31. Waterhouse, *Painting in Britain*, p. 188.
32. *Ibid.*, p. 180.
33. Hazlitt, *Conversations*, p. 20.

❧ EMILIE BUCHWALD

# Gainsborough's "Prospect, Animated Prospect"

UNLIKE Sir Joshua Reynolds who took care to be informed about every matter of aesthetic moment, who corresponded with the poet-painter-gardener William Mason, as well as with other enthusiastic landscape gardenists, and who went so far as to have Sir William Chambers erect a rather wretched country house at Richmond that he also might talk of and sketch a pleasing prospect,[1] Thomas Gainsborough was not interested in "making" landscapes, nor in improving them, nor even in talking about them. He did, however, spend almost a lifetime painting them.

The landscape backgrounds of Gainsborough's portraits are a valuable repository of changing landscape fashion, since Gainsborough was, without question, a fashion reporter of the first order, sensitive to the erratic mechanism that ordains the change in the fabric of a collar, the length of a glove, the components of a landscape. He did not, as was Reynolds's custom, paint his sitters in "fancy dress," but in contemporary costume; similarly, his portrait backgrounds often represent the fashionable landscape, or, at the least, that landscape which harmonized with his noble sitters' conception of an appropriate background. Since the portraits are more reliably dated than are many of the important landscape paintings or the more than five hundred catalogued Gainsborough landscape drawings, an examination of the portraits provides a fairly reliable method of establishing that Gainsborough consciously abandoned the Dutch naturalistic manner of his early work for techniques which resulted in far more generalized and idealized scenes in his later paintings. Furthermore, the portraits and fancy paintings of Gainsborough's last years, warmly admired by Reynolds, are excellent examples of nature seen through the veil of sensibility, fashionable nature; in fact, picturesque nature. These Gainsborough creations fuse his carefully acquired disregard for the minutely realistic with his skill as an interpreter of fashion. Their popularity is another indication that the vogue of the picturesque in the eighties and nineties was not an anticipation of Wordsworthian delight in nature herself, but yet one final manifestation of an aesthetic which sought in some way to codify nature.

Gainsborough's contemporaries fostered the false impression that he was simply a recorder, a great artist who succeeded in spite of his lack of proper training. His earliest biographer Philip Thicknesse talks patronizingly of "his little landscapes" and drawings,[2] probably for the purpose of inflating his own role in forming Gainsborough's taste and abilities. The comment made by William Jackson, one of Gainsborough's numerous musician friends, strengthened the impression of Gainsborough as an unlearned natural: "Gainsborough avoided the company of literary men — who were his aversion, he was better pleased to give than to receive information. . . . so far from writing he scarcely ever read a book."[3]

Reynolds himself was in doubt about the elements of Gainsborough's power. Northcote reports a revealing tidbit: on one occasion when Sir Joshua was standing before one of Gainsborough's paintings, he confessed, "I cannot make out how he produces his effects."[4] Yet he was forced to acknowledge that effects were indeed produced. In his Fourteenth Discourse, Reynolds dismisses the work of recently famous Italian painters, saying "I take more interest in, and am more captivated with, the powerful impression of nature, which Gainsborough exhibited in his portraits and in his landscapes, and the interesting simplicity and elegance of his little ordinary beggar-children than with any of the works of that

1. Derek Hudson, *Sir Joshua Reynolds* (London, 1958), pp. 107, 108.

2. Mary Woodall, *Thomas Gainsborough* (New York, 1949), p. 21. For my discussion of Gainsborough's style I am indebted to Ellis K. Waterhouse's *Gainsborough* (London, 1958), and to Mary Woodall's *Gainsborough's Landscape Drawings* (London, 1939), abbreviated henceforth as *GLD*.

3. Thomas Gainsborough, *The Letters of Gainsborough*, ed. Mary Woodall (New York, 1961), p. 11.

4. George Fulcher, *The Life of Thomas Gainsborough* (London, 1856), p. 155.

[Italian] School." [5] Reynolds wrote this Discourse two years after Gainsborough's death. The rivalries of the past had receded into proper perspective, and Reynolds was attempting to give the devil his due. He was aware that his fellow academicians were not prepared to be as generous in some ways as he was, a fact which is demonstrated by Fuseli's sneering remark "posterity will judge whether the name of Gainsborough deserves to be ranked with those of Vandyke, Rubens, and Claude." [6] But obviously, Sir Joshua wished to give Gainsborough the praise and the place he deserved. On the other hand, one can easily understand why he hesitated to give full praise to a painter whose methods and successes he could not completely account for, and which, in a sense, were affronts to everything that the Royal Academy training stood for. When one compares certain passages from the Discourse devoted to Gainsborough, Reynolds's mental gymnastics are evident: "It is no disgrace to the genius of Gainsborough to compare him to such men as we sometimes meet with, whose natural eloquence appears even in speaking a language, which they can scarce be said to understand." [7] These lines describe an artist who does not understand what he does, but who does it well nevertheless. Reynolds also says that Gainsborough's work shows "a minute observation of particular nature," and that he made "a faithful, if not a poetical representation of what he had before him," [8] once again, a description of a man who did not think, but performed, and, moreover, performed as a literal recorder. The description of Gainsborough as a careful recorder of "particular nature" hardly accords with Reynolds's description of Gainsborough's technique, a technique which obviously perplexed Reynolds, since it ought to have resulted in chaotic paintings; as he confesses, however,

it is certain, that all those odd scratches and marks, which on a close examination, are so observable in Gainsborough's pictures, and which even to experienced painters appear rather the effect of accident than design; this chaos, this uncouth and shapeless appearance, by a kind of magick, at a certain distance assumes form, and all the parts seem to drop into their proper places; so that we can hardly refuse to acknowledge the full effect of diligence, under the appearance of chance and hasty negligence. That Gainsborough himself considered this peculiarity in his manner and the power it possesses of exciting surprise, as a beauty in his works, I think may be inferred from the eager desire which we know he always expressed, that his pictures, at the Exhibition, should be seen near, as well as at a distance. [9]

This passage demonstrates the full extent of Reynolds's uncertainty as well as his desire to be just; he recognizes that what appears to be "chance and hasty negligence" must be something else, something more, although all his training and judgment are opposed to the idea. Further, he realizes that Gainsborough had a definite purpose in mind in making use of this "peculiarity in manner," that his technique was deliberate and careful, and that he was far from a "faithful" recorder of "particular nature." Perceptive and sensitive observer that he was, Reynolds instinctively understood and paid tribute to Gainsborough's ability to create life, that "powerful impression of nature," in what he painted, but instead of following the path of his own acute observations to their conclusion, he felt called upon to explain away that ability. Certainly Gainsborough's was a natural eloquence, but it was by careful study and experiment that he added to the expressive powers of the language he and Reynolds shared. Although his earliest works are indeed quite literal recordings of nature, he proceeded to evolve a method of depicting her which is as general, ideal, and abstract in its way, as are the paintings of Claude Lorraine or Gaspar Poussin.

Mary Woodall's *Gainsborough's Landscape Drawings* ends once and for all the assumption that Gainsborough was unacquainted with and uninterested in learning the landscape techniques of those seventeenth-century artists most admired by his contemporaries: Claude Lorraine, Gaspar Poussin, and Salvator Rosa. Indeed it would have been truly amazing if he had not been acquainted with them in an age when their landscapes were displayed prominently in any noble house worthy of being visited. One of Gainsborough's sketchbooks displays fifty-eight Italian scenes of landscape and architecture, copied perhaps from a series of engravings of Italian paintings in England made by Pond between 1732 and 1736.[10] The influence exerted on Gainsborough by Van Dyck and Rubens, an influence noted by Reynolds, seems to have commenced when Gainsborough moved to Bath in 1759 and was able to visit the collections at Wilton, Bowood, and Longleat, and to see Ralph Allen's adaptation of the gardens of Prior Park based on the paintings of Gaspar

5. Sir Joshua Reynolds, *Discourses on Art*, with an introduction by Robert Lavine (New York, 1961), p. 218.
6. Fulcher, *Life*, pp. 180–81.
7. Reynolds, *Discourses*, p. 227.
8. *Ibid.*, p. 222.
9. *Ibid.*, p. 226.
10. Woodall, *GLD*, p. 10.

Poussin, complete with grottoes and temples.[11] There are, however, in the landscape compositions of the Bath period, resemblances between Gainsborough's composition and brushwork — the spiky brushstrokes of the foliage, for instance — and Claude's, which may legitimately be traced to Gainsborough's close inspection of the Claudes he saw.[12] Among the engravings in Gainsborough's possession at his death were thirty-two made from Claude's paintings, only three less than the number of reproductions of the work of his beloved Van Dyck.[13]

As for the influence of Gaspar Poussin, the fashionable grounds of Prior Park have already been mentioned. A drawing of Gainsborough's in a private collection is inscribed "given to my father . . . in the style of Gaspar Poussin," and other drawings show the same composition in the manner of Poussin.[14] John Hoppner, otherwise an admirer of Gainsborough's work, wrote an evaluation for the *Quarterly Review* after Gainsborough's death which deserves quotation:

His last manner, though greatly inferior to that immediately preceding it, was certainly the result of much practice and knowledge, with some leaning perhaps to the suggestion of indolence. Its principal defects seem to be that it neither presented the spectator with a faithful delineation of nature nor possessed any great pretensions to be classed with the epic works of art. . . . The studies that he made at this time of his life, in chalks, from the works of the more learned painters of landscape, but particularly from the works of Gaspar Poussin, were doubtless the foundation of the style.[15]

In the eyes of a discerning contemporary, Gainsborough had a "last manner"; he was consciously seeking new effects which had little to do with the faithful and particular representation of nature which Reynolds speaks of, and which are to Hoppner annoyingly different from those which he expected. This last manner has absorbed the techniques of the important "learned painters of landscape," but made use of those techniques in a way which Hoppner characterizes as "uncouth," an adjective which seems to mean that the author felt his aesthetic sensibilities threatened. Hoppner's observations indicate that he reacted just as strongly as Reynolds to Gainsborough's ability to project a "powerful impression of nature." Both men recognized a new approach and new techniques, but Hoppner rejects them emphatically, while Reynolds at least grapples with the problems they pose.

Gainsborough's earliest efforts were naturalistic landscapes, and his earliest "portraits" were figures set in a landscape. Gainsborough's backgrounds were the very real woods and parks of Suffolk, and there seems every likelihood that his subjects were sketched out of doors together with the landscape they stood or sat in. One of Gainsborough's first such compositions was *Mr. and Mrs. Andrewes* (following page), painted in 1748 or shortly thereafter. Contrary to popular conventions for handling light, particularly in the foreground, Gainsborough produces the effect of the diffused light of an actual English summer day; the figures are thus sharply outlined and form a compositional unit which helps to balance the expanse of landscape opened before us. The rows of wheat replace the more conventional device of a winding road, leading the eye back to rove into the distance. We are treated to the pastoral view of a flock of sheep in a railed enclosure, and in the left middle ground, the suggestion of a herd of cows under the trees in a similar enclosure. Through the central group of trees, the spire of a church draws the eye; the tower of a long low building is dimly seen in the far distance on the left. The balance in this painting between the figures — they are hardly people, though Gainsborough has obviously tried for natural poses — and the landscape, does not recur until the portraits of Gainsborough's "last manner," when the figures and landscapes are reunited, but in a very different way.

In this painting, Gainsborough has given the Andreweses a pleasant survey of their property. It is interesting to consider the question of how up-to-date that property was. Shaftesbury's attack in 1709 upon the hitherto undisputed sovereignty of Lenôtre's garden of parterre and *rond-point*, the subsequent discussions of the "natural" garden by Addison and Pope, the practical publications of Batty Langley and Stephan Switzer, the application of new principles of garden design by Vanbrugh and Bridgeman at Eastbury and Clermont, the collaborations of Lord Burlington with Bridgeman, and, most notably, with William Kent, made Englishmen of wealth anxious not to be left behind the fashion.[16] In the

11. *Ibid.*, pp. 7, 8.
12. *Ibid.*, p. 22.
13. William T. Whitley, *Thomas Gainsborough* (London, 1915), p. 351.
14. Woodall, *GLD*, p. 23.
15. Fulcher, *Life*, p. 248.
16. A discussion of gardening taste in the first half of the eighteenth century may be found in the following: B. Sprague Allen, *Tides in English Taste* (Cambridge, Massachusetts, 1937), vol. I; Isabel W. U. Chase, *Horace Walpole: Gardenist* (Princeton, 1943), Pt. I, Chapters I, II, III; Margaret Jourdain, *The Work of William Kent* (London, 1948), introduction by Christopher Hussey; Osvald Sirén,

Thomas Gainsborough, *Mr. and Mrs. Andrewes*. Reproduced by courtesy of the Trustees, the National Gallery, London

thirties, Kent was summoned to redesign the grounds of Carlton House, Claremont, Chiswick, Stowe, and Rousham.[17] In a letter from Sir Thomas Robinson to Lord Carlisle in 1734, the "new taste in gardening" in which grounds were laid out "without either level or line" is commended. Sir Thomas remarks, "if this grows a fashion . . . they [the laborers working on the gardens] will run no risk of having time lay on their hands."[18] How accurate a prophet he proved! Thus, while his grounds may have raised an owner's just pride in the breast of Mr. Andrewes, they would have raised a corresponding eagerness to make them modern in the breast of William Kent. First, of course, the railed enclosures would have given way to fosses to create the impression of a unified scene. The central group of trees would have been parted to create a vista terminating in a landscape view of the church with its spire. The small lakes on the bosom of the hill in the right middle ground would have been united and made to serpentine gracefully, and somewhere on the tree-lined furthermost shore, a temple, dedicated perhaps to the Virtues or the Worthies or some particular deity, would have sprung up, not to mention busts, vases, urns, and obelisks scattered with a liberal hand in other woody recesses. The fusion of the lawn with the fields would have been applauded: Kent's plan for Rousham, though still formal, combined lawns with cultivated fields, so that Addison's early visualization of "a whole estate thrown into a kind of garden" is fulfilled.[19]

Once such improvements had been made, however, the same view, because of the very nature of the changes, would seem much more lawnlike, and would certainly appear much less varied. In the midst of his pleasant rhapsodizing about the effects of the new style of gardening, Horace Walpole stops for a few sentences to complain about precisely such a difficulty:

how rich, how gay, how picturesque the face of the country! The demolition of walls laying open each improvement, every journey is made through a succession of pictures. . . . If we have the seeds of a Claude or a Gaspar amongst us, he must come forth. . . . One misfortune in truth there is that throws a difficulty on the artist. A principal beauty in our gardens is the lawn and smoothness of turf: in a picture it becomes

China and the Gardens of Europe of the Eighteenth Century (New York, 1950), Chapter 4.

17. John Summerson, *Architecture in Britain, 1530–1830* (London and Baltimore, 1953), p. 197.

18. Jourdain, *William Kent*, p. 77.

19. *Ibid.*, p. 23.

a dead and uniform spot, incapable of chiaroscuro, and to be broken insipidly by children, dogs and other unmeaning figures.[20]

A painting by Canaletto of the newly-modernized main front of Badminton House in Gloucestershire confirms the accuracy of Walpole's observation. The marvelous expanse of lawn swallows up the scene. Precisely such "unmeaning figures" as Walpole speaks of appear on the great sweep of lawn in Canaletto's painting, dwarfed, made insignificant by the improved landscape. When he painted his portrait of the Andreweses and their property, Gainsborough did not have to contend with the problems that faced Canaletto as he looked out from the modernity of Badminton House. As we shall see, Gainsborough refused to allow himself to become involved with difficulties such as these.

When Gainsborough and his wife removed to Bath in 1759, the great estates in and around that area were already in the midst of fashionable improvement. Longleat was being remodeled by Lancelot "Capability" Brown.[21] A visitor to the house in 1760 wrote: "the gardens . . . are succeeded by a fine lawn, a serpentine river, wooded hills, gravel paths meandering round a shrubbery, *all modernized* by the ingenious and much sought after Mr. Brown." [22] The following year, William, Earl of Sherburne engaged both Robert Adam and Capability Brown, the former to prepare designs for a new house at Bowood, and the latter to remake the grounds; calling for Brown to "enclose the gardens by a sunk fence . . . to re-turf various lawns . . . [to make] a sham bridge . . . and great plantations on either side of the Mausoleum as well as those by which the park was bounded." [23] In 1766, Gainsborough painted David Garrick leaning against a bust of Shakespeare, in a landscape which Walpole identifies as Prior Park, with Capability Brown's newly-completed Palladian bridge visible in the background.[24] Gainsborough might have "thrown it into" the composition as a kind of added attraction, a fashionable extra.

Except for this prominent Palladian bridge, Gainsborough painted none of the "improved" premises he visited so eagerly at Bath for a sight of the Van Dycks and the Rubenses. The obvious reason may have been his financial success. His studio was busy; his portraits had been successful almost immediately, and he appears to have had even more work than he wished to take on.[25] He evidently had no fear of incurring displeasure which would damage his career when he wrote to Lord Hardwicke in 1764 explaining his reasons for declining to paint a specific view of Lord

Hardwicke's estate at Wimpole, perhaps of that hill at the end of the north avenue which was topped by a sham castle ruin of Sanderson Miller's design:[26]

Mr. Gainsborough presents his Humble respects to Lord Hardwicke; and shall always think it an honor to be employ'd in anything for his Lordship; but with respect to *real Views* from Nature in this Country he has never seen any Place that affords a Subject equal to the poorest imitations of Gaspar or Claude. . . if his Lordship wishes to have anything tolerable of the name of G, the subject altogether, as well as figures, etc. must be of his own Brain; otherwise Lord Hardwicke will only pay for Encouraging a Man out of his way and had much better buy a picture of some of the good Old Masters.[27]

Gainsborough's letter may prove little more than an unwillingness to be condescended to by a fine gentleman, for we know that he spent a good deal of time in his Suffolk years doing precisely what this letter denies — copying "*real Views* from Nature." From the testimony of several sketching companions it is clear that he did not give up sketching real views from nature at Bath.[28] But, most important for Gainsborough's future work, we also know that he supplemented these excursions more and more in the Bath years by the device of assembling, on a little table reserved for the purpose, landscapes of stones, sticks, grass, and pieces of looking glass, landscapes which were certainly the artist's own creations.[29] Ellis Waterhouse believes that Gainsborough's answer to Lord Hardwicke stems from his desire to create his own compositions in landscape, "on a level with the great masters of landscape who were admitted by the connoisseurs of the age." [30] Lord Hardwicke can hardly have failed to see that Gainsborough did not intend to be regarded as a mere

20. Horace Walpole, *Anecdotes of Painting in England* (London, 1827), IV, 278–79.

21. The introduction by Christopher Hussey to Dorothy Stroud's *Capability Brown* (London, 1950) provides a thoughtful and most informative summary of Brown's career, including the influence of William Kent upon his "style" of improvement, as well as the bases of the attacks that were launched against Brown's work in the 1790's.

22. *Ibid.*, p. 71.

23. *Ibid.*, p. 121.

24. Whitley, *Thomas Gainsborough*, p. 67.

25. Woodall, *Thomas Gainsborough*, p. 48.

26. Stroud, *Capability Brown*, p. 128.

27. Gainsborough, *Letters*, pp. 87, 91.

28. Woodall, *GLD*, p. 44.

29. Reynolds, *Discourses*, p. 220.

30. Waterhouse, *Gainsborough*, p. 15.

copyist of park improvements. It is certainly significant that Gains-borough mentions the landscapes of Claude and Gaspar Poussin, striving as he was to create his own landscape compositions, which, of necessity, were more ideal than real and more general than particular. Moving as he did within those circles which discussed and imitated the work of the continental artists, he may indeed have revised his earlier attitude toward landscape painting; he may have come, for that matter, to use his sketch-ing excursions to gather motifs and "raw material" which he intended to recompose later. It is not possible to prove the truth of this last supposi-tion. The landscape drawings are undated, and the only way to group them with any kind of coherence is to examine and compare them with the dated paintings, the method Miss Mary Woodall uses. Thus, she groups together three sketches which bear certain definite resemblances to *The Watering Place*.[31] Whether they were all done at the same time is clearly open to stylistic interpretation. The fact remains that Gains-borough did make three sketches, of differing "real" scenes, which he regrouped and altered when he painted *The Watering Place*. In his later works, motifs from other drawings appear singly or in different combi-nations as part of portrait backgrounds.

One of his Bath sitters may have helped to alter Gainsborough's atti-tude toward landscape composition; his subject was Uvedale Tompkyns Price, the father of the gentleman who was to make a name throughout England for his *Essay on the Picturesque*. The elder Price seems also to have been interested in the art of landscape, for he is portrayed with a crayon in one hand and a drawing of trees in the other. Although there is no evidence of the sort of relation existing between Gainsborough and the elder Price, one may reasonably conclude that two men with a common interest in landscape painting would have exchanged views. In any event, Gainsborough often came to sketch trees at Foxley, Price's estate. Writing of his early acquaintance with Gainsborough, Sir Uve-dale Price mentions that he was used to accompanying Gainsborough on sketching trips into the country, and bears witness to the animation the artist displayed when he came upon "cottages and village scenes with groups of children, and objects of rural life,"[32] the sort of scene Price himself praises as contributing to picturesque impressions.

A portrait of Lady Gertrude Alston luxuriously gowned, dated by Waterhouse as a work of the mid-sixties, displays an unusual background. Lady Alston appears to have wandered into a dense forest in all her finery. By the glimmer of light on the left, an urn on a pedestal base is barely visible; the urn and the light itself are indications that Lady Alston has stepped from one part of her property to another, has walked from a sunlit area of the path to " 'a scene of what Mr. Shenstone used to call his forest ground, consisting of wild green slopes peeping through [a] dingle, or irregular groups of trees, a confused mixture of savage and cultivated ground.' " [33] Such landscapes were very much in vogue in the sixties and were cultivated not only at the Leasowes by Shenstone, but also, most notably, at Hagley and at Painshill. Horace Walpole describes with admiration the scene at Painshill where "the walks seem not designed, but cut through the wood of pines; and . . . when you look down on this seeming forest, you are amazed to find it contain a very few acres." [34] Thus, the background of the Alston portrait suggests what Walpole calls "the forest or savage garden";[35] whether Gainsborough or his sitter decided upon this particular background is not so important as the fact that his sitter, obviously interested in fashionable finery, must have considered it modish and in good taste.

Other portraits of the sixties, including those of the Honorable Edmund Craggs Nugent, Sir Benjamin Truman, Lord Rivers, Mary, Countess Howe, and Dr. Ralph Schomberg, have backgrounds which also suggest that the subject has been arrested momentarily in the course of an outing — dressed in his or her best, of course. The most realistically rural background of this period, and unique for a noble lady's portrait at this time in Gainsborough's career, is that in the portrait of Mary, Countess Howe. The scenery, especially the carefully particularized burdock which appears to threaten the lady's gown, and the fence of palings straggling into the distance, is reminiscent of Gainsborough's Suffolk landscapes,[36] and is quite unlike that of any of the other portrait backgrounds of the Bath period. The landscape background of Dr. Ralph Schomberg's portrait, however, is very similar to those Gainsborough drawings imitating the typically Poussinesque landscape composition,

31. Woodall, *GLD*, pp. 61–63.
32. Whitley, *Thomas Gainsborough*, p. 41.
33. Chase, *Horace Walpole*; the quotation is from Robert Dodsley's description of the Leasowes, p. 227.
34. *Ibid.*, from the text of Walpole's "The History of the Modern Taste in Gardening," p. 33.
35. *Ibid.*
36. The burdocks appear in the Suffolk landscape *Cornard Wood* (Woodall, *GLD*, Plate 6) and the fence of palings in a Suffolk landscape drawing (Woodall, *GLD*, Plate 20).

and is a precursor of that generalizing "last manner" which the critic Hoppner found objectionable. While Gainsborough used his years in Bath to study and absorb the courtly elegance, the subtle and intriguing hauteur, the flattering aura of unassailable breeding which he admired in Van Dyck's characterizations, in these same years he also consciously worked to acquire landscape techniques which were equally derived from the seventeenth century.

In 1766, Gainsborough moved his family to London. He continued to make experiments with lighting effects, painting in a kind of twilight which Reynolds believed helped to heighten his color effects, and occupied increasingly with the play of reflected lights on the gowns of his sitters. His frustrations when his paintings were displayed so that these effects were not properly seen at the Royal Academy exhibitions led to his rupture with the Academy in 1772. From that time until his success with the royal family secured him a deluge of commissions in 1777 and thereafter, Gainsborough appears to have painted surprisingly few full-length portraits. Those portrait backgrounds of the seventies which are outdoor scenes are, with few exceptions, conventional, and represent little new compositional effort; certain poses reappear in several portraits, and sometimes when a pose is repeated it is not particularly appropriate: George, second Lord Vernon, was painted in 1767 with his dog pawing his vest. Ten years later, Gainsborough painted Lady Brisco in the very same attitude. Her dog, too, paws her elegant satin gown. The delicate overskirt fluttering at the lady's side is indicative of the fluttering draperies, usually gauze-thin, which are included again and again in the portraits of the eighties that have landscape backgrounds. The landscape behind Lady Brisco is artfully wild, with its winding river culminating in a waterfall, its variety of thickly-wooded hillsides, distant building, and rugged mountain terminating the vista. Gainsborough, busy in London, created this landscape, probably by the rocks-grass-glass-on-the-table method; it is a landscape, however, such as would have commanded the approval of those who admired Hagley and the Leasowes. Richard Sullivan, whose reactions to his travels through England in 1778 are recorded in the form of letters, ostensibly written to a friend, is delighted by the cascades, the glens, the carefully revealed vistas, the "highly picturesque and variegated country" which those two estates possessed.[37] That Gainsborough in London should have painted such a landscape background for Lady Brisco may be an indication of the vogue of these motifs.

The much-admired portrait of the Honorable Mrs. Thomas Graham repeats the pose which Gainsborough had used for a portrait of John Eld in 1772; like Eld, Mrs. Graham rests her left elbow on an architectural prop which abets the effect of restraint and formality. The deep glen behind Mrs. Graham, like the tree and foliage behind Eld, conveys the suggestion of family acres and a noble park, as the columns on the left of these personages are intended to suggest a suitable residence for persons of quality. And yet there is a difference between the two portraits: the Eld portrait is uncompromising in its respectable coldness; Mrs. Graham's is softened by the slightest suggestion of a wistful, a weary expression in her face, heightened by the contrast between her delicate person and the weightiness of the satins and ornaments she wears; the wildness and suggested recesses of the glen unaccountably add to this pensive, almost melancholy, impression.

In the landscape portraits of the eighties, Gainsborough develops the sympathetic relation between subject and background which is hinted at in his painting of Mrs. Graham. No portrait of the seventies, however, even the most conventional, displays that favorite property which Reynolds used almost regularly in his landscape portraits — the baroque swag of drapery hanging between the sitter and the landscape, an interposition which reduced the landscape to the level of a backdrop.

Possibly Gainsborough felt an independence bred of secure fame; perhaps his ambition at last caught up with his talent; whatever the reasons, a few years after he had secured royal patronage and favor, Gainsborough's work exhibited a new freedom, in concept as well as in execution. Although the basic features of his style did not change, there were important changes in technique. Tree forms are more summarily indicated, as, indeed, is landscape form as a whole; usually the basic lines of the drawings are indicated in pencil or black chalk, with washes dashed across in sweeping brushstrokes. The oil sketches for the *Market Cart* and for the *Perdita* resemble the wash drawings in that only the briefest of outlines suggests the composition in thin paint, while flat washes of

37. Richard Joseph Sullivan, *Tour through Parts of England, Scotland and Wales in 1778* (London, 1885), II, 20–30. Sullivan's delight in gloomy thickets, mournful cypresses, rugged mountains, and the like, reveals that by the later years of the seventies, there was an articulate audience who would welcome the doctrines of Uvedale Price and Richard Payne Knight.

Thomas Gainsborough, *Mrs. Richard Brinsley Sheridan.* Courtesy
National Gallery of Art, Washington, D.C.

paint suggest the tones of each area; these oil sketches, as a result, are very much like water colors.[38] Waterhouse suggests that the portraits of these last seven years of Gainsborough's life were "both highly creative and experimental," and that Gainsborough was striving for something other than what the term portrait traditionally implies.[39] Contrasted with his earlier landscape portraits, the work of these years establishes quite a new balance between the figure and the landscape.

Gainsborough's portrait of Giovanna Baccelli, the vivacious dancer with a checkered career, shows the young woman practicing her art, not on the stage, but on the lawn of a park, holding up her fluttering overskirt, her hair slightly disheveled by her exertions. The portrait gives the impression of impending movement, as if at any second, like a sophisticated wood nymph, the Baccelli might twirl on her pointed toe across the lawn and into the woods. This introduction of the impulse to movement into the picture seems to be Gainsborough's attempt to correct what he felt was an intrinsic disadvantage in the portrait as a means of defining character. A letter he wrote in 1771 concludes: "Had a picture voice, action, &c., to make itself known as actors have upon the stage no disguise would be sufficient to conceal a person; but only a face, confined to one view, and not a muscle to move to say, 'Here I am,' falls very hard upon the poor painter." [40] The picture of the Baccelli has no voice, but it does succeed in implying the presence of "action, &c.," to say "Here I am" to the viewer. The possibilities the Baccelli portrait exploited were brilliantly developed the next year in *The Mall*, an exercise in motion. The sway of the trees, the promenading belles, the frisking dogs are captured with that feathery, painterly stroking of Gainsborough's six-foot brush aswim with turpentine. A portrait of Mrs. Sheridan (opposite page), usually dated, like *The Mall*, as a work of 1783, demonstrates the same interest in movement. Waterhouse conjectures that the painting may have been begun as early as 1774; in any event, Gainsborough was still at work on it in 1785 and had not completed it to his own satisfaction at the time of his death.[41] When the portrait was first exhibited in 1783, a critic described it in the following words: "Mr. G. is engaged on a portrait of Mrs. Sheridan. . . . She is painted under the umbrage of a romantic tree, and the accompanying

38. Woodall, *GLD*, p. 74.
39. Waterhouse, *Gainsborough*, pp. 26, 27.
40. Whitley, *Thomas Gainsborough*, p. 75.
41. *Ibid.*, p. 89.

objects are descriptive of retirement. The likeness is powerful, and is enforced by a characteristic expression which equals the animation of nature." [42] To achieve the animation of nature must certainly have been Gainsborough's intent. When the portrait was again exhibited in 1785, the Reverend Henry Bate, a good friend of Gainsborough's, noted that the painter intended to add lambs, to give the painting "an air more pastoral than it at present possesses." [43] But the painting would be unusual even without the added pastoral note of the lambs. Mrs. Sheridan has become almost a landscape object herself. Her hair, the most disarranged hairdress Gainsborough had painted until this time, seems an extension of the wind-blown foliage above her head; the scarf that flutters through her relaxed fingers is only slightly less diaphanous than the luminous clouds. She appears, like the slender trunk of the single tree behind the sheep, a form exposed to the play of elements. The loneliness, the rural solitude, accord perfectly with Mrs. Sheridan's expression of wistful stillness. This pastoral melancholy was suggested in the earlier portrait of the demimondaine Mrs. Perdita Robinson, who is seated in a landscape displaying many points of resemblance to that in the *Mrs. Sheridan*, but with almost none of its life. Mrs. Robinson sits against a skillful stage set, while Mrs. Sheridan sits within and as a part of a landscape.

The famous portrayal of the newly-married Hallets known as *The Morning Walk* has a landscape background similar to that of the *Perdita*, except that it displays the animation of Mrs. Sheridan's landscape. Any disarray of the lady is artful as well as artificial; the plumes of the Pamela hat, the mass of fluffed hair, the wind-touched laces and scarf produce a careful impression of careless elegance. Gainsborough's audience probably saw in this painting of the squire of Canons and his bride the embodiment of youth and affection happily combined with leisure and independent means. Théophile Gautier said of this painting that it produced "a strange retrospective sensation, so intense is the illustration it produces. . . . We really fancy we see the young couple walking arm in arm along a garden avenue." [44] But where are the lawn, the Brownian "clumps" of trees, the gravel path, the temple and obelisk? The scene through which the Hallets walk is one which travelers in search of picturesque beauty would have approved; it is presumably in its natural state, a disarray as luxuriant and artful as Mrs. Hallet's costume. The technique of painting the Hallets and their dog as areas of varying texture admirably unites them with their landscape. The smooth darkness of the Squire's jacket and trouser leg are repeated in the deep shadows of the foliage and tree trunk. Mrs. Hallet's hair, the fluffy mass of foliage of the single tree silhouetted against the clouds, and the dog's curled plume of a tail are echoes of one another in texture and in shape. The agitated ruffles and highlighted roundness of the lady's breast and the blowing puffs of clouds; the plumes of her hat, and the downward plumes of foliage directly behind her; these and several other details masterfully tie together the landscape and its inhabitants. Sir Walter Armstrong comments that this painting is really a subject-picture more than a portrait, a detached idea for a painting in which the faces of the Hallets have been painted.[45] It would certainly seem a further extension of the "motion" picture, of the Baccelli portrait, of *The Mall.*

Similarly, the *Cottage Girl with Dog and Pitcher* is not exactly a fancy-picture, nor a landscape with a figure, nor a portrait. Like the Hallet portrait it is a "detached idea," a painting in which the traditional distinctions of type disappear. In the Bath years Gainsborough had written to his friend Jackson: "do you really think that a regular composition in the *landscape way* should ever be fill'd with History, or any figures but such as fill a place (I won't say stop a gap) or to create a little *business* for the Eye to be drawn from the trees in order to return to them with more glee." [46] The figures which filled "a place" in Gainsborough's landscapes were brought forward for close-ups in the fancy-pictures, for which Gainsborough used actual models.[47] The Reverend Henry Bate records that Gainsborough used a young peasant whom he had met near Richmond Hill for the cottage girl painting.[48] C. R. Leslie, however, is quite sure that "this inimitable work is a portrait, and not of a peasant child but a young lady." [49] Leslie's conclusion is understandable. When the sturdy young peasants Gainsborough painted in the fifties are compared with the cottage girl of the eighties, the difference is remarkable. The paintings of the cottage girl, of the peasant girl gathering sticks, and of the girl with pigs which Sir Joshua

42. *Ibid.*, p. 238.
43. *Ibid.*, p. 265.
44. *Masters in Art: Thomas Gainsborough* (Boston, 1901), p. 35.
45. *Ibid.*, p. 26.
46. Gainsborough, *Letters*, p. 99.
47. Waterhouse, *Gainsborough*, p. 35.
48. Whitley, *Thomas Gainsborough*, p. 243.
49. *Ibid.*, p. 242.

Thomas Gainsborough, *The Woodman*. From an engraving in Chauncey Brewster
Tinker's *Painter and Poet*, ©1938, Harvard University Press

Thomas Gainsborough, *Old Peasant with Donkey*

bought for his own collection represent a new fusion of Gainsborough's aristocratic portrait technique with his idealized and generalized representations of English landscape. The same fashionable attitudes of pastoral melancholy, of wistful pensiveness which appear in the portraits of Mrs. Robinson and Mrs. Sheridan characterize these paintings. Reynolds's admiration for Gainsborough's "little ordinary beggar children" is easier to fathom when one realizes that the children in these paintings are by no means ordinary or beggarly. The poverty in these paintings, and in *Shepherd-Boy in a Storm* and *Jack Hill in his Cottage*, though quite plainly indicated, is — if such a thing can be allowed to exist — a beautiful, a sentimentalized poverty. Chauncey Brewster Tinker admits that the shepherd boy and a few of the other fancy-pictures of this period may be charged with sentimentality, but he puts forward Gainsborough's last painting, and one which he was obviously fond of, *The Woodman*, as a work in which "poverty has . . . no amelioration, no soft and winning touch of ideality." [50] A comparison of *The Woodman* with a painting of the early fifties, *Old Peasant with Donkey*, will show quite clearly the decided touches of "ideality" that Gainsborough injected into *The Woodman*, which, unfortunately, we know only from an engraving made twenty years before the original was burned. The old peasant with his donkey is ugly, coarse, and rude. The woodman with his dog corresponds closely to what Uvedale Price was to define as picturesque ugliness.[51] (See reproductions on pp. 376 and 377.) It is the earlier studies, in which the painter does not editorialize, that the critics of the early nineteenth century preferred. The later fancy-pictures, so popular when Gainsborough painted them, the fruits of his attempts to compose familiar English motifs in a classic style, were rejected by these critics. In 1814 Hazlitt described the cottage girl painting in these words:

there is a consciousness in the turn of the head, and a sentimental pensiveness in the expression which is not taken from nature, but intended as an improvement upon it! There is a regular insipidity, a systematic vacancy, a round, unvaried smoothness to which real nature is a stranger, and which is only an idea existing in the painter's mind.[52]

What a long road Gainsborough had journeyed to achieve that effect of improvement upon nature, that idea which existed only in his own mind!

Paintings such as these appear to have fulfilled a desire which garden planners of the last quarter of the century expressed, for what Walpole calls "prospect, animated prospect." [53] Walpole wisely remarks that static architectural features of the garden and grounds are, after a time, boring. He quotes the comments of a French visitor to Strawberry Hill who wished for "real points of view with moving objects; for instance, here I would have . . . a watering-place." Walpole replies: "I am glad you would like a watering-place, for *there* actually happens to be one; in that creek of the Thames the inhabitants of the village do actually water their horses; but I doubt whether, if it were not *convenient* to them to do so, they would frequent the spot only to enliven my prospect." [54] The fact remains that Walpole included the watering place and other lively scenes as part of his prospect, instead of screening them with trees. The practice of employing a hermit to haunt retired walks, satirized in *Columella*, as well as the less naïve later practice of including the village and its activities in one's view, are other examples of this desire for "prospect, animated prospect." Gainsborough's *Mrs. Sheridan*, *The Morning Walk*, *The Watering Place*, *The Market Cart*, *The Woodman* and his paintings of country children provided his landed audience with canvases which captured what they themselves were attempting in their own garden landscape planning. His long study of the great seventeenth-century European landscape and portrait artists and his ability to link figures and landscape in an emotive bond enabled him to produce paintings which happily and profitably accorded with prevailing taste. Gainsborough held the mirror up to nature — nature as his public liked to imagine her.

50. Chauncey Brewster Tinker, *Painter and Poet* (Cambridge, Massachusetts, 1938), p. 98.
51. Sir Uvedale Price, *An Essay on the Picturesque* . . ., 3 vols. (London, 1794), I, 173, 174, 175.
52. Whitley, *Thomas Gainsborough*, p. 242.
53. Chase, *Horace Walpole*, Walpole's text, p. 34.
54. *Ibid.*, p. 23n.

❧ JAMES SCOGGINS

# The Preface to LYRICAL BALLADS: A Revolution in Dispute

M ODERN literary history has no tolerance for abrupt transitions from one "age" to another, so that scholars today speak of the *Lyrical Ballads* as a "watershed" or "Romantic Manifesto" with amused and urbane apology for the textbook precision of such terms. By now the prefaces of 1800 and 1802 have been with us as literary subjects long enough to permit at least one generalization: the more intensively they have been subjected to the scrutiny of scholars, the less has been asserted of their claim to original and revolutionary features. We can no longer complain, as Arthur Beatty did in 1922, that Wordsworth's early prefaces are "almost unknown documents," [1] nor is it without significance that during the period just before and just after Beatty made this observation, an almost unqualified belief in the fact of the "Revolution of 1798" was general among students of the Romantic period. In the last few years both the prefaces and the poems of *Lyrical Ballads* have undergone careful, and often skeptical, examination, and the older view has so nearly been discredited that instead of assuming with Helen Darbishire that "Wordsworth's discovery of a new poetic world and the revolution he brought about in revealing it are taken now as a matter of course," [2] the scholar today would be following a safer course if he began his discussion, as Stephen Maxfield Parrish did, with the observation that Wordsworth, at any rate, *thought* that he was introducing a new poetry. [3]

This new attitude toward the *Lyrical Ballads* was inevitable, and can be cited, without irony, as a sign of progress, a healthy exchange of enthusiasm for perspective. And if it forces those of us who yet insist that both poems and prefaces are profoundly original to yield positions no longer self-evident, it also invites us to search out those which cannot be discredited and to equip ourselves with arguments suitable to a skeptical audience. The aim of the present essay is to accept this challenge, by identifying the one important and radical departure from earlier aesthetic theories that justifies the reputation of *Lyrical Ballads* as a revolutionary document in the history of literature. I shall begin by relinquishing, to one degree or another, those earlier claims to originality which recent scholarship has called in doubt.

A striking feature of recent studies of the Preface to *Lyrical Ballads* is the search for an underlying principle that would unite the various topics raised in it. These studies seek to demonstrate that the surface arguments — about the real language of men, the essential identity of poetry and prose, the function of meter — can most accurately be subsumed under a single principle. Parrish, for example, has stated that the underlying theme of the Wordsworth-Coleridge dispute over poetic doctrine was "a disagreement about dramatic method," and that to Wordsworth, "the truth revealed in poetry was psychological truth, and it was revealed most plainly in dramatic utterance, in the language really spoken by men in a state of passion." [4] To W. J. B. Owen, the "comprehensive motive behind the Preface," to which "all other motives suggested by Wordsworth, and more especially by his critics, are eventually subordinate," is "the attempt to define a permanent rhetoric" as "a means of aligning poetry with nature, of giving it, as far as possible, a form as 'steady' and as 'perennial' as that of the mountain." [5] Without disputing either of these

1. *William Wordsworth: His Doctrine and Art in Their Historical Relations*, University of Wisconsin Studies in Language and Literature, No. 17 (Madison, 1922), p. 14.
2. *The Poet Wordsworth* (Oxford, 1950), p. 56.
3. "Dramatic Technique in the *Lyrical Ballads*," *PMLA*, LXXIV (1959), 85. Parrish's series of articles on these poems is among the happiest results of reexaminations of the *Lyrical Ballads*. See, in addition to the article cited above, " 'The Thorn': Wordsworth's Dramatic Monologue," *ELH*, XXIV (1957), 153–63; "The Wordsworth-Coleridge Controversy," *PMLA*, LXXIII (1958), 367–74; "Wordsworth and Coleridge on Meter," *JEGP*, LIX (1960), 41–49.
4. Parrish, "The Wordsworth-Coleridge Controversy," 367, 371.
5. Introduction to *Wordsworth's Preface to Lyrical Ballads*, *Anglistica*, IX (Copenhagen, 1957), 12–13. For the sake of convenience I have taken all my quotations from the prefaces from the Selincourt-Darbishire edition of *The Poetical*

statements, I should like to suggest that neither goes quite far enough toward identifying the unifying theme of Wordsworth's preface.[6] And this theme is such that even if we grant that there were anticipations in eighteenth-century aesthetics for almost all those specific doctrines for which Wordsworth has earlier been granted originality, the Preface must still be credited with the introduction of a totally new concept in English poetics, a concept that puts as many worlds between "Tintern Abbey" and *The Seasons* as there are between the *Critique of Pure Reason* and *An Essay concerning Human Understanding*.[7] To explain and support this assertion, I shall begin on a familiar theme: Wordsworth's attempts to define the proper aim of serious poetry and the true relation between the mind of man and the external world.

Of Wordsworth's statements in the Preface that the immediate aim of poetry is to provide pleasure, Owen remarks: "One of Wordsworth's most firmly held tenets." [8] So it certainly was, and yet it is on precisely this ground that Wordsworth was most consistently attacked by his contemporaries. A reviewer of the *Poems* of 1815 defines sharply the basic dispute between poet and critics: "the question about which Mr. Wordsworth's readers are interested is, whether other subjects do not afford equal or superior pleasure, not whether they throw greater or less light upon the 'elementary feelings,' and 'essential passions,' and 'primary laws of our nature.' " [9] The assumption of this reviewer is that Wordsworth had confused the end of poetry with that of metaphysics ("but the fact obviously is, that people do not resort to poetry for metaphysical instruction"), and lest we think to brush aside this criticism as the product of a mediocre intelligence, let us recur to the testimony of the greatest of Romantic critics: "a *biographical* attention to probability, and an *anxiety* of explanation and retrospect" seem "to destroy the main fundamental distinction, not only between a poem and prose, but even between philosophy and works of fiction, inasmuch as it proposes *truth* for its immediate object, instead of *pleasure*." [10]

To Wordsworth, however, the revolutionary feature of his poetry was that it was intended to provide a new *kind* of pleasure, which his prefaces were designed to explain and to justify, and to this end all his comments on the style of his new poetry are subordinate. Because so much of the Preface to *Lyrical Ballads* is directly concerned with style, however, this is the topic which has most occupied Wordsworthian scholarship, and seldom has the relation between end and means been discussed. Most of the blame for this situation must be laid to Wordsworth himself, for, as Coleridge complained, much of the Preface to *Lyrical Ballads* is "obscure beyond any necessity," [11] and nothing in it is more obscure than Wordsworth's attempts to explain the relations among the many topics he discusses in this document. Nevertheless, it is precisely in his theory concerning the relation between style and the new kind of poetic pleasure which he proposed to provide that Wordsworth achieved his signal break with the eighteenth century — a metaphysical break preeminently, but with vast implications for poetry and aesthetics. Some hint of the relation he recognized between the principal aim and the style of his poetry Wordsworth did give, most notably in the familiar passage that follows:

the pleasure which I have proposed to myself to impart, is of a kind very different from that which is supposed by many persons to be the proper object of poetry. Without being culpably particular, I do not know how to give my Reader a more exact notion of the style in which it was my wish and intention to write, than by informing him that I have at all times endeavoured to look steadily at my subject.[12]

To the best of my knowledge, the order of these statements has been passed over without comment, but the implications of that order are profoundly important. It is clear, first of all, that Wordsworth believed that

*Works*, but Owen's edition and commentary are invaluable for serious study of these documents. The texts of both the 1798 and 1800 poems, with excellent introduction, notes, and appendixes, are at long last available in a modern edition: *Lyrical Ballads*, ed. R. L. Brett and A. R. Jones (New York, 1963).

6. Closer to my own view is that of Josephine Miles: "Problems of diction, problems of figure, problems of order, all are subordinated, the usual critic of Wordsworth's diction to the contrary, to problems of what Wordsworth called reality: the literal sympathetic connection between man and nature, between image, feeling, and thought, and between them in just these terms" (*The Primary Language of Poetry in the 1740's and 1840's*, University of California Publications in English, XIX, No. 2 [Berkeley and Los Angeles, 1950], 363). In a sense my essay is an amplification of this statement.

7. This analogy is a modification of one suggested by Samuel Holt Monk, in *The Sublime: A Study of Critical Theories in XVIII-Century England* (New York, 1935), p. 5.

8. *Wordsworth's Preface*, 74n.

9. *Quarterly Review*, XIV (1816), 203.

10. *Biographia Literaria*, ed. J. Shawcross. 1st ed. rev. (London, 1962), II, 103, 104. Subsequent references to this work will be preceded by the abbreviation *BL* and will appear in parentheses in the text of this paper.

11. *Collected Letters of Samuel Taylor Coleridge*, ed. Earl Leslie Griggs (Oxford, 1956), II, 830.

12. *The Poetical Works of William Wordsworth*, ed. Ernest De Selincourt and Helen Darbishire, 2nd ed. (Oxford, 1952), II, 390. Subsequent references to this work will be preceded by the abbreviation *PW* and will appear in parentheses in the text of this essay.

the new pleasure he proposed to impart demanded a style different from that which had by his time achieved almost exclusive legitimacy. We might at first be tempted to invoke, as an explanation of these remarks on style, the hallowed principle of decorum, but what Wordsworth had in mind will not fit that label comfortably. The question was not for him a matter of suiting the style to the form, but of discovering a style to fit *all* forms; and, as Coleridge later came to suspect, Wordsworth was in 1800, and, though more equivocally, in 1802, insisting that there is only one proper style for poetry of serious intention and permanent value (*BL*, II, 29–30). An explanation of Wordsworth's stubborn adherence to his statements about language and style in the Preface is partly disguised in the elliptical argument of the last sentence of the passage I have quoted, but we can assert with reasonable confidence that to ground a style as Wordsworth did on the principle of steady observation of subjects is to imply an attitude toward the external world radically different from that of the eighteenth-century nature poets. Ironically, however, Wordsworth's very insistence on the importance of this principle has led some scholars to draw him rather too tightly into the associationist school of eighteenth-century aesthetics, misled, I believe, by his use of the terminology of Hartley and his followers.[13] When I return to this topic, I shall try to demonstrate that the surface similarity of this passage to familar tenets of earlier doctrines should be attributed to the same "poverty of language" that forced Wordsworth to use the far from satisfactory term *Imagination* as a prose translation for "the vision and the faculty divine" and "Reason in her highest mood."

Since in the Preface Wordsworth attempted to define the new poetic pleasure he proposed to provide by means of contrast with the kind he hoped to displace, I shall defer my further remarks on this topic in order to give a brief account of the literary context into which he believed he was introducing a new element.[14] And perhaps the best way to approach this subject is to determine what Wordsworth's contemporaries most highly praised and most emphatically condemned in both his poetry and doctrine. We shall find, I believe, that these critics were not so whimsical and inconsistent as Coleridge professed to think them (*BL*, I, 50–55).

M. H. Abrams has helped to correct an erroneous view of the eighteenth century that is not confined to casual students of literature: "The assertion that eighteenth-century critics read by reason alone is gross calumny. Readers of no age have demanded more, or more violent, emotion from poetry," including, as Abrams adds, the redoubtable Dr. John-son.[15] Furthermore, as Robert Mayo reminds us, "the accepted masters for many verse-writers" at the turn of the century were Pope, Gray, Prior, Johnson, Gay, Parnell, Akenside, and Thomas Warton, so that the taste of readers of verse, we may assume, was fairly steady throughout at least the last half of the eighteenth century.[16] The implications of these cultural notes for public reaction to the *Lyrical Ballads* are obvious. We might expect that in both their praise and their censure of these new poems Wordsworth's reviewers would reflect an essentially neoclassical temper — more that of Gray, let us say, than of Pope — but neoclassical nonetheless. And this is precisely what we do find.

More than one scholar has remarked that what the late eighteenth-century reader most vigorously applauded was a kind of delicate mixture of the old and the new in poetic traditions. Thus, intensely "romantic" souls like Anna Seward warmed much more readily to the elevated enthusiasms of Scott and Southey than to the daring commonplace of Wordsworth.[17] The foundations for the taste of such readers had been laid by the so-called pre-Romantic poets and critics, who dominate, to the point of distortion, modern surveys of the second half of the eighteenth century. With Lockian psychology and Shaftesburian sensibility as a philosophical framework, and *The Seasons* as their principal text, these writers were able to formulate an increasingly rigid set of criteria for evaluating "elevated" poetry. More than anything else it was this intensely exclusive taste that Wordsworth recognized as the formidable enemy of his new poetry and doctrine. In order, therefore, to bring into sharp focus the rival traditions that met to do battle in 1798, I shall attempt first to reconstruct the standard of taste that Wordsworth in time successfully vanquished, and second to identify in selected reviews of his poems the influence of this older tradition. In the interest of brevity, I

13. See, e.g., Meyer H. Abrams, *The Mirror and the Lamp* (New York, 1953), pp. 103–4; Owen, *Wordsworth's Preface*, p. 107.

14. Robert Mayo gives an excellent account of the poetic tastes of Wordsworth's potential audience in "The Contemporaneity of the *Lyrical Ballads*," *PMLA*, LXIX (1954), 486–522.

15. *The Mirror and the Lamp*, p. 71.

16. "Contemporaneity," 488–89.

17. For an informative study of cultivated taste at the turn of the century, see Samuel Holt Monk, "Anna Seward and the Romantic Poets" in *Wordsworth and Coleridge: Studies in Honor of George McLean Harper*, ed. Earl Leslie Griggs (Princeton, 1939), pp. 118–34.

shall draw exclusively upon critical commentary of the second half of the eighteenth century.

In 1766, Richard Hurd began a famous essay by distinguishing between poetry and all other literary compositions on the grounds that poetry alone has as its immediate end the production of pleasure. From this venerable assumption Hurd was able to deduce some very specific conclusions: "Novelty and variety are certain sources of pleasure; a construction of words which is not vulgar is therefore more suited to the ends of poetry than one which we are every day accustomed to in familar discourse." It follows, then, Hurd goes on, that the purpose of poetry is "not to reflect the real face of things, but to illustrate and adorn it," because "there is something in the mind of man, sublime and elevated, which prompts it to overlook all obvious and familiar appearances, and to feign to itself other and more extraordinary . . ." [18] Given even this brief statement, we should appreciate the difficulty of the task that Wordsworth set for himself when he chose to write poetry with aims and means opposite almost to those which Hurd, and many of his most influential contemporaries, attributed to the art.

It has often been said that Wordsworth is a poet of nature, but if we bear in mind what this term meant to late eighteenth-century admirers of Thomson and Dyer, we must apply it to Wordsworth with the utmost circumspection.[19] A lucid description of nature poetry that fits Thomson, but not Wordsworth, is the following by Thomas Twining, from an essay published in 1789:

there is one particular kind of description that may be said to be, in a great measure at least, peculiar to modern times: I mean that which answers to landscape in painting, and of which the subject is prospects, views, rural scenery, etc., considered merely as pictures — as beautiful objects to the eye . . . that rich profusion of picturesque ideas which every reader of poetry recollects in Shakespeare, Milton, Spenser, Thomson, and almost all the modern poets of any name.[20]

The major saints of English poetry, as recognized by the later eighteenth century, are here invoked, and all are here, even Shakespeare and Milton, as poets of landscape.

By the time of Wordsworth's first major bid for acceptance as a serious poet, the taste of his prospective audience had become restrictive, simplified, and, to an extent, codified, so that in a very real sense the average cultivated reader of his day had available to him only three slots into which he could place new poems. If a poem was not, in both language and sentiment, sublime, or beautiful, or picturesque ("Novelty" had, since Gilpin's essay, acquired this more formal name), it could not be granted major status. Perhaps the chief villain of this false taste was Erasmus Darwin. Wordsworth's choice of this writer for much of his attack in the Preface on the degenerate poetry of the day is quite understandable, for Darwin's "metaphysical" descriptions of natural phenomena had succeeded in convincing readers of their own superior intelligence, while entertaining them with his. From our perspective, however, Darwin's theory and practice of poetry are best seen as simply the culmination, if also the perversion, of a long series of pronouncements by neoclassical spokesmen of the latter half of the eighteenth century. For Darwin the triad of which I spoke had achieved unquestioned authority: "The matter [of poetry] must be interesting from its sublimity, beauty, or novelty . . ." He further displays the new rigidity of this canon by providing the following formulas for the achievement of these three acceptable poetic effects: "The farther the artist recedes from nature, the greater novelty he is likely to produce; if he rises above nature, he produces the sublime; and beauty is probably a selection and new combination of her most agreeable parts." [21] The way to write "nature poetry," then, is to get as far as possible from nature. The effect of such ideas on Wordsworth we need hardly imagine. For good or ill, neoclassical doctrine had become so oversimplified and extreme that Wordsworth found it a conspicuous and vulnerable target. Not for the first time in the history of literature was a Pope to suffer for the sins of a Darwin.

It has become customary of late to reject an earlier assumption that Wordsworth's reviewers attacked his poems in their role as rear-guard defenders of a dying Neoclassicism.[22] The newer attitude, I am confident,

18. "A Dissertation on the Idea of Universal Poetry" in *Eighteenth-Century Critical Essays*, ed. Scott Elledge.
19. So warns Morse Peckham, in *Beyond the Tragic Vision* (New York, 1962), p. 112.
20. "On Poetry Considered as an Imitative Art" in Elledge, *Eighteenth-Century Critical Essays*, II, 998.
21. "Interlude I from *The Loves of the Plants*" in Elledge, *Eighteenth-Century Critical Essays*, II, 1009–10.
22. See, e.g., D. Nichol Smith, ed., *Jeffrey's Literary Criticism* (London, 1910), p. xx; John Wain, ed., *Contemporary Reviews of Romantic Poetry* (London, 1953), p. 32. Of the two modern extended studies of Jeffrey's criticism of the Romantics — Russell Noyes, *Wordsworth and Jeffrey in Controversy*, Indiana University Publications: Humanities Series, No. 5 (Bloomington, 1941), and James A. Greig, *Francis Jeffrey of the Edinburgh Review* (Edinburgh, 1948) — Greig's presents, on the

is essentially the more accurate one, but I am less confident than some of its proponents that a degenerate form of Neoclassicism (what Mayo calls, in another context, "the backwash of the Augustan era") is not the root of most of the reviewers' objections to the new poetry of Wordsworth.[23]

A survey of reviews of Wordsworth's publications from 1798 to 1807 yields this not surprising conclusion: most praise for the poems was bestowed on those of elevated language, sentiment, and subject (preeminently "Tintern Abbey") and most censure, on those of "mean" language, sentiment, and subject (preeminently "The Idiot Boy"). We read, for example, praise for Wordsworth's Petrarchan "splendour and purity of diction . . . harmony . . . solemn sublimity of sentiment," but in the same review, regret for his mistaken belief that "the commonest external thing, the most every day occurrence of life, or the meanest appearance of nature is equally capable of being made the ground-work or subject of poetry with the noblest and most uncommon." [24] More than any other feature of Wordsworth's poems and doctrine, his insistence upon staking his claim to genius on the inherent sublimity of the most commonplace of objects and experiences was the basis for his critics' hostility to the new poetry. Readers who had been carefully instructed by Dennis, Addison, and their successors in the mysterious ways of the Sublime were not about to descend from majestic mountains to small celandines. On this basic issue the battle was joined, and considering the fact that Wordsworth was seeking to overturn more than a century-old tradition, we should hardly be surprised that his victory was so long delayed, or that he failed to explain himself fully in a few relatively brief essays.

Because it is generally acknowledged that the majority of Wordsworth's early reviewers followed the lead of the most influential of their number, it is perhaps possible to use Lord Jeffrey of the *Edinburgh Review* as an epitome, for although he was undoubtedly more extreme than his fellows in his evangelistic opposition to the new poetry and in his fear of its influence, Jeffrey is, in almost every particular, thoroughly representative both in his reluctant praise and in his frequent condemnation of Romantic poetry.[25] Jeffrey had, moreover, perhaps the best claim of his time to the judicial robes that had been worn with more distinction by Dr. Johnson. Politics aside, in his enormous influence, his public common sense and private irrationality, his equal appreciation of Roman nobility and almost maudlin sentimentality, Jeffrey is Johnson writ little — and, ironically, in Scotch-English. No more than his greater predecessor could the Edinburgh reviewer be expected to exhibit patience with Wordsworth's "mysticism," his seeming disdain for traditional modes and values, his violations of decorum in linking mean language to high purpose and elevated sentiment to low objects — like daffodils, owl hoots, idiots, and madwomen. It is easiest to understand Jeffrey's unfeigned exasperation with the "Lake School" (like Johnson, he knew the value of collecting individual targets into one large one) if we think of him as a lesser Johnson suddenly dropped into a world of rapidly disintegrating norms and values. Like Johnson, Jeffrey knew too well the sufferings of man in the real world to be sympathetic with poetry that asserted suffering, or any other intense passion, as a value in itself. The purpose of poetry, he believed, was to offer peace, joy, and above all, hope to men weary of real-life sorrows. For this reason his favorite modern poets were Burns and Crabbe, who, unlike Wordsworth, presented "true" pictures of rustic and humble life; and Rogers and Campbell, who "belonged in spirit to the eighteenth century . . . were polished, sentimental, interested in humanity, and reasonable." [26] And because , like Johnson, he believed that above all poetry should operate as a moral force, as he understood that function, his very favorite of the new writers was the one least new, Walter Scott, who satisfied the highest demand of art that Jeffrey recognized, identified by his modern editor as "the idea that the greatest authors reconcile us to life by showing the good in it." [27]

For Jeffrey, and for most of his colleagues, the admirable traits of Wordsworth's poetry were precisely those for which poets since Thomson had been praised — its "romantic scenery," "beautiful sentiments from a polished mind," "tenderness of heart," and "truest sensibility for the beauties of nature" — along with his announced aim, if not his achieve-

whole, a fairer picture, though he is at times a bit inclined to blame Wordsworth for the excesses of Wordsworthians.

23. "Contemporaneity," 489.

24. *The British Critic*, XI (1819), 584–86. This review, one of the most sympathetic of the time, concludes with praise for Wordsworth's rejection of the false taste of the age "from the restoration down to a late period," but regrets that, inevitably, he has committed "the excesses, from which no manliness or strength of mind seems able to guard the reviver of an old, or the inventor of a new system" (587). Probably no modern student of Wordsworth would disagree with either observation.

25. See Joseph M. Beatty, Jr., "Lord Jeffrey and Wordsworth," *PMLA*, XXXVIII (1923), 221–35; and Thomas M. Raysor, "The Establishment of Wordsworth's Reputation," *JEGP*, LIV (1955), 61–71. See also note 22 above.

26. Beatty, "Lord Jeffrey and Wordsworth," 222.

27. Smith, *Jeffrey's Literary Criticism*, p. xviii.

ment, of a language free from the false refinements of much verse since the mid-century.[28] But if the reviewers were fairly consistent in their praise, they were more nearly unanimous in their selection of targets for censure. Aside from their scorn of the arrogant presumption of this young upstart's setting himself up as the savior of English poetry, the most bitter invective of these writers was called forth by that principle of Wordsworth's doctrine which they dimly, but correctly, perceived to be the keystone of the new poetry. To his reviewers the clearest manifestation of Wordsworth's heretical tendencies was his choice of low and mean subjects, and to Jeffrey at least, the most dangerous implication of this heresy was "the positive and *bona fide* rejection of art altogether."[29] Without quite realizing it, these reviewers had hit upon that which is radically new in Wordsworth's poetic doctrine. Perhaps the most lucid statement of this irreconcilable conflict is the following passage: "It is true that the poetical world talked much some years ago about *the Loves of the Plants* . . . and that, in the bold language of eastern metaphor, the little hills are represented as dancing with joy: — but Mr. Wordsworth disdains metaphor and fable. That which he describes is set forth in the colours of reality, not of fiction."[30]

Wordsworth's heresy is here clearly identified: he refused to accept the universally unquestioned assumption that the province of poetry is the world of fictions. His revolt, then, was not against literature exactly, but against literature conceived of as exclusively fictional. It was on this basis, though never so clearly expressed, that the reviewers' strongest condemnation of Wordsworth was directed against such poems as those included, in the volumes of 1807, under the heading "Moods of My Own Mind." More than any other group this one was the test of Wordsworth's belief that the simplest objects of nature and the humblest experiences of men can yield insights, to an imaginative mind, into a transcendent reality; and even Coleridge singled out two of them — "Gipsies" and "I Wandered Lonely as a Cloud"— to illustrate his objection to what he called Wordsworth's "mental bombast": "a disproportion of thought to the circumstance and occasion" (*BL*, II, 109–14).[31]

In 1808 an outraged reviewer of the *Poems in Two Volumes* expressed a shock, doubtless shared by a majority of his contemporaries, that Wordsworth should imagine that "he has discovered any thing, either in the trivial incidents which he usually makes the subject of his narrations, or in the moral feelings and deductions which he endeavours to associate with them, too sublime for the admission of such decorations as these masters [Vergil and Milton] have not deemed derogatory from the highest themes they ever touched." [32] The fact is that Wordsworth believed that he *had* discovered something new, and he attempted in the Preface to define it.

The new kind of pleasure that Wordsworth proposed for his poetry rested on what we have come to call, in terms much more general than Kant's, the Copernican Revolution of the Mind — "the general concept that the perceiving mind discovers what it has itself partly made." [33] It follows from this concept that the aim of a poetry founded upon it must involve a new interpretation of reality — not that which had passed under the name in earlier times, not the external world as independent of the mind of man, but a reality which is in some measure the very creation of man's mind. It is because of his faith in this concept that Wordsworth insisted upon the importance of the poet's keeping his eye on the subject and seeking a language that would convey the real meaning of an object-mind experience, eschewing those distorting embellishments belonging to a poetic language arbitrarily divorced from the world of real objects and real passions. If we accept this interpretation of Wordsworth's doctrine, we can better understand the point of his much-criticized Appendix to the Preface. The subject of that essay is the gradual dissolution of

28. See Elsie Smith, *An Estimate of William Wordsworth by his Contemporaries* (Oxford, 1932), pp. 35–37 and passim; *Quarterly Review*, XIV, 201.

29. Quoted by Greig, *Francis Jeffrey*, p. 179. This observation has more recently been made by Helen Darbishire (*The Poet Wordsworth*, p. 35) and Roger Sharrock, "Wordsworth's Revolt against Literature," *EC*, III (1953), 396–412. I need hardly add that these modern critics and Lord Jeffrey share little more than the observation itself.

30. *Monthly Review*, LXXVI (1815), 129.

31. See also Smith, *An Estimate of William Wordsworth*, pp. 71, 73–74, 79–81, 84, 87–91, 99–105. Other poems included under the heading "Moods of My Own Mind" were "My Heart Leaps Up," "To the Cuckoo," and "Written in March." For Wordsworth's defense of this group of poems see *The Letters of William and Dorothy Wordsworth: The Middle Years*, ed. Ernest De Selincourt (Oxford, 1937), I, 127–30.

32. *The Annual Review; and History of Literature*, VI (1808), 524. Cf. the following remarks from the *Quarterly Review*, XIV, 209: "the merit of a poet does not essentially consist, as is sometimes supposed, in the possession of sensibilities different from or more intense than those of other people, but in the talent of awakening in their minds the particular feelings and emotions with which the various objects of his art are naturally associated."

33. Abrams, *The Mirror and the Lamp*, p. 58. See also Monk, *The Sublime*, pp. 4–5, 228–32; Peckham, *Beyond*, pp. 112–18 and passim; Harold Bloom, *The Visionary Company* (New York, 1961), p. 124.

what Wordsworth believed to have been an original vital unity of language and emotion, object and mental representation.[34] The argument is not for mimesis, in the traditional sense of that term, but for a rediscovery of the meaning of objects and man's passions, both of which men had ceased to know fully, largely because false poets had substituted their arbitrary and fictional worlds for the real one. In effect, Wordsworth's aim was to remove from men's perceptions the film that had been created by generations of false poets, in order to help them discover anew the profound meaning of commonplace objects and elemental emotions. He hoped in this way to create poetry that would be "a homage paid to the native and naked dignity of man, to the grand elementary principle of pleasure, by which he knows, and feels, and lives, and moves" (*PW*, II, 395).[35]

"Genius," Wordsworth writes, "is the introduction of a new element into the universe"; then he goes on less boldly: "or, if that be not allowed, it is the application of powers to objects on which they had not before been exercised, or the employment of them in such a manner as to produce effects hitherto unknown. What is all this but an advance, or a conquest, made by the soul of the poet?" A bit later in the passage he adds that "to create taste is to call forth and bestow power, of which knowledge is the effect" (*PW*, II, 428).[36] In all such statements of the unique claim of the new poetry, Wordsworth was not invoking the traditional role of the poet as maker, the creator of a golden world greater than the brazen one we live in. He intended to offer, on the contrary, knowledge of this world, a world already golden, its luster hidden only because of man's deadened senses and imagination. One result of this doctrine was his attempt to substitute for the traditional contrast between poetry and prose the "more philosophical" one between poetry and science. As Wordsworth knew, this task was crucial, for the old view appropriated "truth" for prose and left only fiction for poetry. Truth, he insisted, is no less, and even more, the province of poetry than of science. "The Man of science seeks truth as a remote and unknown benefactor," while the poet "rejoices in the presence of truth as our visible friend and hourly companion." Moreover, "The objects of the Poet's thoughts are everywhere," even "though the eyes and senses of man are, it is true, his favourite guides." The man of science, Wordsworth implied, is absolutely confined to the understanding and senses. Unlike him, the poet discovers truth "not standing upon external testimony," the testimony of the senses, "but carried alive into the heart by passion; truth which is its own testimony, which gives competence and confidence to the tribunal to which it appeals, and receives them from the same tribunal" (*PW*, II, 394–96).[37] This tribunal Wordsworth was later to call Imagination. Tucked away in an obscure section of his discussion of meter in the Preface is the following comment on one of the most often ridiculed of the lyrical ballads, "Goody Blake and Harry Gill": "I wished to draw attention to the truth that the power of the human imagination is sufficient to produce such changes in our physical nature as might almost appear miraculous. The truth is an important one; the fact . . . is a valuable illustration of it" (*PW*, II, 401). This is a most revealing statement of Wordsworth's position, yet so far as I know nothing has been said of the distinction implied in it between *fact* and *truth*.[38] The truth illustrated in the poem is that the mind of man is at least partly creative of what he customarily considers to be the world apart from him, and it was to provide illustrations of this truth that the lyrical ballads were conceived.

Probably the best-known passage in the *Biographia Literaria* is Coleridge's explanation of the plan of the *Lyrical Ballads*, yet it is perhaps well-known in a very general way and will, therefore, invite a close reexamination:

our conversations turned frequently on the two cardinal points of poetry, the power of exciting the sympathy of the reader by a faithful adherence to the truth of nature, and the power of giving the interest of novelty by the modifying colors of imagination. The sudden charm, which accidents of light and shade, which moon-light or sun-set diffused over a known and familiar landscape, appeared to represent the practicability of combining both. These are the poetry of nature. (II, 5)[39]

34. This primitivist theory of the origin of language was, of course, common in the eighteenth century, but Wordsworth's deductions from it certainly were not.

35. A true poet, says Wordsworth, believes that to "break in upon the sanctity and truth of his pictures by transitory and accidental ornaments" implies "the assumed meanness of his subject" (*PW*, II, 397).

36. This passage is from the "Essay, Supplementary to the Preface," first included in the 1815 edition of the collected poems.

37. This context should make us question the usual interpretation of the sentence that follows in the Preface, so apparently traditional as to seem a critical commonplace at the time Wordsworth wrote it: "Poetry is the image of man and nature." Does he not mean that poetry, the mind of man, and nature are alike animated by one spirit, and, therefore, alike creative of reality?

38. See Owen's brief comment on this passage, *Wordsworth's Preface*, p. 190.

39. For Wordsworth's similar statement of these principles see *PW*, II, 386. He and Coleridge differed, of course, on the question whether "faithful adherence to

The "these" of the last sentence refers to the natural phenomena that Coleridge had just described, and the key to the passage is an analogy between the "modifying colors of imagination" and the modifying colors of nature, especially by moonlight or sunset, when imperfect light renders the familiar less so. The function of the poetic imagination is to exert on its materials the same modifications that nature exerts on objects of the senses, softening the outlines of apparently discrete things in order to reveal an underlying unity that is hidden in the light of common day, or in the light of man's ordinary understanding. The result of the modifications, in each case, is to permit man to gain a new perspective on reality, and these modifications, though in our terms subjective, because dependent upon human perception, do not distort reality, but rather help to create it. For if the mind of man is at least as "real" as his body, the creations of mind are no less real than what we are accustomed to call objects. The poems of the *Lyrical Ballads*, then, were designed to illustrate that the mind is, in the very strictest sense, constitutive of reality.[40]

Earlier in this essay I quoted from a review of Wordsworth's poems which objected strenuously to the poet's scorn of fable and metaphor, based on a fantastic refusal to believe that poetry is necessarily the creation of fictions. The reviewer's tone is incredulous, and appropriately so, for he was face to face with that which is truly original in Wordsworth's doctrine. Limited, by and large, to a critical vocabulary inherited from a tradition alien to his own views, Wordsworth never fully succeeded in explaining the two most distinctive features of his poetry: the precise functions of the faculty that he called Imagination and the nature of his new kind of poetic symbolism. At the risk of being unfair to Coleridge, I shall have to say that while Wordsworth was illustrating in his poems the principles of the new doctrine which (with few differences at first) they shared, Coleridge was seeking an explanation of them. He came closest to a lucid description of the kind of symbolism that he and Wordsworth introduced into English poetry in a little-read book called *The Statesman's Manual*.[41] Coleridge's conception of the romantic symbol was essentially the same as Wordsworth's during the period when *Lyrical Ballads* occupied them both. That part of Coleridge's discussion of symbolism which is usually quoted as his definition is the following passage:

Now an Allegory is but a translation of abstract notions into a picture-language which is itself nothing but an abstraction from objects of the senses. . . . On the other hand a Symbol . . . is characterized . . . Above all by the translucence of the Eternal through and in the Temporal. It always partakes of the Reality which it renders intelligible; and while it enunciates the whole, abides itself as a living part in that Unity, of which it is the representative.[42]

The context of this important passage has been almost totally ignored, with the understandable result that little progress has been made toward a reasonable interpretation of the definition. Coleridge introduces the topic with this complaint: "It is among the miseries of the present age that it recognizes no medium between *Literal* and *Metaphorical*. Faith is either to be buried in the dead letter, or its name and honors usurped by a counterfeit product of the mechanical understanding, which in the blindness of self-complacency confounds SYMBOLS with ALLEGORIES" (p 36). His distinction between the two terms is further clarified by a remark in the Appendix to the book: "by a symbol I mean, not a metaphor or allegory or any other figure of speech or form of fancy, but an actual and essential part of that, the whole of which it represents" (p. xix). And just after his definition of symbol and allegory, he draws the following analogy to explain more clearly his conception of the latter: these are "but empty echoes which the fancy arbitrarily associates with apparitions of matter, less beautiful but not less shadowy than the sloping orchard or hill-side pasture-field seen in the transparent lake below" (p. 37).

Without underestimating the difficulty of interpreting Coleridge's very complicated attempts at definition, I will assert that at least most of his remarks on the subject are more meaningful than has so far been demonstrated. We should note, first of all, that fancy and understanding are

the truth of nature" requires "a selection of language really used by men." As Coleridge points out, Wordsworth's description of this language is far from clear.

40. In the famous Snowdon episode of *The Prelude*, Wordsworth draws an analogy between the effect of moonlight on a landscape and the shaping power of Imagination (xiv, 11–129).

41. I have chosen to call these symbols "romantic" to distinguish them from those employed by earlier writers (which Coleridge would have called "allegories") and those of later symbolist poets. To distinguish fully between these kinds of symbols is far beyond the scope of the present essay, but I am hopeful that a general sense of what is distinctive about the romantic symbol will be clear from remarks to follow. The best general commentary on the metaphysical background of Coleridge's symbolism remains Shawcross's Introduction to his edition of the *Biographia Literaria*. For a theory of the symbolism of Coleridge and Wordsworth quite different from mine, see George Whalley, "Preface to *Lyrical Ballads*: A Portent," *UTQ*, XXV (1956), 479.

42. (London, 1816), pp. 36–37.

in these passages treated almost as one faculty, and that the essential feature of both is that their functions are mechanical (dead, passive) and arbitrary, rendering not reality, but abstractions dependent upon the products of man's imperfect senses. Fancy, moreover, is compared to a transparent lake, an image that emphasizes the passivity of any faculty dependent upon the senses and bears an obvious family resemblance to the blank tablet of Lockian psychology.[43] Throughout his discussion of symbolism, Coleridge contrasts the living, volitional faculty of symbols, which he called Imagination, to the "unenlivened generalizing Understanding," a faculty, like the Fancy, dependent upon the mere appearances of things (pp. 35–36, xiv-xv).

However much they differed on particular points in their theories of Imagination and Fancy, Wordsworth and Coleridge were at one in opposing to the passive mind of Lockian psychology their conception of a volitional and creative mental power. In fact, the contrast drawn in *The Statesman's Manual* between the symbols of Imagination and the allegories of Fancy underlies also Wordsworth's attempt to distinguish between poetry and "Matter of Fact, or Science." Facts, those dead products of the senses and understanding, are the only materials of the man of science, who, unlike the poet, must *seek* truth as a thing remote and unknown. To the scientist, moreover, truth is a "benefactor," not a familiar and hourly companion, but a beneficent stranger, never seen directly, known only through his gifts. These gifts from the Truth, Wordsworth believed, are facts; that is, only so much of the Truth as man can receive, passively of course, through the senses. Both Wordsworth and Coleridge sought above all to concede the validity of Lockian psychology as an explanation of the manner in which facts are constructed from sense materials, but to insist at the same time upon the existence of another and better source of knowledge. This higher knowledge, in the search for which the human mind is an active partner with the external world, is the source of the new kind of pleasure that Wordsworth proposed for his poems. The faculty for discovering this knowledge he and Coleridge called Imagination, and the means of communicating it was the romantic symbol.

Perhaps the most striking characteristic of the Preface to *Lyrical Ballads* is Wordsworth's consistent attempt to subordinate the subject of his own "particular poems" to the principal thesis he was expounding. Indeed, these poems bear the same relation to the general subject of the Preface as illustrations bear to the truths that they are designed to illustrate. Thus, Wordsworth anticipates and answers a major criticism of his poems by conceding that his "associations must have sometimes been particular instead of general" and that his "language may frequently have suffered from . . . arbitrary connections of feelings and ideas with particular words and phrases," while implying throughout that however his particular illustrations may have fallen short of success, he was certain to succeed, he believed, in his general aim. He had demonstrated in these poems, he believed, that man is not limited to intercourse with facts impressed upon the passive senses and combined mechanically in the associative faculty of understanding, but is an inmate of an active universe which his own imagination partly creates (*PW*, II, 402). Because it was founded on such a faith, Romantic poetry, especially the poetry of Wordsworth, was indeed new. No longer was the poet bound to think himself restricted to the fancy, limited to two essentially unfruitful tasks — adorning, as Pope had done, the dead world of fact as given to the passive understanding, depending for success on wit rather than discovery, and abandoning truth to the man of science; or inventing, as Darwin had done, a world of chimeras that no reasonable man could take seriously. The great distinguishing characteristic of the Romantic poet is his belief in the existence of a mental faculty capable of mediating between the eternal and the finite, by revealing knowledge neither literal nor metaphorical, but at least as real as those material objects that we are accustomed to consider undeniably substantial.

This new concept of poetry was of tragically short duration. It did not last even to the end of Wordsworth's Great Decade, and its decisive influence on Coleridge ended with — some would say before — the composition of "Dejection: An Ode." The abandonment by both men of the unique symbolism that they had developed is reflected in the poetry of the later Romantic period. Roger Sharrock remarks that Wordsworth "never took the step initiated by Coleridge, and adopted by the second generation of romantic poets, into a private poetic universe governed by its own laws." [44] It is ironic that this should be true, but true it is: the poet of the "egotistical sublime" was the most "objective" of the Romantic poets, because he refused to substitute "poetic" for metaphysical truths.[45]

43. The best study of the implications of this image is, of course, Abrams's *The Mirror and the Lamp*.

44. Sharrock, "Wordsworth's Revolt," 409.

45. It is ironic too that Shelley has not been better treated by the new and older "New Critics," for, as Earl R. Wasserman demonstrates, his most successful poetic

Instead, having for some reason, or reasons, lost faith in his own early doctrine, he turned to what he must have regarded as the more worthy of the two alternatives that remained. Refusing to substitute a poetic cosmos for the world he saw around him, he painted to the Fancy, and illustrated by simile, metaphor, fable, and classical myth the "facts" of the understanding, as established in Christian doctrine and poetic tradition.

technique was to create a "cosmos" within a poem; and, as Abrams remarks, "This is the concept, at the heart of much of the 'new criticism,' . . . that a poem is an object-in-itself, a self-contained universe of discourse, of which we cannot demand that it be true to nature, but only, that it be true to itself." See *The Subtler Language* (Baltimore, 1959), and Abrams, *The Mirror and the Lamp*, p. 272.

# BIBLIOGRAPHY

# Key to Abbreviations

OF THE NAMES OF JOURNALS CITED IN
THE BIBLIOGRAPHY AND NOTES

| | |
|---|---|
| ELH | *ELH: English Literary History* |
| JEGP | *Journal of English and Germanic Philology* |
| JHI | *Journal of the History of Ideas* |
| MLN | *Modern Language Notes* |
| MLQ | *Modern Language Quarterly* |
| MLR | *Modern Language Review* |
| MP | *Modern Philology* |
| N&Q | *Notes and Queries* |
| PMLA | *Publications of the Modern Language Association of America* |
| PQ | *Philological Quarterly* |
| SEL | *Studies in English Literature* |
| SR | *The Sewanee Review* |

# Bibliography

## Books, Articles, and Reviews Published
## by Samuel Holt Monk

*The Sublime: A Study of Critical Theories in XVIII-Century England*, Modern Language Association, General Series, New York, 1935. Reprinted, Ann Arbor, 1960.

"Wordsworth's 'Unimaginable Touch of Time'," *MLN*, LII (1937), 503–4.

"Some Recent Historical Scholarship," *Southern Review*, III (1937), 137–51.

"Anna Seward and the Romantic Poets: A Study in Taste," *Wordsworth and Coleridge: Studies in Honor of George McLean Harper*, Princeton, 1939, pp. 118–35.

"From Jacobean to Augustan," *Southern Review*, VII (1941), 366–84.

"A Grace Beyond the Reach of Art," *JHI*, V (1944), 131–50.

"Samuel Stanhope Smith: Friend of Rational Liberty," *The Lives of Eighteen from Princeton*, Princeton, 1946, pp. 86–110.

"Dryden Studies: A Survey," *ELH*, XIV (1947), 46–63. Reprinted, New York, 1963.

"Colleges and Freedom of Opinion in a Revolutionary Era," *Southwestern Bulletin*, Vol. 34, No. 3 (1947), 3–16.

Editor, Nicholas Rowe, *Some Account of the Life of Mr. William Shakespear (1709)*, Augustan Reprint Society Publication No. 17, Los Angeles, 1948.

*John Dryden: A List of Critical Studies, 1895–1948*, Minneapolis, 1950.

Editor, Laurence Sterne, *Life and Opinions of Tristram Shandy*, New York, 1950.

Review of Frank Livingstone Huntley, *On Dryden's "Essay of Dramatic Poesy,"* in *PQ*, XXI (1952), 129–30.

Review of Josephine Miles, *The Primary Language of Poetry*, in *JEGP*, LI (1952), 426–28.

Editor, John Baillie, *An Essay on the Sublime (1747)*, Augustan Reprint Society Publication No. 43, Los Angeles, 1953.

"The Pride of Lemuel Gulliver," *SR*, LXIII (1955), 48–71.

"Dryden's 'Eminent French Critic' in *A Parallel of Poetry and Painting*," *N&Q*, CC (1955), 433.

Editor, with E. N. Hooker, H. T. Swedenberg, et al., John Dryden, *Works*, Vols. I, VIII, Berkeley and Los Angeles, 1956.

Review of John Traugott, *Tristram Shandy's World, A Study of Sterne's Philosophical Rhetoric*, in *MLN*, 71 (1956), 48–50.

"Samuel Johnson Quotes Addison," N&Q, CCII (1957), 154.

" 'Die of a Rose': *Essay on Man*, 199–200," *Huntington Library Quarterly*, XXI (1958), 359–61.

Editor, André Dacier, *Preface to Aristotle's "Art of Poetry" (1905)*, Augustan Reprint Society Publication No. 76, Los Angeles, 1959.

Review of Robert R. Wark, *Sir Joshua Reynolds: Discourses on Art*, in *Criticism*, II (1959), 391–93.

Review of Walter Hipple, *The Beautiful, the Sublime and the Picturesque in Eighteenth-Century British Aesthetic Theory*, in *MLN*, 74 (1959), 257–61.

"A Note in Montague Summers's Edition of 'The Way of the World,' Corrected," N&Q, CCV (1960), 70.

"Shadwell, 'Flail of Sense': 'Macflecknoe' Line 89," N&Q, CCV (1960), 67–68.

Review of Ernest Lee Tuveson, *The Imagination as a Means of Grace: Locke and the Aesthetics of Romanticism*, in PQ, XL (1961), 406–10.

Editor, "The Restoration and the Eighteenth Century," *The Norton Anthology of English Literature*, ed. M. H. Abrams, New York, 1962, I, 1126–1734.

Editor, *Five Miscellaneous Essays of Sir William Temple*, Ann Arbor, 1963.

Review of Bernard Schilling, *Dryden and the Conservative Myth: A Reading of "Absalom and Achitophel,"* in *MP*, LXI (1964), 246–52.

"Dryden and the Beginnings of Shakespeare Criticism in the Augustan Age," *The Persistence of Shakespeare Idolatry*, ed. Herbert Schueller, Detroit, 1964, pp. 49–75.

Editor, Daniel Defoe, *Colonel Jack*, London, 1965.

In preparation: Editor, John Dryden, *Works*, Vol. IX.

# INDEX

# Index

Abington, Mrs.: Reynolds portrait of, 353
Abrams, Meyer H., 193, 384–85
Adam, James, 32, 33
Adam, Robert, 32, 33, 366
Addison, Joseph, 286; idea of sublime in, 4, 94, 102–103, 110, 112–13, 120–21, 301, 302, 388; evolution of criticism of, 12, 94–95, 102, 115, 125–27; on landscape gardening, 25, 363; on Chaucer, 59; compares poetry and prose, 94; on true wit in poetry, 94, 102, 103–11 passim, 115, 116; on Milton, 94, 104, 109, 112, 116–24, 126, 208, 302; preface to Dryden's *Georgics* of Vergil, 94–102 passim, 109, 115; on ornament in poetic style, 94–115 passim; description of the georgic, 95–96; on pleasures of imagination in poetry, 95–96, 100–102, 123, 197–99, 199n, 217; on propriety, 96–97, 98, 110; on vividness, 96–97, 99–102; on poetry as pleasure to the understanding, 99; on Vergil's metaphors, 99–100, 107–108, 124–25; influence of Boileau on, 102–103, 104, 109, 116, 122; notes on his translation of *Metamorphoses*, 102–10 passim, 115, 116; on simplicity in poetry, 104, 109, 110, 112–13, 115, 127; on Dryden, 104, 110, 111; on classical writers, 109, 112, 115, 116; on natural genius, 110, 111–12, 116, 126; Longinus influences, 111, 197; relationship with Joseph Warton, 111; ballad criticism of, 112–15; on representation of nature in poetry, 114–15; "An Account of the Greatest English Poets,"
116, 208; on inadequacies of English language, 118, 119–20, 123; on well-chosen allegories, 123–24; on the sensitive reader, 126–27, 198; discusses use of gallery device, 162; applies painting theory to poetics, 197–200; aesthetic principles of, 197–200, 213, 217, 220; on Shakespeare, 208; on Spenser, 208; admires Renaissance painters, 208–209; Hume on, 245; use of type-characters, 335
Aden, John M., 153
Aeschylus, 210
aesthetic theory: in *18*th c. generally, 11, 228, 231, 387; and associationism, 11, 349; in classical Greece, 13–14; and morals, 74, 81, 83, 88–89; beginnings of, 80, 213; nature as guide to, 82–84, 85–86, 88; and primacy of natural beauty, 92, 215–18, 227, 228; of Addison, 197–200, 217, 220; neglect of, 213–15; modern analytical philosophers on, 214–15, 217–18, 225, 228; of Lord Kames, 217, 220; on objective quality of beauty, 218, 220; role of senses in, 218–20, 222, 224; of Alison, 220; and fallacy of common essence view, 220–21, 223, 225, 228; and development of transitive meanings of terms, 221–25, 228–31; and beauty of imagination, 222–23; and beauty of intellect, 222–23; of Payne Knight, 222–23; and the picturesque, 222–23, 359; of Alexander Gerard, 223–25; of Hume, 225, 236, 237–38, 242; and causes for judgment errors, 225–26; distinction of modes in,